Learning to Cooperate, Cooperating to Learn

Learning to Cooperate, Cooperating to Learn

Edited by

Robert Slavin
Center for Social Organization of Schools
Johns Hopkins University
Baltimore, Maryland

Shlomo Sharan
Tel-Aviv University
Tel-Aviv, Israel

Spencer Kagan
University of California
Riverside, California

Rachel Hertz-Lazarowitz
Haifa University
Haifa, Israel

Clark Webb
Brigham Young University
Provo, Utah

and
Richard Schmuck
University of Oregon
Eugene, Oregon

PLENUM PRESS • NEW YORK AND LONDON

Library of Congress Cataloging in Publication Data

Main entry under title:

Learning to cooperate, cooperating to learn.

Rev. versions of papers originally presented at the Second Conference of the International Association of Cooperation in Education, held at Brigham Young University, Provo, Utah, July 1982. Includes bibliographical references and index.
1. Group work in education—Congresses. 2. Cooperativeness—Congresses. 3. Classroom management—Social aspects—Congresses. 4. Minorities—Education—Congresses. I. Slavin, Robert E. II. International Association for the Study of Cooperation in Education.
LB1032.L36 1985   371.1'02   84-24832
ISBN 0-306-41772-3

This volume is a project of the International Association for the Study of Cooperation in Education (IASCE).

Executive Committee of the IASCE (1982–1985)

President	Shlomo Sharan, *Tel-Aviv University*
Past President	Richard Schmuck, *University of Oregon*
Secretaries and newsletter editors	Nancy and Theodore Graves *University of California at Santa Cruz*
Treasurer	Noreen Webb, *University of California at Los Angeles*
Officers-at-large	Spencer Kagan, *University of California at Riverside* Emmy Pepitone, *Bryn Mawr College* Robert Slavin, *Johns Hopkins University*

Individuals wishing to join the IASCE may receive membership information from Noreen Webb, Graduate School of Education, UCLA, Los Angeles, California 90024.

©1985 Plenum Press, New York
A Division of Plenum Publishing Corporation
233 Spring Street, New York, N.Y. 10013

Printed in the United States of America

Contributors

J. HUGH BAIRD, Department of Secondary Education, Brigham Young University, Provo, Utah

VICTOR BATTISTICH, Developmental Studies Center, 130 Ryan Court, Suite 210, San Ramon, California

YAEL BEJARANO, Everyman's University, Tel Aviv, Israel

CAROLE COOPER, Developmental Studies Center, 130 Ryan Court, Suite 210, San Ramon, California

NEIL DAVIDSON, Curriculum and Instruction Department, College of Education, University of Maryland, College Park, Maryland

NANCY B. GRAVES, Consultants/Trainers in Cooperation, Creativity, and Change, 136 Liberty Street, Santa Cruz, California

THEODORE D. GRAVES, Consultants/Trainers in Cooperation, Creativity, and Change, 136 Liberty Street, Santa Cruz, California

RACHEL HERTZ-LAZAROWITZ, School of Education, Haifa University, Haifa, Israel

JAMES JENKINS, Department of Secondary Education, Brigham Young University, Provo, Utah

DAVID W. JOHNSON, College of Education, University of Minnesota, Minneapolis, Minnesota

ROGER T. JOHNSON, College of Education, University of Minnesota, Minneapolis, Minnesota

SPENCER KAGAN, Department of Psychology, University of California, Riverside, California

PIET KOMMERS, Onderafdeling der Toegepaste Onderwijskunde, Technische Hogeschool Twente, Postbus 217, 7500 AE Enschede, The Netherlands

PETER KUSSELL, Israel Educational Television Center, Ramat Aviv, Tel Aviv, Israel

REUVEN LAZAROWITZ, Department of Education in Technology and Science, Technion-Israel Institute of Technology, Haifa, Israel

GEOFFREY MARUYAMA, Department of Educational Psychology, University of Minnesota, Minneapolis, Minnesota

WIM NIJHOF, Onderafdeling der Toegepaste Onderwijskunde, Technische Hogeschool Twente, Postbus 217, 7500 Ae Enschede, The Netherlands

EMMY A. PEPITONE, Department of Education and Child Development, Bryn Mawr College, Bryn Mawr, Pennsylvania

SHULAMIT RAVIV, Wingate Institute for Physical Education and Sport, Netanya, Israel

WENDY RITCHEY, Developmental Studies Center, 130 Ryan Court, Suite 210, San Ramon, California

ERIC SCHAPS, Developmental Studies Center, 130 Ryan Court, Suite 210, San Ramon, California

RICHARD SCHMUCK, College of Education, University of Oregon, Eugene, Oregon

JOSEPH SCHWARZWALD, Department of Psychology, Bar-Ilan University, Ramat Gan, Israel

SHLOMO SHARAN, School of Education, Tel Aviv University, Tel Aviv, Israel

YAEL SHARAN, Israel Educational Television Center, Ramat Aviv, Tel Aviv, Israel

ROBERT E. SLAVIN, Center for Social Organization of Schools, Johns Hopkins University, Baltimore, Maryland

DANIEL SOLOMON, Developmental Studies Center, 130 Ryan Court, Suite 210, San Ramon, California

JUDITH SOLOMON, Developmental Studies Center, 130 Ryan Court, Suite 210, San Ramon, California

SHELAGH TOWSON, Department of Psychology, Trent University, Peterborough, Ontario, Canada

PATRICIA TUCK, Developmental Studies Center, 130 Ryan Court, Suite 210, San Ramon, California

GARY TYRRELL, Department of Psychology, University of California, Riverside, California

MARILYN WATSON, Developmental Studies Center, 130 Ryan Court, Suite 210, San Ramon, California

CLARK WEBB, Department of Curriculum and Instructional Science, Brigham Young University, Provo, Utah

NOREEN M. WEBB, Graduate School of Education, University of California, Los Angeles, California

KEITH F. WIDAMAN, Department of Psychology, University of California, Riverside, California

G. LAWRENCE ZAHN, Department of Psychology, University of California, Riverside, California

Preface

This book was written and edited as a project of the International Association for the Study of Cooperation in Education (IASCE). It grew directly out of the second conference of the IASCE, held at Brigham Young University, Provo, Utah, in July 1982. The chapters in the book were originally presented in some form at the Provo conference, though most have been considerably revised since that time. This is the second book sponsored by the IASCE; the first, *Cooperation in Education* (Provo, Utah: Brigham Young University Press, 1980), edited by Shlomo Sharan, Paul Hare, Clark Webb, and Rachel Hertz-Lazarowitz, was based on the proceedings of the first conference of the IASCE in Tel Aviv, Israel, in 1979.

The IASCE is a group of educators interested in studying, developing, or applying cooperative methods at various levels of the process of education. It includes researchers, teacher educators, teachers, and school administrators from more than a dozen countries.

A comparison of the first IASCE volume with the present work shows how far the research on cooperation in education has grown in just a few years. In 1980, there was just enough empirical research in the schools to establish that cooperation among students in the classroom was feasible, effective in increasing student achievement, and beneficial for such social outcomes as positive intergroup relations and a wide range of prosocial behaviors and attitudes. However, little was known about how and why these effects came about, and the range of alternative cooperative learning methods was limited.

The present volume goes far beyond the previous work in several ways. It contains both research and theoretical statements greatly extending our understanding of how cooperative learning groups operate and why they produce their characteristic effects. New methods of bringing about cooperative learning are described in these pages. Significant advances in understanding the effects of cooperative learning experiences on cooperative, altruistic, and prosocial behaviors are discussed in several chapters, as are completely new ways of understanding the impact of cooperative learning in the multiethnic classroom. There was every reason for researchers in the area of cooperative learning to be proud of their accomplishments in 1980, but

ix

progress since then, much of it presented in this volume, testifies to the continuing vitality of the field.

The preparation of this volume was supported in part by a grant from the National Institute of Education, No. NIE-G-83-0002. However, the opinions expressed are those of the authors and do not represent NIE policy.

ROBERT E. SLAVIN

Contents

PART III

PART IV

I

Learning to Cooperate, Cooperating to Learn

Basic Concepts

RICHARD SCHMUCK

INTRODUCTION

Cooperation is a fundamental concern of educators. The increasing complexity of social conditions locally and worldwide has brought to the forefront the importance of learning to cooperate. Recent educational thought and research have shown the power of cooperating to learn.

Contemporary living puts emphasis on a citizen's skills in relating well with others. Relationships between the races, the sexes, and nation-states have all become paramount concerns. The future will hold an even more compelling need to deal with interpersonal, intergroup, and intersocietal tensions and conflicts. People should not learn merely to avoid such problems; they should (and can) learn to handle them constructively and creatively if we are to live and work well together in the twenty-first century.

As a consequence of social changes during the past several decades, human beings have been pushed to live closer and closer together. Con sequently, the schools have taken an increased role in helping young people to learn the skills necessary for living successfully with one another. Thus, parallel with the traditional academic curriculum, the schools have concerned themselves with developing students' interpersonal skills. Moreover, because of theory and research from the social sciences, many teachers have become convinced that cooperative activities in the classroom enhance the learning of the traditional academic curriculum. Indeed, many teachers nowadays strive to help students in both learning to cooperate and cooperating to learn.

Current intellectual developments in cooperation and learning have grown out of two streams of historical thought. One of those comes

RICHARD SCHMUCK • College of Education, University of Oregon, Eugene, Oregon 97401.

from the work of John Dewey, who emphasized social aspects of learning and the role of the school in educating students in cooperative democratic living. The other historical stream flows out of the work of Kurt Lewin and subsequent work by scholars of group dynamics, such as Ronald Lippitt and Morton Deutsch. In certain respects, Lewin, Lippitt, and Deutsch have stressed the collection of scientific data that undergirds the philosophical insights of Dewey, although they have seldom explicitly written about that interest. The Lewineans described their effort as *action research,* an expression that Dewey would have accepted.

Dewey and Lewin never met each other so far as I know, nor is there any evidence that they corresponded or even read each other's works. They did, however, share a common interest in taking action to bring about societal improvement. They were activists and optimists. Their intellectual work emphasized taking risks in working for school improvement by initiating action research even in the face of insufficient scientific data. Their pioneering spirit in acting to improve social interaction and cooperation in schools lives on in the minds and hearts of the contributors to this book.

Dewey argued that if humans are to learn to live cooperatively, they must experience the living process of cooperation in schools. Life in the classroom should represent the democratic process in microcosm, and the heart of democratic living is cooperation in groups. Moreover, Dewey argued that classroom life should embody democracy, not only in how students learn to make choices and carry out academic projects together, but also in how they learn to relate to one another. This approach could involve being taught to empathize with others, to respect the rights of others, and to work together on rational problem-solving.

I believe that a key to unlocking Dewey's philosophy about cooperation and learning lies in the development of group dynamics as a discipline. This discipline has added to Dewey's philosophical contributions by creating scientific methods for gathering evidence on the functions and processes of cooperation in groups. The applied action-research strategy of group dynamics was created primarily by Lewin and his students, the most notable of whom were Lippitt and Deutsch, who, more than any other Lewineans, applied Dewey's philosophy and Lewin's theory to cooperation in groups.

Lewin, Lippitt, and Deutsch spearheaded practical, scientific work on group dynamics and cooperation. In order to appreciate their conceptions of group dynamics and cooperation, it is necessary to understand that their self-concept as professionals involved more than that of the pure scientist as defined in conventional terms. For the early Lewineans, intellectual work represented a combination of science, therapy, social reconstruction, intervention, and morality. The validity of a teaching activity or a group exercise depended on its usefulness in improving cooperative activity. If a recorded response or a table of data had no implication for social improvement, then collecting and analyzing them would take on very little value. Such a pragmatic sense of science lives on in this book.

Soon after Lewin died in 1947, Ronald Lippitt wrote about his life as an "adventure in the exploration of interdependence." Lippitt started a commemorative article about Lewin by writing: "At a time when the major problems of continued existence are problems of inter-communication and cooperative action the world can ill afford to lose the contributing force of such a scientist-citizen as Kurt Lewin" (p. 87). Lippitt went on to write about Lewin's interdependent style of life, his exploration into the interdependencies of group life, his emphasis on the interdependence of action and research, and his view of the interdependencies of different research methods. In a very real sense, those sorts of interdependencies live on in this book.

Morton Deutsch was a student of Kurt Lewin's when Lewin died. He remembered one of Lewin's favorite questions as being "What is the essence of the phenomena?" That query was uppermost in Deutsch's mind when he formulated his doctoral dissertation on the effects of cooperation and competition. For it was on the day that Deutsch was to present his dissertation proposal to Lewin that Lewin died. Lippitt took Lewin's place as chair, and Deutsch answered Lewin's questions about the essence of the phenomena to Lippitt:

> The crux of the differences between cooperation and competition lies in the nature of the way the *goals* of the participants in each of the situations are linked. In a cooperative situation the goals are so linked that everybody sinks or swims together, while in the competitive situation if one swims, the other must sink. (1949, p. 129)

That answer lives on today in the research of those who have contributed to this book.

The initial section of the book presents some intellectual and conceptual underpinnings of cooperation and learning in schools. Robert Slavin brings us up-to-date with the terms, concepts, and research of cooperative learning. Emmy A. Pepitone describes a program of research on the origins of self-orientation, cooperation, and altruism in children. Spencer Kagan applies some of the concepts summarized by Slavin to build a typology of cooperative learning methods. The works of Slavin, Pepitone, and Kagan demonstrate the strides that have been made since that creative era of the early Lewineans a half century ago.

REFERENCES

Deutsch, M. A theory of cooperation and competition. *Human Relations*, 1949, *2*, 129–151.

Lippitt, R. Kurt Lewin, 1890–1947: Adventures in the exploration of interdependence. *Sociometry*, 1947, *10* (1), 87–97.

1

An Introduction to Cooperative Learning Research

ROBERT E. SLAVIN

Why have we humans been so successful as a species? We are not strong like tigers, big like elephants, protectively colored like lizards, or swift like gazelles. We are intelligent, but an intelligent human alone in the forest would not survive for long. What has really made us such successful animals is our ability to apply our intelligence to cooperating with others to accomplish group goals. From the primitive hunting group to the corporate boardroom, it is those of us who can solve problems while working with others who succeed. In fact, in modern society, cooperation in face-to-face groups is increasingly important. A successful scientist must be able to cooperate effectively with other scientists, with technicians, and with students. An executive must cooperate with other executives, salespersons, suppliers, and superiors. Of course, each of those relationships also has competitive elements, but in all of them, if the participants cannot cooperate to achieve a common goal, all lose out. It is difficult to think of very many adult activities in which the ability to cooperate with others is not important. Human society is composed of overlapping cooperative groups: families, neighborhoods, work groups, political parties, clubs, teams.

Because schools socialize children to assume adult roles, and because cooperation is so much a part of adult life, one might expect that cooperative activity would be emphasized. However, this is far from true. Among the prominent institutions of our society, the schools are least characterized by cooperative activity. Teaching itself is for many one of the loneliest jobs in the world, because teachers rarely work together. Students have long experienced cooperative activity in laboratory groups, and project groups, but these activities occupy a small portion of a student's schooling. Most of the time, students work independently, and they are continually in competition with one another for grades, praise, and recognition. Such competition does not have the positive features of a contest between well-matched adversaries, be-

ROBERT E. SLAVIN • Center for Social Organization of Schools, Johns Hopkins University, Baltimore, Maryland 21218.

cause in the classroom, winners and losers can be predicted fairly reliably the day they first come into class: those who have succeeded in the
past will probably succeed, and those who have failed will probably fail.
For many low-performing students, no amount of effort is likely to put
them at the top of the class because they have already missed so much in
past years. Thus, the competition for top scores in the classroom is
poorly matched. Because they have such a small chance of success, low
performers may give up or try to disrupt the activity. They can hardly be
expected to do otherwise. High achievers may not do their best because
they know that they will be near the top anyway (see Kukla, 1972). Further, the competition for grades and recognition may set up a pecking
order in the classroom, with high-performing students at the top (Ames,
Ames, & Felker, 1977). This process further alienates low-performing
students, who may turn to delinquency or withdrawal as a means of
maintaining positive self-esteem in the face of what they perceive as a
hostile school environment.

The problems of competitive classrooms have been discussed for
years, but although there have been many complaints, there have been
few practical solutions. Many teachers express frustration with the competitive classroom system, particularly because of what it means for low-
achieving students, but they have felt constrained in their strategies by a
lack of alternatives.

Cooperative Learning Methods

Over the past decade, alternatives to the traditional competitive classroom have emerged. They are instructional methods called *cooperative
learning* (see Sharan, 1980; Slavin, 1983a). Cooperative learning methods are structured, systematic instructional strategies capable of being
used at any grade level and in most school subjects. All of the methods
involve having the teacher assign the students to four- to six-member
learning groups composed of high-, average-, and low-achieving students, boys and girls, black, Anglo, and Hispanic students, and
mainstreamed academically handicapped students as well as their
nonhandicapped classmates. In other words, each group is a microcosm
of the class in academic achievement level, sex, and ethnicity.

All cooperative learning methods are based on social psychological
research and theory, some of it dating back to the early 1900s (see
Johnson & Johnson, 1974; Slavin, 1977a). However, they have been
adapted to one degree or another to meet the practical requirements of
classrooms and to solve problems introduced by the use of cooperation

itself (such as maintaining individual accountability as well as group responsibility). The "engine" that runs cooperative learning is always the same: heterogeneous groups working toward a common goal. In almost every other aspect, however, the methods differ from one another. The most widely researched and used cooperative learning methods are briefly described below (see Chapter 3 for more detailed descriptions of these methods).

STUDENT TEAM LEARNING

An extensively researched and widely used set of cooperative learning methods is called *Student Team Learning* (see Slavin, 1980), which consists of Student Teams-Achievement Divisions (STAD), Teams-Games-Tournament (TGT), and Jigsaw II, in addition to many modifications and special-purpose cooperative methods. In STAD, after the teacher presents a lesson, the students meet in four- to five-member teams to master a set of worksheets on the lesson. Then each student takes a quiz on the material. The scores that the students contribute to their teams are based on the degree to which the students have improved over their individual past averages. The teams with the highest scores are recognized in a weekly class newsletter. TGT is similar to STAD, except that the students play academic games as representatives of their teams instead of taking quizzes. Students compete with others of similar achievement so that, as in STAD, any student who prepares can be successful. Jigsaw II is a modification of Aronson's Jigsaw method. Jigsaw and Jigsaw II are discussed below.

JIGSAW

Jigsaw (Aronson, 1978) was one of the earliest of the cooperative learning methods. In Jigsaw, each student in a five- to six-member group is given unique information on a topic that the whole group is studying. After the students have read their sections, they meet in "expert groups" with their counterparts from other groups to discuss the information. Next, the students return to their groups and teach their teammates what they have learned. The entire class may take a test for individual grades at the end.

Jigsaw II (Slavin, 1980) is designed to integrate original Jigsaw with other Student Team Learning methods and to simplify the teacher preparations required to use the method. In Jigsaw II, students are assigned to four- to five-member teams. They read narrative materials, such as social studies chapters, short stories, or biographies, and each team member is given a special topic on which to become an expert. The students discuss their topics in "expert groups," then return to teach their teammates what they have learned. Finally, the students take a quiz on the material, and the quiz scores are used, as in STAD, to form individual and team scores.

LEARNING TOGETHER

The method that is closest to pure cooperation is called "Learning Together" (Johnson & Johnson, 1975). Students work in small groups to complete a single worksheet, for which the group receives praise and recognition. This method emphasizes (1) training students to be good group members and (2) continuous evaluation of group functioning by the group members.

GROUP-INVESTIGATION

The Group-Investigation method (Sharan & Sharan, 1976) is the most complex of all the cooperative learning methods. It calls for students in small groups to take substantial responsibility for deciding what they will learn, how they will organize themselves to learn it, and how they will communicate what they have learned to their classmates. Each group takes on a different task and then allocates subtasks among the members. The tasks often involve open-ended investigations using a variety of resource materials. Ultimately, the groups prepare reports to present to the rest of the class.

Although cooperative learning methods vary considerably in their features, it is interesting to note that their differences are primarily alternative ways of dealing with the same problems inherent in cooperation. For example, most of the methods avoid making it possible for one student to do most of the group's work. The problem is avoided in STAD and Jigsaw II by having the students take quizzes alone without help from their teammates so that each student must know the material. In TGT, the students play academic games with the members of other teams to add points to their team scores; again, the students must know the material if they are to contribute a high score. The Jigsaw, Jigsaw II, and Group-Investigation methods make it impossible for the group's work to be unevenly distributed because each student must become an expert on some part of the group task.

Another inherent danger in the use of heterogeneous learning teams is that low-achieving students will have little to contribute to the group's efforts, and that high-achieving students will resent this or will belittle the contributions that the low achievers make. This danger is averted in STAD and Jigsaw II by having each student's contribution to the team score represent the degree to which each quiz score exceeds the student's own past average. In TGT, the students compete against equals to add points to their team scores, a method that gives low-achieving and high-achieving students equal chances to contribute to the team score. Jigsaw, Jigsaw II, and Group-Investigation make sure that each student has something of value to contribute by giving students their own areas of expertise.

Making students value group success is vital to cooperation because without an incentive to cooperate, many students will not do so. In STAD, TGT, and Jigsaw II, students receive recognition in a class news-letter if they are on high-scoring teams. In the Johnsons' Learning To-gether methods, the students often receive grades based on their group's performance. Jigsaw uses individual tests on which the students must learn from their teammates to do well, and in Group-Investigation, both class and teacher evaluations of group products serve as means of motivating the groups to pull together.

COOPERATIVE LEARNING: THE RESEARCH

What happens when we change from the traditional classroom to cooperative methods? The effects of cooperative methods have been studied in two principal areas: student achievement and student social relationships. Positive effects on achievement have been anticipated be-cause in a cooperative group, students are likely to encourage and help one another to learn (see Johnson & Johnson, 1974; Slavin, 1977a). Posi-tive effects on social relationships, such as improved race relations and attitudes toward academically handicapped classmates, are also ex-pected because cooperative learning creates the conditions of nonsuperficial, cooperative contact long believed to improve relation-ships across such boundaries as race or ethnicity (see Allport, 1954; Slavin & Hansell, 1983).

ACADEMIC ACHIEVEMENT

Anyone who has seen students working in cooperative groups will note that they enjoy doing so, that working cooperatively makes schoolwork social and exciting. But what are the effects of working cooperatively on student achievement?

Slavin (1983b) has recently identified 46 field experiments in elementary and secondary schools that have studied the effects of cooperative learning on student learning, using control groups, in experiments lasting at least 2 weeks, but more often running for 8–16 weeks. A favorable effect on student achievement was found in 29 of these studies and no differences in 15, and in 2 studies, there was a significant difference favoring the control group.

The pattern of results of those studies on cooperative learning indicates the importance of designing cooperative methods to resolve the problem of individual accountability. The most successful methods for increasing student achievement were the ones in which group scores were composed of the sum of individual achievements, or in which each member had a unique task for which he or she could be held accountable. Of the 27 studies in which all group members studied the same material and group rewards were provided based on the individual achievements of the group members, 24 (89%) showed significantly positive effects on student achievement in comparison with the control groups. In contrast, enhanced achievement was found in none of the 9 studies in which all group members studied the same material and the group was rewarded based on a group product, or in which no group rewards were given. Among the studies in which each student had a unique task, about half found positive effects on achievement. Among these studies, the most successful methods in terms of increasing achievement were those in which the groups were rewarded on the basis of the sum of individual test scores, such as Jigsaw II (Ziegler, 1981), or on the basis of a group product, as in Group-Investigation (Sharan, Hertz-Lazarowitz, & Ackerman, 1980). This pattern of findings, in addition to results of component analyses that supported the same idea, led Slavin (1983b) to conclude that individual accountability and group rewards are necessary if cooperative learning is to have positive achievement effects. If the learning of every group member is not critical to group success, or if group success is not rewarded, achievement is unlikely to be increased above the level characteristic of traditional classrooms.

The positive effects of cooperative learning methods on student achievement appear just as frequently in elementary and secondary schools; in urban, suburban, and rural schools; and in subjects as diverse as mathematics, language arts, social studies, and reading. There is some tendency for blacks and other minority-group students to gain especially in achievement as a result of working cooperatively (Lucker, Rosenfield, Sikes, & Aronson, 1976; Slavin & Oickle, 1981), although whites in cooperative groups also gain more in achievement than whites in traditional classes. Most studies show that high, average, and low achievers gain equally from the cooperative experience; a few have shown greater gains for low achievers; and others have shown the greatest gains for high achievers. Wheeler (1977) found that students who preferred to cooperate learned best in a cooperative program, whereas students who preferred to compete did best in a competitive program.

INTERGROUP RELATIONS

The effect of cooperative learning strategies on relationships between black, white, and Hispanic students in desegregated schools is an outstanding case of social psychology in action. Anyone who visits a junior high school at lunchtime can see that, although we have moved students of different ethnicities into the same school building, we have a long way to go in having them interact on an equal and amicable basis and form friendships. Numerous studies of friendship between students of different ethnic groups (e.g., Gerard & Miller, 1975) have confirmed this observation: students make few friendship choices outside their own racial or ethnic groups, and such preferences do not change of their own accord.

Cooperative learning techniques place students of different races or ethnicities in learning groups where each group member is given an equal role in helping the group to achieve its goals. That is essentially the optimal situation for interracial contact to lead to the positive relationships specified by the most widely accepted theory of positive intergroup relations: Allport's (1954) contact theory of intergroup relations. Allport's theory holds that, if individuals of different races are to develop supportive relationships, they must engage in frequent cooperative activity on an equal footing. Put another way, it is reasonable to expect that if we assign students to work together on a common task toward a common goal, where each individual can make a substantial contribution to the mutually desired goal, the students will learn to like and respect one another.

Research on cooperative learning supports this expectation. Of 14 studies of cooperative learning and intergroup relations, all but 2 found positive effects on this variable (Slavin, 1983a). These studies involved relationships between blacks and whites, Hispanics and Anglos, recent immigrants and Anglo-Canadians, and Middle-Eastern and European Jews in Israel. In every case, cooperation produced similar positive results on cross-ethnic friendships and interactions. Two of these studies (Slavin, 1979; Ziegler, 1981) found that these effects were maintained for as long as nine months after the end of the cooperative programs.

MAINSTREAMING

The barriers to friendship and supportive interaction presented by ethnic differences are serious, but they are small compared to the gap between mainstreamed academically handicapped students and their nonmainstreamed classmates (Gottlieb & Leyser, 1981). However, this is another area in which cooperation could overcome substantial differences. Several researchers have shown that cooperative learning improves relationships between mainstreamed and nonmainstreamed students. In a recent study, Madden and Slavin (1983) found that STAD helped nonmainstreamed students to accept their mainstreamed classmates while also improving the class's achievement and self-esteem. Ballard, Corman, Gottlieb, and Kaufman (1977) introduced cooperation between educable mentally retarded (EMR) students and their nonretarded classmates and found a marked increase in friendship between the EMR and non-EMR students. Armstrong, Johnson, and Balow (1981) and Cooper, Johnson, Johnson, and Wilderson (1980) found positive effects of the Learning Together model on the acceptance of mainstreamed learning-disabled children.

SELF-ESTEEM

Several of the cooperative learning studies have included measures of student self-esteem. Increased self-esteem had been anticipated as an outcome of cooperative learning both because students in cooperative groups feel more liked by their classmates (which they usually are) and because they are likely to feel more successful academically (which they also usually are). Almost every cooperative learning study that included a self-esteem measure found significantly positive effects on this outcome (see Slavin, 1983a).

OTHER EFFECTS OF COOPERATIVE LEARNING

The outcomes discussed above—student learning, intergroup relations, mainstreaming, and self-esteem—have been studied most extensively in the cooperative learning research because they have so much importance as outcomes of schooling. However, there is a wide range of other outcomes that have also been studied in this research.

Not surprisingly, most evaluations of cooperative learning have demonstrated that students who work together like school more than those who are not allowed to do so. They also like their fellow students more. Students who have worked cooperatively are more likely than other students to be altruistic, to be able to cooperate effectively, and to believe that cooperation is good (see, for example, Hertz-Lazarowitz, Sharan, & Steinberg, 1980). They are also likely to say that they want their classmates to do well in school and that they feel that their classmates want them to do well.

One study by Slavin (1977b) found that emotionally disturbed adolescents who experienced cooperative learning were more likely than traditionally taught students to interact appropriately with other students, and this effect lasted for five months after the end of the project. Janke (1978) found enhancing effects of cooperative learning on appropriate interactions among emotionally disturbed students and also found that the program improved these students' attendance.

CONCLUSIONS

The research summarized above shows that cooperative learning programs have positive effects on a wide range of outcomes, including achievement, intergroup relations, attitudes toward mainstreamed academically handicapped students, and self-esteem. Some of the cooperative learning methods, in particular the Student Team Learning methods (STAD, TGT, and Jigsaw II) and the Johnsons' Learning Together methods, are used by thousands of teachers throughout the United States and abroad.

Although the basic findings cited above are now well established, there are many issues yet to be resolved. Recent research on cooperative learning has focused less on documenting basic effects and more on investigations of *why* cooperative learning methods have the effects they do, and *for whom* they work best. New applications to deal with student heterogeneity and to permit cooperation between different groups have been developed, basic research on how students behave under cooperative and competitive conditions has continued, and new conceptualizations of cooperative learning and its effects have been described. It is this "second-generation" research on cooperation and cooperative learning that constitutes the bulk of this book. It includes new research on the effects of cooperative learning on relationships across sex as well as across ethnic lines, descriptions of methods of preparing students for cooperation, and one project designed to increase cooperation and prosocial behavior in an entire community.

The problems confronted in cooperative learning are the central and enduring problems of education. Student achievement, intergroup relations, and mainstreaming have been three principal foci of concern over the past decades. This book makes an important contribution to knowledge about how cooperation among students may help to solve many of these critical problems of education.

REFERENCES

Allport, G. *The nature of prejudice.* Cambridge, Mass.: Addison-Wesley, 1954.

Ames, C., Ames, R., & Felker, D. Effects of competitive reward structures and valence of outcome on children's achievement attributions. *Journal of Educational Psychology,* 1977, *69,* 1–8.

Armstrong, B., Johnson, D. W., & Balow, B. Effects of cooperative vs. individualistic learning experiences on interpersonal attraction between learning-disabled and normal-progress elementary school students. *Contemporary Educational Psychology,* 1981, *6,* 102–109.

Aronson, E. *The Jigsaw classroom.* Beverly Hills, Calif.: Sage, 1978.

Ballard, M., Corman, L., Gottlieb, J., & Kaufman, M. Improving the social status of mainstreamed retarded children. *Journal of Educational Psychology,* 1977, *69,* 605–611.

Cooper, L., Johnson, D. W., Johnson, R., & Wilderson, F. Effects of cooperative, competitive, and individualistic experiences on interpersonal attraction among heterogeneous peers. *Journal of Social Psychology,* 1980, *111,* 243–252.

Gerard, H. B., & Miller, N. *School desegregation: A long-term study.* New York: Plenum Press, 1975.

Gottlieb, J., & Leyser, Y. Friendship between mentally retarded and nonretarded children. In S. Asher & J. Gottman (Eds.), *The development of children's friendships.* Cambridge: Cambridge University Press, 1981.

Hertz-Lazarowitz, R., Sharan, S., & Steinberg, R. Classroom learning styles and cooperative behavior of elementary school children. *Journal of Educational Psychology,* 1980, *72,* 99–106.

Janke, R. *The Teams-Games-Tournament (TGT) method and the behavioral adjustment and academic achievement of emotionally impaired adolescents.* Paper presented at the Annual Convention of the American Educational Research Association, Toronto, 1977.

Johnson, D. W., & Johnson, R. T. Instructional goal structure: Cooperative, competitive, or individualistic. *Review of Educational Research,* 1974, *44,* 213–240.

Johnson, D. W., & Johnson, R. T. *Learning together and alone.* Englewood Cliffs, N. J.: Prentice-Hall, 1975.

Kukla, A. Foundations of an attributional theory of performance. *Psychological Review,* 1972, *79,* 454–470.

Lucker, G. W., Rosenfield, D., Sikes, J., & Aronson, E. Performance in the interdependent classroom: A field study. *American Educational Research Journal,* 1976, *13,* 115–123.

Madden, N. A., & Slavin, R. E. Cooperative learning and social acceptance of mainstreamed academically handicapped students. *Journal of Special Education,* 1983, *17,* 171–182.

Sharan, S. Cooperative learning in small groups: Recent methods and effects on achievement, attitudes, and ethnic relations. *Review of Educational Research*, 1980, 50, 241–271.

Sharan, S., & Sharan, Y. *Small-group teaching*. Englewood Cliffs, N. J.: Educational Technology Publications, 1976.

Sharan, S., Hertz-Lazarowitz, R., & Ackerman, Z. Academic achievement of elementary school children in small-group versus whole class instruction. *Journal of Experimental Education*, 1980, *48*, 125–129.

Slavin, R. E. Classroom reward structure: An analytic and practical review. *Review of Educational Research*, 1977, *47* (4), 633–650. (a)

Slavin, R. E. A student team approach to teaching adolescents with special emotional and behavioral needs. *Psychology in the Schools*, 1977, *14* (1), 77–84. (b)

Slavin, R. E. Effects of biracial learning teams on cross-racial friendships. *Journal of Educational Psychology*, 1979, *71*, 381–387.

Slavin, R. E. *Using student team learning (rev. ed.)*. Baltimore, Md.: Center for Social Organization of Schools, Johns Hopkins University, 1980.

Slavin, R. E. *Cooperative learning*. New York: Longman, 1983. (a)

Slavin, R. E. When does cooperative learning increase student achievement? *Psychological Bulletin*, 1983, *94*, 429–445. (b)

Slavin, R. E., & Hansell, S. Cooperative learning and intergroup relations: Contact theory in the classroom. In J. Epstein & N. Karweit (Eds.), *Friends in school*. New York: Academic Press, 1983.

Slavin, R. E., & Oickle, E. Effects of cooperative learning teams on student achievement and race relations: Treatment by race interactions. *Sociology of Education*, 1981, *54*, 174–180.

Wheeler, R. *Predisposition toward cooperation and competition: Cooperative and competitive classroom effects*. Paper presented at the Annual Convention of the American Psychological Association, San Francisco, 1977.

Ziegler, S. The effectiveness of cooperative learning teams for increasing cross-ethnic friendship: Additional evidence. *Human Organization*, 1981, *40*, 264–268.

2

Children in Cooperation and Competition
Antecedents and Consequences of Self-Orientation

EMMY A. PEPITONE

This chapter first considers several theoretical issues on the conceptualization of competition and cooperation, considerations that were particularly salient in guiding our research. Those concerns have generalizability to group interaction, as we demonstrate here by a focus on interpersonal classroom dynamics.

In the second part of the chapter, we present a series of related studies of elementary school children from different socioeconomic backgrounds. Emphasis is on children's interpersonal behavior and performance as they work under experimentally controlled competitive and cooperative conditions. The need for continued research along these lines is stressed, contrasting value contexts of children's social environments.

Findings from this research lead into an additional examination of the children's self-orientations within a theoretical framework that highlights some possible antecedents and consequences. We argue that children's excessive concern with themselves may prevent growth of an understanding of the needs of others. If so, the introduction of cooperative learning procedures is likely to be less effective unless an effort is made simultaneously to reduce self-oriented behaviors.

DISTINCTIONS BETWEEN AND WITHIN CONDITIONS OF COMPETITION AND COOPERATION

Cooperation and competition constitute certain relationships between two or more persons. Based on his landmark study at MIT on students who were being graded either traditionally by competition or on the ba-

EMMY A. PEPITONE • Department of Education and Child Development, Bryn Mawr College, Bryn Mawr, Pennsylvania 19010.

sis of a grade for their group performance, Deutsch (1949) concluded that both situations are conditions of interdependence. In either case, people's "fates" are intertwined. In classrooms where students learn in a competitive goal structure (such as grading on the curve), interdependence is "contrient." [1] One pupil's aim, or goal, is in opposition to that of all the others in that a pupil's obtaining the highest grade automatically determines to some degree the fate of each of the others, just as the best pupil's fate depends on the others' doing worse. In cooperative situations, where, for instance, learning groups are given a grade based on the group's performance, there is quite a different kind of interdependence; any individual's success depends directly on the success of his or her peers. Not only does one or more pupils' problem solving help all the rest to reach their individual goals (i.e., they are "promotively interdependent"), but one or more pupils' misdirections or failures to perform may hinder all the others.

The Deutsch conceptualization was written from a field-theoretical social-psychological point of view. It emphasizes forces emanating from these two goal structures, contrient and promotively interdependent, which, in turn, he said determined different interpersonal behaviors. This formulation, made under the prevalent behaviorist orientation of the past three decades, underwent subtle changes as the concept of *reward* replaced the concept of *goal*. The more limited concept of reward was perhaps more appropriate when used in classrooms where, from the point of view of most teachers and students, grades were given as rewards for learning. Thus, today, the most widely followed definitions of cooperation and competition, as applied to learning settings, are those proposed by Johnson and Johnson (1974, 1975): A *cooperative* reward structure is one in which two or more individuals are rewarded based on their performance as a group, and a *competitive* reward structure is one in which, from among two or more persons, only those who perform best are rewarded. Additionally, the Johnsons saw the necessity of introducing the concept of an *individualistic* reward structure, in which each individual is rewarded solely for his or her own performance, regardless of others' work.

From the large number of empirical comparisons on the effectiveness of these three classroom reward structures arose the need for yet more refined and specific distinctions. Recent research on various

---

[1] The terms "contrient interdependence" and "promotive interdependence" are used by Deutsch to denote what he considers the salient defining characteristics of competitive and cooperative social conditions: the inherently different goal-relationships among members in these two different situations, as elaborated in the following pages.

cooperative learning methods in classrooms (e.g., Sharan & Hertz-Lazarowitz, 1980; Slavin, 1983a,b) has directed attention beyond comparisons of cooperative, competitive, and individualistic reward structures to an emphasis on a comparison of the effects of *different* cooperative learning strategies. Thus, Slavin (1983b) dealt only with "cooperative incentive structures," in which rewards are given for academic work performed in group settings. In cooperation, Deutsch emphasized only rewards given to "the-group-as-a-whole," stressing the substitutability of members' goal striving activities so that any one member's progress, or lack of progress, toward the goal could move all other members along. Slavin made a distinction between such group rewards, given for the performance of the group as a whole, and group rewards based on each pupil's individual performance (which may then be combined in one form or another to yield a group score). Clearly, this is a refinement of Deutsch's concept of promotively interdependent goal structures.

To my mind, there is a difference between the meaning of *group reward* and *group goal*. The latter, as used in group dynamics theory, denotes the objectives of a group; the focus is what the group wishes to accomplish. This is theoretically different from any additional external evaluation placed on the accomplishment itself, or from rewards given to the group on the basis of the evaluation such as are represented by grade assignments. This distinction may be particularly relevant to learning settings, considering the important literature on extrinsic versus intrinsic motivation (e.g., Condry, 1977; Deci, Betley, Kahle, Abrams, & Porac, 1981). In the latter, self-imposed goals are present in the absence of rewards, and in the former, the focus is on externally imposed goals and rewards. As classroom rewards are generally restricted to grades or evaluations of one kind or another, the Slavin distinction is valuable in learning environments. It allowed Slavin to demonstrate superiority of learning under group rewards based on each pupil's individual performance, as opposed to conditions where individual performance was neglected and the reward was given for the group's final performance.

As stated at the outset, Deutsch's distinction (1949) between cooperative and competitive conditions was based solely on individual goal relationships. Today, the need is being recognized for consideration of task structures as another separate source of interdependence. For instance, Slavin (1983b) made a further distinction within cooperative learning structures between task specialization and group study: In the former condition, each pupil is given a particular part of the group task to carry out; in the latter, such specific and exclusive assignments are absent. By introducing yet another variable, that of presence or absence of group reward, Slavin was able to evaluate the relative contributions of each of these variables within different cooperative learning settings.

The conceptualizations on which my own research is based have evolved over a period of more than a decade (an earlier exposition may be found in Pepitone, 1980, especially Chapter 2). I try to advance Deutsch's conceptualization in several ways. First, two separate sources of interdependence are distinguished: those stemming from goal relationships and those deriving from task structures. Further, each of these relationships varies in degree along a dimension of interdependence. We have found it useful to employ in our research design the additional concept of similarity with regard to both degree of goal similarity among group members and similarity of their respective task assignments. Next, we examine in greater detail how the concept of goal and task similarity allows more exact specification and operationalization of degree of member interdependence along these two dimensions.

ON GOAL INTERDEPENDENCE

A conception of the dimensionality of interdependencies may be said to be implied in the original Deutsch (1949) formulation: Promotive interdependence is defined as "any situation . . . in which a goal region can be entered (to some degree) by any individual . . . if all the individuals . . . can also enter their respective goal regions . . . (to some degree)" (p.132). What is implied here is that member goals are in "overlapping regions"—to stay within the field-theoretical conceptual frame—or, put differently, members share some aspect of each other's goals "to some degree." Parallel considerations appear in the case of competition: In Deutsch's definition "if a goal region is entered by one individual, the other . . . will to some degree be unable to reach his (p.132)." Again, goals are shared "to some degree," but the attainment of one is in opposition to the attainment of another; that is, they are contrient.

Shared goals, then, be they promotive or contrient, by their very nature will resemble each other "to some degree." This similarity of goal structures has important implications for the performance of members, as will be discussed shortly. At this point, it is necessary to understand that the degree of goal similarity is one source of interdependence among persons and that it may be ordered along a dimension from zero similarity (A's and B's goals are completely different), through various degrees of increasing similarity, to identity of goal structure. Such identity of individual goals is often called a *group goal*. Just how, theoretically, individual goals may be transformed into a group goal still remains an unsolved conceptual issue. It is generally assumed that the existence of a highly attractive group goal, accepted by all members, creates the strongest interdependence; hence, experimental research in the area of cooperation—including our own investigations—presents potential collaborators with group goals that are likely to be accepted by each member.

Of course, each person is likely to have in his or her motive structure various different goals, some of which may exist simultaneously. In an analysis of cooperative or competitive group situations, we tend to ignore such diverse personal goals, and concern ourselves only with those that are relevant to the group situation of interest. Thus, for instance, when children prepare for a school play, the common goal for which they strive individually may be assumed to be a successful performance. It is also likely that individual pupils have a number of additional goals that, as a rule, also bear strong resemblance to each other. For example, because children in the same classroom tend to share such factors as developmental stage similarity, exposure to similar classroom instruction and norms, and living in similar neighborhoods, their goals also tend to resemble one another. Individual goals in our school play example might include pleasing the teacher, reaping rewards from relatives and friends, and imagining the performance as a first step toward becoming a famous actor or actress.

Dissimilarity of individual goals may of course also coexist in cooperative situations, and such member disagreement may hinder group progress. In the above example, one or more children may have stage fright, may detest acting, or simply may wish to do something else. The effects of goal dissimilarity depend on how it is handled by both the dissenting member and the rest of the group. Nonparticipation may simply weaken the total resources available to the group; dissenters may be carried along with other members into the goal region of success on the night of performance, regardless of individual goal differences. This assumption follows from Deutsch's definition of positive goal interdependence. More serious consequences may occur when a child not only refuses to participate but also actively seeks to undermine the group's success. She or he may grimace at the audience at a particularly moving moment, trip up another actor, or use other devilish devices calculated to reduce the group's success. In classroom situations, one of the responsibilities inherent in teaching is to induce acceptance of the stated goals, regardless of deviance in the personal goals of pupils.

A summary of these arguments asserts that the greater the similarity of individual goals in cooperative situations, the stronger the positive member interdependence. In competitive situations, similarity of goals, along with task similarity, plays a very special and very different role. We return to this issue after a brief examination of the general effects of task similarity.

Regardless of the type or degree of competitive or cooperative interdependencies, rarely are individuals able to sit back and wait passively to be moved into their goal region. Most of the time, they must *do* something, and what they do is determined to various degrees by the work that must be performed. Thus, the *activity structure*—or task— that requires action on the part of individuals in a group is another source of interdependence relations.

ON TASK INTERDEPENDENCIES

Tasks have been characterized in many different ways, with task difficulty and divisibility being perhaps the most important aspects of activities carried out in cooperative or competitive settings (for further discussion, see Pepitone, 1980, Chapter 2, p. 70 ff.; Steiner, 1972; Hackman and Morris, 1975). In cooperation, the divisibility of tasks is particularly relevant to the distribution of labor in some collaborative groups, as we shall see shortly. A high degree of similarity among the tasks carried out by different members also has important performance implications. This fact was recognized by Deutsch in his second hypothesis, which postulates the substitutability of similarly intended actions of cooperating members. As is the case with goals, tasks may also be ordered along a similarity dimension that may be assumed to vary from zero, where A's and B's tasks are completely different (i.e., no common work features are present), through various degrees of increasing similarity, to identity of work assignments.

Regardless of the degree of task interdependence, each task demands certain specific skills if the particular work is to be executed. Based on existing group dynamics theory, we have distinguished in our research three major sources of the skills needed in competitive and cooperative situations: (1) *task activity requirements*—demands stemming from the properties of tasks that require the manipulation of materials (e.g., how bricks are to be laid); (2) *task role requirements*—interpersonal relationships dictated by the demands of the task (e.g., who needs to have contact with whom to lay the bricks); and (3) *group role requirements*—demands that stem not directly from the properties of the tasks, but from the internal needs of the group to maintain itself for task performance (e.g., one group role may be to settle quarrels, or to initiate and continue discussion; such roles may be essentially the same in situations where the task activity requirements are radically different).

Thus far, we have outlined several concepts and specified two separate dimensions that may give rise to different kinds and degrees of interdependencies among individuals.[2] These basic formal considerations make it possible to distinguish different patterns of the combined goal and task interdependencies that may arise in various types of competitive and cooperative conditions, respectively. Such a beginning classificatory scheme is presented next, with distinctions between the various patterns based on both the kind and the degree of interdependence found in each.

PATTERNS OF INTERDEPENDENCE

COACTION: THE CONDITION OF LEAST INTERDEPENDENCE

The competitive conditions of the least member interdependence on each of the two dimensions are those in which persons each work on a different task by and for themselves, with different goals, yet side by side with others. In conditions of near-zero interdependence, the tasks are considerably different from each other; one person's goal attainment is not dependent on the other's, and no interpersonal interaction is required. Johnson and Johnson (1974) would identify this situation as individualization, but the presence of others introduces an element of competition. Were each person isolated from and wholly unaware of the coacting others, competition would most likely be absent. What makes this a competitive situation is that, as F. H. Allport (1924) so aptly put it, "the mere presence of others" is sufficient to elicit competitive motives and besting behaviors. Empirical evidence, from Allport's work to my own (Pepitone, 1972), indicates that under conditions of such coaction, children and adults alike will start paying attention to "the sights and sounds of others" (again Allport's words).

---

[2]In a recent theoretical analysis that continues his concern with types of interpersonal interdependencies, Deutsch (1982) lists as one of several dimensions the dimension of cooperation–competition. However, he conceives of this dimension as bi-polar, as a "pro-con" distribution, ranging from such relationships as close friends, teammates, co-workers and the like at the cooperative end, to personal enemies, divorced couples, and political opponents. Of course he readily admits to oversimplification inherent in such dichotomizations. I take issue with this categorization not so much on these grounds, but rather because it sets up false opposites. Based on the research evidence presented later in this chapter, it would appear conceptually more correct, and empirically more useful, to consider cooperative and competitive situations as two distinctly different social fields. Different constellations of forces are created—the degree of difference being a function of particular patterns of goal and task interdependence as is described below—but the respective force fields give rise to qualitatively different kinds of social behaviors.

In school settings, this state of affairs is an apt characterization of the most common learning climates that exist in today's classrooms during periods of "seat work." Educators label these instructional methods as "individualized learning," and social psychologists such as Johnson and Johnson (1974) similarly refer to these conditions as "individual goal structures." I consider it theoretically more correct to refer to such situations as *minimal competitive learning situations* because of the comparison processes that are found to occur there and that I assume to be sufficient to initiate a competitive cycle. F. H. Allport merely denoted the phenomenon, referring to the minimal condition—as I interpret him—as "social facilitation," and to conditions of increased contrient dependence as "rivalry," defined as "an emotional reinforcement of movement accompanied by a conscious desire to win" (p. 262). Our series of studies supports the assumption of a tripartite process of social comparison that occurs whenever two or more persons perceive each other as relevant in some way.

The more similar task activities are to each other in coaction, the more information can be gained by comparison. We postulate three interrelated processes that comprise the total comparison. First, in order to assess oneself or another in terms of the progress made, relative success, and so on, attentional processes must be engaged in so that others or their performance outcomes may be observed. Second, these processes are closely followed by and often intermingle with evaluational processes, which allow inferences about relative standings, and about the level of the opponent's abilities, strengths and weaknesses, tactics, and so forth. Third, motivational processes are aroused in the form of achievement-related motives as a result of conclusions drawn from the inferences. The comparison process may be initiated by any one of the three subprocesses. Highly motivated persons will wish to assess their competitors and in so doing attend to their performance. Yet a child's mere attention to another for some point of information about an assignment may evoke the other two processes as well. As the similarity of the activities in which various children engage increases, so does the amount of nonverbal attention paid to others (Pepitone and Hannah, 1980), and this attention is increased still more as the similarity of the goals is increased and goal contriency becomes explicit.

To return to the distinction between individualized learning structures and competitive reward structures, the empirical difference is only in the degree of competitiveness, primarily created by the teacher's explicitness about goal contriency. It follows that it is a mistake to assume that just because pupils are working on different tasks and are graded on their own performance rather than on the sliding scale, competitive motivations and besting are absent. To the extent that there are common elements in such coaction (e.g., each pupil aiming for a high grade, checking true or false on identical worksheets, or turning pages and so on), social comparison predictably occurs. This is not to say that teachers have no control over this situation. Deemphasis of grades certainly may decrease pupil perception of goal contriency, and different worksheets for each pupil will decrease perception of task similarity, consequently decreasing the perception of negative interdependence— not, however, completely so, as long as pupils are in coactive learning arrangements.

COLABOR: THE CONDITION OF LEAST COOPERATIVE INTERDEPENDENCE

Conditions of coaction and colabor resemble each other, differing only in the degree of positive goal-relatedness and goal similarity.

Let us start with coaction. As an example, consider a situation in which each child is asked to draw independently a picture in his or her seat. Task similarity is moderately low—after all, each child may draw whatever she or he wishes; and hence, there are neither shared individual goals nor a common goal. No "reward" is offered, although in the Deutsch sense and our sense there is some goal similarity—that is, each child is to end up with a picture. Other things being equal, we guess that children will start casting glances at their neighbors (the "attention" part of the comparison process). Before long, someone is bound to start an upward cycle of comparison with an "innocent" remark such as "Mine is better than yours" (the evaluation process begins). Some children will refuse to tell what they are making, some may actually cover their page to prevent others from copying. Such hindering behaviors indicate children's increased sense of goal similarity, task similarity, and goal contriency. The drawings will start looking alike in subject matter or style. Clearly, the coactive situation is becoming explicitly competitive.

Now suppose that the teacher informs the class that it is the principal's birthday and suggests that they might want to combine their individual pages into a book as a present for him or her. The chances are, if the response is enthusiastic, that the classroom climate will change. There will be increased communication, each child eager to tell what he or she is making (indicative of decreased goal contriency), perhaps even asking permission to crayon along with another (growing feelings of goal interdependence approaching goal identity). Individual tasks, perceived as more similar, may now even seem substitutable. By changing a situation of low goal contriency and moderate task similarity to one of moderate promotive goal interdependence, collaboration has been accomplished.

It should be apparent that in conditions of colabor, as compared with coaction, the crucial difference lies in the common goal. Interdependence is strengthened to the extent that there is a similarity between individual goals. In our example, the common goal is the final product of the gift of a book for the principal, and the goal similarity may lie in each child's making a picture of flowers for her or him. During the process of working toward a common goal, tasks that may have been seen as individual may actually be perceived as more interdependent (although *colabor*, as our definition implies, denotes situations where a very low degree of task interdependence is created). It is our hypothesis, however, that these situations of lowest group interdependence are fluid and may be changed from one into the other, without encountering much resistance. In our example, by changing a situation of low goal contriency and moderate task similarity to one of moderate promotive goal interdependence, some degree of collaboration has been established. This issue clearly merits further investigation.

COMPETITIVE COUNTERACTION

Some competition does require interaction. In what we call *competitive counteraction*—as in many games, such as singles tennis and chess—absolute goal contriency exists, but the task requirements demand interactive exchange. In Deutsch's competitive groups, the students were required to engage in group discussion, knowing that their contributions would be graded in comparison to those of their classmates. While overtly making positive contributions, the students frequently attempted to put down other students or otherwise denigrated others while "upping" their own standings. The task interdependence here may be strong and may actually require positive interaction; the source of negative interrelationships resides in the basic goal contriency. Rules and regulations in more formal games may serve the purpose of both justifying certain negative interactions and restraining others. It is an intriguing question whether and to what extent in the Deutsch situation there existed a positive shared goal relationship as well, serving as an added source of positive interdependence and counteracting contriency of goals. Along those lines, I have noted classroom patterns where teachers actively gave encouragement for participation and information sharing as an explicit classroom norm, whereas the pupils, perceiving themselves to be operating under conditions of goal contriency, resolved the conflicting expectations by high classroom participation, addressed exclusively to the instructors and wholly neglecting their classmates.

Competitive counteraction is differentiated from coaction not only because it requires overt task-related interaction, but also because of its implied demands for the interactive skills necessary to execute these tasks. These skills require a certain level of development and experience in anticipating the behavior of others. In coaction, where, by definition, interaction is not required, individuals need only to possess simple assessment skills to evaluate their own and their competitor's status: Is he ahead? If so, then I must speed up; he is making a picture of a man—I'll make three men to beat him (the latter was actually a frequent response of second-grade working-class children in Pepitone, Loeb, & Murdoch, 1980).

To be sure, there are coactive situations in which more complex inferential skills are also required. But it is typically in counteraction that formal reasoning and empathic understanding are required, as one competitor must anticipate the other's move, and prepare his or her own defense and the likely response and counterresponse. This point is important to keep in mind because, contrasted with cooperation, competition is often considered a more "natural" response in small children. Not only is there cross-cultural evidence that casts some doubt on this assertion (Graves, 1976), but it must also be remembered that competitive situations may be highly complex, often requiring the ability to assess and negotiate in sophisticated and difficult interpersonal situations.

COORDINATIVE COLLABORATION

A complement to competitive counteraction is found in coordinative collaboration, where some degree of task interdependence is required; it is found where two or more individuals help each other in exchange for reaching their own personal goals, rather than working toward a common, shared goal. In fact, the individual goals of each person may be wholly different, or they may overlap, to various degrees, and vary anywhere along a similarity continuum. The relationship between them may be characterized by the proverbial "You scratch my back and I scratch yours"; agreements may be either spontaneous or contractual within the context of a task-related exchange. It is this task relationship, rather than the goals, that is promotive.

The Nelson and Madsen (1969) marble-pull game serves as an example of identical individual goals reachable only through task interdependence. Each child pulled in a reward only when the other let go of his or her string. Taking turns pulling and letting go was the only equitable solution, and it was the most productive in terms of total rewards. More individualized goals may be involved with older children and adults. Schofield (1980) described such exchange relationships among high-school friends, where Mary allows John to copy her math assignment if he will draw a map for her.

This "coordination of activities in order for individuals to obtain what they want" (Bryan, 1975, p. 130) is frequently accepted as the standard definition of cooperation. Such differentiated task assignments are closely allied to role division, a condition of potentially the greatest interdependence and of such a degree of complexity that we prefer to distinguish it from the other two cooperative conditions.

ROLE-RELATED COOPERATION

This condition is characterized by the strongest task and goal interdependencies. It may be described at its most complex as all members striving to reach a common goal, with each person being utilized in movement toward that goal. In colabor, the only source of interdependence is, by definition, goal commonality on the support dimension, and in coordinative collaboration, it is the interdependent task relationship. However, in role-related cooperation, all of the sources of interdependence combine to make this the condition of greatest potential member interdependence. The stress is on potential interdependence because there is no assurance that, in each situation where such strong requirements for task-role and group-role enactment exist, the individual persons involved will be able and willing to carry them out. Although the model comes closest to Deutsch's "promotive interdependence," there has been relatively little research on the complex interface between task requirements and role relationships.

The label of *role-related cooperation* emphasizes the dominant function of both task roles and group roles in this type of promotively interdependent situation. From a role-theoretical point of view, coordinative cooperation may be described as a situation in which the reciprocal execution of different task roles is expected so that each person may reach his or her own goal. In role-related cooperation, where there is one common goal, the function of different group members in fulfilling different task requirements may be such that each member will be expected to carry out certain activities that may be variously referred to as *role assignments, role responsibilities,* and the like. This model is exemplified in Aronson's Jigsaw program (1978), in which task interdependencies are created by assigning each pupil one part of a learning problem, the solution of which is needed by all the members in a small group. (It may be of interest here that this procedure is, in fact, an operational definition of Slavin's [1983] definition of *task specialization*). For ease of execution, researcher and teacher alike generally assign both tasks and roles to given pupils. The perhaps more typical situation in which a group is given a goal and must evolve its own role divisions deserves at least equal attention.

In "real-life situations," the members usually do not assume equal burdens, and these conditions pose fascinating theoretical issues. Slavin's (1983b) distinction between group rewards based on each individual performance and the rewards given to the group as a whole points to one direction of further study. Another important area is related to the concept of group roles, defined above as roles in which the requirements stem not directly from the task, but from the internal needs of the group to maintain itself in order to accomplish its work. As early as 1948, Benne and Sheats distinguished between task roles and group roles. The latter concept especially has been relatively neglected in both research and practice. In role-related cooperation, though, group roles are essential; it is almost inconceivable that a working group could proceed smoothly without member functions that would, for instance, "break the ice" at the first meeting of a new group, involve nonparticipants, mediate disputes throughout the work process, and so on. Regardless of role distribution—whether roles are assumed by different members or combined in the role of a "leader," a supervisor, or other authority figure—it appears likely that such basic group roles are required to various degrees in all role-related cooperation.

To some extent, role-related cooperation may be said to have a counterpart in competitive counteractive conditions, where the task interdependency is so extensive that each move of one partner is almost wholly contingent on an opponent's move. I am tempted here to speak of "role-related competitive counteraction," were it not for the fact that although the partners must indeed learn to anticipate or "expect" the opponent's behavior (and in that sense develop role expectations, as do group members in cooperative conditions), here the expectations are utilized in order ultimately to eliminate the opponent as a threat to one's own exclusive goal attainment. Although both conditions are thus characterized by extremely complex task interdependencies, the goal relations in the two situations are so diverse as to typify the largest difference between competitive and cooperative conditions.

Task activities in competitive counteraction, however, may be exceedingly similar, and this potential similarity has important theoretical implications. Group dynamics research on interpersonal relations has shown consistently that task similarity increases the attraction between group members (Back, 1948; Byrne, 1971). Another body of research in social psychology has postulated (G. Allport, 1954), and to some extent demonstrated, positive relationships between the personal contact of group members, especially if they are on equal status levels, and liking of each other (Cook, 1978). If we extrapolate from both these trends, we may expect that, given an equal degree of task similarity in a condition of coaction and competitive counteraction, group members would be less attracted to each other in the former condition, as interpersonal contact is absent in coaction by definition. As yet, there is no satisfactory explanation of what variables may mediate between similarity and attraction. Two mediating variables may be suggested: Similarity of task assignment provides a common bond between strangers, increasing the sense of familiarity and its general consequences of increased trust and liking. In competitive counteraction, there is the additional task requirement of having to respond to the opponent's moves. Anticipation requires projection into the other's intentions and more general cognitive structure, possibly even into his or her affective state. If so, such empathic understanding may provide a wider base of similarity, further increasing liking of the opponent. Having to take account of the opponent's ingenuity, prowess, or skills may introduce even an additional component of respect into the adversary relationship. Along these lines, it is not uncommon to note prominent figures—for instance, in the world of sports—publicly expressing admiration for each other, and even developing friendships on the termination of the contest.

Research into these complex counteractive competitive conditions is nonexistent. It must also be left for future research to determine whether it is possible to build a cohesive and mutually supportive group composed of such former arch competitors.

Role enactment skills, along with motivational factors, may be considered the human counterpart of the environmental conditions of cooperation and competition. It is, of course, crucial to understand the skills available to children at different points in their development that will enable them to engage successfully in given tasks. In school settings, curriculum development may be said to constitute attempts to match task requirements with children's mastery of skills at different ages. The goals of our research were to understand children's abilities to fulfill the roles required in competitive and cooperative situations. We feel that this information is crucial for adapting cooperative and competitive instructional strategies to different age levels and societies. In the next section, the experimental methodologies employed to this end are delineated, followed by a presentation of the line of research that we pursued in order to further our understanding of the development of children's interpersonal behaviors in different environments.

STUDIES OF INTERACTIONS OF CHILDREN'S FAMILIAL BACKGROUND, AGE, AND SEX WITH THEIR INTERPERSONAL BEHAVIOR AND PERFORMANCE IN COOPERATIVE AND COMPETITIVE CONDITIONS

Our investigations were carried out almost exclusively within public-elementary-school settings. The first explorations confirmed our belief that the area of interest was of such complexity and diversity that, in order to permit any kind of meaningful general understanding, it was essential to plan a series of studies that would employ a uniform methodology. For the same reasons, it also became evident that, at the beginning at least, controlled experimental research was preferable to naturalistic studies.

What was needed was a task that would be sufficiently flexible to create the different interdependencies in the goal and work structures that make up the different types of cooperative and competitive situations described earlier. Additional important criteria were (1) that the task must be adaptable to children of various ages; (2) that it must be relatively independent of demands on the children's intelligence or other specific abilities; (3) that the task would permit the observation and the recording of the children's behavior and performance throughout the work period; and (4) that the children would find it enjoyable.

What emerged was a methodology that has proved highly satisfactory over the years. It came to be known among the students who were involved in the research as the *Pep Board Task*.

EXPERIMENTAL METHODOLOGY

THE WORK TASK

The task consists of two parts (for details, see Pepitone, 1980, Chapter 3). (1) the Pep Board—a custom-made 40 inch circle of ½-inch Duraply, covered with a blue velvety material commercially known as Velcro; and (2) Pattern Blocks from the Elementary Science Study Program produced by McGraw-Hill and by Creative Publications. The latter are 250 variously shaped and colored flat blocks adapted by us so that each piece can adhere firmly to the board but is easily movable and capable of being placed in different positions. Several of the shapes may be combined to substitute for each other (e. g., six equilateral triangles combine to form a hexagon).

THE INDEPENDENT VARIABLES

Cooperative and competitive environments constituted the major global factors created in the different studies. Depending on the needs of the particular investigation, the task requirements varied from wholly unstructured ("You may make anything you wish") to highly structured ("Copy the design exactly as you see it in front of you").

The procedure involved taking three like-sexed children to a vacant classroom and asking them to work on the Pep Board.

Cooperative goal structures were created by asking the children to make one product together. Additional incentives were sometimes provided by holding out an indivisible group reward. The children were told that if their outcome was "special," they and their product would be photographed, and the picture would be printed in a book. In the competitive condition, several children worked around the board, each making his or her own product, and the reward was promised for "the best" outcome in such competitive coaction.

Actually, a photograph was always taken at the end of each session, as it served as the basis for scoring performance at a later date. Additionally, the photograph proved an excellent debriefing device, as the children were told that they all did so well that each product would be photographed. This outcome put them in a positive mood; they promised not to divulge what had transpired until the others had had a chance to play also; and they returned happily and proudly with their "secret" to the classroom.

But behavior, as Lewin (1935) put it so concisely, is an interaction of personal and environmental variables. Much thought was given to the selection of the individual difference variables. We decided to concentrate at first on the global factors that are generally accepted as indicators of children's growth; that could be reliably isolated, controlled, and measured; and that had proved important in related research. In the series of studies that are examined below, these personal variables included the children's age, sex, and familial socioeconomic status (SES). These variables led to more specific questions, a further refinement of the variables, and further research, some of which is also presented here.

THE DEPENDENT VARIABLES

INTERPERSONAL BEHAVIOR.   In all investigations, at least two observers recorded the behavior in precoded categories. The unit of verbal behavior was taken as the period of a child's speech separated by a pause or by another child's verbalization. Nonverbal behavior was differentiated by a change from one activity to the next. The emphasis was principally on task- and group-role-related behavior. In competitive conditions, this procedure turned out to include mainly various manifestations of social comparison and besting behaviors, whereas in cooperation the focus was on various prosocial behaviors. The specific categories are defined as individual studies are examined.

The observers were trained during pilot studies until their agreement for each category reached 90% or higher. During several of the studies, the second observer alternated between making periodic reliability checks and keeping running records of the quality of the children's verbal and nonverbal behaviors to supplement the precoded categories.

PERFORMANCE.   A variety of measures was explored. These included the quantity of pieces, and various indices of quality, such as product balance, originality, elaborateness of design, and distinctiveness of theme. These separate scores proved highly positively interrelated, so that for most studies the most inclusive measure, that of product complexity, is reported.

RELATIONSHIPS BETWEEN SES, AGE, SEX, AND CHILDREN'S INTERPERSONAL BEHAVIORS AND PERFORMANCE

SAMPLE POPULATIONS

The foundation for this series of studies was provided by two separate parallel doctoral investigations (Murdoch, 1974; Loeb, 1975). The authors collaborated in perfecting a common methodology that was employed in the study of the total pupil population, kindergarten through fifth grade, in two elementary schools from school districts entirely different in socioeconomic status. One sample, designated as working class (WC), came from a North Philadelphia city school whose parent population was almost exclusively white. According to the 1970 census information, over 80% of the parents in this district were classified as blue-collar workers, and only 7% as professionals. The second sample was composed of children from a suburban school located on the Philadelphia "Main Line." The parents in this school district were white, and over 90% were employed in professional and managerial positions. We designated this sample as upper middle class (UMC).

A classification of each child by parental status was not possible in this series. However, the following excerpts from informal observer impressions about the two schools may point to their palpable lifestyle differences:

> In suburbia . . . school building was a modern cinderblock and glass structure . . . . Each classroom had glass walls looking out on three acres of landscaped garden area and surrounding countryside . . . . Fourth wall opened into corridor so teachers and children felt free to move about within classroom or visiting another, often for some enrichment experience . . . . Most children were bused or driven by car . . . . At the end of school day . . . parking lot was filled with oversize station wagons driven by housekeepers, maids, or brightly dressed mothers, chatting . . . . often another young child with his or her own steering wheel strapped in a carseat next to mother.
>
> The working-class school . . . grey stone and brick . . . fenced in, paved yard, not a tree or shrub in sight . . . a miniature fortress . . . inside when classes were in session . . . halls were empty, except for now and then a child sitting on floor outside classroom door, obviously being punished . . . occasional sharp voices of a teacher . . . appearance of a morgue . . . . Only on playground, bedlam broke loose . . . pushing, shoving and running games . . . apparently requiring little skill but sheer brawn. . . . .at the end of school day, older ones escaped for home on foot, younger ones often . . . picked up by mothers pushing baby carriage and/or toddler at side, sometimes wailing from a motherly slap or two. (Pepitone *et al.*, 1980, p. 211)

METHODOLOGY

In each classroom, like-sexed children were randomly grouped into triads, and half of these groups were, in turn, randomly assigned to conditions of competition or cooperation. We would have liked to distinguish between the different conceptual subtypes within each condition; however, even though these two studies were the most extensive in sheer number of subjects—employing 468 WC and 450 UMC children—the final design of 2 (conditions) $\times$ 2 (SES) $\times$ 2 (sex) $\times$ 6 (grades) left only 8–16 groups within each cell. Even these groups consisted of combined groups from different sections of a given grade, so that further subdivision into competitive and cooperative subtypes was methodologically unfeasible.

Hence, it was decided to maximize the differences between the two work environments. In the *cooperative condition* (Coop), a group goal was created so that one common product was required, and the additional group reward was contained in the promise of a photograph of the triad for "special performance." In the *competitive condition* (Comp), individual competitive goal structures were induced as follows: "We want to see which one of you can make the best picture." This instruction was reinforced by the promised individual reward of a photograph to be taken of the best product only.

Different types of task interdependence were operationalized through different task role requirements: In Coop, the children in each triad were asked to work together; in Comp, each child was to work independently of the other two coactors around the Pep Board. However, the task requirements themselves were identical in both conditions: the children were asked to make a flat picture of a person on the board. We wanted to choose performance content that could be handled by children of different ages at their own skill level. We agreed with the rationale of Goodenough (1926), Harris (1963), and Koppitz (1968), who argued for the universality of the human figure and its rich associative store at any age in support of the "draw-a-man" test. Our girl subjects' objections during pilot work convinced us very quickly to request a picture of a *person* instead of a man.

The assignment of this task afforded possibilities of cross-age comparisons of the products, as well as future cross-cultural comparisons.

SOME MAJOR FINDINGS

For each of the dependent variables, a separate 2 (SES) × 2 (sex) × 2 (condition) × 6 (grade) ANOVA, corrected for uneven cells, was performed. As a protection against gaining significance by increasing the number of analyses, a conservative alpha level ($p < .01$) was adopted. All *post hoc* comparisons used the Newman–Kuels procedure. Our definitions of the dependent variables are given below.

FREQUENCY AND TYPE OF INTERACTIONS IN CONDITIONS

One of the strongest main effects found was that, for each of the major dependent variables, there were significant condition differences ($p < .001$) (see Table 1). There was significantly less overall interpersonal interaction in Comp than in Coop; in the process observation records, one finds continuous reference to the fact that the triads who had entered the room chatting away and enjoying their initial exploration of the task fell into uncomfortable silence when the Comp conditions were introduced. Initially, we attempted to employ various group dynamics techniques to try to put the children at ease, but we have since accepted this reaction as typical of these competitive condi-

TABLE 1. Mean Behavior and Performance, by Condition, Sex, and Social Class[a]

Behavior and performance	Condition				Sex				Social class			
	Cooperative	Competitive	F[b]	p	Boys	Girls	F[b]	p	Upper middle class	Working class	F[b]	p
Nonverbal attention	13.48	30.84	45.40	< .001	22.37	21.96	0.03	n.s.	18.67	25.66	7.37	<.008
Task-oriented	24.10	11.64	26.05	< .001	19.40	16.34	1.57	n.s.	18.73	17.01	.49	n.s.
Other-oriented	19.11	0.90	152.05	< .001	10.41	9.60	0.30	n.s.	6.50	13.60	23.08	<.001
Performance	32.26	25.16	41.04	< .001	28.21	29.21	0.83	n.s.	31.15	26.28	19.35	<.001

[a]From Children in Cooperation and Competition: Toward a Developmental Social Psychology by E. A. Pepitone. Lexington Mass.: D. C. Heath and Company. Reprinted by permission.
[b]df (1,258).

tions. Along these lines, the most frequent behavior in the Comp condition was *nonverbal attention paid to others*, consisting mostly of looking at the coactors' product-in-process. This occurred over twice as frequently as it did in Coop. We interpreted these behaviors as being indicative of various aspects of the social comparison process postulated to occur in coactive Comp conditions, where no interaction is required. By contrast, there was over twice as much *task-oriented* behavior (verbal task-specific comments that were positive, neutral, or negative) in Coop as contrasted with Comp (average Coop = 24.10 vs. 11.64 in Comp; $F = 26.05$, $p < .001$). *Other-oriented* behaviors (consisting mostly of various forms of helping others, such as making verbal suggestions, actively showing the others how to place certain pieces, or placing pieces for them) were virtually absent in Comp, less than *one* other-oriented interaction in Comp (mean = .10), in contrast to a mean of 19.11 other-oriented behaviors in Coop.

It must be remembered here that we attempted to maximize the differences between the conditions in attempting to create pure coactive competitive conditions, on the one hand, and highly interdependent cooperative conditions, on the other. Apparently, we succeeded in doing so, and the postulated differences follow.

OTHER MAIN EFFECTS AND INTERACTIONS

Interestingly, the only consistent non-significant main effects on any of the dependent variables were those attributable to sex. We return to this important issue in our consideration of some later studies.

By contrast, the children's behaviors differed significantly as a function of their familial SES background. Of interest here is the fact that there were nonstatistically significant differences between the SES groups in task-oriented behaviors (averaging 18.73 for UMC children vs. 17.01 for WC children), suggesting that task involvement was about equal in the children from both samples. Nonverbal attention was the largest interaction category for both groups of children in Comp, but it was significantly higher for WC children (WC mean = 25.66 vs. 18.67 for UMC; $F = 7.37$; $p < .008$). In the light of the performance differences in the Comp condition to be examined next, we interpreted this nonverbal attention to be related to information seeking, betraying perhaps either a greater uncertainty of the WC children when working under Comp conditions, or the greater self-assurance of the UMC children (see Table 2).

There were several interactions between age (expressed through grade) and SES, both in the children's interpersonal behaviors and in

TABLE 2. Percentage of Children Making Stick Figures and Complete Persons, in Competitive Condition, by Grade[a]

		Grade					
		K	1	2	3	4	5
Stick figures[b]							
UMC	Boys	100	83.3	72.2	62.5	60	16.7
	Girls	83.3	83.3	58.3	94.1	75	45.8
WC	Boys	48.3	50.1	81	80	53.2	20
	Girls	53	85.7	77.4	77.8	73.3	60.7
Complete figures[b]							
UMC	Boys	0	12.5	27.8	37.5	26.7	66.7
	Girls	0	8.3	33.3	0	16.7	37.5
WC	Boys	0	14.3	4.8	20.0	40.0	20.7
	Girls	0	0	19.0	16.7	6.7	33.3

[a]From *Children in Cooperation and Competition: Toward a Developmental Social Psychology* by E. A. Pepitone. Lexington, Mass.: D. C. Heath, p. 225. Copyright 1980 by D. C. Heath and Company. Reprinted by permission.
[b]Where percentage figures do not total 100%, products fall into the additional categories of nonrecognizable or incomplete figures.

their performance. The following figures help to explicate these relationships. Figure 1 shows the mean performance complexity of WC and UMC children for each grade level in the Comp conditions. The products of the children from both schools improved up to second and third grade, where the asymptote was reached. At each grade level, the UMC children's performance surpassed that of the WC children. These performance differences received additional support from data on the nature of the products made by the children. The developmental trends in human figure drawing found stick figures appearing before complete figures. Indeed, in kindergarten, 100% of the UMC boys' groups, and almost all the girls' groups, composed stick figures with blocks. Only about half the WC kindergartners produced recognizable stick figures. They reached the level of the UMC kindergartners only approximately two years later.

Lest we jump to oversimplified explanatory theories of intelligence or cultural deficit, let us turn to Figures 2 and 3, which show trends in class differences in performance and other-oriented behaviors telling quite a different story.

There was a significant interaction between grade and SES ($F = 3.02$; $p < .01$), an interaction that was absent under Comp conditions. In Coop, the superiority of the UMC children's performance persisted, but only through second grade; by third grade and thereafter, the WC children performed as well as their UMC counterparts did. This trend might be interpreted to mean that the WC children, especially the older ones,

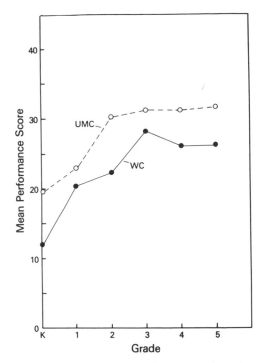

FIGURE 1. Competitive condition: Mean performance of working-class and upper-middle-class children. (From *Children in Cooperation and Competition: Toward a Developmental Social Psychology* by E. A. Pepitone. Lexington, Mass.: D. C. Heath, p. 224. Copyright 1980 by D. C. Heath and Company. Reprinted by permission.)

were able to work together better than their counterparts. And, indeed, Figure 3 demonstrates that at each grade level except the second grade, the WC children engaged in more other-oriented behaviors. This difference became highly significant at third grade and beyond.

We were left with questions that revolved around two major issues: (1) How can we account for the differences in behavior and performance of the children from these different familial backgrounds? (2) To what extent were the results in the Comp condition due to the specific condition of coaction that we had devised?

From the perspective of related research, our results pertaining to socioeconomic differences are not startling. Investigators employing game-theoretical methodologies with children have demonstrated that, in general, urban middle-class children are less "other-oriented" than are rural lower-class children (e.g., Shapira & Lomrantz, 1972; Kagan, 1977; Knight & Kagan, 1977). That is, the middle-class children

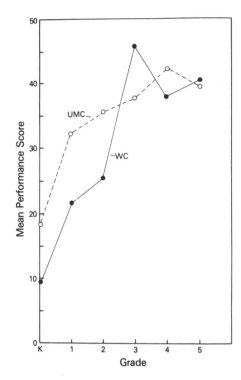

FIGURE 2. Mean performance of working-class and upper-middle-class children in cooperative condition. (From *Children in Cooperation and Competition: Toward a Developmental Social Psychology* by E. A. Pepitone. Lexington, Mass.: D. C. Heath, p. 240. Copyright 1980 by D. C. Heath and Company. Reprinted by permission.)

preferred to "maximize their own profits" (in game-theoretical language) as opposed to being willing to share them equally with others, or to give to others even more than to themselves. What the Loeb and Murdoch research contributed to this issue was, above all, a demonstration that (1) on the whole children from affluent suburban backgrounds *can function better* in competitive work situations than can children from less privileged urban working-class environments; and (2) when asked to collaborate, young "preoperational" WC children function at least as well as their UMC counterparts. From about the time when children are known to be capable of greater empathy for others (i.e., to have "decentered"), WC children collaborate with their peers significantly more when asked to do so. There are many possible interpretations of these findings; they are discussed in the last part of this chapter.

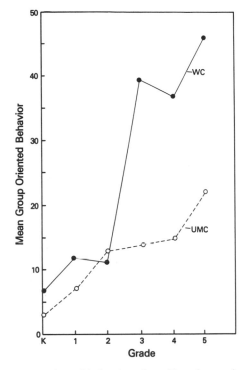

FIGURE 3.   Mean group-oriented behavior of working-class and upper-middle-class children in cooperative condition. (From *Children in Cooperation and Competition: Toward a Developmental Social Psychology*. Lexington, Mass.: D. C. Heath, 1980, p. 241. Copyright 1980 by D. C. Heath and Company. Reprinted by permission.)

Answering the second question posed above is basic to tackling the larger issue just raised. The outstanding finding that very little interaction took place in our Comp condition is in all likelihood a function of the individual goal contriency that required no interaction and of the fact that the task requirements did not impose such interactive roles. If we wish to discover how children will behave overtly in Comp conditions, then we must create Comp conditions that require interaction, at least to some degree, a requirement that is difficult to set up experimentally without turning it into a Coop condition.

The set of studies described below explored competitive conditions in which some interaction between students was necessary. The design developed to achieve these ends involved a conflict situation in which considerable goal contriency existed, which could be resolved only through some form of counteraction among the members. The experimental device involved creating a scarcity of material goods, a condition that may be defined as one in which there are fewer needed resources than there are individuals who need these resources.

UMC CHILDREN'S BEHAVIORS IN SCARCITY CONDITIONS

Economists call their study the "science of scarcity" in the sense that their problems derive from, and must solve, questions of the distribution of economic goods. No society can produce as many economic goods as can satisfy all of its people, so from that perspective scarcity is present in every society. In the United States, scarcity has been thus far of relatively little concern to the average citizen and scientists, perhaps because it has principally affected, up to now, only certain isolated segments of society. But the likelihood that the scarcity of a variety of resources will become a national problem increases daily. This may be one of the reasons for a recent upsurge in research in this area by leading social scientists, primarily into issues of the allocation of scarce resources (e. g., Lerner & Lerner, 1981). This area is of considerable theoretical interest because shortages may be remedied in different ways. Solutions may range from collaborative decisions with regard to equitable distribution practice to fierce competitive struggles over scarce goods (an extended discussion of the many conceptual issues surrounding conditions of scarcity may be found in Pepitone, 1980, Chapter 8).

Children, of course, experience scarcity and must resolve distribution problems in their own world, be they problems of parental affection, of teacher attention, or of sharing toys and other possessions with siblings and friends. Systematic studies of children's behaviors in such situations are also scarce.

We tried to exploit the fact that shortages in a group setting demand some kind of interpersonal interaction, be it competitive counteraction or coordinative cooperative exchange. The study that we decided on would, it was hoped, tell us something about what happens in situations where goal contriency exists (as it does in scarcity), but where, theoretically at least, solutions other than competition are possible. Further, if competitive solutions dominated (as was expected with the UMC sample involved), we would learn something about interpersonal behaviors in competitive counteractive situations.

THE SAMPLE

The subjects were 117 predominantly UMC second-graders from another elementary school in the same suburban school district previously described.

PROCEDURES

Because the basic procedures were in all respects identical to those described earlier, we detail here only the features unique to this study. Each child in a triad was asked to make an exact replica of a design with block pieces on the Pep Board. The box containing blocks was placed in the center of the board, and all three children had to remove from it the needed pieces.

To ensure that each child would perceive a state of scarcity, expectations of potential shortages were created through experimental instructions. To define the degree of existing scarcity, we introduced the criterion of substitutability. That is, in addition to the number of needed objects available in relation to the number of needy people, the substitute objects had the potential of serving as equivalents and thus reducing the scarcity. So, at the outset of the session, the children were introduced to the possibility of substituting various blocks for other blocks. They were encouraged (and helped, if needed) to explore different kinds of substitutions until they fully understood. This procedure was followed by instructions about the sequence to be followed in copying the design, which ensured that each child would need the same blocks at approximately the same time. Thus, the stage was set for the scarcity conditions to make their impact.

In this study, we also began to differentiate some of the global variables studied before. Thus, two degrees of competitive motivation were created, crossed with two degrees of scarcity threat.

Competitive motivation was varied independently of the goal contriency created by the scarcity threat. In the low-competition condition (LoC) the children were told that this was not a test, that we wanted to learn from them how teaching children about colors and shapes helps them to remember more about designs. In the *high-competition condition* (HiC), the children were told that we wanted to see who could come closest to making the exact picture and that the winner would be the one who used the blocks of the exact same colors and shapes.

In the *low-scarcity condition* (LoSc), the children were given assurance that there would be more than enough block pieces for all. In the *high-scarcity condition* (HiSc), they were told that there would not be enough block pieces for all three children to make the exact replica with exactly the same shapes and colors, and that substitutions would have to be employed to complete the picture.

The final design involved five boys' groups and five girls' groups assigned to each cell, except for the LoC-LoSc condition which lacked one boys' group. The observers again scored the children's behaviors in precoded categories, this time in relation both to the blocks and to each other. These behaviors are described in conjunction with the major results.

FINDINGS

Postsession interviews indicated that the desired conditions had indeed been established. In LoSc, the mean rating in answer to whether there had been sufficient blocks available was between 1 ("more than enough") and 2 ("enough"); in the HiSc condition, it was between 2 and 3 ("somewhat short"). It should be noted that even the HiSc condition was perceived as only moderately high in scarcity.

Our first question was whether the UMC children, placed in a LoC-LoSc condition where there was no threat of tests and where the supplies were ample, would show evidence of other-orientation (such as helping others) and concern about a fair distribution of the materials that were needed by all. For this purpose, we created a category of "concern about justice in distribution practice." On the verbal level, this comprised children's enunciation of distribution principles, such as equity and equality. Nonverbally, the category was reserved for eventualities such as one member's distributing the blocks among all three children, taking substitutes for herself or himself, and giving scarce items to others. Table 3 shows under "Equity concerns" that no group, in any of the four conditions, and not a single child in any of the groups, made any attempt to distribute the needed blocks more equitably. Similarly, the "Helping" category, which included assistance in the correct placement of the blocks, as well as various verbal suggestions with regard to improving performance, also averaged only a fraction of one interaction in each condition. A surprisingly significant increase in the "Helping" category may be noted in the HiSc condition. This was traceable to a small group of boys in that condition in the following way: In all groups, the children who had completed their task were asked to sit down at another table and to wait for the others who were still working. A number of boys who had already finished and had sat down returned to the table and helped the losers to complete the design. This behavior cannot, of course, be counted as helping in the strict sense, as the boys who did so had already completed their assignment and were the "first" to finish. Whether the boys' return was prompted simply by boredom, a need to assert their superiority once more, guilt or remorse over taking more than an equal share, or other motives cannot be determined here. The winning boys may have been the ones most highly motivated and, having battled their way to victory by amassing the blocks quickly and by any means available, were the ones who could subsequently afford to atone by being helpful to those whom they had caused to lose.

TABLE 3. Second-Graders' Mean Behaviors in Different Conditions of Motivation and Scarcity Threat[a]

Dependent behaviors	Sex			Experimental conditions						Significant interaction effects[b]	F
				Competition			Scarcity				
	Boys	Girls	F	LoC	HiC	F	LoSc	HiSc	F		
Sensitization											
Verbalization during work	.54	.52	n.s.	.63	.38	n.s.	.18	.87	11.34***	Sx × C × Sc	4.81*
Postwork ratings	2.33	2.05	n.s.	2.15	2.22	n.s.	1.96	2.40	5.52*		
Hoarding											
Simultaneous search	.84	1.30	3.18*	1.09	1.07	n.s.	.82	1.32	3.56*		
Amassing materials	1.32	1.28	n.s.	1.23	1.37	n.s.	1.04	1.55	4.44*		
Distributive justice											
Equity concerns	0.00	0.00	n.s.	0.00	0.00	n.s.	0.00	0.00	n.s.		
Hoarding attributions	.37	.38	n.s.	.14	.60	7.56**	.11	.63	9.83**	Sc × C	5.59*
Unfairness attributions	19.18	13.52	25.39***	17.09	15.50	n.s.	12.93	19.45	33.27***		
Achievement-related acts											
Desire to win	2.65	2.63	n.s.	2.37	2.90	5.34*	2.23	3.03	11.72***	Sx × C	5.48***
Verbal besting	1.67	.62	5.33**	.51	1.72	8.02**	.19	2.02	21.15***	Sx × C	3.65*
										Sx × Sc	4.35*
										C × Sc	4.67***
										Sx × C × Sc	9.65**
Mild aggressivity	.39	.12	4.88*	.25	.25	n.s.	.16	.33	n.s.		
Strong aggressivity	.79	.10	14.56***	.51	.37	n.s.	.05	.80	16.88***	Sx × Sc	9.58***
Helping	.46	.50	n.s.	.61	.35	n.s.	.21	.80	12.11***		

[a]From *Children in Cooperation and Competition: Toward a Developmental Social Psychology* by E. A. Pepitone. Lexington Mass.: D. C. Heath, p. 312. Copyright 1980 by D. C. Heath and Company. Reprinted by permission.

[b]Sx = Sex, C = Competitive condition, Sc = Scarcity condition.

*$p < .05$. **$p < .01$. ***$p < .001$.

Not only helping behaviors, but also "verbalization during work" was negligible, with a mean interaction again of less than 1 in each of the four conditions. This outcome confirms our earlier findings that coactive group conditions restrict interpersonal interaction. Though not significant, in the same verbalization during work category, there was even a trend of decreased interaction in HiC conditions as compared with LoC conditions. This trend was in line with earlier data on inverse relations between competitive motivation and interpersonal communication. However, as scarcity was increased, there was a highly significant increase in task-oriented verbalizations (LoSc = .18 vs. HiSc = .87; F = 11.34, $p < .001$). Here is the first indication that experience of scarcity forces children to interact more with each other.

In our earlier studies, we attributed the ever-present large amount of nonverbal attention paid to co-workers and the occasional snatching of blocks to underlying competitive motivation. In this study, the nonverbal indicators of competitive motivation were extended to the category of "Hoarding." This consisted of two subparts, both particularly relevant to scarcity conditions: (1) "simultaneous search" behavior was scored when a child inserted one or often both hands into the box while the other members were also rummaging for pieces. Although this action appeared entirely justified and proper, one could discern ulterior purposes. The simultaneity of rummaging could prevent others from obtaining the desired blocks, and the child could casually withdraw several pieces without appearing obviously possessive. This search for materials was closely allied to the second type of behavior, characterized as "amassing materials"; sometimes as many as a dozen pieces at a time would emerge in a grubby little hand after such a rummaging bout. On the average, both of these behaviors occurred in triads just a little more than once during the session in each condition. However, both types of hoarding were found again significantly more often in the HiSc condition. Some children omitted the first phase of hoarding; they waited until no hands were in the box and then, with lightning speed, collected all the blocks that they expected to need. Along with these silent but purposive searches, the children also accused each other openly of being unfair or of hoarding, again primarily in the HiSc condition. "Unfairness attributions" were found more frequently than any other verbal or nonverbal interactions. (It is noteworthy here that such accusations demonstrate an understanding of an underlying equity norm about the distribution of the blocks; however, in this situation, the children brought this norm into play only when *others* were in violation. It was not applied to a child's own behavior.)

The above trend toward significant increases in hoarding and interpersonal accusations in the HiSc condition suggests a difference between scarcity conditions and competitive conditions. In the former, a relatively greater need for required objects may be experienced. This need, as hypothesized, then stimulates increased verbal interaction. Accusations of unfairness may be seen as functional in the sense that there is an implied demand to cease taking scarce materials for oneself without consideration of others. Most of the time, however, these behaviors merely escalate the conflict rather than resulting in explicit agreements about equitable distribution practices. The significant interaction for the attribution of hoarding indicated that when high goal contriency (HiC) was combined with high scarcity threat (HiSc), the children reacted to each other as competitors for scarce goods, rather than looking for collaborative solutions.

Further evidence of the apparent differences and similarities between the competitive conditions and those of scarcity is presented under the category of "Achievement-related acts." They included verbal expressions of a "Desire to win" and "Verbal besting." Table 3 discloses that the children in both the HiC and HiSc conditions showed significantly higher levels of both these motivations than did the children in the corresponding low conditions. Yet, in the HiC condition, this strong motivation to win did not elicit aggressive behavior. Two levels of aggressivity were distinguished: "Mild aggressivity" was restricted primarily to verbal insults or minor skirmishes; "Strong aggressivity" was reserved for the occurrence of physical assaults. Both of these forms occurred with low frequency across conditions but, again significantly, more often in the HiSc condition. The children's most frequent attribution of unfairness to others in the HiSc condition, in fact, appears to have been objective.

It is important to recall that in this study the scarcity level was, relatively speaking, very low. Even in the HiSc condition, substitutes were available so that each child was able to complete the task. The children's achievement needs and aspirations to complete the model exactly as depicted, combined with the threat of a potential scarcity of the needed materials, were sufficient to elicit competitive counteractions expressed as accusations and other forms of verbal hostility and aggressive physical contacts.

May the same type of behaviors be expected under the same conditions in different samples of children? This issue and others are taken up in the last part of this chapter. First, however, a brief examination is in order of the strong sex differences also found in this study.

SEX DIFFERENCES

In contrast to the Loeb (1975) and Murdoch (1974) findings of no differences between boys' and girls' behaviors in competitive coaction, sex differences were found in this third study. In line with other research (Maccoby & Jacklin, 1974), the boys in the HiSc conditions, which were set up to elicit potential counteraction, indeed expressed significantly more physical aggression, verbal besting, taunting of competitors, unfairness attributions, and the like. In other words, the boys dispensed with polite pretense and expressed their needs physically and directly. In all these categories, the boys in the HiSc conditions exceeded the girls in the same conditions. Interestingly, the only category in which the girls significantly exceeded the boys was that of simultaneous search under the general category of hoarding. Rummaging behaviors may, in fact, be seen as a type of "semipassive" resistance, a preventive measure rather than an active attempt to assert one's own rights. The girls hoarded as much as the boys, and in postinterviews, they expressed as strong motivations to win as did the boys. The various interaction effects for both verbal besting and aggression leave no doubt that when boys are highly motivated to win and the needed supplies are scarce, they especially wish to maximize their own gain and and actively fight to obtain it. In the combined HiSc—HiC conditions, the boys had an average of 8.00 for verbal besting and 1.33 for strong aggressivity, as opposed to the girls' 0.53 and 0.00, respectively. On the whole, the data suggest that girls may be as achievement-oriented as boys but respond in more subtle, less aggressive ways. The next study offers additional supportive data for this hypothesis.

ANTECEDENTS AND CONSEQUENCES OF SELF-ORIENTATIONS

DEFINITION AND MEASUREMENT OF SELF-ORIENTATION

It must be emphasized that, in the research that we have presented thus far, we were not interested in SES differences *per se* from the sociologists' point of view. Rather, we became increasingly focused on the behaviors consistently displayed by the more privileged children, as compared with their less affluent counterparts. Most important appeared the demonstration that, at each elementary grade level, the UMC children's performance was superior to that of the WC children under competitive conditions and that, from third grade on, the UMC children helped each other less in cooperative conditions. Rounding out this pattern further was our finding in subsequent research that, even with the moderate degree of scarcity that we had created, another UMC sample responded in anything but prosocial ways: second-graders accused each other of being "selfish." Indeed, they were selfish in the sense of taking for themselves, rather than giving to others. It is also of interest to note that although this concept apparently had some meaning to the accusers, they themselves behaved no differently from those whom they accused.[3]

What caught our interest in this series of SES studies was what we refer to as "self-orientation," and what game-theoretical researchers label "self-maximizing."[4] We chose the term *self-orientation* because it places the basic emphasis on the *self*, specifically on favoring the self at the expense of others. If others are noticed at all, they are seen primarily as obstacles in one's path, or as means of comparison with oneself, for one's own purposes. We noted how much of the time the children seemed to be oblivious of their coactors—who were literally no more than a few inches away—and of *their* requirements. We began to put forth the hypothesis that, in children from affluent backgrounds, self-orientation interferes with consideration of others' needs in that it actively prevents concern for others as equally deserving persons.

This is not a wholly new interpretation. As early as 1967, Madsen demonstrated that if children are disposed to make self-maximizing responses, they continue to do so even if these responses prove maladaptive (Madsen, 1967). The most direct evidence pertaining to the interference effects of individualistic orientations has been provided by Kagan and Madsen (1972), who showed that inductions of a self-oriented set greatly increased competition, which then prevented children from obtaining a reward that they could have obtained otherwise. This interpretation is also in line with a subset of data from Loeb's research (1979), indicating that prior individual experiences with the Pep Board task resulted in negative transfer in terms of less complex figures

[3]Even though this is a well-known dynamic, going as far back as Hartshorne and May (1928), it is generally ignored in theories of moral development. It would seem important to incorporate into these theories the idea that, at some developmental periods at least, children appear quite able to recognize and condemn lying, cheating, stealing, and other antisocial behaviors *in others*, while simultaneously justifying or denying, or possibly not even recognizing, their own antisocial behaviors.

[4]In some sense, of course, all behavior may be characterized as "self-maximizing." This has been recognized by philosophers and even contemporary psychologists in their preoccupation with the "altruistic paradox," which asserts that all supposedly "self-less" behavior in fact contains its own rewards. Because this issue, as stated, cannot be disproved, and operational definitions are provided in our research for both self-oriented and other-oriented behaviors, it need not concern us further.

produced in subsequent cooperative work situations. Still, one needs to ask: What *is* this self-orientation conceptually?

Kagan (1977) and Knight and Kagan (1977) have substantially expanded the limited choices originally provided by gaming methodology by increasing both the range and the exactness with which diverse self- and other motivations may be specified. Restricting his analysis to two-person situations in which the choices of A will determine something about A's outcome as well as that of B (i.e., conditions of *outcome interdependence*), Kagan (1977) was able to infer from specific choice strategies different types of social behaviors with which different types of social motivations are coordinated. Thus, for instance, where the choice is such as to obtain absolute gains for the self, the specific motive is considered that of self-gain. Avoidance of absolute losses for the self is referred to as self-defense, and the presence of both patterns is considered a major individualistic motive. The opposite patterns—obtaining absolute losses for the self, or avoiding absolute gains for the self—are seen as self-sacrifice and humility, respectively, and more generally as self-diminution. When absolute gains are obtained for others, the motive is called helping, and it, as well as the pattern of protecting others by avoiding absolute losses for them, is specified as being altruistic.

From these examples (3 out of a total of 16 such different behavior outcomes possible in Kagan's "social motive matrix"), it is evident that a considerable range of behaviors may be specified and accompanying motives inferred. The limitations are those inherent in all forced-choice game models, involving, principally, restriction to dyadic interactions only. Because the dependent behavior is still a choice made from a choice card with only two alternatives at a given time, the diversity of the behaviors that may be studied is severely limited. From that perspective, our own methodology complements Kagan's approach nicely, in that it provides opportunities for the systematic observation of less limited and hence more varied interpersonal behaviors among more than two children in small-group settings. Because there are no explicitly required behaviors around the construction task, and because the range of interpersonal behaviors is not limited in any way, our research may be subject to question. First, how reliably observed were the behaviors that occurred and second, how can valid motivational dynamics be inferred from these behaviors?

The first consideration can be put aside quite easily. In the scarcity study discussed earlier, interobserver reliabilities over 85% were obtained on behavior that prevented others from making progress, on behavior that amassed resources at the expense of others, and on various manifestations of aggression, both verbal and physical. Reference to related motivations as "Self-oriented" appears justified: The children were clearly concerned with their own progress at the expense of others, a finding that indeed satisfies our definitional requirements. Psychodynamically, though, it left us unsatisfied.

ANTECEDENTS OF SELF-ORIENTATION

Interestingly, there are several convergent psychodynamic theoretical formulations that have been causally linked as antecendents to the self-oriented tendencies associated with higher socioeconomic positions. In social psychology, the most relevant conceptualization is that of Lerner (1974) and Lerner, Miller, and Holmes (1976), whose research examined the assumption that children's expectations about what is their due— that is, their "deservedness" or "entitlement"—are influenced by what they generally receive and are asked to give in return.

Extending the argument to children raised in different socioeconomic environments, we start with the assumption that how children deal with material resources is related to the material environment to which they are exposed. Children surrounded by abundance, "indulged" by their parents and relevant others, may come to expect that their needs will be met noncontingently and may feel justified in taking what they want when they want it, believing they are entitled to such treatment. Their self-concept with regard to their own deservedness will be vastly different from children raised in leaner environments, who are likely to accept their state as "just," no matter how small the "slice of pie" to which they feel themselves entitled.[5] Coordinated with this concept of entitlement, then, may be a variety of behaviors that we have denoted as self-oriented. They are characterized by an active pursuit of material resources for personal use and by various degrees of aggressiveness and appropriation of what is needed, either with no apparent thought given to equally needy other coactors or with an explicit determination to best them. The concept of personal entitlement is central to our research: It links the material context of the home surroundings, on the one hand, and children's behaviors that involve objects in interpersonal contexts, on the other hand.

---

[5]This is true only to the extent that less privileged children are raised in homogeneous environments. According to social evaluation theory, exposure to "better-off" others may call forth comparison with them (presumably on the material possessions, the psychological features, and so forth on which they may differ). Unfavorable outcomes from such comparisons may then leave less well-off children with feelings of dissatisfaction and "relative deprivation."

Over the last decades, clinical professionals have been pointing to another variety of self-oriented syndrome referred to as the *narcissistic personality* (Masterson, 1981; Nelson, 1977; Akhtar & Thomson, 1982); its breeding ground is referred to as the *culture of narcissism* (Lasch, 1978; Sampson, 1977, 1980). Here, the expectation is also one of instant gratification, and the connection is also made with material affluence, as described in great detail by Coles (1977):

> They . . . grow up surrounded by possessions, animate as well as inanimate. They have learned to look after them, and to depend upon them for support. . . . The quantitative difference in their material acquisitions prompts a qualitative psychological difference: an enhanced expectation of what life has to offer. (p. 391)

Parents are described as often constituting strong normative role models, with

> continuous and strong emphasis put on the self . . . its display, its possibilities, its cultivation and development, even the repeated use of the word (p. 381). These privileged ones are children who live in homes with many mirrors. They have mirrors in their rooms, large mirrors in adjoining bathrooms. When they were three or four, they were taught to use them. (p. 384)

Some of the children of the affluent, proudly fulfill parental expectations:

> I've got lots of chores. We're not spoiled here! I have to clean out the stalls and brush the horses carefully before we go riding. I have to pick up my room (p. 384).

However, in many of the case histories, Coles also identified a predominant attitude of passivity. He exemplified this attitude of entitlement aptly as a child's

> seem[ing] to be sitting on a throne of sorts—expecting things to happen, wondering with annoyance why they don't . . . reassuring himself that they will, or if they haven't, shrugging his shoulders and waiting for the next event. (pp. 367–412)

This clinical analysis is an intriguing notion in the sense that self-orientation has been generally located only at the active, aggressive end. It may, in fact, be that, as Lerner seemed to imply, when much is given to children but also much is asked, giving provides the entitlement component, and the demand for a response creates self-expectations of the exertion of active, self-assertive behaviors. Coles's descriptions suggest that, where much is given, and little is asked in return, passivity is the result. This formulation opens up the possibility that, for experimental purposes, the individual expression of self-orientation may be ordered along a continuum that varies on an active-passive dimension, with one pole represented by aggressive competition against others, and the other by passive withdrawal from others.

CONSEQUENCES OF SELF-ORIENTATION

Both types of concern with the self may be said to have the effect of depersonalizing the other. Active self-orientation considers others simply obstacles to be circumvented or eliminated as competitors inhibiting one's own goal attainment; in the passive stance, others are seen merely as suppliers of personal satisfactions. Both types have negative consequences in group situations. Where group members are made interdependent in reaching a common goal through task role division, passive nonparticipation may act as a barrier to group success as much as intense preoccupation with one's own goals leads to activity on behalf of the self and neglect of the needs of others. In situations where individual and group goals may coincide, passively oriented members may reach their own goals by simply being carried along by the group. Under these circumstances, passivity may be functional to one's own goal attainment.

At the other pole of active self-orientation, group members may often appear to be high contributors to the group's success when, in fact—from their own point of view—they perform needed tasks for their own goal attainment to which the group's goal attainment is purely incidental. However, self-oriented persons of either extreme type will not be able to remain acceptable and functional group members in role-related situations because of their obliviousness to the needs of others. Where task interdependence is high and participation is required from each member, nonresponsiveness to others will be damaging both to one's own goal attainment and to that of others.

The study with which we end this chapter begins to explore the admittedly complex hypothetical structure that we have outlined. To examine the antecedents of self-orientations, we involved children in structured individual interviews that inquired into their family structure and their lifestyle, including their favorite possessions, their aspirations, and their wishes. The consequences of probable self-orientations were examined by creating an experimental situation that required sensitivity to the needs of others and in which either aggressive competition or passivity would prove maladaptive.

SELF-ORIENTATION AND RESPONSES TO LIMITATIONS BY OTHERS

This study was in some sense a variant of the study examined in the previous section. Instead of the scarcity-of-blocks situation, where one person's taking needed blocks reduced another's probability of success, here the movement of one person in pursuit of his or her own goals interfered with the goal-directed movements of the other. The standard condition required the children to compete to see who could make the longest train, the beginning of which was depicted on a model. In fact, the task was designed so that it was difficult to complete the individual assignment without encountering the other subject's product looming ahead as an obstacle. (Only mature foresight and advanced planning could prevent these head-on clashes, and we found only one child in the primary grade age group who could anticipate the problem before starting to build.)

In the standard condition, the children were shown a picture composed of cutout shapes of exactly the same size, colors, and shapes as the blocks needed to make a train consisting of one engine and two attached wagons. In the competitve condition (Comp), the following instructions were given: "First, I would like each of you to copy exactly each part of this train as it is shown here on the model. Then, when you are finished, you may add as many different wagons of your own as you can. *I want to see which one of you can make the longest train."* No additional rewards were promised, yet the children were explicitly instructed to compete, and after the first few groups had been observed, it became very clear that they did.

To study the effects of spatial opposition alone, we created a control condition called *coaction* that used instructions identical with those above, except that the competitive instructions were omitted. We told the children to copy the model: "Then, when you are finished, you may add as many different wagons of your own as you wish."

THE SAMPLE

The subjects were taken from the same affluent school district as before. The specific elementary school in which the research was carried out is located in the center of the area with the highest real-estate values on the whole Main Line. Of the 81 subjects from the first and second grades, aged 6–8½, 45 were girls and 36 boys. Of the fathers, 57% were in professional occupations and 22% in managerial and business positions. This time, we were able to associate the specific father's position with his child from extended postinterviews with each child, occasionally supplemented by information from a teacher. The remaining 21% could not be established reliably. However, compared with other like-aged children from lower socioeconomic backgrounds whom we have studied in the past, we were struck by the accuracy with which the children from professional familial backgrounds could describe their fathers' occupation. For instance, over half the fathers were medical doctors, whose specialties—including neurosurgery, osteopathy, cardiology, and anesthesiology—could be detailed exactly and with considerable pride even by first-graders. Less than 8% of the mothers were said to work.

Measurement of Dependent Variables

Although a variety of measures were employed, we concentrate here only on two types of measures: (1) a performance score of the number of wagons constructed by each child and (2) two sets of interpersonal behaviors. Here, we explored the possibility of measuring self-oriented behaviors along a dimension varying from passive to active; other-oriented behaviors were conceived of as varying from least interdependent to most interdependent. In both types of behavior, the focus was on how each child dealt with spatial limitations vis-à-vis her or his coactors. The two sets of behavior categories are described below:

SELF-ORIENTATION

1. *Passive, withdrawn:* Member perceives that she or he is blocked and comes to an impasse.
2. *Minor accomodation to other:* Member circumvents another and continues in same direction on own path.
3. *Major bypass:* Member makes major change in direction to circumvent other.
4. *Expressing entitlement:* Member requests other to adjust, that is, to move.
5. *Asserting entitlement:* Member moves some of other's products to make room for self.
6. *Active, aggressive entitlement:* Member attempts to eliminate other as obstacle by dismantling other's product, taking blocks, and so on.

OTHER-ORIENTATION

1. *Least interdependence:* To avoid infringement on other, each member restricts self to staying on own part of product.

2. *Minor accommodation to other:* Member dismantles some of own product to make room for other.

3. *Search for equitable solution:* Member helps other to move around; reciprocal actions occur.

4. *Proposals for common solution:* Creation of group goal is suggested but fails; connection of wagons is considered but rejected.

5. *Pro forma common goal created:* Products are joined, but there is low task interdependence; members continue separate work.

6. *Role-related cooperation:* Individual products are joined, and members work on common product and/or embellish each other's work; task interdependence and goal interdependence are present.

RESULTS

We are presenting here largely a descriptive overview of some of the more interesting and important trends, rather than including detailed statistical analyses.[6]

It took an average of seven minutes from the start to the point when at least two of the children reached an impasse as their trains met up with each other. Among the 27 triads that were studied, not 1 decided to change the competitive structure into a cooperative one by making a long train with the others. Conceptually, this means that none of the groups engaged in role-related cooperation. There were 5 groups that stopped working when they reached an impasse, thus falling into the passive, withdrawn category; 4 were girls' groups, and 3 of these were made up of first-grade girls who, perhaps because of their young age, lacked the skills necessary to find alternative solutions. Only 3 groups (all boys) fell at the active, aggressive pole. The remaining 19 groups tried to avoid head-on clashes but took matters into their own hands, looking for a solution that would allow the pursuit of their goal to emerge as winner. Thus, by far the dominant response when blocked was a major bypass—behavior that, according to our classificatory scheme, may be seen to fall into the moderately self-oriented category.

The actual behaviors involving bypassing took several forms. Almost all the children started around the periphery of the board at three

---

[6]In this exploratory study, a descriptive treatment of the children's behavior patterns was indicated, especially because the use of inferential statistics proved impossible in comparisons that we made with children from a small rural elementary school. In the latter, the total numbers—47 children in all, large age differences ranging over six grades, failure to return parental permission slips for participation in the research, and other reasons for exempting some children—prevented testing for sample differences.

assigned equidistant points from each other. When a child was blocked, the simplest response was to move his or her wagons above the other's train, to increase speed to regain the time lost while dismantling, and to continue on that level. Quite often, the children encountered yet a third blocking wagon and had to circumvent it again to capture space to expand their train. Others twisted their wagons into the board in spiral fashion; another favorite was to cut boldly across the board, at right angles to the original direction on the periphery.

The children were quite aware of the other coactors. They compared the length of their own train with that of others, and some groups used up inordinate amounts of time counting and recounting their own and others' wagons, arguing about exact numbers. The degree of inventiveness that they employed was astounding. For instance, one of the favorite means of amassing more wagons was simply to make each smaller, thus gaining in absolute numbers.

There was almost no evidence of one child's being supportive of another's success. Occasionally a child (more often a girl) would suggest to another how she or he could move around and avoid being stopped altogether, but it was noted that in almost all of these cases, the one who appeared so other-oriented stood to profit by having the other move away from his or her own train. Requests to move one's blocks were generally ignored or emphatically refused. To be sure, no one actively destroyed another's total construction, though attempts to move or to steal others' blocks were not uncommon.

In 10 of the groups, there were individual children who invited their co-workers to "hitch our trains together" (falling at Point 4, moderate interdependence on our other-oriented dimension). Some even repeated the offer several times; however, their suggestions were ignored and were sometimes decisively rejected. In a few cases, loud objections or small skirmishes ensued when a persistent child actually tried surreptitiously to connect his or her wagon to that of another. The child in question was told in no uncertain terms to "take your hands off my train"; the other child made it perfectly clear that she or he wanted to make her or his own train by herself or himself. In five of these cases— three girls' groups and two boys' groups—a dyad agreed to join trains; but having connected them perfunctorily, with merely one or two blocks, they did not know what to do next to continue the collaboration. The connection was allowed to stand, but each turned back to working on his or her own train. Thus, although these children had reached Point 5 of other-oriented behavior, for all practical purposes they were still working by themselves and for themselves.

The argument that the children may have cooperated more were it not for the explicit competitive instructions is largely invalidated by

comparisons with the control Coaction condition, where the same over-
whelming preference for individualistic bypass solutions was found.
However, the average amount of time spent working on the train was
significantly longer in the Comp (18.35) than in the Coaction (12.70, $F =$
30.26, $p <.001$) conditions, and the same trend was also seen in the average number of wagons made during this time (6.47 vs. 4.07, $F = 25.27$, p
$< .001$). Although competitive motivation added a further challenge apparently absent in coaction, individualistic solutions were clearly equal
in both.

SEX DIFFERENCES

There was a main effect of sex; the boys worked significantly longer than
did the girls. This finding is of interest especially in the light of a recent
compilation of cross-cultural data that shows decisively that in all studies that used Anglo-Saxon children and were exclusively based on
game-theoretical methodology, competition was greater among boys
than among girls (Strube, 1981). Our data suggest the possibility of more
subtle differences, for there was also a significant interaction of condition and sex. In the Comp condition, the boys and the girls worked
equally long at their task (mean time for boys was 19.50 min vs. the girls'
17.00 min, n.s.). In the Coaction condition, the mean for the boys was
19.22 min, whereas the girls' mean dropped significantly to a low of 9.83
min. In other words, the boys apparently found coaction as challenging
as competition, whereas the girls lost interest in coaction. Supportive of
this relationship are the data from behavioral besting. In the Comp condition, the boys and the girls had mean besting scores of 6.44 and 5.63,
respectively. Again, these are nonsignificant differences. In the Coaction condition, the boys' mean besting fell somewhat, to 3.75, significantly higher than the girls' score of 1.67.

The importance of the above relationships is that they suggest that
girls *can* compete as much as boys and *do* compete equally if explicitly
asked to do so. Recently, the argument and some evidence have been
put forth pertaining to boy–girl lifestyle differences. Presumably, girls
prefer "relational" styles as opposed to the dominant male
achievement-oriented modes (Gilligan, 1982). But if so, why did the girls
in our sample apparently lose interest earlier than the boys in Coaction,
the condition that was less competitive and hence ought to appeal more
to girls? And, more crucially, why did the girls not engage in more
other-oriented behaviors altogether? There is the fact that the three actively and aggressively self-oriented groups in the present study were
all composed of boys. This trend is in line with the more overt and more

frequent aggression also found among boys in our earlier scarcity study. It is clear that matters are more complex and that answers must await further study.

A Second Glance at the Antecedents of Self-Orientation

We return to our original hypothetical assumptions about affluence, a sense of entitlement, and self-orientation. Postexperimental interviews with the children dispelled any lingering doubts about whether parental affluence meant *ipso facto* that these children were surrounded by material comforts. One page of the interview consisted of a checklist of possessions. This list was subsequently collapsed into categories that included privacy in living arrangements ("a room of your own"); books; toys; sports equipment; and an assortment of "machines" (record player, television, calculator, bicycle, electronic games, musical instruments). Almost all of the children listed several possessions within each of the categories.

The children were also requested to state their favorite wishes (after Dembo, 1960), and whether or not they expected these wishes to come true. They were allowed five wishes, but as the wishes at different ranks mirrored essentially the same trend, only the first wishes are reported here. Of the primary wishes, 63% fell into a materialistic category, and 25% fell into a category of "pets" (mostly for girls). From among the many findings, one of the most interesting deals with the type of materialistic wishes. They were subdivided into categories of "modest," "expensive," and "excessive." The latter were defined as including a collectivity of objects, for instance, "all the toys at XX" (a large department store specializing in expensive toys). Excessive materialistic fantasies also contained wishes for imaginary or impossible objects for example, "that everything would be made of chocolate" or "to have a tree that grows cars so that I could pick one whenever I want."

No differences in type of wish were found between children of professional parents and of nonprofessional parents. It is not clear whether the differences were simply too small to be significant in this small sample; whether the children of nonprofessionals were equally surrounded by affluence; or whether, as we had hypothesized elsewhere (Pepitone, 1982a, b), less privileged children who attend classrooms in which affluent children constitute the majority come to accept the value systems of the more affluent. Regarding the latter hypothesis, it was noteworthy that, when asked whether their wishes would come true, 53% of the children from professional backgrounds answered affirmatively, whereas only 25% of the rest of the children did so (a significant difference). My favorite example is the 7-year-old son of a cardiologist whose wish was for "all the Nobel prizes in the world." The coders had no difficulty agreeing that this wish should be categorized as excessive, but they had quite a discussion about whether it was imaginary or realistic. The young boy had to think hard when asked whether his wish would come true. He shook his head sadly from side to side, then brightened up and asserted: "Well, maybe *one* Nobel prize at least."

We have selected only a handful of findings to convey the sense that these children resembled in many ways the privileged children described by Robert Coles—including the calm, realistic assessment of what one owned; the pleasure in personal possessions; and above all, the taking of one's lifestyle for granted. The sense of personal entitlement certainly was there and, the observers agreed, could be seen in the matter-of-fact style with which many of the children barreled their way through and around the constructions of others. They were not desperate to win; they had simply been given a task in the school setting, and they proceeded to pursue it in a competent, efficient, self-assured, and self-oriented manner. In fact, these children's behavior was not as aggressively self-oriented as we had expected; but neither were they concerned with the fate of others. Rather, they seemed to display a little of the "blunted affect" attributed to receiving frequent and instant gratification. It appeared that their self-sufficiency and self-oriented set indeed prevented openness to alternatives and to more interdependent group problem-solving.

But, one may well ask, would not all children proceed in a similar fashion when told to compete? Obviously, an informed response requires study across different social groups, cultural comparisons, and systematic variations that could pinpoint familial values at home, the specific normative climates in given schools, and the group standards of the larger community in which the children live.

We have the beginning of an answer to the question of whether all children are likely to behave in the observed manner. It was derived from a pilot study done in a Vermont village of 361 persons, 46 of whom attended a three-room schoolhouse that included kindergarten through sixth grade, and whose parent population ranged in occupation from teacher and skilled carpenter downward. It is seldom that such children are found in environments identical to those of the privileged, and so they are rarely compared. But when we created exactly the same task environment for them, we saw 6-year-olds politely asking each other, "*Please* could you move your wagon just a little bit?" The ones addressed, to our amazement, made room for the other by dismantling one or more whole wagons to make it possible for the other to pass. Certainly, this is other-orientation operationalized. Several 7- and 8-year-old boys' groups talked about how much fun it might be to make one big long train. They turned to the experimenter to ask permission first and then proceeded to launch with gusto into a truly cooperative performance that featured role division and common planning, which resulted in tracks for the whole train, a roundhouse for the night, and, above all, feelings of accomplishment and camaraderie all around the Pep Board.

As the identical methodology was used with Philadelphia suburban and Vermont rural children, these widely different yet internally consistent findings are not likely to be accounted for by experimental chance or other extraneous effects. Yet, these results are not surprising with children's groups as diverse as these. Kagan, Knight, Martinez, and Espinoza Santana (1981) have reviewed some of the most frequently offered explanatory models for the generally stronger competitiveness found in urban environments. We are in agreement with their argument that many differences between urban and rural environments could singly or in combination account for these effects. In post-task interviews, we dwelled on the Vermont children's home environments; again, not surprisingly, there were the expected differences in material possessions. For the most part, the Vermont children's possessions and wishes were modest, including such objects as paperdolls, clothing items, kites, skates, sleds, or, at most, wishes for "a dollar." Their Philadelphia counterparts tended to refer to the brand names of toys and clothes that were, objectively, more expensive. The counterpart of the dollar was "to have lots and lots of money . . . to buy anything I want." None of the Vermont children's wishes fell into the "excessive" category.

There were also considerable similarities between these disparate samples, and yet, within the surface similarities, shades of differences could be discerned. A high percentage of both groups wished for pets, ranging in both cases from kittens to horses. (More Vermont children already had pets and fully expected more. In suburbia, one frequently heard sadness was that "my mommie won't let me have a pet in the house.") The suburban children received an allowance for responsibilities that typically involved keeping their room neat, setting and clearing the table, or bringing in the newspaper from the curb. The Vermont children told of somewhat more after-school responsibilities, typically without pay, which included feeding and taking care of the animals, bringing in wood, and helping with the hay.

Surprisingly, both groups of children spent the major part of after-school time alone or with siblings or grandmothers (maids in suburbia), in front of a television set having milk and cookies.

We had expected the affluent children to have a more diverse and larger life space in terms of places and foreign countries visited, yet the responses from both samples were, again, surprisingly similar. Familial travel patterns had much in common: Many children from both populations visited their distant grandparents once a year but otherwise spent summers at home, although for different reasons. The Vermont adults utilized the relatively short season for outdoor work that needed to be done before the long winter ahead, and so they spent the summers at home. Professional duties kept the suburban parents city-bound during the summers. When these parents did take a vacation during the year, it tended to be brief and without their children, who continued to attend school and were left at home under the care of various housekeepers. Thus, in the summers, these children spent their time in their family swimming pools with preselected neighbors' children, whereas the children from the Vermont sample reported going swimming in the nearby lake.

On first impression, there was even some overlap in the teaching populations: In both cases, the teachers appeared very well prepared, had attended first-rate teacher-training institutions, and verbalized their responsibilities as socializers of the children. In the suburban school observed, the teachers appeared to be especially lavish with praise for any signs of minimal effort on the part of a child. In Vermont, socializing took the form of firm and loving reinforcement of norms about peaceful settlement of disputes and daily reinforcement of prosocial acts. The latter school difference hints at differences that are in line with the postulated antecedent of differences in self-orientation, and that were observed in the two diverse samples of children. There were also indications that, as the children grew older, the observed similarities in the lifestyles of the two samples would diminish and the differences would deepen.

It should be clear from this chapter that we have barely made a beginning in the study of these two socioeconomically diverse populations of children. We deliberately selected two rather homogeneous populations; one high-priority issue is to pursue the effects on each other when the children from these different populations are placed in one classroom. There is also one striking similarity in both samples that may turn out to be of overriding significance: Both made wishes almost exclusively *for themselves only*. It is tempting to attribute these findings to the instructions that told each child to ask for "anything you wish." Yet the same invitation was issued to a sample of Greek children, even slightly younger—ages 5–6½ (Prattos, 1983). These children made frequent wishes for different members of their family, and the children from an island community in Greece seemed to do so more frequently than did Athenian children. The wishes of the former have a touchingly, empathetic quality (e.g., "a chair for my mommie so her back won't hurt her so much"). Clearly, cross-cultural studies are needed that include samples from urban and rural areas, and from different socioeconomic levels. It is possible that the individualistic-competitive cultural heritage of American children will manifest itself in interaction with the other social variables. If self-orientations indeed tend to prevent other-orientations, it would follow that, along with the introduction of cooperative learning practices, an active effort must be made in American schools to reduce self-orientations that interfere with effective functioning in interdependent situations.

REFERENCES

Akhtar, S., & Thomson, A., Jr. Overview: Narcissistic personality disorders. *American Journal of Psychiatry*, 1982, *139*(1), 11–20.

Allport, F. H. *Social Psychology*. Boston: Houghton Mifflin, 1924.

Allport, G. W. *The nature of prejudice*. Reading, Mass.: Addison-Wesley, 1954.

Aronson, E., Bridgeman, D. L., & Geffner, R. The effects of a cooperative classroom structure on student behavior and attitudes. In D. Bar-Tal, & L. Saxe (Eds.), *Social psychology of education: Theory and research*. Washington: Hemisphere Publishing, Halsted Press, Wiley, 1978.

Back, K. W. Interpersonal relations in a discussion group. *Journal of Social Issues*, 1948, *4*, 61–65.

Benne, K., & Sheats, P. Functional roles of group members. *Journal of Social Issues*, 1948, *4*, 41–49.

Bryan, J. H. Children's cooperation and helping behaviors. In E. M. Hetherington (Ed.), *Review of child development research*, Vol. 5. Chicago: University of Chicago Press, 1975.

Byrne, D. *The attraction paradigm*. New York: Academic Press, 1971.

Coles, R. Privileged ones: The well-off and the rich in America. In *Children of crisis*, Vol. 5. Boston: Little, Brown, 1977.

Condry, J. Enemies of Exploration: Self-initiated vs. other-initiated learning. *Journal of Personality and Social Psychology*, 1977, *35*, 7.

Cook, S. W. Interpersonal and attitudinal outcomes in cooperating interracial groups. *Journal of Research and Development in Education*, 1978, *12* (1), 97–113.

Deci, E. L., Betley, G., Kahle, J., Abrams, L., & Porac, J. When trying to win: Competition and intrinsic motivation. *Personality and Social Psychology Bulletin*, 1981, *7* (1), 79–83.

Dembo, T. A theoretical and experimental inquiry into concrete values and value systems. In B. Kaplan & S. Wapner (Eds.), *Perspectives in psychological theory: Essays in honor of Heinz Werner*. New York: International University Press, 1960.

Deutsch, M. A theory of competition and cooperation. *Human Relations*, 1949, *2*, 129–151.

Deutsch, M. Interdependence and psychological orientation. In V. J. Derlega & J. Grzelak (Eds.), *Cooperation and helping behavior: Theories and research*. New York; Academic Press, 1982.

Gilligan, C. *In a different voice*. Cambridge: Harvard University Press, 1982.

Goodenough, F. L. *Measurement of intelligence by drawings*. New York: Harcourt, Brace and World, 1926.

Graves, N. B. *Egocentrism and cultural deprivation: Empirical evidence for the ethnocentric bias of Piagetian theory*, Vol. 12. Auckland, New Zealand: South Pacific Research Institute, 1976.

Hackman, J. R., & Morris, C. G. Group tasks, group interaction process and group performance effectiveness: A review and proposed integration. In L. Berkowitz (Ed.), *Advances in experimental social psychology*, Vol. 8. New York: Academic Press, 1975.

Harris, D. B. *Children's drawings as measures of intellectual maturity*. New York: Harcourt, Brace and World, 1963.

Hartshorne, H., & May, M. A. Studies in the nature of character. *Studies in deceit*, Vol. 1. New York: Macmillan, 1928.

Johnson, D. W., & Johnson, R. T. Instructional goal structure: Cooperative, competitive or individualistic. *Review of educational research*, 1974, 4, (2), 213–240.

Johnson, D. W., & Johnson, R. T. *Learning together and alone: Cooperation, competition and individualization*. Englewood Cliffs, N.J.: Prentice-Hall, 1975.

Kagan, S. Social motives and behaviors of Mexican American and Anglo American children. In J. L. Martinez (Ed.), *Chicano psychology*. New York: Academic Press, 1977.

Kagan, S., Knight, G. P., Martinez, S., & Espinoza Santana, P. Conflict resolution style among Mexican children: Examining urbanization and ecology effects. *Journal of Cross-Cultural Psychology*, 1981, 12 (2), 222–232.

Kagan, S., & Madsen, M. C. Rivalry in Anglo American and Mexican children. *Journal of Personality and Social Psychology*, 1972, 24, 214–220.

Knight, G. P., & Kagan, S. Development of prosocial and competitive behaviors in Anglo American and Mexican American children. *Child Development*, 1977, 48, 1385–1394.

Koppitz, E. *Psychological evaluation of human figure drawings*. New York: Grune and Stratton, 1968.

Lasch, C. *The culture of narcissism: American life in an age of diminishing expectations*. New York: W. W. Norton, 1978.

Lerner, M. J. The Justice Motive: "Equity" and "parity" among children. *Journal of Personality and Social Psychology*, 1974, 29, 539–550.

Lerner, M. J., & Lerner, S. C. (Eds.). *The justice motive in social behavior: Adapting to times of scarcity and change*. New York: Plenum Press, 1981.

Lerner, M. J., Miller, D. T., & Holmes, J. G. Deserving and the emergence of forms of justice. In L. Berkowitz, & E. Walster (Eds.), *Advances in experimental social psychology: Equity theory: Toward a general theory of social interaction*, Vol. 9. New York: Academic Press, 1976,

Lewin, K. *Dynamic theory of personality*. New York: McGraw-Hill, 1935.

Loeb, H. W. *Social interactions and performance under competitive and cooperative working conditions: A developmental study of elementary school children*. Unpublished doctoral dissertation, Bryn Mawr College, 1975.

Loeb, H. W. *An exploration of transfer effects on performance between cooperative and competitive working conditions*. Paper presented at the International Conference on Cooperation in Education, Hertzlia, Israel, July 1979.

Maccoby, E. E., & Jacklin, C. N. *The psychology of sex differences*. Stanford, Calif.: Stanford University Press, 1974.

Madsen, M. C. Cooperative and competitive motivations of children in three Mexican subcultures. *Psychological Reports*, 1967, 20, 1307–1320.

Masterson, J. F. *Narcissistic and borderline disorders: An integrated developmental approach*. New York: Brunner/Mazel, 1981.

Murdoch, E. M. *A developmental study of social behaviors which are related to performance under competitive and cooperative working conditions.* Unpublished doctoral dissertation, Bryn Mawr College, 1974.

Nelson, L. I., & Madsen, M. C. Cooperation and competition in four year olds as a function of reward contingency and subculture. *Developmental Psychology,* 1969, *1,* 340–344.

Nelson, M. *Narcissistic condition: A fact of our lives and times.* New York: Human Science Press, 1977.

Pepitone, E. A. Comparison behavior in elementary school children. *American Educational Research Journal,* 1972, *9* (1), 45–63.

Pepitone, E. A. *Children in cooperation and competition: Toward a developmental social psychology.* Lexington, Mass.: D. C. Heath, 1980.

Pepitone, E. A. *Effects of children's self-orientation on cooperative problem solving.* Paper presented at the Second Conference of the International Association for the Study of Cooperation in Education: Brigham Young University, Provo, Utah, 1982. (a)

Pepitone, E. A. *Social comparison, relative deprivation and pupil interaction: Homogeneous vs. heterogeneous classrooms.* Paper presented as part of a symposium on Social Comparison: Implications for Education, at the American Educational Research Association Annual Meetings. New York, March 1982. (b)

Pepitone, E. A., & Hannah, B. H. Exploration of comparison behaviors in third grade children. In E. A. Pepitone, (Ed.), *Children in cooperation and competition,* Lexington, Mass.: D. C. Heath, 1980.

Pepitone, E. A., Loeb, H. W., & Murdoch, E. M. Age and socio-economic behavior and performance in cooperative and competitive working conditions. In E. A. Pepitone, (Ed.), *Children in cooperation and competition.* Lexington, Mass.,: D. C. Heath, 1980.

Sampson, E. E. Psychology and the American ideal. *Journal of Personality and Social Psychology,* 1977, *35,* 767–782.

Sampson, E. E. Justice and social character. In G. Mikula (Ed.), *Justice and social interaction: Experimental and theoretical contributions from psychological research.* New York: Springer Verlag, 1980.

Schofield, J. W. Cooperation as social exchange: Resource gaps and reciprocity in academic work. In S. Sharan, P. Hare, C. D. Webb, & R. Hertz-Lazarowitz (Eds.), *Cooperation in education.* Provo, Utah: Brigham Young University Press, 1980.

Shapira, A., & Lomrantz, J. Cooperative and competitive behavior of rural Arab children in Israel. *Journal of Cross-Cultural Psychology,* 1972, *3,* 352–359.

Sharan, S., & Hertz-Lazarowitz, R. A group-investigation method of cooperative learning in the classroom. In S. Sharan, P. Hare, C. D. Webb, & R. Hertz-Lazarowitz (Eds.), *Cooperation in education.* Provo, Utah: Brigham Young University, 1980.

Slavin, R. E. *Cooperative learning.* New York: Longman 1983. (a)

Slavin, R. E. When does cooperative learning increase student achievement? *Psychology Bulletin,* 1983, *94,* 429–445. (b)

Steiner, I. D. *Group process and productivity.* New York: Academic Press, 1972.

Strube, M. J. Meta-analysis and cross-cultural comparison. *Journal of Cross-Cultural Psychology,* 1981, *12* (1), 3–20.

3

Dimensions of Cooperative Classroom Structures

SPENCER KAGAN

The case for cooperative learning has been made on many grounds; it usually (1) enhances student achievement, especially the achievement of minority and low-achieving students; (2) improves cross-ethnic relations; (3) aids in the successful mainstreaming of handicapped students; (4) facilitates the maintenance of minority cultural values; (5) promotes positive social relations and prosocial development; and (6) increases the liking among students for class, school, learning, and self. The theoretical arguments and the empirical data that support such claims have been presented in various forms (Aronson, 1978; Johnson & Johnson, 1975; Johnson, Maruyama, Johnson, Nelson, & Skon, 1981; Johnson, Rynders, Johnson, Schmidt, & Haider, 1979; Kagan, 1980, 1983; Sharan, 1980; Sharan & Sharan, 1976; Slavin, 1980a, 1983).

The methods of cooperative learning have certain elements in common that distinguish them from traditional instructional formats, such as the division of the whole class into small teams of students who are made positively interdependent by the systematic application of principles of reward and/or task structure. Nevertheless, the various methods of cooperative learning have among them considerable diversity. Some embody a very different philosophy of education from others and, as a consequence, employ different task structures and forms of classroom social organization. Each cooperative learning method is to some extent a unique solution to the problem of how to structure a classroom. It is my intent here to delineate the dimensions along which the different methods of cooperative learning differ. An analysis of the dimensions of cooperative classroom structures has implications for theoretical, empirical, and applied work in cooperative learning, and it is a second intent of this chapter to draw out and discuss those implications.

For purposes of analysis, six cooperative learning methods were selected. The cooperative learning methods—STAD, TGT, the original Jigsaw (called Jigsaw I), Jigsaw II, Group Investigation, and Co-op Co-op—

SPENCER KAGAN • Department of Psychology, University of California, Riverside, California 92521.

were selected because each has been articulated sufficiently to support a detailed analysis and because they represent a range of cooperative learning structures. Each of these six cooperative learning methods was analyzed along each of 25 dimensions. The dimensions are presumed to be the major dimensions along which cooperative-learning classroom structures differ. The dimensions fall into six categories: philosophy of education, nature of learning, nature of cooperation, student roles and communication, teacher roles, and evaluation. The analysis is similar to, but broader and more detailed than, that made by Sharan (1980) in which Group Investigation and peer tutoring were contrasted along 11 dimensions.

Before analyzing how the cooperative learning methods differ, a brief overview of each of the methods is presented, and following the analysis of the methods, the implications of the analysis are drawn out. Thus, the chapter is divided into three parts: (1) a very brief presentation of the essentials of the cooperative learning methods; (2) an analysis of how the methods differ along the 25 dimensions of cooperative classroom structures; and (3) a discussion of the implications of the analysis.

THE COOPERATIVE LEARNING METHODS

A full presentation of each of the six cooperative learning methods chosen for analysis is beyond the scope of the present chapter. What is intended in this section is only to present the essential elements of each method, to facilitate the analysis of the methods that follows. A detailed description of each method is available in published material, as indicated, and those wishing to learn how to carry out the techniques or the details of the techniques should consult the references indicated.

STUDENT TEAMS-ACHIEVEMENT DIVISIONS (STAD)

Student Teams-Achievement Divisions (STAD) has been described in detail by Slavin (1980c). There are five components of STAD, as follows:

CLASS PRESENTATIONS

The material to be learned is initially presented to the whole class by the teacher or in an audiovisual presentation.

TEAMS

The teams are composed of four or five students who are carefully selected to represent a cross section of the class; the teams are as heterogeneous as possible with regard to the sex, the ethnic background, and the ability level of the students.

The team members work together in a peer-tutoring format to master the material of the learning unit. Most often, the team members quiz each other, working from worksheets that consist of problems and/or information to be mastered.

QUIZZES

The students are evaluated via individual quizzes. The quizzes assess individual achievement on the material presented in the class and practiced in the teams.

INDIVIDUAL IMPROVEMENT SCORES

A detailed scoring system allows the students to earn points for their teams based on improvement over a running average of past scores. The scoring system is based on a periodically readjusted "base score" for each student; each student earns points for his or her team based on improvement over past performance.

TEAM RECOGNITION

The teachers use newsletters, bulletin boards, or other forms of social recognition and rewards to teams for high individual weekly performance and/or high cumulative standings. Recognition is provided for individuals who perform exceptionally well or who are most improved.

TEAMS-GAMES-TOURNAMENTS TGT

Teams-Games-Tournaments (TGT) is identical to STAD except that quizzes are replaced with academic game tournaments and individual improvement scores are replaced with a bumping system (Slavin, 1980c), as follows:

GAME TOURNAMENTS

The students play games in which they win points by demonstrating knowledge of the academic material which has been practiced in teams. The games have simple rules which allow students to take turns answering content-relevant questions. A student can earn extra points by correctly challenging the answer of another student. The students play the academic games at tournament tables consisting of three students of similar ability level. The highest scorer from each tournament table earns six points for his or her team; the middle scorer earns four points; and the lowest scorer earns two.

BUMPING SYSTEM

To ensure that students have an equal opportunity to earn points for their team, tournament tables are homogeneous with regard to ability level. Initially the teacher assigns students to tournament tables. Later, a bumping system reassigns students to tournament tables: following each tournament the highest scorer at each table advances to a higher ability-level table and the lowest scorer moves to a lower ability-level table.

JIGSAW

JIGSAW I

The original Jigsaw method was developed to place students in situations of extreme interdependence. Each student is provided with only part of the materials of an academic unit but is evaluated on how well he or she masters the whole unit. In a sense, each student on a learning team has but one piece of a jigsaw puzzle; the learning task for each student is to obtain the information from every piece of the puzzle. To do well, the students have to learn the unique information possessed by every other member (see Aronson, 1978). The elements of the original Jigsaw method include the following:

SPECIALLY DESIGNED CURRICULUM MATERIALS. The curriculum materials are designed or rewritten so that each member of a learning team has a unique source that is comprehensible without reference to the other sources.

TEAM-BUILDING AND COMMUNICATION TRAINING. Because communication among team members is an essential part of Jigsaw, special team-building and communication-training activities are included to prepare the students to cooperate and communicate in groups. Team building is extensive; it involves role playing, brainstorming, and specially designed group activities.

STUDENT GROUP LEADER. During the extensive team building, the importance of a group leader is stressed. Group leaders are selected by the teacher, and they receive special training, including discussions and role playing. The group leader is expected to help organize the group, to keep the group on task, to serve as the group–teacher liaison, to model productive social and academic behaviors, and to help resolve conflicts.

TEAMS.   Teams range in size from three to seven members but five- or six-member teams are recommended. The students are assigned to teams so that the teams will be heterogeneous with regard to ability level, race and sex, and personality factors such as assertiveness. The teachers are to use their knowledge and intuition in forming groups.

EXPERT GROUPS.   Each team member is assigned to an expert group composed of the members of other teams who have been assigned the same expert topic. The students meet in expert groups to exchange information and to master the material each student is to present to his or her team.

INDIVIDUAL ASSESSMENT AND REWARD.   The students take individual tests or quizzes covering all of the material of the learning unit; there is no group reward.

JIGSAW II

Jigsaw II was adapted from the original Jigsaw method to use existing curriculum materials and to take advantage of some of the features of STAD that are not part of the original Jigsaw (Slavin, 1980c). The typical sequence of events in Jigsaw II is as follows: The students are assigned to teams as in STAD; they are assigned to expert topics within the teams; they read the whole learning unit, with emphasis on their expert topic; they meet in expert groups to discuss and master their topics; they report to their teams; they take an individual quiz, which contributes to a team score; and they receive individual and team recognition. Jigsaw II differs from Jigsaw I in a number of important respects, including the following:

USE OF EXISTING CURRICULUM MATERIALS AND UNIVERSAL ACCESS. Because all students have access to all learning materials, interdependence among students is lessened. The use of existing curriculum materials, however, makes Jigsaw II practical and economical.

USE OF STAD SCORING AND TEAM RECOGNITION TECHNIQUES.   Jigsaw II uses base scores, improvement scores, team scores, and individual and team recognition techniques used in STAD, which are not part of the original Jigsaw. Also, Jigsaw II uses four-person teams in contrast to the original Jigsaw, which usually uses five- or six-member teams. The teams in Jigsaw II are formed as in STAD and TGT; personality factors and teacher intuition are not part of the formula used to form the teams.

ABSENCE OF TEAM BUILDING AND DIFFERENTIATED STUDENT ROLES. Unlike original Jigsaw, Jigsaw II does not include team building and communication training. No attempt is made to have students become differentiated with regard to their roles within the teams; no team leader is appointed.

GROUP-INVESTIGATION

Group-Investigation was designed to provide students with very broad and diverse learning experiences, quite in contrast to the STAD, TGT, and Jigsaw techniques, which are oriented toward student acquisition of predetermined facts and skills. A detailed presentation of the philosophy and technique of Group-Investigation has been presented by Sharan and Hertz-Lazarowitz (1980). The method requires the coordination of four dimensions of classroom life: (1) the organization of the classroom into a "group of groups"; (2) the use of multifaceted learning tasks for cooperative group investigation; (3) the inclusion of multilateral communication among pupils and active learning skills; and (4) teacher communication with and guidance of the groups.

In Group-Investigation, pupils progress through six consecutive stages, as follows:

Stage I: Identifying the Topic and Organizing the Pupils into Research Groups. Various techniques are used to have students identify and classify topics to form inquiry groups. The students join the group of their choice within the limits of forming three- to six-member groups. Ideally, the groups are composed of pupils of both sexes, with different abilities, and from varying ethnic backgrounds. Although the student choice of inquiry groups and the ethnic and ability-level heterogeneity within the groups are sometimes initially inconsistent goals, they are reconciled over time with discussion and the active assistance of the teacher.

Stage II: Planning the Learning Task. Group members or pairs of group members determine subtopics for investigation. Tasks that are appropriate for Group-Investigation pose problems that can be dealt with in a variety of ways; they are complex tasks, unlike the information- and skill-acquisition tasks toward which STAD and TGT are oriented. The groups decide what is to be studied and how it is to be studied, and they determine the goal of their study.

Stage III: Carrying Out the Investigation. The students gather information, analyze and evaluate the data, and reach conclusions. Multilateral learning is stressed, which includes communication with collaborators, the teacher, and other sources of information, including feedback loops among the participants.

Stage IV: Preparing a Final Report. The group must engage in activities that culminate in a report, an event, or a summary. Organizing, abstracting, and synthesizing information are stressed. There is an opportunity for the members of different groups to coordinate their activities.

The steering committee, consisting of representatives of each group, meets and is active in coordinating time schedules, reviewing requests for resources, and ensuring that the ideas of the groups will be realistic and interesting. The steering committee also makes sure that all pupils are involved and contributing to the group's work. The groups decide the content and the method of their presentation.

Stage V: Presenting the Final Report. The final presentation may take various forms, including exhibitions, skits, debates, or reports. Members of the class may participate in various reports. The presentation involves multilateral communication and interaction and is often a moving emotional experience.

Stage VI: Evaluation. Assessment of higher level learning is emphasized, including applications, synthesis, and inferences. Affective experiences should be evaluated also, including the levels of motivation and involvement. Various forms of evaluation are possible. Teachers and pupils can collaborate on evaluation, including the formulation of exams. The steering committee may work with the teacher in selecting from the exam questions that are submitted by the groups.

Co-op Co-op

The essence of Co-op Co-op is structuring the classroom so that students work in cooperative teams toward a goal that will help the other students in the class. A detailed presentation of the philosophy and the technique of Co-op Co-op is presented by Kagan (see Chapter 16 of this book). Like Group-Investigation, Co-op Co-op is oriented toward complex, multifaceted learning tasks and student control of what and how to learn. There are important differences between the techniques, however, as Co-op Co-op involves a simpler classroom organization—there is no steering committee, and there is little interrelation among the groups.

The 10 steps of Co-op Co-op are as follows:

1. Student-centered class discussion. Initial experiences, including class discussion, are designed to uncover and stimulate student curiosity.
2. Selection of student learning teams. As in STAD, this step usually is designed to maximize heterogeneity within the teams

along the dimensions of ability level, sex, and ethnic background.

3. Team building. As in the original Jigsaw, team building is incorporated to increase within-team cooperation and communication skills.

4. Team topic selection. The students divide the learning unit into topics, so that each team is responsible for one aspect of the learning unit and the work of each team will complement that of the others in moving the whole class toward mastery of the learning unit.

5. Minitopic selection. As in Jigsaw, each student becomes an expert in one aspect of the team learning goal; unlike in Jigsaw, the students determine how to divide the topic, and the minitopics are selected by the students rather than being assigned by the teacher.

6. Minitopic preparation. The students individually gather and organize materials on their minitopics.

7. Minitopic presentations. As in Jigsaw, each student presents to the group what he or she has learned on the chosen topic. A second round of minitopic presentations follows an opportunity to respond to the group's discussion of each individual minitopic and its relation to the whole topic.

8. Preparation of team presentations. Teams prepare presentations to the whole class of what they have learned on their team topic.

9. Team presentations. The presentations are made to the whole class. Nonlecture presentations, such as demonstrations, role plays, and the use of audiovisual media, are preferred.

10. Evaluation. Evaluation is made of the individual presentations to the team (usually by teammates); of the team presentations to the whole class (usually by classmates); and of each individual paper or project by each student on his or her minitopic (usually by the teacher).

DIMENSIONS OF COOPERATIVE CLASSROOM STRUCTURES

In order to differentiate and analyze cooperative classroom structures, it is useful to distinguish the various dimensions along which they differ. As indicated, for the present analysis 25 dimensions of cooperative learning structures were selected; the dimensions fall into six categories: philosophy of education, the nature of learning, the nature of cooperation, student roles and communication, teacher roles, and evaluation. In Table 1, the six cooperative learning methods are contrasted along the 25 dimensions of cooperative classroom structures. In the following sections, the six categories of classroom structure dimensions are discussed.

PHILOSOPHY OF EDUCATION

In his classic work on experience and education, John Dewey (1938) contrasted traditional and progressive education, indicating that the traditional curriculum contained rigid discipline that ignored the capacities and interests of the student. The challenge that Dewey presented for progressive education was to provide a structure within which students could have beneficial learning experiences. Although all of the cooperative learning methods in some ways might be considered progressive, they provide different amounts and kinds of structure for students and, in turn, quite different kinds of learning experiences. In fact, the cooperative learning methods differ so radically in their structures that they embody distinct philosophies of education. Methods providing a great detail of structure, extrinsic motivation for learning, and predetermined, teacher-defined learning objectives are closer to the "traditional" side than are methods that emphasize learning experiences tailored to the interests and abilities of the individual student.

The aim of education implied by STAD, TGT, and to a large extent Jigsaw is to increase the general knowledge and the basic skills of students. This aim can be described as a *product orientation* and is measured by standardized achievement tests. The product is achievement. In contrast, Group-Investigation and Co-op Co-op, although concerned with achievement, can be described as having also a strong *process orientation*. The concern is not only about how many facts or basic skills the students acquire, but also about how the students develop as persons. The goal is for students to become actively identified with learning so that they naturally express their curiosity and pursue their interests via communication with others. The process orientation is viewed not as the fixed acquisition of predetermined knowledge, but as facilitation of a student's personal development. Emphasis is placed not only on *what* is learned but also on allowing students to learn *how* to learn. It is assumed that once a person identifies with being a learner and has success in learning, learning about himself or herself and the world will occur in several ways. Learning, then, will not be separated from life, or "for" a better life, but will be part of the process of living.

Student control of the goals and means of learning in Co-op Co-op and Group-Investigation is designed to stimulate student curiosity,

TABLE 1. Dimensions of Cooperative Learning Classroom Structures

| | Cooperative learning classroom structures | | | |
Dimensions	STAD and TGT	Jigsaw I and II	Group-Investigation	Co-op Co-op
Philosophy of education				
1. Why learn? (student perspective)	Learning is instrumental to winning in team competition and to individual success on quizzes.	In Jigsaw I, learning is instrumental to high individual scores for self and teammates; in Jigsaw II, learning is instrumental to winning in team competition and to individual success in quizzes.	Learning, satisfying curiosity about the world and oneself, is a primary goal. Learning is also a means of helping teammates and classmates.	
2. Why cooperate? (student perspective)	Cooperation helps teammates to learn and so facilitates winning.	Cooperation in expert groups and in learning teams helps self, teammates, and classmates to learn; it is instrumental to high scores in Jigsaw I and to team winning in Jigsaw II.	Cooperation, helping teammates and classmates to reach their individual and collective learning goals, is a primary goal. Cooperation is also a means of helping self and others to learn. Students cooperate in order to learn and learn in order to cooperate; learning and cooperation are intertwined primary goals.	
3. Goals of education (teacher perspective)	Learning basic skills and information. Improvement of social skills and peer relations. Learning is viewed from a product orientation; it is primarily skills and information acquisition.		To facilitate the inquisitiveness and resourcefulness of individuals, with emphasis on higher level learning. Learning is viewed from a process orientation: The primary aim is to influence important aspects of what a person	Variable: In some classes, limited goals like those of STAD and TGT can be adopted; in other classes, the goals of Group Investigation are adopted. Yet other classes may emphasize the development of creative, expressive, and in-

			is, not just the skills and information he or she has. Learning is an integral part of the life process; learning is broadly defined to include social skills.	trospective aspects. A broad process interpretation of learning is usually adopted.
4.	Teacher orientation toward students	Manipulative: Students are made to learn by making learning instrumental to obtaining points, obtaining high test scores, and/or winning. Students are viewed as perfectible products; the teacher, through the classroom structures, manipulates students into learning teacher-selected materials.		Humanistic: Unique individual development is allowed and encouraged. Students are viewed as persons; their learning goals are solicited and respected.	
5.	Assumptions about cooperation, learning, and competition	Competitive motives are stronger than motives to cooperate and learn, and so competitive motives are used to facilitate cooperation and learning.		Learning and sharing are inherently rewarding; between-team competition is not necessary to "drive" within-team cooperation and learning.	
Nature of learning					
6.	Source of learning objective	Teacher	Teacher	Students	Students and/or teacher
7.	Source of learning content	Teacher	Teacher	Students	Students and/or teacher
8.	Complexity of learning task	Simple	Medium	Complex	Simple to complex
9.	Diversity of learning sources	Little	Little	Great	Little to great
10.	Differentiation of learning objectives among students	No	No	Yes	Yes or no, usually yes
11.	Differentiation of learning objectives among teams	No	No, in learning teams. Yes, in expert teams	Yes	Yes
12.	Types of learning fostered	Information, basic skills, minimal social skills	Information, basic skills, some interpretation and synthesis, some social skills	Analysis, synthesis, application, some information and basic skills; many social skills	Same as Group Investigation plus sometimes creative expression and/or self-discovery

continued

TABLE 1. (*continued*)

	Cooperative learning classroom structures			
Dimensions	STAD and TGT	Jigsaw I and II	Group-Investigation	Co-op Co-op
Nature of cooperation				
13. Within-team task structure	Helping: Usually dyadic peer-tutoring. No division of labor. Positive facilitation.	Sharing: Presentations by experts. Division of labor. Positive interdependence in Jigsaw I; positive facilitation in Jigsaw II.	Cooperation: Various forms of cooperative interaction to set and reach group goals, may include helping and sharing. Division of labor. In theory, positive interdependence; in practice, only positive facilitation likely.	Individualistic/cooperative: Groups are encouraged to share resources. Division of labor possible. Each group may contribute essential component to learning unit or groups may be independent. Positive facilitation possible.
14. Between-team task structure	None or competitive: In STAD, no interaction, interdependence facilitation, or division of labor; in TGT, intensely competitive, negative interdependence and no division of labor.	Sharing: Between-team sharing via expert groups. No division of labor across learning groups; division of labor across expert groups. Positive facilitation.	Cooperative: Steering committee oversees between-team cooperation. Division of labor: Class is group of groups. Ideally, positive interdependence; actually, only positive facilitation likely.	
15. Within-team reward structure	Individualistic/cooperative: Highly developed reward structure. Individual grades contribute to team score. No interdependence or facilitation with regard to individual grades, but interdependence due to team score.	In Jigsaw I, individualistic: Individual grades contribute to individual score only; no team score. No interdependence or facilitation with regard to individual grades. In Jigsaw II, individualistic/cooperative; same as STAD and TGT.	Cooperative, variable: Not highly developed reward structure. If team score present, positive facilitation. If no team score, intrinsic reward facilitation: Students invested in group effort rewarded by successes of teammates. Individualistic rewards sometimes included.	
16. Between-team reward structure	Competitive: Highly developed reward structure; negative interdependence.	Competitive or none: In Jigsaw I, no highly developed reward structure and no between-	Cooperative or none: No highly developed between-team reward structure. If assimilation of group presentations by other groups assessed, informal positive interdependence created (good presentations yield	

continued

		team rankings; in Jigsaw II, same as STAD and TGT.		successes for members of other teams) If groups identify with each other, they may take pleasure in success of other groups, so there may be an informal intrinsic cooperative between-team reward structure.

Student roles and communication

17. Inclusion of team building	No	Yes, in Jigsaw I; no, in Jigsaw II	Yes	Yes
18. Types of student groups	Peer tutoring; class audience (during teacher presentations)	Peer tutoring; expert; group audience (during expert presentations); class audience (during teacher presentations)	Investigative team; steering committee; class audience (during team and teacher presentations)	Co-op Co-op team; group audience (during minipresentations); class audience (during team and teacher presentations)
19. Types of student roles	Student; tutor; tutee	Student; expert consultant (in expert group); expert tutor (in team); tutee; team leader (in Jigsaw I)	Student; investigator; team topic presenter; steering-committee member (possibly); additional roles in group	Student; resource gatherer; minitopic presenter; team topic presenter; additional roles in group
20. Types of student communication	Tutor–tutee dyadic drill; mutual support	Expert presentations to learning group; exchange, analysis, and discussion among experts; mutual support.	Mutual exchange; planning; decision making; critical analysis and synthesis; feedback; mutual support; and others.	Same as Group Investigation with the addition of formal expert presentations of minitopics within groups and possibility of creative expression and disclosure.
21. Status hierarchy among students	Largely unequalized: Tutor–tutee roles are to rotate, but because of assignment of high and low achievers to teams, status hierarchy likely to emerge.	Largely equalized: Every student given high status because of expert status in one area. In Jigsaw I, in which only the experts have expert material, equal status ensured more than in Jigsaw II, in which all members have access to expert material.	Variable, somewhat equalized: To the extent that each team member is responsible for a unique aspect of the group product, status hierarchy is equalized. In practice, however, status hierarchy is likely to emerge during discussion, analysis, synthesis, and planning. Status hierarchy is accepted as natural and inevitable when students are allowed free expression and free access to materials.	

TABLE 1. (*continued*)

	Cooperative learning classroom structures			
Dimensions	STAD and TGT	Jigsaw I and II	Group-Investigation	Co-op Co-op
Teacher roles				
22. Types of teacher roles	Lecturer; director; consultant to learning teams and individual students	Lecturer; director; consultant to learning teams, expert groups, and individual students. In Jigsaw I, human relations trainer	Consultant to investigative teams; member of steering committee; human relations trainer	Consultant to Co-op Co-op team and individual students; lecturer; human relations trainer in some classes
23. Teacher–student status hierarchy	Highly hierarchical: Teacher is source of learning of objectives, learning materials, and evaluation.	Hierarchical: Teacher is source of learning objectives, learning materials, and evaluation, but students do assume some of the traditional roles of teachers when they become experts.	Relatively equal status: Teacher and students together determine learning objectives, learning materials, and evaluation. Students to a very high degree assume the traditional roles of teachers.	Relatively equal status: Teacher and students together determine learning objectives, learning materials, and evaluation. Students to a very high degree assume the traditional roles of teachers.
Evaluation				
24. Source of evaluation	Teacher	Teacher	Students and teacher.	Students and teacher.
25. Evaluation	In STAD, individualistic quizzes; in TGT, competitive tournaments	Individualistic tests	Individualistic tests on learning unit; class and/or teacher evaluation of Group Investigation	Individualistic tests on learning unit; class and/or teacher evaluation of Co-op Co-op presentation; teammate and/or teacher evaluation of minitopic presentation and contribution to team effort; teacher evaluation of paper based on minitopic.

understanding, and communication. Learning in Co-op Co-op and Group-Investigation is student-directed; the students learn because they want to understand. Student-directed learning is intrinsically rewarding and is quite different from instrumental learning, where the aim is to gain points, approval, or victory in a competitive tournament.

Cooperation and learning are complementary in Co-op Co-op and Group-Investigation. The students cooperate in order to learn better, and they learn in order to help others. The students become identified with the goal of sharing with others what they have learned. The reward for this type of cooperation is intrinsic; it is pleasurable to communicate one's understanding to others, and there is joy in seeing another person helped. Cooperation comes to be viewed as an efficient and natural way to learn, and students learn to share with others what they have learned, for the sake of the others. Thus, in Co-op Co-op and Group-Investigation, cooperation is a goal, not just a means of obtaining a competitive victory.

Many students can perceive and are influenced by the assumptions underlying classroom structures. If students are treated as objects to be manipulated into learning what the teacher wants them to learn, they will be more likely to treat others as objects. If they see that the reason for cooperating and learning is to compete better, they can end up placing greater value on competition than on cooperation or learning. Perhaps one of the most important dimensions that distinguishes Co-op Co-op and Group-Investigation from the other cooperative learning structures is the metacommunication of the methods. The methods differ radically in the attitudes that they communicate toward learning, cooperation, and the value of a humanistic as opposed to a manipulative orientation toward others. To an important degree, Co-op Co-op and Group-Investigation embody a more democratic philosophy of education than the other techniques because they give greater control to students over what is to be learned and how it is to be learned.

NATURE OF LEARNING

Co-op Co-op and Group-Investigation emphasize involving students in learning; STAD and TGT, in contrast, are more exclusively oriented toward content acquisition. Jigsaw, like STAD and TGT, is heavily oriented toward content acquisition, but it also often includes the learning of interpersonal skills. In Co-op Co-op and Group-Investigation, students learn to be learners: They deal with complex learning tasks by formulating questions, locating resources, and solving problems using analytic and synthetic processes. There is room for students to manifest their own ingenuity. The learning tasks of the students in these methods are differentiated so that higher ability students may have much more difficult tasks than lower ability students; it is assumed that the best learning experience takes into account the interests and the abilities of the student. In STAD, TGT, and Jigsaw, in contrast, the learning tasks tend to be simpler, uniform across students (with the exception of the division of labor in Jigsaw), and predetermined by the teacher. The resources are also predetermined, and there is little room for creativity or for the unique expressions of individual students. In short, the learning tasks and the procedures differ among the cooperative learning methods according to their different philosophies of education.

Whereas the learning tasks in the STAD, TGT, and Jigsaw methods always involve skill or content acquisition, Co-op Co-op and Group-Investigation can be used also for creative expression, or in group discussion where an attempt is made to synthesize and then verbalize the group members' opinions, rather than dealing exclusively with facts about an external reality. Thus, a group-produced play, mural, or poem might be the product in Co-op Co-op or Group-Investigation.

NATURE OF COOPERATION

The nature and the extent of within- and between-team cooperation in different methods of cooperative learning differ markedly. The reason is that the methods create different task and reward structures and, consequently, different amounts and kinds of interdependence and social facilitation among the students. The term *task structure* refers to how the students do the work. It is important to distinguish learning tasks from evaluation tasks. For example, in TGT, the learning task usually includes dyadic drill in teams, and the evaluation task involves competition in a tournament. The term *reward structure* refers to the positive or negative consequences of the successful or unsuccessful completion of the learning and evaluation tasks. Distinguishing among learning tasks, evaluation tasks, and reward structures helps us compare the different cooperative learning methods. For example, STAD and TGT have similar learning tasks (dyadic drill in groups), dissimilar evaluation tasks (quizzes vs. tournaments), and similar reward structures (individual points contribute to team scores).

Cooperative task and reward structures are characterized by mutual positive interdependence or mutual positive facilitation among students. If the success of each teammate is necessary for the success of every other, mutual positive interdependence exists. The students are dependent on each other to achieve success and will most likely cooperate because they realize that the success of their teammates is necessary for their own success. If the success of the teammates contributes to but is not necessary for one's own success, mutual positive facilitation exists. When there is mutual positive facilitation, students will often, but not always, cooperate; sometimes they may attempt to succeed on their own.

The amount and kind of interdependence and facilitation among students depends on the nature of the task and reward structures. In general, positive interdependence in learning depends on the extent to which each member contributes a unique and indispensable component to the group product and/or the extent to which learning depends on mutual helping or cooperation. Positive interdependence in evaluation exists if the team members are assessed as a group rather than individually and if the performance of each team member contributes to the group grade. Positive interdependence in the reward structure exists when individual points contribute to a group score or grade, or when the group receives a grade on a group product to which all the members contribute. There are, however, numerous variables within the reward and task structures of cooperative learning methods that influence the salience and the extent of the positive interdependence and facilitation among students. Those variables include (1) group size and composition; (2) the method of determining group scores (e.g., combining individual scores or grading a group product); (3) the method of combining individual scores, if used, to produce a group grade or score (e.g., summing, giving all members the grade of the lowest achiever, or requiring all members to reach a certain criteria); (4) the presence or absence of a competitive between-team reward structure; (5) the percentage of the total grade for a unit that the group grade comprises; and (6) the percentage of the total grade for a class that the grade in the cooperative unit comprises. None of the cooperative learning methods maximizes the extent of positive interdependence among students across the learning task, the evaluation task, and the reward structure. Some methods rely more on the learning-task structure to produce cooperation. While other methods rely more on the reward structure. This observation suggests the possibility of modifying the existing cooperative learning methods to increase positive interdependence and cooperativeness among students—a topic to be discussed later.

WITHIN-TEAM TASK STRUCTURE

If the successful completion of a team's learning task depends on cooperation among the teammates, by definition, the within-team task structure is cooperative. Although all the cooperative learning methods adopt cooperative within-team task structures, they differ in the type of cooperation that they stress. STAD and TGT emphasize a peer-tutoring structure: One student *helps* another, usually through dyadic drill in groups. In contrast, Co-op Co-op and Group-Investigation emphasize the putting together of a team product and its presentation by the group: Students *cooperate* to reach a common goal. Jigsaw emphasizes elements of both cooperation and sharing: Students cooperate in their expert groups to arrive at a common understanding of their topic and sometimes even at a common format for presenting that understanding to their teammates; they also return to their groups to *share* what they have learned.

The within-team task structure is characterized by positive interdependence if a team cannot be successful without help or cooperation from every member. In fact, most of the existing methods have within-team task structures better characterized by positive facilitation. In STAD and TGT, students can choose not to work with teammates and can learn the material alone. In Co-op Co-op and Group-Investigation, each team member ideally makes a unique contribution to the group so that its members are positively interdependent. In fact, though, a very weak team member can be "carried," so that the group fills in or makes up for the weak component, and the task structure is characterized by positive facilitation rather than positive interdependence. Only in some cases can teachers assure a complete division of labor among students within teams so that each student has an absolutely indispensable contribution to make to the group effort. In Jigsaw I, because division of the learning task into separate components is the essence of the method, it can be characterized as having positive interdependence within the task structure of the team. In Jigsaw II, help from each expert becomes less essential for the completion of the learning task because each student has access to all the learning materials, so only positive facilitation exists.

BETWEEN-TEAM TASK STRUCTURES

In general, the cooperative learning methods differ far more on their between-team task structures than on their within-team structures. The between-team structures range from intensely competitive to highly cooperative.

In TGT, an intensely competitive between-team task structure is set up in the evaluation task: Students attempt to win points for their team in tournaments in which the success of one student is enhanced by the failure of another. Maximum points are earned in the tournaments by the students who challenge other students who miss a question. In such a situation, students may learn to hope for the failure of others. The task for students is to obtain more than others as they actively compete in direct interpersonal interaction. In contrast, STAD involves no interaction of students across teams, and it therefore has no between-team task structure.

The between-team task structures of Co-op Co-op, Group-Investigation, and Jigsaw, unlike those of STAD and TGT, are highly cooperative. In Group-Investigation, a steering committee ensures coordination of the efforts of the various groups and efficient and complementary division of labor. Each group serves a unique role in the complex social organization of the classroom, which is viewed as a group of groups serving a common goal. In Co-op Co-op, there is less emphasis on between-group task structure. The groups are encouraged to choose topics of interest to the whole class, to share resources, and sometimes to give feedback and/or help to other groups. Between-group cooperation is created, but there is little in the formal task structure or the classroom organization to make the groups work together. In Jigsaw, it is the expert groups that create between-group cooperation. Although the groups do not cooperate as whole entities, their members send a representative to each expert group so that all members are aided by the efforts of others both directly in the expert groups and indirectly in their teams as teammates share what they have learned from the experts of other teams.

WITHIN-TEAM REWARD STRUCTURES

In STAD, TGT, and Jigsaw II, each team member receives an individual score that contributes to the team score, so the reward structure is probably best described as individualistic and cooperative. In contrast, in Co-op Co-op and Group-Investigation, if team grades are given, it is to the team as a whole; individuals, however, may also receive a grade for their individual contributions to the group effort, so the reward structure can be described as cooperative and possibly individualistic. The nature of the reward can also differ across methods. In STAD, TGT, and Jigsaw II, there is an extrinsic reward: publicly displayed team standings to which all teammates contribute. The reward to teammates for the success of individual team members in Co-op Co-op and Group-Investigation, rather than points and an improved team standing, is understanding of the learning material and an improved group presentation. Thus, if students identify with their team and with their team presentation, they will find it intrinsically rewarding if their teammates are successful in their individual learning tasks. If the group presentations are formally evaluated, an extrinsic cooperative within-team structure is also created because the success of each teammate contributes to the reward for all team members.

Jigsaw I and Jigsaw II differ radically with regard to their within-team reward structures. In Jigsaw I, there is no team score; individual grades in no way contribute to the rewards of others, and so there is no positive interdependence or facilitation in the reward structure. The within-team reward structure is thus best described as individualistic. In Jigsaw II, as in STAD and TGT, individual grades contribute to a team score as well as to an individual score, so the reward structure is best described as individualistic and cooperative. In those techniques, therefore, there is positive interdependence in relation to the team score, but there is no interdependence or facilitation among teammates in relation to their individual scores. Although it would seem that the absence of a team score in Jigsaw I would produce less cooperation than is found in STAD, TGT, and Jigsaw II, Jigsaw I, unlike these other techniques, has a highly interdependent task structure that could make up for the lack of interdependence in the reward structure.

It is possible that the presence of both a team score and an individual score in STAD, TGT, and Jigsaw II produces less cooperation than if only a team score were derived. If no individualistic elements are introduced, and if the team score is based on the evaluation of a team product rather than on combining the scores of individuals, a greater sense of team identity and positive interdependence may result.

BETWEEN-TEAM REWARD STRUCTURES

Between-team reward structures differ far more across the different learning methods than do the within-team reward structures. STAD, TGT, and Jigsaw II have highly competitive between-team reward structures in which the success of one team is dependent on the failure of other teams as the teams compete to be highest in the standings. Competition is encouraged in trying for the best scores and the highest standings. Jigsaw I is far less competitive than Jigsaw II because in Jigsaw I there is no emphasis on between-team comparisons. Further, both Jigsaw methods soften between-team competition because of their cooperative between-team task structure. Jigsaw II represents the interesting case of a mixed task and reward structure: The between-team task is largely cooperative, but the between-team reward structure is competitive.

The extrinsic between-team reward structures in both Co-op Co-op and Group-Investigation are generally not highly developed. Consistent with the philosophy of these techniques, the teams are encouraged to help each other not for improved grades or points, but because cooperation between teams is a natural and efficient way to master the whole topic. When these techniques are running well, the groups identify with each other and take pleasure in the successful presentations of other groups. If a formal evaluation of the students is made on the basis of how well they master the material presented in the team presentations, an extrinsic cooperative between-team reward structure exists because good presentations by a team lead to content mastery and better grades for members of other teams. In Co-op Co-op and Group-Investigation, there is no use of extrinsic classroom rewards that are contingent on having all groups reach some criterion; that kind of cooperative between-team reward structure would be possible and might even increase between-team cooperation, but it runs counter to a philosophy of education that emphasizes the intrinsic rewards associated with learning and sharing.

It is surprising to note that none of the cooperative learning methods adopts a formal extrinsic cooperative between-team reward structure. Such a structure would be easy to put into place: A reward for the whole class could be provided if all the groups reached criterion, or the amount of a class reward could be made to depend on the sum of the points earned by all the teams. Such a reward structure could dramatically increase between-team cooperation and in no way would run counter to the philosophy of education in STAD, TGT, or Jigsaw II.

RELIANCE ON TASK VERSUS REWARD STRUCTURE

Interestingly, the various methods differ in how much reliance they place on the task relative to the reward structure for producing cooperation among students. STAD, TGT, and Jigsaw II do not have highly developed cooperative task structures. Students, in fact, can choose to work alone rather than in dyads within teams. There is no division of labor: No student has a unique contribution to make to the group. Students help each other in those methods not because the task demands cooperation but because of the cooperative reward structure. Students hope for the success of their teammates and offer them help when possible because they contribute to a common team score, and the success of each improves the team score for all.

In contrast, Co-op Co-op, Group-Investigation, and Jigsaw I reverse the priorities placed on reward and task structures: The cooperative task structures are highly developed, but generally, little reliance is placed on the reward structures. Teachers attempt to make each student responsible for a unique and important part of the learning task so that all students will have to cooperate. Generally, there is far less emphasis on team scores or group grades.

It may be that the greater reliance of STAD and TGT on the reward structure and the greater reliance of Co-op Co-op and Group-Investigation on the task structure are appropriate for the learning materials and the learning tasks usually encountered in these methods. Perhaps the acquisition of basic skills and information, which often involves drill, is best encouraged by a well-defined external reward structure, whereas in complex learning tasks, which may be inherently more interesting, external motivation is perhaps not as important. It is interesting to speculate, however, on how cooperation might be increased by including a cooperative task structure in STAD or TGT or by adding a highly developed cooperative reward structure to Co-op Co-op or Group-Investigation.

STUDENT ROLES AND COMMUNICATION

All of the methods provide students with role experiences from which they are constrained in traditional classrooms. Whereas in traditional classrooms students are confined to the role of "student," which too often translates into being a passive recipient of information and methods, in cooperative activities students experience role diversity. It is likely that such diversity has beneficial effects on student development. Students can experience a change in self-concept when they are expected to become tutors, expert consultants, investigators, and presenters. Students in cooperative learning classrooms may become better prepared to assume a diversity of roles outside the educational setting.

In general, there is greater role constraint in STAD and TGT than in Group-Investigation and Co-op Co-op; Jigsaw occupies a middle position. To some extent, the nature of roles and student communication depends on the complexity of the learning task. In Jigsaw, for example, if the material to be mastered in expert groups is quite complex, the students in a Jigsaw classroom may have to engage in complex analysis and discussion. If the material is simple, the role of the experts may be confined to listing facts to share with their groups.

Interestingly, the status hierarchy among students is far more equalized in Jigsaw, especially Jigsaw I, than in the other methods. In theory, there is equal status among the students in Co-op Co-op and Group-Investigation because each has a unique contribution to make to the group. In practice, however, a status hierarchy often emerges in these methods when students are allowed free expression and access to materials, and the group may give more weight to the ideas and areas of interest of some students than to those of others. In STAD and TGT, a status hierarchy often emerges because students have been assigned to groups so that high achievers can tutor low achievers. Only in Jigsaw I is the status hierarchy among students formally equalized because equal weight is given to the expert area of all students, ensuring that they will have a unique and indispensable contribution to make.

The presence of team-building techniques in Jigsaw I, Co-op Co-op, and Group-Investigation, but not Jigsaw II, STAD, and TGT, is consistent with the differences in their task and reward structures. In the methods that do not include team building, there is greater emphasis on the external reward structure. The learning tasks are generally simpler in those methods, and it is assumed that the cooperative reward structure will produce sufficient cooperation so that team building is not necessary. In the absence of a highly defined cooperative reward structure, and because complex communication among students is necessary in Group-Investigation, Co-op Co-op, and Jigsaw I, team building is stressed. It is assumed that social interaction skills, at least for some students, must be taught; without them, high levels of cooperation are unlikely.

TEACHER ROLES

As the students adopt the roles traditionally reserved for the teacher, the teachers using cooperative learning also adopt new roles. In STAD and TGT, the teacher is available to work with individual students or with groups while most of the class is involved in tutor–tutee relations. Similarly, in Jigsaw, the teacher has time to consult with the expert and learning groups to facilitate their mastery of the material. The teacher is freed even more in Group-Investigation and Co-op Co-op because the students assume the responsibility for the whats and hows of teaching and learning. Typically, the teacher consults with the groups, suggesting ideas or possibilities to be explored. The teacher must ensure an equitable and reasonable division of labor in the groups, but this is often done by asking a question of a group rather than by taking over the decision making.

EVALUATION

The source of evaluation is the teacher in STAD, TGT, and Jigsaw I and II, whereas student involvement in evaluation is often expected in Group-Investigation and Co-op Co-op. In the former methods, the form

of evaluation is individual performance in tournaments and on quizzes
and tests. In the latter, the forms are more varied, including teacher and
student evaluations of group products and presentations, teacher evaluations of student papers based on their individual contributions to the
group, and teammate evaluations of the contributions of individual
team members to their team.

IMPLICATIONS OF THE ANALYSIS

An analysis of the dimensions of cooperative learning within classrooms
provides a conceptual framework for viewing cooperative learning
methods and has a number of implications.

The analysis points out the similarities and differences among the
techniques, indicates the ways in which the existing techniques might
be modified, and suggests interesting new techniques that might be
generated. The analysis also suggests a number of critical problems that
need to be answered by research.

DIFFERENTIATING CO-OP CO-OP AND GROUP-INVESTIGATION

Co-op Co-op and Group-Investigation share the same philosophy of education and provide similar student and teacher roles. Nevertheless, the
two techniques can be differentiated along several important dimensions, including the complexity and the flexibility of classroom organization and the type of roles that are adopted within the groups.

COMPLEXITY OF CLASSROOM ORGANIZATION

After the initial selection of topics by the teams in Co-op Co-op, during
which the teacher attempts to ensure that the work of each group will
complement that of the others, there is little between-team cooperation.
The groups are viewed as independent entities, each pursuing its own
learning objective. In contrast, in Group-Investigation, the groups are
viewed as part of a larger class organization; they are all working together to solve a common problem. Thus, in Group-Investigation, there
is need for a steering committee to ensure that there will be an ongoing
coordination of efforts across groups. In this complex organization, the
class is viewed as a "group of groups," and ideally, there is positive interdependence in the task structure. That is, a problem for investigation
is selected for the whole class, and the tasks are divided among the
groups in ways that make it impossible for any group to fully reach its

learning objective without the information provided by the other groups. In Co-op Co-op, there may be some positive facilitation among the groups as they informally share resources and information, but the groups are relatively independent, and the success of one is not dependent on the success of others. Co-op Co-op calls for a simpler form of classroom organization.

FLEXIBILITY OF CLASSROOM ORGANIZATION

Co-op Co-op is more flexible than Group-Investigation along a number of dimensions. Teachers can use Co-op Co-op for a variety of learning objectives other than investigation, including the mastery of informational content, value clarification, concept mastery, and self-discovery. Co-op Co-op can be used with only one text or resource as the source of learning, or with a broad range of learning sources, as in Group-Investigation. Whereas Group-Investigation stresses a certain kind of learning experience and therefore emphasizes a multiplicity of student-generated learning sources, Co-op Co-op is designed as a framework within which a variety of experiences and materials can be placed.

MINITOPICS

Students in Co-op Co op make a formal presentation within their group on their individual minitopic. Thus, Co-op Co-op shares with Jigsaw a certain kind of teaching experience for students that is not present in Group-Investigation. The minitopics of Co-op Co-op, however, are different in important ways from the expert topics of Jigsaw. Whereas each student in Jigsaw shares an expert topic with the experts of other groups and can learn about his or her expert topic without consulting original resources, each student in Co-op Co-op is solely responsible for an individual minitopic and so must make an original contribution. The formal presentations by members on their minitopics in Co-op Co-op are also different from the informal group discussions in Group-Investigation. Further, minitopics ensure that each individual will make a substantial "content" contribution to the group, whereas that may not always be the case in Group-Investigation.

MODIFYING COOPERATIVE LEARNING TECHNIQUES

Changing an existing cooperative learning technique on any one of the 25 dimensions of classroom structures can have an impact on the nature of social relations and learning among students. The analysis of the dimensions of cooperative learning structures provides a basis for systematically modifying an established technique in order to adapt it to the aims or needs of a class. For example, if a teacher liked the Jigsaw structure but wanted to include student-generated learning sources in order to increase depth of understanding and to familiarize the students with resource gathering and assimilation, the teacher might assign expert topics, as is usually done in the Jigsaw methods, but would make available time and a variety of resources for the students to gather information on their expert topics independently. This change would radically alter the nature of student communication in the expert groups: Each student would have unique materials and a fresh perspective, and there could be in the expert groups of Jigsaw the kind of analysis and synthesis that is now found only in the learning teams of Co-op Co-op and Group-Investigation. No longer would students be attempting to organize and assimilate teacher-assigned materials that they had all read; they would be confronted with the tasks of choosing what to learn and of assimilating a diversity of material. Positive interdependence would be created in the task structure within the expert groups, not just within the teams, and the expert group meetings would involve high-level cooperation and learning. Such an alteration in Jigsaw would probably have an important effect on between-team relations and on certain kinds of learning.

It is striking to note that some techniques place an emphasis on the reward structure (STAD, TGT, and Jigsaw II), whereas other techniques (Co-op Co-op, Group-Investigation, and Jigsaw I) place relatively more emphasis on the task structure to produce cooperation. It would be possible to modify those techniques that emphasize reward structure to include a division of labor in the task structure, probably with positive effects. Similarly, it would be possible to institute a formal team-reward structure in those techniques that do not have one, also possibly with positive outcomes.

GENERATING NEW COOPERATIVE LEARNING TECHNIQUES

It is very surprising to note that none of the cooperative learning techniques has a well-defined, explicit cooperative between-team reward structure. If a class received a reward contingent on all groups reaching some learning criterion, a between-team cooperative reward structure would be established, probably with profound effects on between-team relations among students and on sense of class identity.

New within-team reward structures can be generated to suit specific purposes. For example, teachers who are particularly concerned about improving the achievement of low achievers might try giving each team member a score that consisted of the sum of his or her own achievement score and the achievement score of the lowest achiever in the group. Such a reward structure would make every team member positively interdependent with the lowest achiever (part of each team member's grade would depend directly on how well the lowest achiever performed). Almost certainly, this approach would induce efforts among teammates to help the team member who most needed help.

It is very simple to alter the evaluation task structure in a traditional classroom and to create a new cooperative learning structure. For example, if two midterm exams are given, a teacher can inform the students that, for the second midterm, those scoring above the median on the first midterm have an option of tutoring those who scored below, and that tutors can earn credit for the improvement scores of tutees. Such a simple alteration creates positive interdependence among students and would create a considerable amount of positive peer tutoring.

RESEARCH IMPLICATIONS

The analysis of the dimensions of classroom structures points to both basic and applied research questions that remain to be answered. A program of research is needed to determine the differential processes and outcomes that are a consequence of established and new cooperative learning techniques. Another program of research is needed to determine the basic principles related to cooperative learning structures.

APPLIED RESEARCH

Existing cooperative learning methods differ on numerous dimensions that should influence group processes and academic and nonacademic outcomes. For example, as noted, Jigsaw I and II differ on a critical dimension: positive interdependence in the within-team task structure. Because students in Jigsaw II do not necessarily have to depend on each other to do well, it is possible that their attitudes toward each other and toward the need for cooperation are quite different compared with those in Jigsaw I, in which true interdependence is set up by the task structure.

Numerous important questions beg for answers. For example, do students have a different attitude toward learning in those techniques in which learning is established as the goal? It certainly would seem that attitudes toward cooperation should be different in techniques in which cooperation is instrumental in winning in between-team competition from techniques in the methods that make helping others a primary goal. The effects of intrinsic and extrinsic reward systems in the various techniques also merit research.

It seems that the cooperative learning methods that stress basic skill mastery rely on a cooperative reward system, and that those that stress learning in lower consensus areas rely more on a cooperative task structure. It is possible that such a divergence is functional: Perhaps the basic skills that often involve boring drill need an exciting extrinsic reward structure, whereas the lower consensus areas provide more intrinsic rewards. It remains, however, for empirical research to establish the types of learning tasks for which each type of cooperative learning method is best suited.

BASIC RESEARCH

There is a need to analyze the effects of specific elements within cooperative learning structures. A program of research that systematically dismantles or modifies the existing structures might provide insight into basic principles regarding cooperative learning. If, for example, Co-op Co-op were run twice, once with student choice of learning topics and minitopics and once with teacher-assigned team topics and minitopics, the effects of student versus teacher control of learning goals might be analyzed. The independent contribution of each of the 25 elements of cooperative classroom structures merits research attention: It would be important to generate empirically based principles that could serve as guidelines for predicting the probable effect of modifications of cooperative learning methods. For example, it may be that changes in the reward structure tend to influence student achievement, whereas changes in the task structure tend more to influence peer-group processes.

In a very suggestive first step toward analyzing the independent contribution of the various components of cooperative learning methods, Slavin (1980c) tested the separate effects of reward and task structures. Four classroom structures were contrasted: Students either worked together (group task) or alone (individual task), and they received rewards either as a group (team reward) or as individuals (individual reward). The results indicated that, for both task structures, the group reward produced greater achievement, and for both reward structures, the individual task structures produced the greater gains. The most striking finding, however, was the interaction of task and reward structures: Actually all the conditions produced approximately equal gains, with the exception of the condition that combined group task and individual reward. In that condition, the students showed the greatest time off-task and the lowest gains. Apparently an individual reward structure may undermine the motivation of students to work together. Thus, the various elements of cooperative-learning classroom structures appear to interact: Certain elements may contribute to gains only if they are found in combination with other elements. Although to some extent it may make sense to regard the cooperative learning methods as integrated packages, Slavin's (1980c) component analysis demonstrated that peer tutoring was not a critical component of the STAD package in producing academic gains. Clearly, this finding challenges our basic assumptions about why cooperative learning methods produce the gains that they do, and it points to the need for more component analyses.

To date, cooperative learning methods have been treated almost exclusively as intact packages of variables and have been contrasted almost exclusively with traditional classroom structures. Although this approach has been valuable in establishing the effectiveness of cooperative learning, it provides no evidence regarding the relative importance of the various elements of the cooperative learning methods. Having documented the very profound and positive impact of cooperative learning methods, researchers must now aim for a fuller understanding of how the methods achieve their outcomes.

REFERENCES

Aronson, E. *The jigsaw classroom*. Beverly Hills, Calif.: Sage, 1978.

Dewey, J. *Experience and education*. New York: Macmillan, 1938.

Johnson, D. W., & Johnson, R. T. *Learning together and alone*. Englewood Cliffs, N.J.: Prentice-Hall, 1975.

Johnson, D. W., Maruyama, G., Johnson, R., Nelson, D., & Skon, L. Effects of cooperative, competitive, and individualistic goal structures on achievement: A meta-analysis. *Psychological Bulletin*, 1981, *89*, 47–62.

Johnson, R., Rynders, J., Johnson, D. W., Schmidt, B., & Haider, S. Interaction between handicapped and nonhandicapped teenagers as a function of situational goal structuring: Implications for mainstreaming. *American Educational Research Journal*, 1979, *16*, 161–167.

Kagan, S. Cooperation-competition, culture, and structural bias in classrooms. In S. Sharan, A. P. Hare, C. Webb, & R. Lazarowitz (Eds.), *Cooperation in education*. Provo, Utah: Brigham Young University Press, 1980.

Kagan, S. Social orientation among Mexican-American children: A challenge to traditional classroom structures. In E. Garcia (Ed.), *The Mexican American child: Language, cognition, and social development*. Tempe, Ariz.: Center for Bilingual Education, 1983.

Sharan, S. Cooperative learning in small groups: Recent methods and effects on achievement, attitudes, and ethnic relations. *Review of Educational Research*, 1980, *50*, 241–271.

Sharan, S. & Hertz-Lazarowitz, R. A Group-Investigation method of cooperative learning in the classroom. In S. Sharan, P. Hare, C. D. Webb, & R. Hertz-Lazarowitz (Eds.), *Cooperation in education*. Provo, Utah: Brigham Young University Press, 1980.

Sharan, S. & Sharan, Y. *Small-group teaching*. Englewood Cliffs, N.J.: Educational Technology Publications, 1976.

Slavin, R. E. Cooperative learning. *Review of Educational Research*, 1980, *50*, 315–342. (a)

Slavin, R. E. Effects of student teams and peer tutoring on academic achievement and time on-task. *Journal of Experimental Education*, 1980, *48*, 252–257. (b)

Slavin, R. E. *Using student team learning*. Baltimore: John Hopkins Team Learning Project, 1980. Also available as *Student team learning: A manual for teachers*. In S. Sharan, A. P Hare, C. Webb, & R. Lazarowitz (Eds.), *Cooperation in education*. Provo, Utah: Brigham Young University Press, 1980. (c)

Slavin, R. E. *Cooperative learning*. New York: Longman, 1983.

II

Internal Dynamics of Cooperative Learning

RACHEL HERTZ-LAZAROWITZ

INTRODUCTION

This section, entitled "Internal Dynamics of Cooperative Learning," emphasizes a recent new direction in research on cooperative groups. Although research on groups in general is a well-established area in social psychology, research on groups in the classroom is fairly new. The social psychology of school learning, in general, and the social psychology of cooperative learning, in particular, constitute a stimulating field of research, in which many sociocognitive variables await empirical investigation. The three chapters in this section deal with this area of inquiry in three different ways. Each of the chapters supplies the reader with data and also poses questions for future thinking and research. The chapter by David W. Johnson and Roger T. Johnson draws conclusions from 10 years of research on cooperation in the classroom. Noreen M. Webb's chapter summarizes her oyotomatic research on giving and receiving help in variously composed groups. The chapter by the Dutch researchers Wim Nijhof and Piet Kommers investigates the effects of group member heterogeneity on group problem-solving and individual change. These chapters represent a growing tendency to investigate small and precise units of behavior, and all three chapters in this section emphasize the search for an understanding of the cognitive and social processes that correlate with academic achievement. The following section of the introduction discusses each of the three chapters.

The chapter by Johnson and Johnson integrates a decade of research on cooperative learning. The Johnsons have expanded the social psychological concepts of cooperative, competitive, and individualistic motives for goal accomplishment postulated by Kurt Lewin and Morton Deutsch. The long reference list at the end of their chapter attests to their remarkable contribution to applied social psychology in the implementation of cooperative learning in hundreds of classrooms. The

RACHEL HERTZ-LAZAROWITZ • School of Education, Haifa University, Haifa, Israel.

Johnsons have added conceptual clarity to the research on goal structures in general by studying intensively the effects of cooperative, competitive, and individualistic goal structure on a broad array of academic and social variables. Most of the studies reported in their chapter involve comparisons between two or three learning modes, usually cooperative compared with competitive and/or individualistic goal structures. The bulk of their research findings documents the effectiveness of cooperative learning in producing greater gains in academic and social outcomes. Generally, this tendency is consistent with findings from research on the effects of other cooperative methods, such as TGT, STAD, Jigsaw, and Group-Investigation.

The chapter by Johnson and Johnson presents a conceptual framework that includes 11 internal dynamics of cooperative learning groups that mediate or moderate the relation between cooperation and social and/or academic gains. Each of the 11 dynamic variables was researched to some extent by Johnson and Johnson. They can be further grouped into three general clusters: (1) *cognitive process variables,* such as quality of learning strategy, controversy, and oral rehearsal; (2) *social variables,* such as peer regulation, encouragement and feedback, active involvement, support and acceptance, and positive attitudes; and (3) *instructional variables,* such as the type of learning task, the time on the task, the ability level of the group members, and the fairness of the grading. It is interesting that in a study conducted in Israel by Hertz-Lazarowitz, Shahar, and Sharan (1981), hundreds of elementary-school pupils were asked to write an open-ended essay about their perceptions and evaluations of, feelings about, and attitudes toward cooperative learning after experiencing two years of cooperative learning in the Group-Investigation method. The pupils' responses provided an insight into the internal dynamics of group work. Their responses referred to the cognitive, social, instructional, and motivational domains. Future research will hopefully be capable of systematic and detailed analysis of these variables as related to developmental and individual differences between group members experiencing cooperative learning.

The comparative research designs used in the Johnsons' studies have some limits that should be noted. First, a distinction should be made between two clusters of variables being studied. Academic gains as measured by achievement tests are important variables on which to compare the effectiveness of different methods, as academic learning takes place in all the learning modes under investigation. However, some variables are more characteristic of one or another learning mode, and thus, a comparison of the different methods on such variables poses some logical and conceptual problems. Examples of such variables are verbal communication among peers, helping in the learning task, and exchanging ideas, which are maximized in cooperative learning and minimized in individualistic learning. A comparison of cooperative with individualistic or competitive learning modes on these process variables has limited usefulness; comparisons on such variables should instead be conducted within and between various cooperative methods.

The extensive research conducted by the Johnsons is a substantial part of the basic empirical data representing the first-generation research on cooperative learning. The comprehensive meta-analysis conducted by Johnson, Maruyama, Johnson, Nelson, & Skon (1981) represents a summary of this research. The contribution of the Johnsons is much broader than conducting research. They have made a difference in many schools and classrooms, and their center for cooperative learning produces instructional materials, conducts workshops for teachers, and publishes manuals for implementing cooperative learning.

The focus of the chapter by Nijhof and Kommers is on an analysis of cooperation in heterogeneous and homogeneous groups. They composed their 10 experimental groups on the basis of the students' prior knowledge of urban planning, which was the problem that these fifth-graders had to solve. The learning task was open-ended, and many alternative solutions were correct. The interactive behaviors under investigation in this study were various types of discussion that were observed and coded in the cooperative phase of the study. Nijhof and Kommers make a distinction among three levels of argumentation: (1) no argumentation; (2) exchanging ideas without argumentation; and (3) offering opinions with argumentation. In the definition of *argumentation*, they include giving reasons for some actions, giving explanations, and giving background information. In general, the results of the study showed that the heterogeneous groups, in which pupils began with different prior knowledge and different opinions on urban planning, produced more argumentation and a discussion of more topics. However, these findings were not statistically compared because of the small numbers of groups involved in this study.

The principal contribution of the Nijhof and Kommers chapter is its focus on critical issues that have been neglected thus far. First, I agree with their emphasis on the importance of the nature of the learning task, which is often neglected. More research attention should be devoted to the task under study (Sharan & Hertz-Lazarowitz, 1980; Sharan, Hertz-Lazarowitz, & Hare, 1981). Second, the research design is quite original. The pupils came to the cooperative group *after* they had planned the town individually. Thus, the group project involved equal individual input based on the prior experience of each member in the problem being worked on. The finding that more argumentation was found in groups with controversial knowledge and opinions is not surprising, but the tendency of those argumentations to be higher in the heterogeneous groups is interesting. Future research should focus on improving the understanding and the predictive power of such behaviors.

The chapter by Webb is a fine example of a systematic plan of research composed of a series of interrelated studies. Webb investigated three significant topics in the area of the internal dynamics of cooperative learning. First, she used a process–outcome approach to examine the relationship between achievement gains and giving and receiving help in academic tasks. Second, the effect of group composition, as defined by ability, gender, and personality measures, was studied in relation to interactive behaviors and achievements. Last, the issue of the stability of group interaction over time was investigated. Each of these three topics makes a significant contribution to the theory and the application of cooperative learning. From these studies, researchers as well as classroom teachers can get initial answers to questions about cooperative learning that are often posed. Webb found that help, defined as "giving explanations," is positively related to group achievement, and that receiving explanations, or giving and receiving terminal responses (i.e., help without explanations), is negatively related to achievement. This finding demonstrates the power of explanatory behaviors utilized by peers in the group to affect achievement. This topic is of particular importance because we have yet to study the frequency and the nature of giving explanations on an individual level. The literature on prosocial behavior in the classroom suggests that the frequency of helping in the typical classroom is relatively low. In observational studies conducted in Israel and the United States, we found that helping behavior between students in typical classrooms accounts for only 3%–7% of total interactions (Hertz-Lazarowitz, 1983; Hertz-Lazarowitz & Fuchs, 1983; Fuchs, Hertz-Lazarowitz, Eisenberg & Sharabany, 1984). On the other hand, the recent literature on peer tutoring suggests that the tutor, not the tutee, is the one who benefits, and some research raises doubts about whether "helping is always such a good thing" (De Paulo, Webb, & Hoover, 1983). The finding of a positive correlation between achievement and *giving* help, combined with Webb's finding that high-ability students gave more explanations and with conflicting correlations between receiving help and achievement (Studies 4 and 5), indicates the complexity of helping interactions in the group and raises the question of who benefits from such help. Webb's research opens a stimulating and important line of investigation. Her findings regarding group composition as a predictor of interaction and achievement suggest that group composition is a key factor in cooperative learning. The repeated finding that mixed-ability groups (as opposed to uniform-ability groups) facilitate giving explanations and thus facilitate behaviors that are positively correlated with achievement supports the theoretical claims of all cooperative learning methods. Webb further compared mixed-ability groups of two levels (high and medium or medium and low) and of three levels (high, medium, and low) and found that, in all three studies, questions were answered more frequently in mixed-ability groups than in uniform groups. These findings suggest that groups composed of two ability levels seem to be the most beneficial for all students. The reader has to bear in mind that Webb's findings are based on relatively short interventions and involved only mathematics. Future research should examine these issues in other school subjects. Webb's chapter also presents a detailed analysis of such other variables as group gender composition, extraversion-introversion, and intellectual achievement responsibility, and their correlations with various types of giving and receiving help.

Finally, Webb studied the stability of group interaction over time. Study 5 was conducted in classrooms employing a cooperative learning method, and the researcher was able to observe the same groups over a three-month interval, in contrast with Study 4, in which the groups worked cooperatively only in the experimental setting. The results of Studies 4 and 5 are important for the understanding of cooperative learning and the internal dynamics of the learning groups. First of all, the highest correlations between achievement and giving help in general, as well as offering explanations in particular, were found in Study 5. However, student behavior was relatively unstable over time. Webb suggested that there may be day-to-day fluctuations in behavior within stable long-term patterns. She recommends observing "group work several times during each instructional unit as well as several instructional units over time."

Undoubtedly, the second generation of research on the internal dynamics of cooperative learning, represented by the chapters in this section, has accomplished much. Just as clearly, much theoretical and empirical work remains to be done in this critical area.

References

DePaulo, B. M., Webb, W., & Hoover, C. *Reaction to help in a peer-tutoring context*. Paper presented at the annual meeting of the American Educational Research Association, Montreal, Canada, 1983.

Fuchs, I., Hertz-Lazarowitz, R. Eisenberg, N., & Sharabany, R. *Prosocial reasoning and behavior of kibbutz and city children.* Paper presented at the annual meeting of the American Psychological Association, Toronto, Cannada, September 1984.

Hertz-Lazarowitz, R. Prosocial behavior in the classroom. *Academic Psychology Bulletin,* 1983, *5*, 319–338.

Hertz-Lazarowitz, R., & Fuchs, I. *Prosocial behavior of kibbutz and city children in two types of classrooms: Traditional vs. open-active classroom.* Unpublished manuscript, Haifa University, 1983. (In Hebrew)

Hertz-Lazarowitz, R., Shahar, H., & Sharan, S. What do children think of small-group teaching? In S. Sharan, & R. Hertz-Lazarowitz, (Ed.), *Changing schools: The small-group teaching (SGT) project in Israel.* Tel Aviv: Ramot Educational Systems, 1981. (In Hebrew)

Johnson, D. W., Maruyama, R., Johnson, R., Nelson, D., & Skon, L. Effects of cooperative, competitive and individualistic goal structure on achievement: A meta-analysis. *Psychological Bulletin,* 1981, *89*, 47–62.

Sharan, S., & Hertz-Lazarowitz, R. A group-investigation method of cooperative learning in the classroom. In S. Sharan, P. Hare, C. Webb, & R. Hertz-Lazarowitz, (Eds.), *Cooperation in education.* Provo, Utah: Brigham Young University Press, 1980.

Sharan, S., Hertz-Lazarowitz, R., & Hare, P. The classroom: A structural analysis. In S. Sharan, & R. Hertz-Lazarowitz, (Ed.), Changing schools: The small-group teaching (SGT) project in Israel. Tel Aviv: Ramot Educational Systems, 1981 (In Hebrew).

4

The Internal Dynamics of Cooperative Learning Groups

DAVID W. JOHNSON
AND
ROGER T. JOHNSON

Introduction

For the past 10 years, we have been conducting a systematic program of research on the relative impact of cooperative, competitive, and individualistic learning experiences on such variables as achievement and relationships among students. One major focus of our research program has been to illuminate the internal processes within cooperative learning groups that mediate or moderate the relationship between cooperation and (1) productivity and (2) interpersonal attraction among students.

In this chapter, we shall first outline the theoretical framework and the conceptual definitions from which we have worked and the research procedures that we have employed. Second, we shall review the evidence from our studies concerning the relative impact of the three types of instructional situations on achievement and relationships among students. Third, we shall review the results of our studies delineating the internal dynamics of cooperative learning groups. Finally, we shall outline the implications of our results for educators who wish to maximize the effectiveness of cooperative learning.

Social Interdependence

Lewin's (1935) theory of motivation postulates that a state of tension within an individual motivates movement toward the accomplishment of desired goals and that it is a drive for goal accomplishment that motivates cooperative, competitive, and individualistic behavior. In formulating a theory of how the tension systems of different people may be interrelated, Deutsch (1949, 1962) conceptualized three types of goal

DAVID W. JOHNSON AND ROGER T. JOHNSON • College of Education, University of Minnesota, Minneapolis, Minnesota 55455.

structures that organize interpersonal behavior: cooperative, competitive, and individualistic. In a *cooperative* goal structure, the goals of the separate individuals are so linked together that there is a positive correlation among their goal attainments. Under purely cooperative conditions, an individual can attain his or her goal if and only if the other participants can attain their goals. Thus, a person seeks an outcome that is beneficial to all those with whom he or she is cooperatively linked. In a *competitive* social situation, the goals of the separate participants are so linked that there is a negative correlation among their goal attainments. An individual can attain his or her goal if and only if the other participants cannot attain their goals. Thus, a person seeks an outcome that is personally beneficial but that is detrimental to the others with whom he or she is competitively linked. Finally, in an *individualistic* situation, there is no correlation among the goal attainments of the participants. Whether an individual accomplishes his or her goal has no influence on whether other individuals achieve their goals. Thus, a person seeks an outcome that is personally beneficial, ignoring as irrelevant the goal accomplishment efforts of other participants in the situation.

OUR RESEARCH EFFORTS AND PROCEDURES

In our work on the relative impact of cooperative, competitive, and individualistic learning experiences, we chose basically to conduct well-controlled field-experimental studies in actual classrooms and schools. Our typical study lasted three weeks, compared cooperative learning situations with individualistic and/or competitive learning situations, and involved students from different ethnic groups and ability levels. We typically obtained the help of three classroom teachers who agreed to assist us in conducting the study. In order to ensure that there would be no differences among the students in each condition, we randomly assigned students, making sure that there was an equal number of males and females, majority and minority members, and high-, medium-, and low-ability students in each condition. To make sure that high-quality teaching occurred in each condition, the teachers received a minimum of 90 hours of training on how to implement cooperative, competitive, and individualistic learning situations and were given a daily script to follow. In order to make sure that any differences among conditions that we found were not due to differences in teaching ability, the teachers were rotated across conditions, so that each teacher taught each condition for one week. To make sure that the study did, in fact, test our theory, the ways in which we implemented cooperative, competitive, and individualistic learning were carefully structured to be unambiguous. To make sure that any differences among conditions that we found were not due to differences in curriculum materials, the students studied the identical curriculum. To verify that the teachers were, in fact, teaching the conditions appropriately, we observed them daily. Finally, we collected observations of how the students interacted with each other. We were determined to conduct our research in as highly controlled and careful a way as possible so we could be confident about the results.

In addition to our field-experimental work, we have conducted several large-scale surveys of school districts and several laboratory-experimental studies. The combination of our field-experimental, laboratory-experimental, and survey studies adds to the richness of our research findings.

SOCIAL INTERDEPENDENCE AND ACHIEVEMENT

In our studies, we have found considerable evidence that cooperative learning experiences promote higher achievement than do competitive and individualistic learning experiences (see Table 1). Of the 26 studies that we have done that include achievement data, in 21 studies cooperative learning promoted higher achievement, 2 studies had mixed results, and 3 found no differences among conditions. These studies have included college students and students from every grade but the eighth grade. They have used curriculums in math, English, language arts, geometry, social studies, science, physical science, and physical education. The studies have lasted from one day to nine months. They have included both males and females; upper-middle-class, middle-class, working-class, and lower-class students; gifted, medium-ability, and low-ability students; students with mild to very severe handicapping conditions; and students from a number of minority groups. The length of the instructional sessions has varied from 15 to 90 minutes.

The adaptability of cooperative learning is illustrated by the fact that, in these 26 studies, high-, medium-, and low-ability students were mixed within the cooperative learning groups, Clearly, the high-ability students did not suffer from working with medium- and low-ability students. In the 4 studies that measured the achievement of gifted students separately, 3 found that they achieved higher when collaborating with medium- and low-ability students, and 1 found no difference in achieve-

TABLE 1. Summary of Characteristics of Studies[a]

	S. Johnson & D. Johnson, 1972	Johnson, Johnson, Johnson, & Anderson, 1976	Johnson & Ahlgren, 1976	D. Johnson, R. Johnson, & Anderson, 1978	Johnson & Tjosvold, 1978	R. Johnson, Rynders, D. Johnson, Schmidt, & Haider, 1979
Length of study	1 day	17 days	1 day	1 day	1 day	6 days
Grade level	College	5	1–12	4–12	College	7, 8, 9
Subject area	Attitude measure	Basic skills; language	Attitude measure	Attitude measure	Moral issue	Bowling
Group size	—	4	—	—	—	10
Type of heterogeneity	Sex	Sex; ability	Suburban/rural/urban	Suburban/rural/urban	Sex	Public/private school; sex; handicap (mentally retarded)
Length of instructional session	—	40–60 min	—	—	60 min	60 min
Sample size	32	30	6,000	8,183	45	30
Conditions	C; Comp	C; Ind	C; Comp	C; Comp; Ind	C/con; Comp/con; no controversy	C; Ind; LF
Achievement	—	Mixed	—	—	—	—
Interpersonal attraction	C > Comp	C > Ind	C > Comp	C > Comp+Ind	C/con > Comp/con + no controversy	C > LF > Ind

	Martino & Johnson, 1979	D. Johnson, R. Johnson, & Tauer, 1979	D. Johnson, R. Johnson, & Skon, 1979	R. Johnson & D. Johnson, 1979	D. Johnson, Skon, & R. Johnson, 1980	Cooper, Johnson, Johnson, & Wilderson, 1980
Length of study	9 days	5 days	6 days	3 days	6 days	15 days
Grade level	2, 3	4, 5, 6	1	5	1	7
Subject area	Swimming	Geometry	Math; reading	Math	Math; spatial reasoning; categorization; retrieval	English; science; geography

Group size	2	4–5	3	4	3	—
Type of heterogeneity	Sex; ability; handicap (learning disabled)	Sex; ability	Sex; social class; ability	Sex; social class	Sex; ability	Sex; ability; ethnic membership; handicap (emotionally disturbed)
Length of instructional session	45 min	60 min	40 min	60 min	60 min	90 min
Sample size	12	69	64	66	45	60
Conditions	C; Ind	C; Comp; Ind	C; Comp; Ind	C; Comp; Ind	C; Comp; Ind	C; Comp; Ind
Achievement	C > Ind	C > Comp > Ind	C > Comp > Ind	C > Comp > Ind	C > Comp > Ind	—
Interpersonal attraction	C > Ind	Mixed	—	—	C > Comp > Ind	C > Comp > Ind
	Nevin, Johnson, & Johnson, 1982	Nevin, Johnson, & Johnson, 1982	Nevin, Johnson, & Johnson, 1982	Nevin, Johnson, & Johnson, 1982	D. Johnson & R. Johnson, 1982a	D. Johnson & R. Johnson, 1982b
Length of study	30 days	10 days	17 days	9 months	15 days	15 days
Grade level	1	7	9	1	4	4
Subject area	Reading	Math	Math	All	Social studies	Math
Group size	3	3	3	3	4	4
Type of heterogeneity	Sex; ability; handicap (learning disabled)	Sex; ability; handicap (learning disabled; emotionally disturbed)	Sex; ability; handicap (learning disabled; emotionally disturbed)	Sex; peer status; handicap (emotionally disturbed)	Sex; ability; ethnic membership	Sex; ability; ethnic membership; handicap (hearing impaired)
Length of instructional session	60 min	45 min	45 min	120 min	45 min	55 min
Sample size	11	16	16	22	76	30
Conditions	C; Ind	C; Ind	C; Ind	C; Ind	C; Comp; Ind	C; Ind
Achievement	C > Ind	C > Ind	C > Ind	C > Ind	—	—

continued

TABLE 1. (Continued)

	Nevin, Johnson, & Johnson, 1982	Nevin, Johnson, & Johnson, 1982	Nevin, Johnson, & Johnson, 1982	Nevin, Johnson, & Johnson, 1982	D. Johnson & R. Johnson, 1982a	D. Johnson & R. Johnson, 1982b
Interpersonal attraction	—	C > Ind	C > Ind	C > Ind	C-;Comp > Ind	C > Ind
	Rynders, Johnson, Johnson, & Schmidt, 1980	Skon, Johnson, & Johnson, 1981	Armstrong, Johnson, & Balow, 1981	D. Johnson & R. Johnson, 1981a	D. Johnson & R. Johnson, 1981b	R. Johnson & D. Johnson, 1981
Length of study	9 days	3 days	17 days	16 days	16 days	16 days
Grade level	7, 8, 9	1	5, 6	4	4	3
Subject area	Bowling	Categorization; retrieval; language acquisition; math	Language arts	Social studies	Social studies	Math
Group size	10	3	4	4	4	4
Type of heterogeneity	Sex; ability; handicap (Down's Syndrome)	Sex; ability	Sex; ability; handicap (learning disabled)	Sex; ability; ethnic membership	Sex; ability; handicap (learning disabled; emotionally disturbed)	Sex; ability; peer status; handicap (learning disabled; emotionally disturbed)
Length of instructional session	60 min	45 min	90 min	55 min	45 min	25 min
Sample size	30	86	40	51	51	40
Conditions	C; Comp; Indiv	C; Comp; Ind	C; Ind	C; Ind	C; Ind	C; Ind
Achievement	—	C > Comp > Ind	Mixed	—	—	—
Interpersonal attraction	C > Comp > Ind	C > Comp > Ind	C > Ind	C > Ind	C > Ind	C > Ind

	D. Johnson & R. Johnson, 1982c	Smith, Johnson, & Johnson, 1982	D. Johnson, R. Johnson, Tiffany, & Zaidman, 1983	R. Johnson, D. Johnson, DeWeerdt, Lyons, & Zaidman, 1983	R. Johnson & D. Johnson, 1983	D. Johnson, R. Johnson, Roy, & Zaidman, 1983
Length of study	5 days	5 days	15 days	10 days	15 days	15 days
Grade level	6	6	4	7	3	4
Subject area	Social studies; science	Social studies	Social studies	Science	Math	Social studies
Group size	4	4	4	4	4	4
Type of heterogeneity	Sex; ability; handicap (EMR; learning disabled)	Sex; ability; handicap; (learning disabled; gifted)	Sex; ability; social class; ethnic membership	Sex; ability; handicap (mentally retarded)	Sex; handicap (hearing impaired)	Sex; ability
Length of instructional session	65 min	65 min	55 min	40 min	55 min	55 min
Sample size	55	55	48	48	30	48
Conditions	C; Ind	C; Ind	C; Ind	C; Ind	C; Ind	C; Ind
Achievement	C > Ind	C > Ind	C > Ind	No difference	No difference	Mixed
Interpersonal attraction	C > Ind	C > Ind	C > Ind	C > Ind	C > Ind	C > Ind

	D. Johnson & R. Johnson, 1984a	D. Johnson & R. Johnson, 1984b	D. Johnson & R. Johnson, 1984c	D. Johnson & R. Johnson, in press (a)	D. Johnson & R. Johnson, in press (b)	R. Johnson, Bjorkland, & Krotee, 1984
Length of study	15 days	11 days	15 days	10 days	10 days	6 days
Grade level	4	6	4	6	4	College
Subject area	Social studies; science	Social studies	Social studies	Science	Science	Golf skill of putting
Group size	4	4	4	4	4	4

continued

TABLE 1. (Continued)

	D. Johnson & R. Johnson, 1984a	D. Johnson & R. Johnson, 1984b	D. Johnson & R. Johnson, 1984c	D. Johnson & R. Johnson, in press (a)	D. Johnson & R. Johnson, in press (b)	R. Johnson, Bjorkland, Krotee, 1984
Type of heterogeneity	Sex; ability; social class; handicap (learning disabled)	Sex; ability; handicap (learning disabled; behavior problems)	Sex; ability; handicap (learning disabled; behavior problems)	Sex; ability; ethnic membership	Sex; handicap	Physical ability
Length of instructional session	55 min	55 min	60 min	55 min	55 min	45 min
Sample size	48	72	59	48	51	115
Conditions	C; Ind	Con; De; Ind	C; Comp; Ind	C; Comp	IC; IComp	C; Comp; Ind
Achievement	C > Ind	—	—	—	—	C > Comp > Ind
Interpersonal attraction	C > Ind	Con > De > Ind	C > Comp+Ind	C > Comp	IC; IComp	C > Coomp+Ind

	D. Johnson, R. Johnson, & Tiffany, 1984	Johnson, Johnson, Pierson, & Lyons, 1984	Smith, Johnson, & Johnson, 1984	Roon, Van Pilsum, Harris, Rosenberg, Johnson, Liaw, & Rosenthal, 1983
Length of study	11 days	15 days	10 days	5 months
Grade level	6	4, 5, 6	College	College
Subject area	Social studies	Social studies	Science	Biochemistry
Group size	4	4	4	4
Type of heterogeneity	Sex; ability; ethnic membership	Sex; ability; age; homerooms	Sex; ability	Sex; ability
Length of instructional session	55 min	40 min	60 min	180 min
Sample size	72	112	36	50

Conditions	Conflict; De; Ind	Con; ConSeek	Con; ConSeek	C; Ind
Achievement	—	Con > ConSeek	No difference	C > Ind
Interpersonal attraction	Con > De > Ind	Con > ConSeek	No difference	—
	Yager, Johnson, Johnson, & Snider, 1984	Warring, Johnson, Maruyama, & Johnson, 1984	Warring, Johnson, Maruyama, & Johnson, 1984	R.Johnson, D. Johnson, Scott, & Ramolae, 1984
Length of study	54 days	11 days	10 days	21 days
Grade level	4	6	4	5, 6
Subject area	Science	Social studies	Social studies	Science
Group size	4	5–6	4–5	4–5
Type of heterogeneity	Sex; ability; ethnic membership; handicap	Sex; ability; ethnic membership	Sex; ability; ethnic membership	Sex; ability; grade level; handicap
Length of instructional session	45 min	55 min	55 min	45 min
Sample size	69	74	51	154
Conditions	C; C/Ind; Ind	C/Con; C/De; Ind	IC; IComp	Single-sex cooperative; Mixed-sex cooperative; Ind
Achievement	—	—	—	C; Ind
Interpersonal attraction	C > C/Ind > Ind	C > Ind	IC > IComp	C > Ind

[a] C = cooperative, Comp = competitive, Con = controversy seeking, ConSeek = concurrence seeking, De = debate seeking, IC = intergroup cooperation, IComp = intergroup competition, Ind = individualistic, LF = laissez-faire.

ment. In the 13 studies that measured the achievement of academically handicapped students, 12 found that they achieved higher in the cooperative condition, and 1 found no difference in achievement. It is evident, therefore, that cooperative learning procedures can provide appropriate instructional experiences for diverse students who work together.

Since the 1920s, there has been a great deal of research on the relative effects of cooperative, competitive, and individualistic efforts on achievement and productivity. Our work is only a small part of this research effort. Despite the large number of studies conducted, however, social scientists have disagreed about the conclusions that may be drawn from the literature. The traditional practice seemed to be to select a subset of studies that supported one's biases, to declare that they are the only studies that are relevant to the question, to place them in a review, and to give one's summary impressions of their findings.

In order to resolve the controversies resulting from such reviews on social interdependence and achievement, we conducted a meta-analysis of all the studies that had been conducted in the area (D. Johnson, Maruyama, Johnson, Nelson, & Skon, 1981). We reviewed 122 studies conducted between 1924 and 1981, which yielded 286 findings. Three methods of meta-analysis were used: the voting method, the effect–size method, and the z-score method. The results indicate that cooperative learning experiences tend to promote higher achievement than do competitive and individualistic learning experiences. The average person working within a cooperative situation achieves at about the 80th percentile of the students working within a competitive or individualistic situation. These results hold for all age levels, for all subject areas, and for tasks involving concept attainment, verbal problem-solving, categorizing, spatial problem-solving, retention and memory, motor performance, and guessing-judging-predicting. For rote-decoding and correcting tasks, cooperation seems to be as effective as competitive and individualistic learning procedures.

Social Interdependence and Relationships among Students

In our studies, we have found considerable evidence that cooperative learning experiences promote greater interpersonal attraction and more positive relationships among students than do competitive and individualistic learning experiences (see Table 1). Of the 37 studies that we have done that include interpersonal attraction data, in 35 studies cooperative learning promoted greater interpersonal attraction, and in 2 the results were mixed. These findings resulted for a wide variety of age levels, subject areas, diverse students, and instructional sessions.

Although the above studies represent considerable validation of the basic proposition of our theoretical model, there remained the need to verify that other researchers were finding similar results. Research reviews commonly examine only subsets of the existing studies, allowing different reviewers to come up with contradictory conclusions. The use of the summary-impression method of reviewing literature has been severely criticized recently. Therefore, we recently completed a meta-analysis of all existing research on the relative impact of cooperative, cooperative with intergroup competition, interpersonal competitive, and individualistic learning experiences on interpersonal attraction among homogeneous and heterogeneous samples of students (D. Johnson, R. Johnson, & Maruyama, 1983). We reviewed 98 studies conducted between 1944 and 1982, which yielded 251 findings. Three types of meta-analysis procedures were used: the voting method, the effect-size method, and the z-score method. The results of all three analyses provide strong validation for the proposition that cooperative learning experiences, compared with competitive or individualistic ones, promote greater interpersonal attraction among homogeneous students, students from different ethnic groups, and handicapped and nonhandicapped students.

INTERNAL DYNAMICS OF COOPERATIVE LEARNING GROUPS

Despite the large number of studies comparing the relative impact of cooperative, competitive, and individualistic learning situations on achievement and relationships among students, the processes that mediate or moderate the relationship between cooperation and productivity, and interpersonal attraction have been relatively ignored. We have examined a number of potentially explanatory variables to illuminate the internal dynamics of cooperative learning groups. Some of the potentially mediating or moderating variables that we have studied are

1. The type of learning task assigned
2. The quality of the learning strategy used to complete learning tasks
3. The occurrence of controversy (academic disagreement) among group members
4. The time on task used in completing the learning tasks

5. The oral rehearsal engaged in while interacting about the learning tasks
6. The peer regulation, encouragement, and feedback engaged in while interacting about the learning tasks
7. The active involvement in learning occurring while completing the learning tasks
8. The ability levels of the group members
9. Feelings of psychological support and acceptance
10. More positive attitudes toward subject areas
11. Greater perceptions of fairness of grading

TYPE OF TASK

In our original reviews of the literature (D. Johnson & R. Johnson, 1974, 1975a), the evidence indicated that for simple, mechanical, previously mastered tasks that require no help from other students, competition promoted a greater quantity of output than did cooperative or individualistic efforts. Believing that the type of task being used might be an important explanatory variable, the authors and their students conducted a series of studies examining the relative effects of cooperative, competitive, and individualistic goal structures on achievement on a variety of school-related tasks (Garibaldi, 1979; D. Johnson, R. Johnson, & Skon, 1979; D. Johnson, Skon, & R. Johnson, 1980; R. Johnson & D. Johnson, 1979; Skon, Johnson, & Johnson, 1981). The studies focused on white first- and fifth-grade students from both urban and suburban settings and black high-school students from an urban setting. The results are surprisingly consistent. Cooperation promoted higher achievement than did either competitive or individualistic efforts on mathematical and verbal drill-review tasks; spatial-reasoning and verbal problem-solving tasks; pictorial and verbal sequencing tasks; tasks involving a comparison of the attributes of shape, size, and pattern; and a knowledge-retention task. On a specific knowledge-acquisition task both cooperation and competition promoted higher achievement than did individualistic efforts. These findings are all the more important as care was taken to optimize the constructiveness of the operationalizations of competitive and individualistic instruction.

Currently, there is no type of task on which cooperative efforts are *less* effective than are competitive or individualistic efforts, and on most tasks (and especially the more important learning tasks, such as concept attainment, verbal problem-solving, categorization, spatial problem-solving, retention and memory, motor, and guessing-judging-predicting), cooperative efforts are more effective in promoting achievement. We therefore left this area of study and moved to an examination of the quality of the strategies being used in learning situations.

QUALITY OF LEARNING STRATEGY

The next potentially explanatory variable that we studied was the quality of the reasoning strategy that students used to complete their assignments. In a pair of studies done in collaboration with Linda Skon (D. Johnson et al., 1980; Skon et al., 1981), we found that the students in the cooperative condition used strategies superior to those used by the students in the competitive and individualistic conditions. These strategies included using category search and retrieval strategies, intersectional classification strategies, the formulation of equations from story problems, and the formulation of strategies for avoiding repetitions and errors in a spatial reasoning task. From these findings, we can conclude that the discussion process in cooperative groups promotes the discovery and the development of higher quality cognitive strategies for learning than does the individual reasoning found in competitive and individualistic learning situations. In a later study (D. Johnson & R. Johnson, 1981a), we found that students working in a cooperative condition reported using higher thought processes than did students working individualistically.

CONTROVERSY VERSUS CONCURRENCE SEEKING

Involved participation in cooperative learning groups inevitably produces conflicts among the ideas, the opinions, the conclusions, the theories, and the information of group members. When such controversies arise, they may be dealt with constructively or destructively, depending on how they are structured by the teacher and what the level of social skills of the students is. We have conducted a series of studies (Lowry & Johnson, 1981; D. Johnson & R. Johnson, in press b; D. Johnson, R. Johnson, & Tiffany, 1984; Smith, Johnson, & Johnson, 1981, 1982, 1984) and have reviewed the research literature (D. Johnson, 1980; D. Johnson & R. Johnson, 1979) on controversy. When managed constructively, controversy promotes epistemic curiosity or uncertainty about the correctness of one's views, an active search for more information, and, consequently, higher achievement and retention of the material being learned. Individuals working alone in competitive and individualistic situations do not have the opportunity for such a process, and therefore, their achievement suffers.

TIME ON TASK

Another possible explanation for the superiority of cooperation in promoting higher achievement than do competitive or individualistic efforts is that students in cooperative learning groups spend more time on task than do students in competitive and individualistic learning situations. In a number of studies, we observed the amount of on-task time in the three types of learning situations (Nevin, Johnson, & Johnson, 1982; D. Johnson & R. Johnson, 1981a, 1982a; D. Johnson, R. Johnson, Roy, & Zaidman, 1984; R. Johnson & D. Johnson, 1981, 1982). Our results indicate that in two of the studies more on-task behavior was found in the cooperative condition, whereas in four of the studies no significant difference in on-task behavior was found. From these results it may be concluded that cooperative learning situations may promote more on-task behavior than the other two goal structures, but probably, there is little difference in observed actual on-task behavior among the three goal structures.

COGNITIVE PROCESSING

One of the most promising mediating variables identified in our meta-analysis (D. Johnson et al., 1981) as explaining part of the relationship between cooperation and achievement was that the oral rehearsal of the information has been found to be necessary for the storage of information into memory, as promoting long-term retention of information, and as increasing achievement. Two of our students, Virginia Lyons (1982) and Patricia Roy (1982), developed an observational instrument that measured the amount of low-level (repetition of information), intermediate-level (stating of new information), and high-level (explanations, rationales, and integration) rehearsal within learning situations. Our studies (D. Johnson & R. Johnson, 1983; D. Johnson, R. Johnson, Roy, & Zaidman, 1984; R. Johnson, D. Johnson, DeWeerdt, Lyons, & Zaidman, 1983) indicate that cooperative efforts contain more low-, intermediate-, and high-level oral rehearsal of information by low-, medium-, and high-ability students than do individualistic efforts.

PEER SUPPORT, ENCOURAGEMENT, REGULATION, AND FEEDBACK

Peer regulation, feedback, support, and encouragement of task-related efforts are often viewed as important in task engagement and in the motivation of less "mature" learners (who may need an external agent to provide more guidance and monitoring of their progress through the steps required to complete a task). Within cooperative situations, the participants benefit from facilitating each other's efforts to achieve, whereas, in competitive situations, the participants benefit from obstructing each other's efforts to achieve, and in individualistic situations, the success or failure of others is irrelevant. There is more frequent helping and tutoring in cooperative than in competitive or individualistic learning situations (Armstrong, Johnson, & Balow, 1981; Cooper, Johnson, Johnson, & Wilderson, 1980; D. Johnson & R. Johnson, 1981a, b, 1982a, b, 1983; D. Johnson, R. Johnson, Tiffany, & Zaidman, 1983). There is also more facilitative and encouraging interaction among students in cooperative than in competitive or individualistic learning situations (D. Johnson & R. Johnson, 1981a, b, 1982a, b, 1983; D. Johnson, R. Johnson, Tiffany, & Zaidman, 1983; D. Johnson, R. Johnson, Roy, & Zaidman, 1984; R. Johnson & D. Johnson, 1981, 1982, 1983; R. Johnson, Rynders, D. Johnson, Schmidt, & Haider, 1979; Martino & Johnson, 1979; Nevin et al., 1982; Rynders, Johnson, Johnson, & Schmidt, 1980). There is evidence, furthermore, that individuals like those who facilitate their goal accomplishment and dislike those who obstruct their goal accomplishment (D. Johnson & S. Johnson, 1972; S. Johnson & D. Johnson, 1972). Expectation that another person will facilitate one's goal accomplishment (D. Johnson & S. Johnson, 1972) and perceptions that another person is exerting an effort to facilitate one's goal accomplishment (Tjosvold, Johnson, & Johnson, 1981) are enough to induce liking.

ACTIVE MUTUAL INVOLVEMENT IN LEARNING

Cooperative learning situations promote a mutual, active oral involvement in learning situations within which students work silently on their own. Within a cooperative learning situation, students are required to discuss the material being learned with one another (D. Johnson & R. Johnson, 1983). In our recent study (D. Johnson, R. Johnson, Tiffany, & Zaidman, 1983; D. Johnson, R. Johnson, Roy, & Zaidman, 1984), we directly observed the active oral involvement of students in completing assigned learning tasks. There is considerably more active oral involvement in cooperative than in individualistic learning situations. The active engagement of providing task-related information was found to be significantly correlated with achievement in the cooperative condition.

There is evidence that the more cooperative students' attitudes are, the more they express their ideas and feelings in large and small classes and the more they listen to the teacher, whereas competitive and individualistic attitudes are unrelated to indices of active involvement in instructional activities (D. Johnson & Ahlgren, 1976; D. Johnson, R. Johnson, & Anderson, 1978). There is evidence that cooperative learning experiences, compared with competitive and individualistic ones, result in a greater desire to express one's ideas to the class (D. Johnson, R. Johnson, J. Johnson, & Anderson, 1976; Wheeler & Ryan, 1973). Cooperative learning experiences, compared with competitive and individualistic ones, promote greater willingness to present one's answers and thus create more positive feelings toward one's answers and the instructional experience (Garibaldi, 1979; Gunderson & Johnson, 1980).

ABILITY LEVELS OF GROUP MEMBERS

Another potentially mediating variable within cooperative learning groups is the interaction among students from diverse ability levels. There may be an important advantage in having high-, medium-, and low-ability students work together on completing assignments and learning material. A number of our studies have compared the achievement of high-, medium-, and low-ability students involved in cooperative learning activities with the achievement of their counterparts working alone individualistically or competitively (Armstrong et al., 1981; D. Johnson & R. Johnson, Roy, & Zaidman, 1984; Martino & Johnson, 1979; Nevin et al., 1982; Smith et al., 1981, 1982, 1984; Skon et al., 1981). There can be little doubt that the low- and medium-ability students, especially, benefit from working collaboratively with peers from the full range of ability differences. There is also evidence that the high-ability students are better off academically when they collaborate with medium- and low-ability peers than when they work alone; at the worst, it may be argued that high-ability students are not hurt by interacting collaboratively with their medium- and low-ability classmates. One of the important internal dynamics of cooperative learning groups, therefore, may be the opportunity for students with different achievement histories to interact with one another in order to complete assigned learning tasks.

PSYCHOLOGICAL SUPPORT AND ACCEPTANCE

Cooperative learning experiences, compared with competitive and individualistic ones, have been found to result in stronger beliefs that one is personally liked, supported, and accepted by other students, that other students care about how much one learns, and that other students want to help one learn (Cooper et al., 1980; Gunderson & Johnson, 1980; D.

Johnson & R. Johnson, 1981a, b, 1982b, 1983, 1984a, b, c; D. Johnson, R. Johnson, J. Johnson, & Anderson, 1976; D. Johnson et al., 1980; D. Johnson, R. Johnson, Tiffany, & Zaidman, 1983; D. Johnson, R. Johnson, Roy, & Zaidman, 1984; R. Johnson et al., 1983; R. Johnson, Bjorkland, & Krotee, 1984; Skon et al., 1981; Smith et al., 1981; Tjosvold, Marino, & Johnson, 1977). Attitudes toward cooperation, furthermore, are significantly related to believing that one is liked by other students and to wanting to listen to, to help, and to do schoolwork with other students (D. Johnson & Ahlgren, 1976; D. Johnson, R. Johnson, & Anderson, 1978).

Thus, it may be assumed that the more cooperative experiences tend to promote the occurrence of these variables, the greater is the resulting interpersonal attraction among students.

ATTITUDES TOWARD SUBJECT AREAS

Cooperative learning experiences, compared with competitive and individualistic ones, promote more positive attitudes toward the subject area and the instruction experience (Garibaldi, 1979; Gunderson & Johnson, 1980; D. Johnson, R. Johnson, & Skon, 1979; R. Johnson & D. Johnson, 1979; Lowry & Johnson, 1981; Smith et al., 1981; Wheeler & Ryan, 1973).

FAIRNESS OF GRADING

Within many schools, the teachers are concerned that when the students work cooperatively and receive the same grade or a joint reward for their efforts, they will believe that the grading system is unfair. Having students work together on a joint product is often seen as being less fair to each student than is having each student work alone to produce an individual product for which he or she receives an individual grade. Although students who "lose" in a competitive learning situation commonly perceive the grading system as being unjust and consequently dislike the class or teacher (D. Johnson & R. Johnson, 1975b), it is of considerable importance for students within cooperative learning situations to perceive the distribution of grades and other rewards as being fair. Otherwise, they may withdraw from the group's efforts to achieve and to maintain effective working relationships among the members. Deutsch (1979) presented data from a number of experiments indicating that before a task is performed, there is a general perception that a competitive grading system is fairest, but after a task is completed, a cooperative grading system, where all group members receive the same grade or reward, is viewed as the fairest. In two large-scale studies (D. Johnson & R. Johnson, 1983; D. Johnson, R. Johnson, & Anderson, 1983), we found that the more students experienced long-term cooperative learning experiences, and the more cooperation they perceived in their classes, the more they believed that everyone who tries has an equal chance to succeed in class, that students get the grades they deserve, and that the grading system is fair. In an earlier study, Wheeler and Ryan (1973) found that students preferred group grades over individual ones. Related to these results are our findings that the vast majority of students tend to prefer cooperative over competitive or individualistic learning experiences (D. Johnson & R. Johnson, 1976; D. Johnson, Johnson, Johnson, & Anderson, 1976; R. Johnson, 1976; R. Johnson, D. Johnson, & Bryant, 1973; R. Johnson, Ryan, & Schroeder, 1974). In the real world of the classroom, joint grades and rewards seem to be perceived as fairer by students than the traditional competitive and individualistic grading systems.

CONCLUSIONS

From our research on the processes that mediate or moderate the relationship between cooperative learning experiences and (1) productivity and (2) interpersonal attraction among students, a number of conclusions may be drawn. Although the type of learning task may not matter a great deal, the processes that promote higher achievement and liking among students may include the promotion of high-quality reasoning strategies, the constructive management of conflict over ideas and conclusions, increased time on task, more elaborative information-processing, greater peer regulation and encouragement of efforts to achieve, more active mutual involvement in learning, beneficial interaction between students of different achievement levels, feelings of psychological support and acceptance, more positive attitudes toward subject areas, and greater perceptions of fairness of grading.

The implications of these results for teachers interested in using cooperative learning procedures are as follows:

1. Cooperative procedures may be used successfully with any type of academic task, although the greater the conceptual learning required, the greater will tend to be the efficacy of cooperation.
2. Whenever possible, cooperative groups should be structured so that controversy among group members is possible and is managed constructively.

3. Students should be encouraged to keep each other on task and to discuss the assigned material in ways that ensure elaborative rehearsal and the use of higher level learning strategies.

4. Students should be encouraged to support each other's efforts to achieve, to regulate each other's task-related efforts, to provide each other with feedback, and to ensure that all group members will be verbally involved in the learning process.

5. As a rule, cooperative groups should contain low-, medium-, and high-ability students.

6. Positive relationships and feelings of acceptance and support should be encouraged.

7. The more positive attitudes toward subject areas should be capitalized on by encouraging students to take further math, science, foreign language, and other classes of interest.

8. The fairness of joint outcomes should be discussed and pointed out to students.

REFERENCES

Armstrong, B., Johnson, D. W., & Balow, B. Effects of cooperative versus individualistic learning experiences on interpersonal attraction between learning-disabled and normal-progress elementary school students. *Contemporary Educational Psychology,* 1981, *6,* 102–109.

Cooper, L., Johnson, D. W., Johnson, R., & Wilderson, F. The effects of cooperation, competition, and individualization on cross-ethnic, cross-sex, and cross-ability friendships. *Journal of Social Psychology,* 1980, *111,* 243–252.

Deutsch, M. An experimental study of the effects of cooperation and competition upon group process. *Human Relations,* 1949, *2,* 199–232.

Deutsch, M. Cooperation and trust: Some theoretical notes. In M. R. Jones (Ed.), *Nebraska symposium on motivation.* Lincoln: University of Nebraska Press, 1962.

Deutsch, M. A critical review of equity theory: An alternative perspective on the social psychology of justice. *International Journal of Group Tensions,* 1979, *9,* 20–49.

Garibaldi, A. The affective contributions of cooperative and group goal structures. *Journal of Educational Psychology,* 1979, *71,* 788–795.

Gunderson, B., & Johnson, D. W. Building positive attitudes by using cooperative learning groups. *Foreign Language Annals,* 1980, *13,* 39–46.

Johnson, D. W. Group processes: Influences of student-student interactions on school outcomes. In J. McMillan (Ed.), *Social psychology of school learning.* New York: Academic Press, 1980.

Johnson, D. W., & Ahlgren, A. Relationship between students' attitudes about cooperative learning and competition and attitudes toward schooling. *Journal of Educational Psychology,* 1976, *68,* 29–102.

Johnson, D. W., & Johnson, R. Instructional structure: Cooperative, competitive, or individualistic. *Review of Educational Research,* 1974, *44,* 213–240.

Johnson, D. W., & Johnson, R. *Learning together and alone: Cooperation, competition, and individualization.* Englewood Cliffs, N.J.: Prentice-Hall, 1975. (a)

Johnson, D. W., & Johnson, R. Students' perceptions of and preferences for cooperative and competitive learning experiences. *Perceptual and Motor Skills*, 1975, *42*, 989–990. (b)

Johnson, D. W., & Johnson, R. T. Student perceptions of and preferences for cooperative and competitive learning experiences. *Perceptual and Motor Skills*, 1976, *42*, 989–990.

Johnson, D. W., & Johnson, R. Conflict in the classroom: Controversy and learning. *Review of Educational Research*, 1979, *49*(1), 51–70.

Johnson, D. W., & Johnson, R. Effects of cooperative and individualistic learning experiences on interethnic interaction. *Journal of Educational Psychology*, 1981, *73*, 454–459. (a)

Johnson, D. W., & Johnson, R. The integration of the handicapped into the regular classroom: Effects of cooperative and individualistic instruction. *Contemporary Educational Psychology*, 1981, *6*, 344–353. (b)

Johnson, D. W., & Johnson, R. Effects of cooperative, competitive, and individualistic learning experiences on cross-ethnic interaction and friendships. *Journal of Social Psychology*, 1982, *118*, 47–58. (a)

Johnson, D. W., & Johnson, R. Effects of cooperative and individualistic instruction on the relationships and performance of handicapped and nonhandicapped students. *Journal of Social Psychology*, 1982, *118*, 257–268. (b)

Johnson, D. W., & Johnson, R. Social interdependence and perceived academic and personal support in the classroom. *Journal of Social Psychology*, 1983, *120*, 77–82.

Johnson, D. W., & Johnson, R. Building acceptance of differences between handicapped and nonhandicapped students: The effects of cooperative and individualistic problems. *Journal of Social Psychology*, 1984, *122*, 257–267.

Johnson, D. W., & Johnson, R. *Mainstreaming hearing-impaired students: The effect of effort in communicating on cooperation*. Manuscript submitted for publication, 1984.

Johnson, D. W., & Johnson, R. *Classroom conflict: Controversy versus debate in learning groups*. *American Educational Research Journal*, in press. (a)

Johnson, D. W., & Johnson, R. Cross-ethnic relationships in intergroup cooperation and intergroup competition. *Journal of Social Psychology*, in press. (b)

Johnson, D. W., & Johnson, R. The effects of intergroup cooperation and intergroup competition on ingroup and outgroup cross-handicap relationships. *Journal of Social Psychology*, in press. (c)

Johnson, D. W., & Johnson, S. The effects of attitude similarity, expectations of goal facilitation on interpersonal attraction. *Journal of Experimental Social Psychology*, 1982, *8*, 197–206.

Johnson, D. W., & Tjosvold, D. Controversy within a cooperative or competitive context and cognitive perspective taking. *Contemporary Educational Psychology*, 1978, *3*, 376–386.

Johnson, D. W., Johnson, R., Johnson, J., & Anderson, D. The effects of cooperative versus individualized instructions on student prosocial behavior, attitudes toward learning and achievement. *Journal of Educational Psychology*, 1976, *104*, 446–452.

Johnson, D. W., Johnson, R., & Anderson, D. Relationship between student cooperative, competitive, and individualistic attitudes toward schooling. *Journal of Psychology*, 1978, *100*, 183–199.

Johnson, D. W., Johnson, R., Pierson, W., & Lyons, V. *Controversy versus concurrence-seeking in multi-grade and single-grade learning groups*. Manuscript submitted for publication, 1984.

Johnson, D. W., Johnson, R., & Skon, L. Student achievement on different types of tasks under cooperative, competitive, and individualistic conditions. *Contemporary Educational Psychology*, 1979, *4*, 99–106.

Johnson, D. W., Johnson, R. T., & Tauer, M. Effects of cooperative, competitive, and individualistic goal structures on students' attitudes and achievement. *Journal of Psychology*, 1979, *102*, 191–198.

Johnson, D. W., Skon, L., & Johnson, R. The effects of cooperative, competitive, and individualistic goal structures on student achievement on different types of tasks. *American Educational Research Journal*, 1980, *17*, 83–93.

Johnson, D. W., Maruyama, G., Johnson, R., Nelson, D., & Skon, L. Effects of cooperative, competitive, and individualistic goal structures on achievement: A meta-analysis. *Psychological Bulletin*, 1981, *89*, 47–62.

Johnson, D. W., Johnson, R. T., & Anderson, D. Social interdependence and classroom climate. *Journal of Psychology*, 1983, *114*, 135–142.

Johnson, D. W., Johnson, R., & Maruyama, G. Interdependence and interpersonal attraction among heterogeneous and homogeneous individuals: A theoretical formulation and a meta-analysis of the reserch. *Review of Educational Research*, 1983, *53*, 5–54.

Johnson, D. W., Johnson, R., Tiffany, M., & Zaidman, B. Are low achievers disliked in a cooperative situation? A test of rival theories in a mixed-ethnic situation? *Contemporary Educational Psychology*, 1983, *8*, 189–200.

Johnson, D. W., Johnson, R., Roy, P., & Zaidman, B. *Oral interaction in cooperative learning groups: Speaking, listening, and the nature of statements made by high-, medium-, and low-achieving students.* Manuscript submitted for publication, 1984.

Johnson, D. W., Johnson, R., & Tiffany, M Structuring academic conflicts between major ity and minority students: Hindrance or help to integration. *Contemporary Educational Psychology*, 1984, *9*, 61–73.

Johnson, R. The relationship between cooperation and inquiry in science classrooms. *Journal of Research in Science Teaching*, 1976, *10*, 55–63.

Johnson, R., & Johnson, D. W. Type of task and student achievement and attitudes in interpersonal cooperation, competition, and individualization. *Journal of Social Psychology*, 1979, *108*, 37–48.

Johnson, R., & Johnson, D. W. Building friendships between handicapped and nonhandicapped students: Effects of cooperative and individualistic instruction. *American Educational Research Journal*, 1981, *18*, 415–424.

Johnson, R., & Johnson, D. W. Effects of cooperative and competitive learning experiences on interpersonal attraction between handicapped and nonhandicapped students. *Journal of Social Psychology*, 1982, *116*, 211–219.

Johnson, R., & Johnson, D. W. Effects of cooperative, competitive, and individualistic learning experiences on social development. *Exceptional Children*, 1983, *49*, 323–330.

Johnson, R., Johnson, D. W., & Bryant, B. Cooperation and competition in the classroom. *Elementary School Journal*, 1973, *74*, 172–181.

Johnson, R., Ryan, F., & Schroeder, H. Inquiry and the development of positive attitudes. *Science Education*, 1974, *58*, 51–56.

Johnson, R., Rynders, J., Johnson, D. W., Schmidt, B., & Haider, S. Producing positive interaction between handicapped and nonhandicapped teenagers through cooperative goal structuring: Implications for mainstreaming. *American Educational Research Journal*, 1979, *16*, 161–168.

Johnson, R., Johnson, D. W., DeWeerdt, N., Lyons, V., & Zaidman, B. Integrating severely adaptively handicapped seventh-grade students into constructive relationships with nonhandicapped peers in science class. *American Journal of Mental Deficiency*, 1983, *87*, 611–618.

Johnson, R., Bjorkland, R., & Krotee, M. The effects of cooperative, competitive and individualistic student interaction patterns on the achievement and attitudes of the golf skill of putting. *The Research Quarterly for Exercise and Sport*, 1984, *55*(2).

Johnson, R., Johnson, D. W., Scott, L., & Ramolae, B. *Effects of single-sex and mixed-sex cooperative interaction on science achievement and attitudes and cross-handicap and cross-sex relationships.* Manuscript submitted for publication, 1984.

Johnson, S., & Johnson, D. W. The effects of others' actions, attitude similarity, and race on attraction towards the other. *Human Relations*, 1972, *25*, 121–130.

Lewin, K. *A dynamic theory of personality.* New York: McGraw-Hill, 1935.

Lowry, N., & Johnson, D. W. The effects of controversy on students' motivation and learning. *Journal of Social Psychology*, 1981, *115*, 31–43.

Lyons, V. *A study of elaborative cognitive processing as a variable mediating achievement in cooperative learning groups.* Unpublished doctoral dissertation, University of Minnesota, 1982.

Martino, L., & Johnson, D. W. Cooperative and individualistic experiences among disabled and normal children. *Journal of Social Psychology*, 1979, *107*, 177–183.

Nevin, A., Johnson, D. W., & Johnson, R. Effects of groups and individual contingencies on academic performance and social relations of special needs students. *Journal of Social Psychology*, 1982, *116*, 41–59.

Roon, R., Van Pilsum, J., Harris, I., Rosenberg, P., Johnson, R., Liaw, C., & Rosenthal, L. *The experimental use of cooperative learning groups in a biochemistry laboratory course for first year medical students.* Manuscript submitted for publication, 1983.

Roy, P. *Analysis of student conversation in cooperative learning groups.* Unpublished master's thesis, University of Minnesota, 1982.

Rynders, J., Johnson, R., Johnson, D. W., & Schmidt, B. Effects of cooperative goal structuring in productive positive interaction between Down's Syndrome and nonhandicapped teenagers: Implications for mainstreaming. *American Journal of Mental Deficiencies*, 1980, *85*, 268–273.

Skon, L., Johnson, D. W., & Johnson, R. Cooperative peer interaction versus individual competition and individualistic efforts: Effects on the acquisition of cognitive reasoning strategies. *Journal of Educational Psychology*, 1981, *73*, 83–92.

Smith, K., Johnson, D. W., & Johnson, R. Can conflict be constructive? Controversy versus concurrence seeking in learning groups. *Journal of Educational Psychology*, 1981, *73*, 651–663.

Smith, K., Johnson, D. W., & Johnson, R. Effects of cooperative and individualistic instruction on the achievement of handicapped, regular, and gifted students. *The Journal of Science Psychology*, 1982, *116*, 277–282.

Smith, K., Johnson, D. W., & Johnson, R. Effects of controversy on learning in cooperative groups. *Journal of Social Psychology*, 1984, *122*, 199–209.

Tjosvold, D., Marino, P., & Johnson, D. W. Cooperation and competition and student acceptance of inquiry and didactic teaching. *Journal of Research in Science Teaching*, 1977, *14*, 281–288.

Tjosvold, D., Johnson, D. W., & Johnson, R. Effect of partner's effort and ability on liking for partner after failure on a cooperative task. *The Journal of Psychology*, 1981, *109*, 147–152.

Warring, D., Johnson, D. W., Maruyama, G., & Johnson, R. *The impact of different types of cooperative learning on cross-ethnic and cross-sex relationships.* Manuscript submitted for publication, 1984.

Wheeler, R., & Ryan, F. Effects of cooperative and competitive environments on the attitudes and achievement of elementary school students engaged in social studies inquiry activities. *Journal of Educational Psychology*, 1973, *65*, 402–407.

Yager, S., Johnson, R., Johnson, D. W., & Snider, B. *The effect of cooperative and individualistic learning experiences on positive and negative cross-handicap relationships.* Contemporary Educational Psychology, in press.

5

An Analysis of Cooperation in Relation to Cognitive Controversy

WIM NIJHOF
AND
PIET KOMMERS

INTRODUCTION

At the end of the 1960s, several research projects on intraclass grouping were begun in the Netherlands and in other European countries. Some were aimed at mastery learning, and others at ability grouping and setting procedures such as those described by Hillson (1967) and Yates (1966). The majority of the studies became feasibility studies. Among the important questions that most of these research projects hoped to solve was how to implement some form of classroom grouping and then to detect the consequent problems for teachers, students, and the whole school organization. Central topics in these research projects became (1) the conditions within the school organization necessary to realize intraclassroom grouping, (2) factors influencing the behavior of teachers, (3) the role of learner resources (i.e., curriculum materials) in implementing intraclassroom grouping, and (4) the effects of mixed-ability grouping and homogeneous-ability grouping on student learning capabilities.

Most of these studies were finished in the mid-1970s. However, several projects have continued into the 1980s, especially those concerning the implementation of intraclass grouping in secondary education. The following conclusions emerged from the earlier studies:

1. Intraclass grouping is only a partial and very restricted means of individualizing instruction.
2. Most kinds of grouping procedures demand from teachers high levels of organizational and technical skills, skills in observational and diagnostical procedures, skills in planning and logistics, and skills in making the optimal use of time, learner resources, and evaluation procedures.

WIM NIJHOF AND PIET KOMMERS • Onderafdeling der Toegepaste Onderwijskunde, Technische Hogeschool Twente, Postbus 217, 7500 AE Enschede, The Netherlands.

125

3. Teacher training should be changed. More attention must be given to the skills mentioned above, especially those concerned with the organization of homogeneous and heterogeneous groups or combinations of them.
4. Individualized instruction based on intraclassroom grouping is more expensive than conventional instruction.

A striking conclusion of this research was that student cognitive performance and skills were neither better nor worse in the various grouping methods than in the conventional system. However, the research indicated that the affective components of student behavior might be better realized in more individualized systems of education, such as in intraclass grouping procedures. Students in classes using intraclass grouping increased in self-concept, were more social, and developed better communication techniques. These findings hint that one gain of intraclassroom grouping might be found in the socioaffective components of student behavior (Appelhof, 1979; Educational Product Information Exchange, 1974; Nijhof, 1978).

Another striking conclusion of this research was that classes have the typical characteristics of small groups. However, research still does not have any evidence or explanation for the processes, procedures, and effects of different kinds of grouping. Although there is much speculation and controversial theory about group problem-solving, there is no convergent view, nor is there full insight into the cognitive and affective procedures within group problem-solving in relation to a variety of group tasks.

These conclusions led us to set up a study that focused on an analysis of the cognitive functioning of students within small groups. Before implementing grouping procedures within schools, we have to know how these groups function and especially how students behave in relation to them. In our view, learning is a process of interaction with objects and with other people. It is worthwhile to analyze the process of interaction in terms of communication with others. In this process, we think that the cognitive background of the members of a group is highly important not only in problem-solving procedures, but also in individualizing and socializing procedures (the integration of the roles and norms of group behavior). There is an ongoing process of information exchange within groups, verbal as well as nonverbal. We are interested in the verbal part of information exchange, in the way in which students go about solving a problem in relation to a specific learning task. In general, we want to know what kind of communication there is and if there is any communication structure. We also wish to investigate the role of the individual. Information exchange between individuals can be seen as and can be reconstructed in terms of interaction between the states of knowledge that are active in the minds of students. It can also be interpreted as the input information that triggers the prior knowledge of the participants.

In order to describe and to analyze the exchange of information as an ongoing problem-solving process in a cooperative setting, it is necessary to explore the interaction of group members in relation to an open problem-solving task (i.e., a question with no single right answer). We wished to analyze communication exchange to investigate the effects of diversity of prior knowledge on the solution of open questions. Cooperation is a collective process in which formal and informal knowledge play an important role. In our industrialized society, students have to learn to solve common problems. We think that the school has a role in teaching students to cope with philosophical, technological, and political issues. We have to learn to listen to each other, and to learn to cooperate to solve common problems. Therefore, we think that it is important to see cooperation in relation to individualization as a personalizing process, and also in terms of socialization. In presenting an open task with open-ended solutions, we will have to teach students planning, communication, and problem-solving techniques in order to raise their capability to cope with controversial issues.

In order to understand how grouping procedures will operate in the school curriculum, we must know how groups will behave when confronted with a variety of tasks. In setting up a research program, we have to restrict our area of study. Therefore, as main topics for our study, we want to focus on two basic questions:

1. Is the level of communication influenced by group composition in terms of prior knowledge of a task domain?
2. What is the shift in perspective of the individual member of a group due to a cooperative learning experience?

The first question deals with the relationship between group composition (homogeneous and heterogeneous) and the art of communication in terms of the use of arguments to solve a group task. The second has to do with the influence of the group on the individual student in terms of his or her problem-solving approach. We elaborate on these questions in the next section, where we give a short presentation of research trends and models and arguments for the formulation of our questions.

THEORETICAL BACKGROUND

In the recent European research on grouping, we find two main streams. The first is learning to cooperate as an educational goal. In this research tradition, much attention has been given to the training of such social competencies as social cognition (Lieshout, 1977; Gerris, 1981). The second is learning by cooperation, where much research has been done on the relationship between cooperation and intelligence. Several experiments of this type have been done in the tradition of the Geneva school of Piaget and his students, basically oriented on epistemological questions (see Doise, 1978).

Although we recognize both traditions in recent cooperative learning research, we prefer to restrict ourselves to the learning-by-cooperation approach, which we see as complement to learning to cooperate. Several researchers in this area maintain that the degree of cooperation is determined only partly by the frequency of interaction. Cooperation as a way of learning together seems to be successful insofar as it stimulates students to externalize their thoughts, expectations, and arguments (Sharan, 1980; Johnson, 1981, Johnson & Johnson, 1979). This fundamental concept can be found in the work of Vygotsky (1962). He proposed as an essential feature of learning the zone of proximal development, in which a stimulating environment awakens a variety of developmental processes within the student, leading to a higher level of cognition. Such a stimulating environment can be organized by way of cooperative learning in relation to a complex and intriguing open task. Once these processes are internalized, they become part of the student's independent developmental achievement. In analyzing learning by cooperation studies, we see a change from models accentuating the relation between prerequisites and cognitive results to models in which motivational and attentional variables dominate and to models designed for information processing, which emphasize the relationship between task-specific information and prior knowledge. Before formulating our research questions about communication in groups, we explore several previously designed models.

ALLEN'S MODEL FOR GROUP BEHAVIOR

Allen (1976) raised the question: What are the specific mechanisms in the interaction process that determine learning performance and the resulting social reactions? To analyze this question, he developed a model that categorized the main conditional factors. He distinguished among

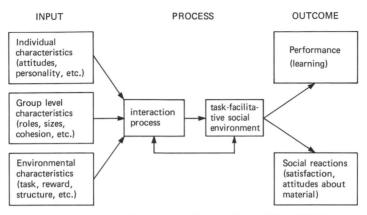

FIGURE 1. Model for group behavior. (From Allen, 1976.)

three groups of variables: variables on the individual, the group, and the environment level (see Figure 1).

What Allen presented is basically an input–output model. The input factors are individual characteristics (e.g., attitudes, aptitudes, and personality); group level characteristics (e.g., role taking, size, cohesion, and homogeneous-heterogeneous); and environmental characteristics (e.g., task and reward structure). He recognized two dominant output factors: performance and social reactions. The first is the cognitive component of behavior, the second the more socioaffective considerations of satisfaction, self-concept, and attitudes. Between the input and the output factors, Allen placed the interaction process as a task-facilitative social environment. The way in which the input factors operate in or interfere with the interaction process and help or hinder cognitive and social outcomes, though, is questionable. The process remains a black box, and the distinction between the cognitive and the social outcomes remains artificial. Nevertheless, the model can be used to illustrate the relevance of the input factors in relation to the interaction process. To be understood, the interaction process needs a more thorough analysis in terms of cognitive or social psychology. Also, the relation of the input factors and the interaction processes in relation to a specific task is not clear. On the whole, the model is too general. It does not consider task-specific variables, nor does it specify communications structures.

THE HACKMAN AND MORRIS MODEL

The model described by Hackman and Morris (1978) is a more specific analysis of the group process in relation to the individual level of functioning and the use of prior knowledge. This model is a combination of an input–output model and a contingency model. Much attention is give to so-called summary variables (input factors on the individual level), which are intermediate entities between "input variables" (factors on the group level) and output (group performance effectiveness). The main difference from the Allen model is the role of the critical task in group-level performance outcomes. Allen's model stipulates individual performance and socioaffective outcomes as a result of group interaction process. Figure 2 shows how the summary variables interact with the focal input variables and the critical task contingencies. They dominate the process of group interaction by way of the level and the utilization of member knowledge and skill, the nature and utilization of task performance strategies, and the level and coordination of member effort.

This model states explicitly the relationship between the group variables and the individual variables in terms of prior knowledge and skills, task performance strategies, and member effort, but it neglects to show how these input factors operate in a group interaction process. To orient our hypothesis toward prior knowledge as a critical input factor in a communication process and toward the flow of information within the group, we need a more detailed model in which the relation between the cognitive functioning of the group members at the individual level has been worked into the group communication process.

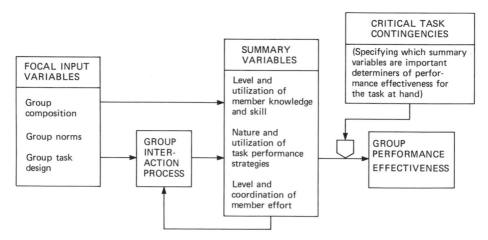

FIGURE 2. Framework showing the relations among the focal input variables, the group interaction process, and the three summary variables in affecting group effectiveness. (From Hackman & Morris, 1978.)

THE JOHNSON AND JOHNSON MODEL

One would expect that most cooperative learning studies have focused on task-specific communication. However, this is not the case. The literature that we reviewed did not show that cooperative learning can take place if the necessary precondition occurs at the individual level. In our opinion, this condition can be described in terms of prior knowledge and problem-solving strategies. We think that the knowledge base is most crucial to problem solving within groups. Apart from group characteristics, declarative and procedural knowledge are the two essential ingredients for problem solving.

Johnson and Johnson (1979) presented a model with which it is possible to formulate more definite expectations about inter- and intrapupil information exchange. In this model, the concept of controversy is seen as a central mechanism in the process of externalizing and internalizing ideas during group work (see Figure 3).

In Figure 3 we find a cyclical process that is based on four components: (1) involvement in controversy (disagreement with another's conclusion), (2) experiencing conceptual conflict, (3) searching for more information and a more adequate cognitive perspective and reasoning process, and (4) deriving conclusions from present information and experiences.

Controversy is a process of perceiving and reasoning. It is highly cognitive in nature and is oriented around conclusions formed from arguments, information experiences, and other data. It is a process of con-

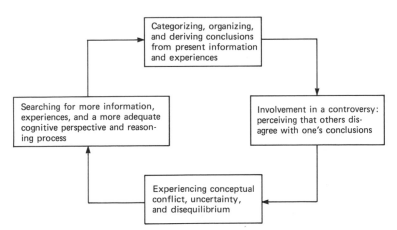

FIGURE 3.   The process of controversy. (From Johnson, 1981.)

vincing other people of a particular cognitive perspective. Johnson's model presents a reasoning process with conceptual conflicts and uncertainty that act as strategies to solve cognitive conflicts. Although this model details the reasoning process and proposes a sequence of phases that counterbalance controversy, it is unclear about the role of prior knowledge. In our view, the perception that others disagree with one's conclusions is based upon prior knowledge and a cognitive perspective. As one participates in a group, he or she does not know if his or her prior knowledge will be integrated or mixed into the communication beforehand, so that others will perceive a discrepancy between their own ideas and those of other members. Thus, controversy has to be made explicit. The Johnson and Johnson model supposes conflicts or controversies about types of problems that are not quite clear. We think that they should be open-ended questions on a higher cognitive level.

As a point for further investigation, we propose to analyze task-related communication and the role of individual prior knowledge within this framework. Johnson and Johnson supposed a dynamic, self-driven cognitive process in confronting and integrating conflicting ideas. We expect that the exchange of information is more intensive and has more impact on the set of individual ideas if it reaches a certain level of discrepancy between the group members. The other models are more explicit about the role of the individual and the group variables in the group problem-solving process. We used them in formulating our experimental design.

Before we describe our experimental design, we want to give a short description of a pilot study that we did with graduate students at the State University of Utrecht. The function of this pilot study was to investigate whether the process of controversy, as described earlier, would show up in a closed task. We were also interested how prior knowledge would be used in solving the problem presented.

PILOT STUDY

In our investigation, we used eight six-student groups, five of which we analyzed in detail. Males and females were equally divided among the groups. Because no other criteria were used in group formation, we felt that the groups were heterogeneous in every way. We presented a closed problem-solving task by way of a short introduction, and then some paper-and-pencil work. The problem was a simulation game of "how to survive in the desert after an airplane crash." The game consists of four phases: (1) an individual ranking procedure of 15 objects (e.g., a small mirror and a bottle of whiskey) that gave priority to the objects necessary for survival, (2) a group discussion about the best way of ranking the objects, (3) a correction procedure at the individual level after group discussion, and (4) a check consisting of an expert ranking compared with the individual ranking. Basically, this experiment consisted of building up prior knowledge before entering the group problem-solving procedure. No learner resources could be used. The only tools that the subjects had were any items of knowledge already available in their minds. The closed character of the task was given by the expert's score. There was only one solution based on the empirical evidence of the number of people that survived after an air crash in the desert.

Both the individuals and the groups succeeded in solving "their" problem, but they did not reach the expert solution. Our main interest lay in an analysis of the communication pattern. We used video recordings to detail the verbal interaction. We came to the conclusion that the closed problem-solving task had provoked a rather rigid means of argumentation, presumably based on a significant lack of adequate prior knowledge and a low degree of participation in the group communication process (Kommers, 1981). Because we could not relate the results to the degree of prior knowledge or to factors of group composition, our conclusion was rather tentative. Nevertheless, we got some ideas about the function of a closed task and about the relationship of prior knowledge to the specific task. We used students in educational psychology with poor scientific knowledge and poor problem-solving strategies in chemistry and geography. One can't solve this problem with common sense alone. The group process had some influence on the individual ranking procedure; some students persisted in their original rankings, but most of them changed their ranks on the basis of group discussions. The group discussion, however poor it may have been, had some effects on the cognitive perspective of the individual members.

SUMMARY

In the preceding sections, we have given a short overview of the results of our literature search and of a pilot study. Our main conclusion is that we do not have sufficient knowledge about group processes, nor do we know what is going on in groups in terms of information exchange. We do not know what role prior knowledge plays, but we are convinced that it plays a very important one. We also think that group problem-solving tasks can facilitate cooperative learning. This might be the case particularly if these tasks promote a variety of cognitive strategies and cause a shift in perspective on the basis of information exchange. Although several input–output models could not help us in analyzing the communication process, they gave us some ideas about the relevant input and output variables. They also indicated the relevance of task-specific contingencies. Also, they suggested that controversy is a highly important mechanism, serving as a motor in idea exchange.

We decided to reformulate the questions that we posed at the beginning of this chapter:

1. Is the level of communication influenced by group composition in terms of prior knowledge in a task domain?
2. What is the shift in perspective of the individual member of a group due to a cooperative learning experience?

As we saw in the pilot study, the composition of a group in terms of prior knowledge can be a very decisive criterion. The more heterogeneous a group is, the more we expect a variety of background information to operate in the communication process. From the pilot study, we found that a closed task might restrict the number of relevant solutions, because it would restrict the scope and the quality of reasoning. Therefore, we decided to use an open task. Finally, we feel that the cognitive development of students can play an important role. In the pilot study, we used students between the ages of 20 and 25. This was a choice determined by convenience. We decided to use students in primary education at the ages of 10–12 for a more systematic experiment. Our main hypothesis for the experiment was that cognitively heterogeneous groups will be more apt to elaborate task-related knowledge and will reflect this variety of background information in their communication.

DESIGN OF A COOPERATIVE TASK

In order to describe the setting in which we tried to initiate an exchange of ideas, opinions, and arguments, we shall first present the constraints on the characteristics and the construction of a group task. In following the "flow-of-information" view, we chose an open problem-solving task. In contrast to competitive, reward-oriented group tasks, we focused on the following characteristics of small-group learning:

1. *Problem task.* A problem can be defined as a situation in which prior knowledge cannot be used directly and an adequate response cannot be grasped immediately.

2. *Initiation of verbal exchange.* Cooperation is not the same as "doing things together," or "having the same opinion." Reflection and argu-

mentation are necessary to raise the group process to the level of learning by participation and deliberation.

3. *Motivation of participants.* The danger of many cooperative tasks is the lack of attention given to the task-specific expertise of the group members. Unequal expertise could lead to unbalanced participation, so that only one or two students would be active.

4. *Suitability of task for participants.* The task must be suited to being performed by individuals as well as by groups. Individual task performance is necessary in order to distinguish the individual from the collective part of the problem-solving approach.

5. *Suitability of task to setting.* The task must be suitable to performance in a normal classroom setting. Teachers must be capable of handling these kinds of problem-solving tasks in a normal setting within the regular curriculum. To guarantee the ecological validity of the experiment and the use of the results in practice, we used a normal classroom situation.

On the basis of these characteristics, we designed an urban planning task for groups of four students. The task used a map of a town (80 × 100 cm) and 24 wooden blocks and pieces of colored paper for the different functions of the town. The planning objects can be divided into five categories:

1. Objects for living: houses and flats
2. Objects in the service and commercial sectors: shops, schools, and hospitals
3. Social and leisure-time objects: playgrounds, cinemas, and parks
4. Traffic objects: roads, bridges, and parking places
5. Work objects: factories and offices

The main goal for the individual as well as for the group was to place every object on the map to represent a city in which it would be pleasant to live. For the sake of analysis, the objects were labeled so that we could make and then interpret pictures and the video recordings. During the group session, each student was allowed to handle the complete set of materials, so that participation for everyone was guaranteed.

EXPERIMENTAL DESIGN

Earlier we formulated our main hypothesis for this experiment: Cognitively heterogeneous groups will be more apt to elaborate task-related knowledge and will reflect this variety of background information in the communication process. Our question is thus whether prior knowledge is a crucial variable for the way in which students can communicate in a cooperative planning task. In the earlier sections, we introduced the intermediate variable of "controversy" as the process of perceiving disagreement and cognitive conflict. In order to vary prior knowledge systematically over the groups, we used a pretest to determine the group's cognitive heterogeneity or homogeneity for use as an independent variable. The operationalization of the cooperative process was termed *level of communication*. This dependent variable was measured by distinguishing three levels of communication:

1. *Basic*: The students participate only by manipulating objects on the map (nonverbal communication; no arguments or opinions).
2. *Medium*: The students participate by making remarks, but without argumentation (no form of reasoning could be inferred).
3. *Upper*: The students participate by giving arguments or by referring to antecedent in the communication process.

The independent variable was measured by pretesting prior knowledge, ideas, and opinions, about "ideal living." In setting up the two conditions, we formed groups with divergent and convergent ideas. In the heterogeneous groups, the participants typically preferred a wide variety of objects in the planning task. The cognitive pretest consisted of multiple-choice questions organized around the five categories of functions. Using open-ended questions would surely have induced creative problem-solving behavior. We wanted to determine available prior knowledge. The following are two examples from the cognitive pretest:

1. What do you like best?
   a. To live in a district with a big distance between houses?
   b. To live in a district where the houses are close to each other?
   c. To live in a district with long rows of houses and flats?
2. What is the best district to live in?
   a. A district in which the shops are in the center?
   b. A district where the shops are along the borderline?
   c. A district where you have to shop by car?
   d. A district where there are no shops at all?

In addition to the cognitive pretest, we tested the social preferences of the students by means of a sociometric test. This test was used to ensure that cohesion within the groups would help to focus on the planning problem. We used an adapted version of the Syracuse Sociometric Scale (1970). All groups were organized on the basis of the cognitive and sociometric tests. The first was used for setting up groups according to cognitive heterogeneity or homogeneity, and the second was used to determine optimal social homogeneity. The students who chose the same classmates as referents for opinion were put into the same group. In the next section, we give an overview of the phases of the experiment.

PHASES OF THE EXPERIMENT

GROUP FORMATION

As noted above, we tested each student on prior knowledge on urban planning and sociometric position in the entire group. Using these data, we created five homogeneous and five heterogeneous groups, all of which met the requirements for a good social climate.

INDIVIDUAL PROBLEM-SOLVING PROCEDURE

Each student had to solve the urban planning task by himself or herself. The planning product was photographed. The product stayed intact so that each student would be able to revise his or her product after the cooperative planning task.

COOPERATIVE PLANNING TASK

Immediately after the individual planning task, the group members met with each other and were given the following instruction: "Try to make a town by working together. The town must be as comfortable as possible for the inhabitants. You will get 15 minutes to complete your plans." No procedural hints were given, nor was a group leader proposed. If a group finished the task in a very short time because the group members didn't oppose each other, the experimenter asked, "Are you all content with the solution?"

To analyze the information exchange, we had to develop an observation technique that enabled exact time assignments for the observations. For this task we used a computer-controlled video recorder. The episodes recorded on video were scored in three levels of communication (see p. 136).

SECOND INDIVIDUAL PROBLEM-SOLVING PROCEDURE (CONFRONTATION)

Each group member went back to his or her planning product and was allowed to revise the first solution. A picture was made of the final solution.

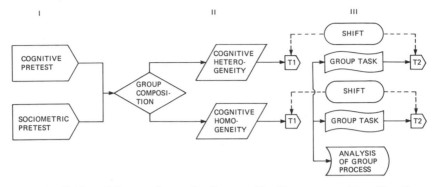

FIGURE 4. Design of the experiment. I = Pretests; II = Group composition; III = Group process; T1 = Individual planning tasks before group task; T2 = Individual planning tasks after group task.

Figure 4 summarizes the research plan. The experiment was conducted in Grades 4 and 5 of a primary school in Utrecht (The Netherlands).

RESULTS

In this section, we present the data and examine the information on the flow in groups. This approach will give us more insight than presentations of the statistical differences between the two conditions. The time spent on communication is analyzed in terms of the content of the discussion as a function of group composition.

ANALYSIS OF TIME SPENT IN COMMUNICATION

A comparison of argumentation time in relation to the conditions was our first indication of the intensity and the frequency of the communication process. Because we were interested in the influence of the two conditions on communication, we scored the episodes in which the students used arguments. Table 1 shows the percentage of argumentation time in relation to the time spent on verbal communication. Table 2 presents the percentage of argumentation time in relation to the total time on task.

As explained earlier, argumentation represents the upper level of communication. This means that the students had to make their logic or value arguments (i.e., economic, psychological, sociological, ecological) explicit. In any case, there had to be some kind of reasoning in terms of

TABLE 1. Argumentation Time in Relation to Verbal Communication Time

Homogeneous groups		Heterogeneous groups	
Number	Percentage	Number	Percentage
1	32.2	6	36.7
2	20.0	7	36.0
3	16.6	8	35.0
4	34.7	9	26.1
5	17.1	10	48.2
Mean	25.8	Mean	33.5
SD	7.7	SD	4.3

conclusions. Sometimes, this took the form of a syllogism, sometimes a combination of arguments without a syllogistic structure. Neither the manipulation of objects on the map nor conversation during the planning task have been included in this analysis. A comparison of the average proportions of argumentation in Table 1 shows a clear and statistically significant tendency toward the heterogeneous condition. (Mann-Whitney U Test, $U = 2$, $n_1 = n_2 = 5$; $p < .016$). The difference between the two conditions seems to have been the same if we relate argumentation time to total time on task. The difference between the two conditions shows the same tendency, with the same degree of statistical significance, at $p < .016$.

For the homogeneous condition, about 85% of the on-task time was spent on verbalizations other than argumentation; for the heterogeneous condition, it was 77%. The homogeneous groups manipulated objects on the map an average of 75% of the time, whereas the heterogeneous groups did so 66% of the time. Although these data fail to sustain our hypothesis that cognitive controversy provokes a higher level of communication in the heterogeneous condition, the tendency in the

TABLE 2. Argumentation Time in Relation to Total Time on Task

Homogeneous groups		Heterogeneous groups	
Number	Percentage	Number	Percentage
1	22	6	25
2	11	7	19
3	10	8	25
4	16	9	21
5	9	10	36
Mean	14.9	Mean	22.5
SD	4.84	SD	5.88

data is clear. Apart from the time used on argumentation and discussion, the content of communication is also very important. We present data about the use of content and formal categories within the group discussions.

ANALYSIS OF CONTENT AND FORMAL ARGUMENTATION AS A FUNCTION OF GROUP COMPOSITION

For the analysis of the video recordings, we formulated 12 content categories and 6 formal reasoning categories.

At first glance, we see that the heterogeneous condition reached a higher spread in categories (Table 3). The dominant categories in the heterogeneous condition were 1, 7, 9, and 11. In the homogeneous condition, 1, 7, and 11 were dominant. In the heterogeneous condition, we find no empty categories, in contrast to the homogeneous condition. The mean percentage of all categories was 9.2% and 9.2%, respectively. Generally speaking, there was no difference between the two conditions. The correlation between the two was .91 (Spearman, r_s), in line with the first conclusion. On the basis of these data, we can't sustain the hypothesis that heterogeneous composition leads to a higher level or to a different way of communicating. Nevertheless, there are some qualitative differences. Categories 5, 8, 9, and 10 give a somewhat different picture for both conditions. We cannot offer a good explanation for these differences. They might be random differences, or it may be that the discussion within the two conditions led to a shift in perspective at the individual level.

TABLE 3. Use of Content Categories (percentage) by Homogeneous and Heterogeneous Groups

Category	Homogeneous	Heterogeneous
1. Space	19.8	16.3
2. Social contact	2.4	0.9
3. Privacy	0	0.9
4. Security	5.2	3.6
5. Quietness	8.4	5.0
6. Easiness	0.9	0.9
7. Leisure time	16.3	13.3
8. Working conditions	1.1	4.5
9. Pollution	7.0	13.8
10. Aesthetics	6.5	4.5
11. Attainability	25.9	32.8
12. Distance	8.6	7.6
Spread in categories	$S_1 = 7.8$	$S_2 = 8.95$

TABLE 4. Use of Formal Categories (percentage) by Homogeneous and Heterogeneous Groups

Formal category	Homogeneous	Heterogeneous
1. Pseudoargument	11.3	11.1
2. Situation-specific argument	45.1	35.5
3. Experience	2.8	3.1
4. Knowledge of rules	25.9	30.0
5. Value argument	7.4	5.6
6. Hypothetical argument (if . . . then)	7.6	14.7
Spread in categories	$S_1 = 14.6$	$S_2 = 16.7$

Next we will look at the use of formal categories in the group discussion. Table 4 indicates two dominant categories for both conditions: the use of situation-specific arguments and the knowledge of rules. The difference between the two conditions in Category 2 is significant. The homogeneous condition took 45.1% of the time for using arguments inherent to the map itself or related to the ongoing process of communication exchange. The heterogeneous condition took 35.5% of the time for these kinds of arguments, a remarkable difference. In the same sense, we can look at Category 4. The use of rules to find a solid solution for the planning task took between 25.9% and 30% of the time available for the two conditions. It is a very decisive category in normal life in making decisions. The heterogeneous condition scored higher in this category. The result in Category 2 concerning the use of "experience" was most unexpected. In four of the five homogeneous groups, there was no use of arguments based on experience in their own life situations. This result is striking. Although the score in the heterogeneous condition was very low, too, every group used some arguments. It seems that the planning task didn't elicit reactions related to the immediate experience of these children. The Spearman correlation between both conditions is .94, which means that there was no dominant way of using the categories in either of the two conditions. Nevertheless, we think that there was a stronger qualitative difference in the formal than in the content categories used by both conditions. The heterogeneous condition used Category 6 (hypothetical argument) twice, the highest formal category that we detected. But our general conclusion on the basis of these data is that there is no significant difference between the two conditions. When we tested the difference in diversity of the discussed categories, we saw a slight tendency in favor of the heterogeneous condition, but the difference was too weak to be significant. The standard deviations are for the homogeneous groups, 14.6, and for the heteroge-

TABLE 5. Shift in Perspective Measured by the Absolute Number of Changes in the Map between Time 1 (T1) and Time 2 (T2)

Homogeneous groups		Heterogeneous groups	
Number	Changes	Number	Changes
1	70	6	31
2	24	7	48
3	77	8	106
4	74	9	64
5	77	10	97
Total	322	Total	346
Mean	64.4	Mean	69.2
SD	20.4	SD	28.5

neous groups, 16.7. In tests (one-tailed) by the F test, we find $F = .76$, not significant.

In concluding this section, we present some data about the shift in perspective on the group level. As stated before, we think that a group communication process might affect the cognitive set of every student. Therefore, we measured the individual solution before starting the group planning task. We took pictures of the product (see "Phases of the Experiment," above). After the group procedure, every student had an opportunity to change the map. We supposed that a change in the map would be effected by the group process because there was no time lag between the group process and individual task performance. Consequently, we can analyze the effect of both conditions on the individual level within each condition (see Table 5).

On the basis of these data, we can conclude that there is no significant difference between the two conditions. The means did not differ significantly. The diversity in the heterogeneous condition was greater than in the homogeneous condition. Our hypothesis that the heterogeneous condition would effect more change (more shifts in perspective as a consequence of participation and of use of arguments) is not supported in this case.

CONCLUSIONS AND DISCUSSION

In this exploratory study, we tried to find out if prior knowledge has any influence on communication processes and on the shift of perspective on the individual level. We formed two conditions: one homogeneous and one heterogeneous, based on cognitive pretest scores. Both conditions were matched on sociometric scores. No other aptitude measures were used. We tried to find out if there were significant differences between the conditions in terms of the use of communication levels and the amount of argumentation at the highest level related to a problem-solving task on urban planning. We found one significant effect: The heterogeneous groups spent significantly more time on arguments at the highest level in relation to verbal communication time, as well as in relation to total time on task. Prior knowledge may have been responsible for this difference. A plausible explanation might be that intelligence, motivation, or other aptitudes play an important role. It might be possible that the heterogeneous groups consisted of brighter students with a variety of ideas. However, we didn't match conditions on intelligence scores or motivation scores, nor did we use a criterion for setting up conditions with different scholastic scores. This might be an approach for a further project. Therefore, we can say only that diversity in prior knowledge might be contaminated with intelligence.

Shift of perspective on the individual level must be attributed to the group process and/or to the structure of prior knowledge. However, we did not find significant effects on this variable. The use of content and formal arguments did not reveal a significant difference, although we found some qualitative differences. Without the use of "think aloud" or related procedures, we cannot trace back the cause of differences. The concept of controversy was operationalized as heterogeneity of prior knowledge as a variable that would influence the information exchange within the group formations. It might be that the task itself narrowed the perception of the problem or diminished the number of relevant aspects. Such situation-specific variables play a role in these kinds of experiments (Parreren, 1970). We found that the students hardly used their own experiences of everyday life. The distance between the planning task and their own experiences might have been too great. Moreover, they did not receive any form of instruction or training in planning techniques or similar skills, so we had to proceed with their available capabilities. We think that it might be useful in further research in this area to include some kinds of systematic instruction in the means of handling such problems as the use of learner resources and planning techniques. In the present experiment, spontaneous behavior was measured, and we did not know if the prerequisites for systematic planning behavior were available. This might be a direction for further experiments. Communication in relation to a well-structured task on the basis of different ideas might not lead automatically to a higher level of reasoning or information exchange when compared with a condition with few ideas. Barnes and Todd (1977) stipulated logical and verbal techniques to help students in formulating their ideas. The concrete material possibly induced some kind of low- or medium-level argumentation. A group leader—an expert, for instance—might be helpful in summarizing the arguments and in reformulating the planning questions at a higher level. In other words, the presence of a discussion leader might raise the level of communication.

We tried to measure a shift in perspective as a consequence of the information exchange within the group at the individual level. We did not find significant results. Therefore, the shifts that we got can be seen as the persistent behavior of students when they are confident in their own solution. The fact that there was no criterion of corrections gave rise to the opinion that everybody could freely give his or her own solution. The knowledge base necessary to find the best solution was determined by the available knowledge. So the importance of prior knowledge might have been rather small, even though the two conditions differed in the number of ideas. Task analysis (Gagne & Briggs, 1979) could be helpful in finding the prerequisites as a source of information in setting up more standardized measurements. The measurement of controversy by means of the number of different ideas as a variable in setting up two conditions is possibly a valid way of thinking. Which other aptitudes will interfere is not quite clear. Aptitude treatment research does not indicate what kind of aptitudes are most suitable in relation to closed tasks. Intelligence, anxiety, and motivation are most frequently cited as significant ones (Snow, 1977), as is the way of structuring a task. In fact, many questions (methodological, cognitive psychological, and sociopsychological) have now been raised. Why groups behave as they do remains an unsolved question. Nevertheless, we think that prior knowledge is an important factor in problem solving in groups, and that further research in this important area will further bear out this conclusion.

REFERENCES

Allen, V., & Feldman, R. S. Research on children tutoring children: A critical review. *Review of Educational Research*, 1976, 46(3), 355–385.

Appelhof, P. N. *Begeleide onderwijsvernieuwing*. Evaluatie van een curriculum-innovatie gericht op differentiatie van het aanvankelijk leesonderwijs, Zwijsen, Tilburg, 1979.

Barnes, D., & Todd, F. *Communication and learning in small groups*. London: Routledge and Kegan Paul, 1977.

Educational Product Information Exchange, *Evaluating instructional systems: PLAN, IGE, IPI*, EPIE Educational Product Report (VII), No. 58, 1974.

Gagne, R. M., & Briggs, L. J. *Principles of instructional design*. New York: Holt, Rinehart & Winston, 1979.

Gerris, J. R. M. *School Education and social development: A time sequence inquiry into the effects of a training program*. Lisse: Swets and Zeitlinger, 1981.

Hackman, R. J., and Morris, C. G. Group tasks, group interaction process and group performance effectiveness: A review and proposed integration. In L. Berkowitz (Ed.), *Group processes*. London: Academic Press, 1978.

Hillson, M. *Change and innovation in elementary school organization*. New York: Holt, Rinehart & Winston, 1967.

Johnson, D. W. Student-student interaction: The neglected variable in education. *Educational Researcher*, January 1981, 5–10.

Johnson, D. W., & Johnson, R. T. Conflict in the classroom: Controversy and learning. *Review of Educational Research*, Winter 1979, 49(1).

Kommers, P. *Communication and problem solving as elements in cooperative learning* (first draft), Department of Education, Utrecht, 1981.

Lieshout, C. F. M. Stimulation of social cognitive development from infancy to adolescence. In C. F. M. Lieshout, & H. J. Ingram (Eds.), *Stimulation of social development in school*. Lisse: Swets and Zeitlinger, 1977.

Nijhof, W. J. *Interne differentiatie als een innovatie*. Den Haag: Staatsuitgeverij, 1978.

Parreren, C. F., van. *Psychologie van het leren, I en II*. Deventer: Van Loghem Slaterus, 1970.

Sharan, S. Cooperative learning in small groups: Recent methods and effects on achievement, attitudes and ethnic relations. *Review of Educational Research*, 1980, 50(2), 241–271.

Vygotsky, L. S. *Thought and language*. Cambridge, Mass.: M.I.T. Press, 1962.

Yates, A. *Grouping in education*. Stockholm—New York: Almquist and Wiksell, 1966.

6

Student Interaction and Learning in Small Groups
A Research Summary

NOREEN M. WEBB

A key feature distinguishing cooperative settings from other learning settings is the opportunity for interaction among students. Yet, a look at the last several decades of research on classroom interaction and achievement reveals that researchers have only recently begun to devote much attention to interaction among students in cooperative groups. Recent studies of student interaction in small groups have uncovered some significant relationships between student interaction and achievement. Although some studies have produced significant results, the overall picture of the importance of student interaction in achievement is somewhat mixed. Part of the reason for the mixed picture is the generality of the measures of student interaction. Most studies have not used specific measures of student interaction that reflect the amount of elaboration contained in students' interaction with one another. Further, the measures of student interaction used in most studies have typically reflected isolated behaviors rather than sequences of interaction among students.

The purpose of the present chapter, then, is to summarize the research conducted by the author and her colleagues that demonstrates the power of specific interaction variables and sequences of behavior in predicting achievement in small groups. The structure of the chapter is a two-stage system linking interaction to achievement (process to outcome) and linking the characteristics of the individual and the group to interaction (input to process). The first four sections focus on the process–outcome link, the fifth section focuses on the input–process link, and the sixth section looks at the stability of group interaction over time.

The first section reviews the research by other authors that bears on the relationship between student interaction and achievement. The sec-

NOREEN M. WEBB • Graduate School of Education, University of California, Los Angeles, California 90024.

ond section describes the program of five studies that form the basis of the analysis and integration presented here. The third section summarizes and integrates the results of analyses of the relationship between student interaction and achievement. The categories of interaction examined here are nonspecific interaction, giving help, receiving help, and sequences of behavior (responses to requests for help). The fourth section shows how conflicting results from other studies on student interaction and learning may be reinterpreted in light of the importance of specific variables and sequences of behavior. The fifth section summarizes the author's and others' research predicting interaction in the group from characteristics of the individual and the group. The sixth section describes data bearing on the stability of student interaction over time. The final section discusses implications for research and practice.

RELEVANT RESEARCH[1]

The research bearing on the relationship between student interaction and achievement can be grouped into three categories: (1) studies examining nonspecific interaction among students; (2) studies examining the level of helping behavior in the group without distinguishing between giving help and receiving help; and (3) studies that have distinguished between giving help and receiving help.

NONSPECIFIC INTERACTION

Only one study fits this category. Johnson (1979) examined peer interaction and achievement in two-person groups instructed to work together. Nonspecific interaction, defined by the amount of time spent talking with other members of the group, did not relate to acheivement.

PEER TUTORING

The studies of peer tutoring produced a single score on helping behavior for each person. In five studies, the data on helping behavior came from observations of groups at work (Hanelin, 1978; Johnson, 1979; Slavin,

---

[1]The following four sections are based in whole or in part on "Predicting Learning from Student Interaction: Defining the Interaction Variables" by Noreen M. Webb, 1983, *Educational Psychologist 18*, 33–41. Copyright 1983 by Division 15 of the American Psychological Association, Inc. Used here with permission.

1977, 1978a, b). Helping behavior (also called *peer tutoring* or *peer-task behavior*) was the proportion of time spent in on-task interaction with other group members. In three other studies, the data on helping behavior came from questionnaires asking students to write the names of students in the group who had helped them and whom they had helped (DeVries & Mescon, 1975; DeVries, Mescon, & Shackman, 1975; Edwards & DeVries, 1975). The number of names served as the behavior variable.

Two of the above studies correlated helping behavior and achievement in two-person groups. The results were mixed. Johnson (1979) reported a correlation of .26 ($p < .01$), whereas Hanelin (1978) reported nonsignificant correlations ($-.29$ for easy tasks, .13 for difficult tasks).

The other studies that examined general helping behavior without distinguishing between giving and receiving help did not attempt to correlate helping behavior and achievement but measured both as outcome variables. The evidence from these studies about the relationship between helping behavior and achievement is therefore indirect. These studies measured the helping behavior and the achievement of four- or five-member teams in two reward conditions: group and individual. In the group reward condition, all group members received the same score in achievement. The team's score was typically the average of the scores of its members on the achievement test administered individually after group work. In the individual reward condition, the students received their own scores on the achievement test. Six studies yielded results for helping behavior that were in the same direction as those for achievement: more helping and greater achievement in the group reward condition than in the individual reward condition (DeVries & Mescon, 1975; DeVries et al., 1975; Edwards & DeVries, 1975; Slavin, 1978b) and equal helping behavior and achievement in the two conditions (Edwards & DeVries, 1975; Slavin, 1977).[2] In the other study, however, group rewards produced more helping behavior than individual reward but did not produce greater achievement (Slavin, 1978a). Although the results of the majority of these studies are consistent with a positive relationship between helping and achievement, the one study that manipulated the amount of helping behavior produced results that do not support this conclusion. Slavin (1978b) compared the achievement of students instructed to work with others to the achievement of students instructed to work individually. Students in the group condition showed lower achievement than students in the individual condition.

[2]The study by Edwards and DeVries (1975) carried out the same comparison in mathematics and social studies classrooms and so is mentioned twice.

GIVING AND RECEIVING HELP

As is the case with the research on peer tutoring, the results of the studies distinguishing between giving help and receiving help are also mixed. Peterson and colleagues at the University of Wisconsin conducted a series of three studies of small-group learning in elementary-school mathematics classrooms. All three studies observed groups at work and coded information about giving help and receiving help for each student. The data on student behavior were then correlated with scores on achievement and retention tests.

Two of the three studies (Peterson & Janicki, 1979; Peterson, Janicki, & Swing, 1981) reported significant positive correlations between giving explanations and achievement ($r = .29$, $p < .05$, and $r = .24$, $p < .05$, respectively). However, when partial correlations were computed and ability was controlled for, the significant relationship disappeared in both studies (Peterson, 1982). When partial correlations were computed within ability levels, there was evidence of a positive relationship between giving explanations and achievement for low-ability students but not for medium-ability and high-ability students.

The third study (Swing & Peterson, 1982) distinguished among three types of help—giving conceptual/sequencing explanations, giving directions, and giving answers— and correlated the scores on these variables with scores on three achievement tests (division, fractions, and a retention test). The correlations (partial correlations controlling for ability) among helping scores and achievement test scores were computed separately at three ability levels: high, medium, and low. Giving conceptual/sequencing explanations related to scores on the fractions test for low-ability students (Kendall's tau ranged from .43 to .59, p <.05). Giving directions did not relate to achievement on any test at any ability level. Giving answers was negatively related to retention test scores for medium-ability students (Kendall's tau = $-.28$, $p < .05$).

The same three studies by Peterson and colleagues were used to investigate the relationship between receiving help and achievement. The first two studies found no relationship between receiving help and achievement (Peterson & Janicki, 1979; Peterson et al., 1981). When partial correlations controlling for ability were computed within ability level, receiving help was found to be positively related to achievement for low-ability students (Peterson, 1982). Swing and Peterson (1982) found that receiving conceptual/sequencing explanations was positively related to fractions scores for low-ability students (Kendall's tau = .43, p < .05), and receiving directions was positively related to division scores for low-ability students (Kendall's tau = .41, $p < .05$).

In summary, the research relating student interaction and achievement in small groups appears to be inconsistent. The next sections summarize and integrate the results of a program of five studies and show how they can be used to help resolve some of the inconsistencies in the research described above.

DESCRIPTION OF THE RESEARCH PROGRAM

In all five studies, the students worked on academic tasks in four-person groups. The instructions to the small groups stressed the importance that all the students in the group learn the material and deemphasized speed. The students in a group were told to work together and not to divide the work, to help group members experiencing difficulty, and to ask for help if they needed it. They were instructed to ask the teacher for help only if no one in the group could solve the problem. To further promote cooperation among the group members, the groups in most studies participated in an intergroup competition in which each group received a score based on the average of the group members' scores on the achievement test administered individually at the end of the curriculum unit. The group with the highest average score received recognition or a tangible prize. The reward structure in most of the studies was therefore intergroup competition–intragroup cooperation (see Michaels, 1977); the groups competed for rewards, but the group rewards were distributed equally within each group. Deutsch (1949, 1960) had found that this reward structure promoted cooperation, helpfulness, and coordination of efforts among group members. The reward structure in other studies combined group and individual rewards.

In most studies, the teacher gave a brief introduction to the topic, including one or two practice problems. Then, the students worked on additional problems in small groups for the rest of the class period.

At the beginning of every study, data were collected on each student's ability. In one study, the students took a complete battery of achievement and intelligence tests. In the other studies, the students were administered tests of mathematics achievement, including computation and mathematical reasoning. The students in a few studies completed personality scales hypothesized to relate to interaction in group settings, including extraversion-introversion and intellectual achievement responsibility. At the end of every study, the students were given achievement tests. The tests consisted of items similar in content and form to problems that the students had completed during the class work.

Peer interaction was observed in all groups while they worked on the academic material. In two studies, peer interaction was coded directly from observations of the groups at work. The observation instrument used in these studies was designed to assess interaction among the students in a group and interaction between the teacher and the students. Each observer wrote notes about all interaction in the group, noting the speaker and the recipient of each interchange, the observation category, and the content of the interchange. The notes were taken in one-minute blocks to allow the approximate duration of the interchanges to be determined. The number of occurrences of each observation category for each student were entered into the analyses. Among the observation categories that were coded were giving help, receiving help, asking questions, asking questions and receiving responses, and asking questions and receiving no responses.

In the other three studies, the group work was tape-recorded, and the peer interaction was coded from written transcripts of the tapes. The transcripts provided information about the interaction among students, as well as the identity of the speaker and the recipient in each interchange. Tallies were made of the number of occurrences of each interaction variable for each student. The major interaction variables coded in these studies included giving explanations, giving information other than explanations, receiving explanations, receiving information other than explanations, asking for help, and various responses to requests for help (explanations vs. information only vs. no response).

The students in all five studies learned mathematical material, but the grade level of the students, the topic learned, the learning setting, and the duration of the group work varied across the studies. In the first study (hereafter labeled Study 1), 48 eleventh-grade students learned material on probability, algebra, and geometry (Webb, 1980a, c; see also Webb, 1980b). The study took place in four weekly sessions in a special setting outside school. In the second study (hereafter labeled Study 2), 96 seventh-, eighth-, and ninth-grade students in four general mathematics classes learned a one-week unit on consumer mathematics (Webb, 1982a). The study took place in a classroom adjacent to the students' own mathematics classroom. In the third study (hereafter labeled Study 3A and 3B), two samples of students learned the area and perimeter of geometric figures (the first sample, $n = 51$) or probability (the second sample, $n = 52$) in a classroom near the students' own mathematics classroom (Webb & Cullian, 1983). The duration of this study was one week. In the fourth study (hereafter labeled Study 4), 77 seventh- and eighth-grade students in two above-average general mathematics classrooms learned a two-week unit on exponents and scientific notation (Webb, 1982b). These students worked in small groups in their own classroom. In the fifth study (hereafter labeled Study 5), 69 seventh- and eighth-grade students in two average-ability general mathematics classrooms learned a three-week unit on the area and perimeter of geometric figures (Webb & Kenderski, 1984). This study, like Study 4, took place in the students' own classrooms. What distinguishes this study from the previous four studies, however, was that it took place in the context of a year-long program of small-group work. In the first four studies, the students were assembled in small groups for the duration of one curriculum unit. In the last study, in contrast, the students worked in small groups throughout most of the school year.

A key variable examined in all the studies was the ability composition of the group. It was hypothesized that the mixture of ability in the group would influence the interaction among the group members and, consequently, how much each student learned. All the studies, therefore, compared two or more group compositions. The students were assigned to the groups in the following way. The ability scores were used to define three ability strata: high, medium, and low, corresponding to the top 25%, the middle 50%, and the bottom 25% of each sample. The students within each ability stratum were randomly assigned to uniform-ability or mixed-ability groups. The uniform-ability groups had students at the same ability level (uniform-high, uniform-medium, or uniform-low). The mixed-ability groups had students from more than one ability level. There were two kinds of mixed-ability groups: groups with students from all three ability levels (high-ability, medium-ability, and low-ability students) and groups with students from two ability levels (high-ability and medium-ability students *or* medium-ability and low-ability students). All the studies had uniform-ability groups. Studies 1, 4, and 5 had mixed-ability groups with highs, mediums, and lows. Studies 2, 3, and 5 had mixed-ability groups with highs and mediums or mediums and lows.

In summary, the five studies focused on student interaction and learning of topics in general mathematics. Four of the five studies took place in natural classroom settings; the other took place in a setting outside school. The grade level of the students in these studies ranged from junior high school to high school. The duration of the studies ranged from one to three weeks.

RELATIONSHIP BETWEEN STUDENT INTERACTION AND ACHIEVEMENT

Four categories of student interacton are examined here: (1) nonspecific interaction; (2) giving help; (3) receiving help; and (4) sequences of behavior: responses to requests for help. The relationship between student interaction and achievement in the four studies was assessed by means of correlations: zero-order correlations and partial correlations controlling for ability. Partial correlations are included to help clarify the causal direction of the relationship between interaction and achievement. In particular, the hypothesized direction is that interaction influences achievement, rather than that interaction is a function of ability level or of previous achievement. For example, a significant zero-order correlation between the giving of explanations and achievement could mean that giving explanations helps students to learn, or it could mean that the students who give explanations show high achievement because they are the most able students to begin with. A significant partial correlation controlling for ability provides support for the first interpretation. The results and the hypothesized explanations of the results are presented for each category of student interaction in turn.

Nonspecific Interaction

Nonspecific interaction is defined here as the frequency of general participation in peer interaction. In all the studies, nonspecific interaction was calculated by summing all instances of verbal interaction in group work, regardless of the type or the purpose of the interaction. Nonspecific interaction, then, included all instances of giving help, receiving help, asking questions, making errors, correcting errors, and providing answers to exercises. In no study was the relationship between nonspecific interaction statistically significant: the zero-order and partial correlations ranged from $-.17$ to $-.04$.

Giving Help

The studies examined here distinguished between three types of help given: (1) all instances of help; (2) explanations; and (3) terminal responses. An explanation typically consisted of a step-by-step description of the solution to a problem or a detailed account of how to correct an error. An example of an explanation given during a unit on exponents and scientific notation is "Okay, look: 63,000,000 times 8,500,000. This is 63 with 6 zeroes. So, in parentheses, 63 times 10 to the sixth and then times 85 times 10 to the fifth . . . 535" (Webb, 1982b, p. 646). Terminal responses consisted of help that did not include detailed descriptions, for example, giving the correct answer to an exercise without explaining how to obtain it ("It's 10^{-7}") or pointing out that another student's answer or procedure for obtaining the answer was incorrect without providing the correct answer and explanation ("No, it's 10 to the negative 2''). The category designated as all instances of giving help was the sum of giving explanations and giving terminal responses.

The data on the relationship between giving help and achievement appear in Table 1. Although every study did not distinguish among all three types of help, a clear pattern emerges in the results of Table 1. Most important is that whether giving help was beneficial for achievement depended on the type of help given. Giving explanations was consistently and positively related to achievement. Giving terminal responses, on the other hand, tended not to be related to achievement.

The different effects on achievement of giving explanations and giving terminal responses help to explain the inconsistent results for giving all kinds of help and, furthermore, suggest that the composite helping variable may not be meaningful. Whether the composite helping variable has a significant relationship to achievement in a particular study seems to depend on the strength of the relationship between giving explanations and achievement. Because the relationship between the composite helping variable and achievement is a combination of the relationships for giving explanations and giving terminal responses, the stronger the result for giving explanations, the greater the likelihood of a significant result for the composite helping variable.

Hypotheses concerning the greater benefit of giving explanations than of giving terminal responses come from cognitive theories of learning and studies of cognitive processes. Particularly relevant here is Wittrock's model of generative learning, in which the learner generates associations between new information and concepts already learned (Wittrock, 1974a, b). Giving explanations not only involves verbalizing associations between new and learned information but may also involve generating new elaborations. A recent study on the cognitive benefits of teaching by Bargh and Schul (1980) also supports the efficacy of giving explanations. Bargh and Schul compared the achievement of persons studying the material only to learn it themselves. Students studying to teach the material learned more than did students studying only to learn. Bargh and Schul suggested that preparing to teach another person may produce a more highly organized cognitive structure than trying only to learn the material for oneself. As an extension of their hypothesis, they suggested that not only may someone *preparing to teach* reorganize the material for clearer presentation, but also a person *actively teaching* someone else may reorganize or clarify the material to allow

> the teacher to see the issue from new perspectives, enabling him or her to see previously unthought of new relationships between the discrete elements. It may be this building of new relationships that facilitates a better fundamental grasp of the material. (Bargh & Schul, 1980, p. 595)

TABLE 1. Correlations between Giving Help and Achievement[a]

Type of help given	Study 1		Study 2		Study 3A		Study 3B		Study 4		Study 5	
	r	Partial r^c	r	Partial r^c	r	Partial r^c	r	Partial r^c	r	Partial r^c	r	Partial r^c
Explanations	—[b]	.39**	—	—	—	—	—	—	.26**	.22**	.47***	.47***
Terminal responses	—	—	—	—	—	—	—	—	−.01	−.02	.11	.07
All help	—	—	.18	.22	.03	.02	.11	.05	.09	.06	.27**	.28***

[a]Adapted from "Predicting Learning from Student Interaction: Defining the Interaction Variables" by Noreen Webb, *Educational Psychologist*, 1983, *18*, 33–41. Copyright 1983 by Division 15 of the American Psychological Association. Adapted here with permission.
[b]— indicates information not available.
[c]Controlling for ability.
**$p < .05$. ***$p < .01$.

Although the hypothesis has not been tested directly, it is likely that giving explanations may involve cognitive restructuring, whereas giving terminal responses may not.

RECEIVING HELP

The definitions of the variables and the patterns of results for receiving help are similar to those for giving help. The three types of help received include (1) all instances of help; (2) explanations; and (3) terminal responses. The correlations between receiving help and achievement appear in Table 2. In the studies that distinguished terminal responses from explanations, receiving terminal responses was negatively related to achievement. The results for receiving explanations, although not entirely consistent, suggest that receiving explanations is beneficial for achievement. Based on the opposite influences of receiving explanations and receiving terminal responses, one would expect the positive and negative effects to cancel out in the findings for the composite help variable. This prediction held in Studies 2, 3, and 4, but not in Study 5. In Study 5, the strong negative effect of receiving terminal responses, combined with no effect of receiving explanations, yielded an overall negative effect of receiving all instances of help.

Hypotheses can be formed to account for the negative effect of receiving terminal responses and the positive (but somewhat inconsistent) effect of receiving explanations. Merely being supplied with the correct answer to a problem or being told that one's answer is incorrect would not be expected to help the learner to discover the correct procedures for solving the problem. Furthermore, receiving terminal responses may frustrate the learner, causing him or her to lose interest in the task and, consequently, to devote less effort to learning the material (see Berkowitz & Levy, 1956; Hammond & Goldman, 1961; Steiner, 1972). Receiving explanations, on the other hand, would be expected to help the learner to correct misunderstandings and to learn the correct procedures. In addition, receiving explanations may be perceived by the learner as positive support for her or his efforts, which in turn would lead to increased individual effort (see Slavin, 1978b).

A hypothesis can also be advanced to account for the lack of a significant relationship between receiving explanations and achievement in Study 5. The efficacy of receiving explanations may be related to the ability level of the student giving the explanations. The average ability level of the students in the fifth study (about average on national norms) was lower than that of the students in the first four studies (above-average on national norms). The students in the last study, then, may

TABLE 2. Correlations between Receiving Help and Achievement[a]

Type of help received	Study 1		Study 2		Study 3A		Study 3B		Study 4		Study 5	
	r	Partial r^c	r	Partial r^c	r	Partial r^c	r	Partial r^c	r	Partial r^c	r	Partial r^c
Explanations	—[b]	.63**	—	—	—	—	—	—	.22**	.21**	.02	-.01
Terminal responses	—	—	—	—	—	—	—	—	-.32***	-.35***	-.43***	-.42***
All help	—	—	.05	-.06	-.22	-.17	.11	.11	-.15	-.17	-.36**	-.36**

[a]Adapted from "Predicting Learning from Student Interaction: Defining the Interaction Variables" by Noreen Webb, *Educational Psychologist*, 1983, *18*, 33–41. Copyright 1983 by Division 15 of the American Psychological Association. Adapted here with permission.
[b]— indicates information not available.
[c]Controlling for ability.
**$p < .05$. ***$p < .01$.

have been less able to produce coherent or complete explanations than the students in the other studies.

SEQUENCES OF BEHAVIOR: RESPONSES TO REQUESTS FOR HELP

Whereas the previous section examined all help received, including solicited and unsolicited help, this section examines the consequences for learning of all types of responses to requests for help. This section, therefore, focuses on *solicited help*. In the discussion here, all indications of need, including questions and errors, are considered requests for help (the former being explicit, the latter being implicit). Responses to requests for help include (1) all responses (explanations and terminal responses); (2) explanations; (3) terminal responses; and (4) no response.

Information bearing on the relationship between solicited help and achievement appears in Table 3.[3] The information provided for Study 1 focuses on a specific mathematical problem and refers to the percentage of students receiving help in response to requests who solved the test problem correctly. The information presented for the last three studies are correlations, as in the previous tables. The most striking result in Table 3 is the strong negative effect on achievement of receiving *no* response to a request for help. Receiving terminal responses, as in the previous section, was uniformly detrimental to achievement. Interestingly, receiving terminal responses had nearly as great an impact on achievement as receiving no response. Receiving explanations tended to be positively related to achievement but, as before, was not consistent across studies.

Receiving all responses, including explanations and terminal responses, had mixed relations with achievement across the studies, including significantly positive and negative correlations and correlations not significantly different from zero. This result is not surprising considering the different relationships for different specific responses. The correlation between all responses and achievement is a combination of the correlations between specific responses and achievement. In Study 4, a combination of significant positive and negative correlations for specific responses yielded no overall effect for all responses combined. In Study 5, a combination of significant negative correlations and zero correlations yielded a negative effect overall. In Study 2, which yielded a significant positive effect overall, one would expect a strong positive relationship between receiving explanations and achievement.

[3]Because Table 2 focuses on all help received without distinguishing between solicited and unsolicited help and Table 3 focuses on solicited help, the correlations in the two tables are not identical for the same categories of help.

TABLE 3. Relationship between Responses for Help and Achievement[a]

Response to request for help	Study 1		Study 2		Study 3A		Study 3B		Study 4		Study 5	
	%[b]	r	r	Partial r[c]	r	Partial r[c]	r	Partial r[c]	r	Partial r[c]	r	Partial r[c]
Explanations	100	—[d]	—	—	—	—	—	—	.22**	.21**	.02	−.01
Terminal responses	0	—	—	—	—	—	—	—	−.43***	−.44***	−.47***	−.47***
No response	0	−.54***	—	−.55***	−.41***	−.39***	−.42***	−.41***	−.57***	−.55***	−.48***	−.51***
All responses	56	.19**	—	.15*	−.34**	−.32**	.10	.10	−.16	−.17	−.26**	−.28**

[a]Adapted from "Predicting Learning from Student Interaction: Defining the Interaction Variables" by Noreen Webb, *Educational Psychologist*, 1983, *18*, 33–41. Copyright 1983 by Division 15 of the American Psychological Association. Adapted here with permission.
[b]Percentage of students receiving this response to a request for help who solved the test problem correctly.
[c]Controlling for ability.
*$p < .10$. **$p < .05$. ***$p < .01$.

Unfortunately, however, this hypothesis cannot be tested because the data are not available. Study 2 coded information about peer interaction directly from group work rather than from tape recordings, and the explanations could not be reliably distinguished from the terminal responses.

SUMMARY

The results of the five studies described above suggest that giving explanations is beneficial to achievement, whereas giving terminal responses (for example, giving correct answers to exercises or pointing out errors without also giving explanations) is not related to achievement. Furthermore, receiving explanations tends to be positively related to achievement, whereas receiving terminal responses and receiving *no* response to a request for help are detrimental to achievement. Not surprisingly, there are no consistent relationships between giving all kinds of help and achievement and receiving all kinds of help and achievement.

REINTERPRETATION AND RESOLUTION OF CONFLICTING FINDINGS

An earlier section of this paper described conflicting findings from studies investigating nonspecific interaction, peer tutoring, and giving and receiving help. The present section reinterprets those findings and helps to resolve the inconsistencies using the distinction between explanations and terminal responses.

NONSPECIFIC INTERACTION

The finding of no relationship between nonspecific interaction (defined by the amount of time spent talking with other members of the group) in the Johnson (1979) study is not surprising. Talking may have included explaining to others or receiving explanations (positively related to achievement) and receiving terminal responses or no responses to requests for help (negatively related to achievement), which may have canceled out. In any case, the lack of a relationship between nonspecific interaction and achievement can *not* be interpreted as indicating a lack of relationship between interaction and achievement.

PEER TUTORING

The studies examining peer tutoring looked at the total amount of help given and received. The lack of findings consistent with a positive relationship between peer tutoring and achievement in some studies has been used to question the role of helping behavior in learning in small groups (Slavin, 1978a). The results described in the previous section suggest an alternative interpretation. The help given in the studies showing no relationship may have been a combination of explanations and terminal responses, with the positive and negative effects canceling out. In the studies finding a positive relationship between peer tutoring and achievement, the help given and received may have been predominantly explanations instead of terminal responses.

GIVING AND RECEIVING HELP

The findings of no relationship between giving explanations and receiving explanations and achievement in the first two Peterson studies (Peterson & Janicki, 1979; Peterson et al., 1981) can be reinterpreted based on the definition of "explanations" in those studies. Explanations in those studies included answers and procedural information as well as descriptions of how to solve the problem (Peterson, 1982). The combination of positive effects (giving and receiving explanations), zero effects (giving terminal responses), and negative effects (receiving terminal responses) could produce nonsignificant correlations overall.

The findings of the Swing and Peterson (1982) study conform nicely to the distinction between explanations and terminal responses. Swing and Peterson's conceptual/sequencing explanations correspond to the explanations defined here, and their directions and answers correspond to terminal responses. The significant correlations between giving and receiving explanations and achievement in the Swing–Peterson study were all positive. All of the correlations between giving "terminal responses" except one did not differ significantly from zero; one was negative. The significant correlations between receiving "terminal responses" and achievement were predominantly negative. These findings provide support for the conclusion that giving and receiving explanations are both beneficial to achievement, that giving terminal responses is not related to achievement, and that receiving terminal responses is detrimental to achievement.

In summary, the apparent inconsistencies among the findings from research on nonspecific interaction, peer tutoring, and giving and receiving help can be resolved by means of the distinction between explanations and terminal responses.

PREDICTORS OF INTERACTION

The previous sections probed the kinds of verbal interaction that relate to achievement. Some interaction, such as giving or receiving explanations, was shown to be beneficial to achievement, whereas other interaction, such as receiving terminal responses to questions, was shown to be detrimental to achievement. These findings are of limited utility for educators, however, unless clues are also provided about which students are likely to experience different kinds of interaction, and about how to design the group context to promote beneficial interaction and to discourage detrimental interaction. This section focuses on individual and group characteristics that may help to predict interaction among group members. The individual characteristics are ability, extroversion-introversion, and intellectual achievement responsibility. The group characteristics are group ability composition and group gender composition.

ABILITY

Three studies (1, 4, and 5) investigated the relationship between ability and giving explanations. In Studies 1 and 4, the relationship was positive and statistically significant: The correlations ranged from .25 (p <.05) to .78 (p < .001). These results suggest that the most able students tend to give the most explanations. The findings in Study 5, however, give a slightly different picture. In that study, although the correlation between ability and giving explanations was not significant, the correlation between *relative ability within the group* and giving explanations was significant ($r = .23, p < .04$). Here, *relative ability* was defined as the difference between an individual's ability and the mean of his or her group. This relationship suggests that the most able person within the group tends to become the "explainer," regardless of his or her absolute ability.

Two studies (1 and 5) examined the relationship between ability and receiving explanations. Only the first found a significant relationship (the correlations ranged from $-.54$ to $-.71, p < .01$). In the first study, the low-ability students tended to receive the most explanations. Study 5 also related receiving explanations to relative ability within the group, but the correlation was not statistically significant.

All of the studies except Study 1 looked at the relationship between ability and receiving *no* explanation in response to a request for one (or receiving no response to an informational question). In none of the studies was the correlation significant. The tendency of students to fail to obtain help when needed cannot, therefore, be tied to ability level.

It should be noted that the positive relationship between ability and giving explanations and the lack of relationship between ability and receiving explanations has been found in other studies. Peterson and colleagues (Peterson & Janicki, 1979; Peterson et al., 1981) reported correlations of .24 ($p < .05$) for giving explanations and nonsignificant correlations for receiving explanations. A third study, however, reported significant relationships for both giving and receiving explanations: High-ability students gave more explanations than low-ability students, and medium-ability and low-ability students received more explanations than high-ability students (Swing & Peterson, 1982).

In summary, ability was a consistent predictor only of giving explanations; the most able students tended to be the explainers. The results of Study 5, however, suggest that the most able students *in a group* tended to be the explainers even if their absolute level of ability was not high.

EXTROVERSION-INTROVERSION

Because social psychologists have often found that extroversion-introversion is a good predictor of interaction in nonacademic group situations (see, for example, Bass, Wurster, Doll, & Clair, 1953; Bass, McGehee, Hawkins, Young, & Gebel, 1953; Grosz & Wagoner, 1971; Stern & Grosz, 1966), Studies 2–5 administered the extroversion–introversion scale of Eysenck's Personality Inventory (Eysenck & Eysenck, 1968). The general hypothesis was that the students who scored high on the scale (indicating extroversion) would be more active in group interaction than the students who scored low on the scale. Specifically, it was expected that introverted students would be more likely to fail to obtain help when needed than would extroverted students. This hypothesis was confirmed in two studies but not in the other three. In Study 2, there was a negative relationship between extroversion-introversion and asking a question and receiving no response ($r = -.19$ $p < .03$), suggesting that introverted students were more likely than extroverted students to be ignored when they asked for help. In Study 4, the correlation between extroversion-introversion and receiving explanations was positive ($r = .22$, $p < .03$), indicating that extroverted students were more likely than introverted students to receive help. In the other studies, the correlations were not significant.

The evidence for extroversion-introversion as a predictor of interaction in the group is in the expected direction but is not consistent. Furthermore, even the significant relationships are fairly weak.

INTELLECTUAL ACHIEVEMENT RESPONSIBILITY

The intellectual achievement responsibility scale was designed to assess "children's beliefs that they, rather than other people, are responsible for their intellectual-academic successes and failures" (Crandall, Katkovsky, & Crandall, 1965, p. 91). The scale has two parts. The positive subscale refers to academic successes, and the negative scale refers to academic failures. This scale was administered to the students in Study 5 to test the hypothesis that students with high intellectual-achievement responsibility would be active in group interaction. The results were surprising. The students who perceived that the responsibility for positive achievement outcomes resided within themselves (internals) gave *fewer* explanations than the students who perceived that the responsibility for their academic success resided in others (externals) ($r = -.22, p < .04$). The negative scale showed a similar result ($r = -.29$, $p < .01$). The internals may have assumed that because they learned well by their own efforts, others did, too, so that it was unnecessary to explain to others. The externals, on the other hand, may have perceived that help from others played an important role in their own learning and, consequently, saw the utility in giving explanations to help others learn.

GROUP ABILITY COMPOSITION

The results of the group composition analyses suggest that the mixture of ability in the group governs processes operating in the group. Study 1 had the most complex design: mixed-ability groups (high-, medium-, and low-ability students in each group); uniform medium-ability groups; and uniform low-ability groups. At the group level of behavior, there was more helping behavior in mixed-ability groups and uniform medium-ability groups than in uniform high-ability and uniform low-ability groups. The results for individual behavior were more complicated, showing that students at a particular level of ability were better off in some group compositions than in others. Because the helping behavior in mixed-ability groups consisted of the highs helping the lows in a teacher–learner relationship, high-ability and low-ability students were quite active in mixed-ability groups. In uniform high-ability groups, on the other hand, students assumed (incorrectly) that everyone in the group knew how to solve problems and did not make much effort to explain the material. In uniform low-ability groups, few students understood the material well enough to give adequate explanations. Medium-ability students, who tended to be ignored in mixed-ability groups, were very active in uniform-ability groups. In sum, high-ability students gave more explanations in mixed-ability groups than in uniform-ability groups; low-ability students received more explanations in mixed-ability groups than in uniform-ability groups; and medium-ability students gave more and received more explanations in uniform-ability groups than in mixed-ability groups.

Study 4 was designed to replicate the above finding that medium-ability students are less active in mixed-ability groups than in uniform-ability groups. The two group compositions investigated in this study, therefore, were mixed-ability groups (highs, mediums, and lows in each group) and uniform-ability groups (all mediums in a group). This finding was replicated for receiving explanations: medium-ability students received more explanations in uniform-ability groups than in mixed-ability groups. The finding was also replicated in Study 5, which included mixed-ability groups (highs, mediums, and lows) and uniform-ability groups (all mediums). Medium-ability students gave more explanations in uniform-ability groups than in mixed-ability groups.

Studies 2, 3A, and 3B were designed to investigate the effects of the other kind of group composition: mixed-ability groups with high-ability and medium-ability students *or* medium-ability and low-ability students. These three studies compared this kind of mixed-abilty group with uniform-ability groups (high, medium, or low). In all three studies, questions were answered more frequently in mixed groups than in uniform groups. In contrast to the mixed groups with highs, mediums, and lows, the mixed groups with students at only two ability levels did not have any students "caught between highs and lows." Consequently, few students were ignored when they asked for help.

For a complete comparison of different kinds of group compositions, Study 5 included uniform medium-ability groups; mixed groups with highs, mediums, and lows; and mixed groups with highs and mediums *or* mediums and lows. All groups had equal means on ability. This design allowed the comparison across group compositions to be made for medium-ability students. Consistent with the results of the above studies, medium-ability students gave the most explanations in mixed-ability groups with students from two ability levels and gave the fewest explanations in groups with students from three ability levels.

In summary, the results of group ability composition present a consistent picture. Mixed-ability groups with students from two ability levels seem to be beneficial for all students, whereas mixed-ability groups with students from three ability levels seem to be beneficial for the highest and the lowest students but not for those in the middle. In the former type of mixed-ability groups, all students seem to participate in the teacher–learner relationship, whereas in the latter type of mixed-ability group, the range of ability is great enough to allow students to make a distinction between students in considerable need of help (low-ability students) and students in moderate need of help (medium-ability students). Because the groups in these studies concentrated on the most needy, they ignored those who needed less help. A tentative recommendation for classroom practice is to compose groups with (1) the highest- and lowest-ability students in the class but not those with medium ability; (2) groups with a moderate range of ability (highs and mediums *or* mediums and low); and (3) groups with only medium-ability students.

GROUP GENDER COMPOSITION

One study (Study 4; see Webb, 1984a) investigated the effects of the gender composition of the group on achievement and interaction patterns. The gender composition factor varied the ratio of females to males in a group. Three kinds of mixed-gender groups were studied: groups with two females and two males; majority-female groups (typically, three females and one male); and majority-male groups (typically, three males and one female). Interaction between students of the same gender and between male and female students coded for six interaction variables: giving, asking for, and receiving explanations, and giving, asking for, and receiving procedural information.

The achievement and interaction results depended on the ratio of females to males in a group. The achievement of females and males was nearly identical in the groups with two females and two males. In the majority-female groups and the majority-male groups, however, the males showed higher achievement than the females.

The interaction patterns paralleled those of achievement. In the groups with two females and two males, the females and the males showed similar interaction patterns. In the other group compositions, the females and the males had dramatically different experiences in group interaction. In the *majority-female* groups, the females focused much of their attention on the males. They asked the males for more explanations and more procedural information than expected, but few of these requests were answered. The females in this group composition also gave more explanations and procedural information to the male than expected. In the *majority-male* groups, the males focused their attention on the other males and tended to ignore the females.

In summary, then, the females experienced interaction that was detrimental to achievement in the groups in which they outnumbered the males or were outnumbered by the males. When they outnumbered the males, they singled out the males for attention, asking them for help and giving them help. The males in these groups rarely reciprocated, however, and as a result, the females received less help than needed. When the females were outnumbered by males, the males tended to ignore the females by not asking them for help and not giving them help.

Possibly as a consequence of these experiences, the females did not learn as much as the males in these group compositions. In the groups with equal numbers of females and males, on the other hand, the females and the males had similar experiences and learned the same amount.

It is interesting that when all the students were pooled in the same analysis without distinguishing between group compositions, the achievement of the males was significantly higher than that of the females ($p < .001$), and the males received more help than the females (most comparisons were significant at $p < .10$). The overall analysis is misleading, however, because these results did not apply to all group compositions. The results of this study suggest that including group composition factors in analyses of data from small groups may help to provide informative and meaningful results.

STABILITY OF GROUP INTERACTION OVER TIME

Establishing a link between group interaction and achievement has little practical value if the interaction patterns are unstable or unpredictable. Two studies examined the stability of group interaction over time (the observations of group work were performed approximately three months apart in both studies), with conflicting results. The first study (Webb & Cullian, 1983) found that students' behavior tended to be fairly stable over time: Specifically, students who had not received answers to their questions on one occasion tended to have the same experience on another occasion. The second study (Webb, 1984b) found student behavior to be relatively unstable over time, even though the *relationships* between students interaction and achievement were similar over time.

The conflicting results in the two studies may be explained by differences in their design. In the first study, the students did not work in groups during the months between the observations. Moreover, the students worked in different groups at the two times. In the second study, in contrast, the students worked in small groups throughout the months between the observations and stayed in the same groups. The differences in the design of the two studies suggest that the lack of stability in the second study may reflect changing roles in the group process over time. As students become adjusted to the small group, they may change their perceptions of the group and their behavior.

Clearly, the findings regarding the stability of group interaction over time are not conclusive. It is possible, for example, that the instability of behavior in the second study was due to short-term fluctuations of student and group behavior. There may be day-to-day fluctuations in behavior within stable long-term patterns. The observations made in the second study may merely have been an unlucky sample. To clarify this issue, it is necessary to observe group work several times during each instructional unit, as well as several instructional units over time.

SUMMARY AND DISCUSSION

This chapter has described research conducted by the author that has focused on students' experiences in small-group interaction. The research has sought to determine which interaction processes relate to achievement, and which characteristics of the student (ability, extroversion-introversion, and intellectual achievement responsibilty) and the group (group ability and gender composition) predict interaction processes. These studies showed that giving explanations is beneficial to achievement, whereas giving only information without explanations is not related to achievement. Similarly, receiving explanations tends to be beneficial to achievement. Receiving information without explanations, in contrast, and receiving *no* help when it is needed are detrimental to achievement.

The data on the predictors of interaction in the group show that few characteristics of the student consistently related to interaction. The most consistent finding was that high-ability students tended to give the most explanations. There was some tendency for extroverted students to be more successful than introverted students in obtaining help when it was needed, but the evidence was weak. The results of group ability composition suggest that mixed-ability groups with high-ability, medium-ability, and low-ability students are beneficial to the highs and the lows, but not to the mediums. Two other group compositions, on the other hand, seem to be beneficial to all group members: mixed-ability groups with high-ability and medium-ability students *or* medium-ability and low-ability students; and uniform-ability groups with all medium-ability students. The results of group gender composition showed that females experienced interaction that was detrimental to achievement in unbalanced groups: majority-female groups and majority-male groups. The females did not have this experience in groups with an equal number of females and males.

The results of the research presented here show the importance of examining specific categories of student interaction. Even differentiating between such categories as giving help and receiving help is not enough. The findings of positive relationships between giving and receiving explanations and achievement, and the negative relationships between receiving terminal responses and receiving no responses to requests for help and achievement highlight the need to differentiate between different types of help and to examine whether requests for help are answered. Investigating giving and receiving help without distinguishing between different types of help will not be informative and may be misleading.

The specificity of the peer interaction variables that best predict achievement in small groups has several implications for observation procedures. Because detailed information about peer interaction is needed, verbatim audio or video records may be essential. Observation systems, whether time-based rotating sampling systems in which a single student is observed at a time, or systems in which all students are observed simultaneously, are unsatisfactory for several reasons. First, it is difficult to reliably distinguish between explanations and terminal responses without hearing the same response several times. Second, it is difficult to capture sequences of interaction among the different members of a group, particularly when one student's request for help and another student's response are often separated in time or by other interaction. Finally, in classroom settings, in which multiple groups typically work simultaneously, verbatim recording can capture most or all of group interaction, whereas an observer watching the group may have difficulty distinguishing voices or understanding what is said.

The results of the studies discussed here also have implications for the unit of observation. Observation studies often record the frequency of a certain behavior (e.g., helping) in a group without identifying the specific group members. Information at the group level has limited utility, however, for predicting and understanding the impact of the group experience on the achievement of individual members. For example, a high frequency of giving explanations in a group may not be beneficial for the achievement of all group members if the explanations are not directed to those who need them most. Furthermore, even a high correlation between the frequency of giving explanations in a group and achievement sheds no light on the effects of giving explanations separate from those of receiving explanations.

In conclusion, it is clear that student interaction is important for achievement in small groups. One of the next steps of research and practice is to explore how students can be encouraged to give each other explanations instead of terminal responses and to be sensitive to other students' need for help. Among the possible strategies are helping students to be aware of the distinction between explanations and terminal responses, training programs for cooperative work, and group compositions (by ability, personality, and demographic characteristics) designed to maximize students' tendencies to help each other, or, more likely, a combination of these strategies.

REFERENCES

Bargh, J. A., & Schul, Y. On the cognitive benefits of teaching. *Journal of Educational Psychology*, 1980, *72*, 593–604.

Bass, B. M., McGehee, C. R., Hawkins, W. C., Young, P. C., & Gebel, A. S. Personality variables related to leaderless group discussion behavior. *Journal of Abnormal and Social Psychology*, 1953, *48*, 120–129.

Bass, B. M., Wurster, C. R., Doll, P. A., & Clair, D. J. Situational and personality factors in leadership among sorority women. *Psychological Monographs: General and Applied*, 1953, *67*, 1–23.

Berkowitz, L., & Levy, B. Pride in group performance and group-task motivation. *Journal of Abnormal and Social Psychology*, 1956, *53*, 300–306.

Crandall, V. C., Katkovsky, W., & Crandall, V. J. Children's beliefs in their own control of reinforcements in intellectual-academic achievement situations. *Child Development*, 1965, *36*, 91–106.

Deutsch, M. An experimental study of the effects of cooperation and competition upon group process. *Human Relations*, 1949, *2*, 199–231.

Deutsch, M. The effects of cooperation and competition upon group process. In D. Cartwright & A. Zander (Eds.), *Group dynamics: Research and theory* (2nd ed.). New York: Row, Peterson, 1960.

DeVries, D. L., & Mescon, I. T. *Teams-Games-Tournament: An effective task and reward structure in the elementary grades* (Rep. No. 189). Center for Social Organization of Schools, The Johns Hopkins University, 1975.

DeVries, D. L., Mescon, I. T., & Shackman, S. L. *Teams-Games-Tournament in the elementary classroom: A replication* (Rep. No. 190). Center for Social Organization of Schools, The Johns Hopkins University, 1975.

Edwards, K. J., & DeVries, D. *The effects of Teams-Games-Tournament and two instructional variations on classroom process, student attitudes, and student achievement* (Rep. No. 172). Center for Social Organization of Schools, The Johns Hopkins University, 1975.

Eysenck, H. J., & Eysenck, S. B. G. *Eysenck Personality Inventory*. San Diego, California: Educational and Industrial Testing Service, 1968.

Grosz, H. J., & Wagoner, R. MMPI and EPPS profiles of high and low verbal interactors in therapy groups. *Psychological Reports*, 1971, *28*, 951–955.

Hammond, L. K., & Goldman, M. Competition and non-competition and its relationship to individual and group productivity. *Sociometry*, 1961, *24*, 46–60.

Hanelin, S. J. *Learning, behavior and attitudes under individual and group contingencies*. Unpublished doctoral dissertation, University of California, Los Angeles, 1978.

Johnson, J. A. Learning in peer tutoring interactions: The influence of status, role change, time-on-task, feedback, and verbalization. (Doctoral dissertation, University of

California, Los Angeles, 1978). *Dissertation Abstracts International*, 1979, *38*, 5469A–5470A. (University Microfilms No. 79-06, 175)

Michaels, J. W. Classroom reward structures and academic performance. *Review of Educational Research*, 1977, *47*, 87–98.

Peterson, P. L. Personal communication, October 19, 1982.

Peterson, P. L., & Janicki, T. C. Individual characteristics and children's learning in large-group and small-group approaches. *Journal of Educational Psychology*, 1979, *71*, 677–687.

Peterson, P. L., Janicki, T. C., & Swing, S. R. Individual characteristics and children's learning in large-group and small-group approaches: Study II. *American Educational Research Journal*, 1981, *18*, 453–473.

Slavin, R. E. *Student learning teams and scores adjusted for past achievement: A summary of field experiments* (Rep. No. 227). Center for Social Organization of Schools, The Johns Hopkins University, 1977.

Slavin, R. E. Effects of student teams and peer tutoring on academic achievement and time on-task. *Journal of Experimental Education*, 1978, *48*, 252–257. (a)

Slavin, R. E. Student teams and achievement divisions. *Journal of Research and Development in Education*, 1978, *12*, 39–49. (b)

Steiner, I. D. *Group process and productivity*. New York: Academic Press, 1972.

Stern, H., & Grosz, H. J. Personality correlates of patient interactions in group psychotherapy. *Psychological Reports*, 1966, *18*, 411–414.

Swing, S. R., & Peterson, P. L. The relationship of student ability and small group interaction to student achievement. *American Educational Research Journal*, 1982, *19*, 259–274.

Webb, N. M. An analysis of group interaction and mathematical errors in heterogeneous ability groups. *British Journal of Educational Psychology*, 1980, *50*, 1–11. (a)

Webb, N. M. Group process: The key to learning in groups. *New Directions for Methodology of Social and Behavioral Science: Issues in Aggregation*, 1980, *6*, 77–87. (b)

Webb, N. M. A process-outcome analysis of learning in group and individual settings. *Educational Psychologist*, 1980, *15*, 69–83. (c)

Webb, N. M. Group composition, group interaction and achievement in cooperative small groups. *Journal of Educational Psychology*, 1982, *74*, 475–484 (a)

Webb, N. M. Peer interaction and learning in cooperative small groups. *Journal of Educational Psychology*, 1982, *74*, 642–655. (b)

Webb, N. M. Sex differences in interaction and achievement in cooperative small groups. *Journal of Educational Psychology*, 1984, *76*, 33–44. (a)

Webb, N. M. Stability of small group interaction and achievement over time. *Journal of Educational Psychology*, 1984, *76*, 211–224. (b)

Webb, N. M., & Cullian, L. K. Group interaction and achievement in small groups: Stability over time. *American Educational Research Journal*, 1983, *29*, 411–424.

Webb, N. M., & Kenderski, C. Student interaction in small group and whole class settings. In P. L. Peterson, L. C. Wilkinson, & M. Hallinan (Eds.), *The social context of instruction: Group organization and group processes*. New York: Academic Press, 1984.

Wittrock, M. C. Learning as a generative process. *Educational Psychologist*, 1974, *11*, 87–95. (a)

Wittrock, M. C. Mathematics learning as a generative process. *Journal for Research in Mathematics Education*, 1974, *5*, 181–196. (b)

III

Cooperative Learning in Mathematics and Science

CLARK WEBB

INTRODUCTION

Several recent analyses of American schooling have concluded that although our society requires cooperative effort for success—whether in the world of work, in recreation, or in the family—our classrooms do little to foster the skills of collaboration toward a common goal (Brandwein, 1981; Goodlad, 1983; Joyce, Hersh, & McKibbing, 1983). Such a finding is disheartening, considering the nature of the problems that we confront in a world of distrust, misunderstanding, and intolerance. The research reported in this section offers an intriguing—if somewhat restricted—glance into a classroom world where cooperation is a normal, rather than an unusual, practice. The cognitive and affective outcomes in such classrooms typically are positive and give us substantial grounds for optimism about an educational future less dedicated to individualistic and competitive practices.

Reports of cooperative approaches in the curriculum areas of mathematics and the sciences are provocative because conventional wisdom predicts more than the usual difficulty in arranging for collaborative efforts in these classes (see Davidson, 1980). Although most math and science classes are more individualistically or competitively oriented than classes in other subjects in American schools, the experiments reported in this section demonstrate that, although no panacea, cooperation in such classrooms is feasible and generally has positive effects.

In the first chapter of this section, Robert E. Slavin reports the results of seven experiments evaluating a cooperative approach called Team-Assisted Individualization, or TAI. These experiments took place in math classes in grades 3–6 in suburban, rural, and inner-city schools. TAI was developed in part in response to the difficulty of using "standard" cooperative methods in heterogeneous mathematics classes.

CLARK WEBB • Department of Curriculum and Instructional Science, Brigham Young University, Provo, Utah 84602.

Progress in math depends on the mastery of hierarchical skills; consequently, group-oriented learning activities that ignore individual pace differences put certain class members at risk. A related factor influencing the development of TAI was the potential for assisting mainstreamed academically handicapped pupils. This potential arises because these learners generally are benefited more by placement in academically, socially, and racially heterogeneous classes than in homogeneous ones, but they are less likely to be placed in such classrooms unless the instructional methods in use can accommodate diverse needs. Therefore, a combination of individualization and cooperation attends more satisfactorily to the needs of handicapped students than an exclusively cooperative method.

The structural features of TAI allow teachers to capitalize on the strengths of both individualized and cooperative approaches to classroom work. The four- or five-member teams provide a setting where pupils can call on each other for assistance as they work through individualized curriculum materials. Team scores and team recognition are included, as is daily opportunity for the teacher to work with small groups of students to introduce major math concepts.

In general, Slavin found in TAI classes (1) an increase in subject-related cognitive understanding; (2) improved acceptance of handicapped students by their nonhandicapped classmates, as well as improved behavior of mainstreamed students; (3) improved intergroup relations (including the interesting finding of increased cross-racial ratings of "smartness" by whites of blacks); (4) improvement of cross-gender relations; and (5) positive teacher and student reactions to TAI.

In the second chapter in this section, Neil Davidson reviews research on four methodologies of classroom cooperation: small-group instruction, Teams-Games-Tournament, Student Teams-Achievement Division, and Team-Assisted Individualization. Davidson's findings come from mathematics classes at the elementary, secondary, and college levels in a number of content areas, for example, calculus, remedial arithmetic, algebra, review of math concepts and manipulations, and geometry. Generally, the material is dealt with at the basic skills level.

Davidson's review concludes that small-group instructional methods in general do not produce significant differences in learning when compared to standard, large-group teaching. However, he emphasizes that teaching that rewards groups while maintaining individual accountability for learning does provide superior learning, at least when the outcomes sought are those generally denominated "basic skills," such as computational skills and simple concept learning and applications.

Three other conclusions of interest are reported. First, the students varied in their preference of one teaching method over another. Sometimes, the experimental procedure was favored, sometimes the control. Second, when the students functioned as teachers—giving explanations, helping other pupils, and so on—they showed higher achievement than did students in the same class who did not engage in such instructional behavior. Third, in common with most of the research findings in cooperative classroom instruction, Davidson found that group or ethnic relations improved under the experimental, cooperation-oriented approaches, as compared to traditional whole-class teaching.

In assessing the utility of a modified form of Aronson's Jigsaw classroom (Aronson, Blaney, Stephan, Sikes, & Snapps, 1978), Reuven Lazarowitz, J. Hugh Baird, Rachel Hertz-Lazarowitz, and James Jenkins report three investigations conducted in secondary science classrooms. The unique characteristic of Jigsaw is that the students are given a portion of the total learning task to master and then teach that segment to the other members of their team. Until all of the pieces of the learning "puzzle" are in place, meaningful learning cannot occur; hence, the name Jigsaw.

The modifiations to Jigsaw implemented by Baird, Lazarowitz, Hertz-Lazarowitz, and Jenkins are principally extensions and enlargements of Aronson's original methodology. Whereas previous Jigsaw research has involved exclusively elementary-classroom implementation, these authors implemented the program in secondary schools. Further, whereas Jigsaw is typically done in units interspersed with other non-Jigsaw learning activities, Modified Jigsaw (MJ) became the exclusive teaching approach for science concepts for at least two weeks (and sometimes longer periods). Also, the complexity of the materials studied by the students was greatly increased. Finally, the role of the teacher in MJ was changed, in that he or she (particularly in Experiments 1 and 2) simply monitored the students' learning experiences, rather than directing them actively.

In general, the authors conclude that MJ in the secondary science classroom produces cognitive learning approximately equal to more traditional methods. They suggest that MJ probably should be used in conjunction with other teaching approaches. Apparently, the students felt the need for more interaction with the teacher and for more individual study time. The authors also suggest, on the basis of their experience with MJ, that cooperative approaches may be less favored by students who succeed well in science classes than by those who do less well. The social skills emphasized in the Jigsaw procedures are seen as relatively unimportant by good science learners. Not surprisingly, this finding varied with the teachers' attitudes about what was important in their classrooms. With regard to the self-perceptions reported by the high-school students, a higher self-esteem index was found for the MJ partici-pants. This finding may reflect, however, as the authors suggest, a short-term "spike" effect rather than an enduring change.

A major point made in this chapter is that learning to be dependent on the teacher may be as achievable a learning outcome as any other, whether it is intended or not. When the students were not used to tak-ing the responsibility for their own learning, they fought the implemen-tation of Modified Jigsaw. This reaction implies that teaching-centered instruction (as contrasted with learning-centered instruction) may re-duce the value of mutual effort, as perceived by students. Such a possi-bility, corroborated in Goodlad (1983, Chapter 3), should not be wel-comed by educators.

In summary, the three papers that follow offer us an introduction to the use of cooperative methods in mathematics and science classrooms, at all levels of schooling, and to how they can enhance certain outcomes, how students react to them, what cautions should be observed regard-ing their use, and how effective they are.

References

Aronson, E., Blaney, N. Stephan, C., Sikes, J., & Snapp, M. *The Jigsaw classroom*. Beverly Hills, Calif.: Sage Publications, 1978.

Brandwein, P. *Memorandum: On renewing schooling and education*. New York: Harcourt Brace Jovanovich, 1981.

Davidson, N. Small-group learning and teaching in mathematics: An introduction for nonmathematicians. In S. Sharan, P. Hare, C. D. Webb, & R. Hertz-Lazarowitz (Eds.), *Cooperation in education*. Provo, Utah: Brigham Young University Press, 1980.

Goodlad, J. *A place called school*. New York: McGraw-Hill, 1983.

Joyce, B., Hersh, R., & McKibbin, M. *The structure of school improvement*, New York: Longman, 1983.

7

Team-Assisted Individualization

Combining Cooperative Learning and Individualized Instruction in Mathematics

ROBERT E. SLAVIN

The past decade has seen an important and dramatic change in research on cooperative incentive and task structures (see Slavin, 1983a), in which individuals work in small groups and are rewarded based on the group's performance. Before the early 1970s, this research took place primarily in the social psychological laboratory, or in short-term field experiments in locations set up to resemble the laboratory. The systematic use of instructional methods involving cooperation among students was rarely seen, and when it did occur, the methods used tended to be drawn directly from the laboratory (see, for example, Johnson & Johnson, 1974; Slavin, 1977).

In the early 1970s, there began to appear instructional methods incorporating principles of cooperation among students, but designed specifically to meet the practical requirements of instruction in elementary and secondary classrooms. These were no longer the "pure" cooperative strategies evaluated in the laboratory but, to one degree or another, included other incentive and task structures and various accommodations to the realities of the classroom. For example, Johnson and Johnson's (1975) "Learning Together" model specifically incorporates competitive and individualistic incentive structures along with cooperative ones, and includes group process and group evaluation procedures designed for use in classes expected to be working cooperatively for some time. Teams-Games-Tournament, or TGT (DeVries & Slavin, 1978), combines within-team cooperation with competition between teams and between individual representatives of different teams. Student Teams-Achievement Divisions, or STAD (Slavin,

ROBERT E. SLAVIN • Center for Social Organization of Schools, Johns Hopkins University, Baltimore, Maryland 21218. The research summarized here was supported by grants from the National Institute of Education (No. NIE-G-80-0113) and from the Office of Special Education (No. G-00-80-1494), Department of Education. The opinions expressed are those of the author and do not represent Department of Education policy.

1978b), also uses within-team cooperation and between-team competition but replaces the individual competition of TGT with individual quizzes. STAD also uses an individualistic reward-for-improvement scoring system. Jigsaw teaching (Aronson, 1978) combines within-group cooperation with an individualistic grading system, and both Jigsaw and Sharan and Sharan's (1976) Group-Investigation model give students individual tasks and responsibilities within their cooperative groups.

Most of these "mixed" strategies are designed to remedy problems inherent in "pure" cooperation. For example, one problem characteristic of cooperative goals is the problem of individual accountability (see Slavin, 1983b). If individuals' contributions to their group's product are difficult to quantify, or if all group members' efforts are not required to complete the group task, then some group members may feel that, as others will do most of the work, their own active participation or learning efforts are unnecessary. STAD and TGT avoid this problem by the use of team scores composed of the sum of individual quiz scores (STAD) or scores from individual competitions with members of other teams (TGT). Jigsaw and Group-Investigation solve the problem by giving group members individual responsibility for subtasks, so that each group member's participation is essential. A recent review of cooperative learning research (Slavin, 1983b) concluded that cooperative learning methods that use such techniques for increasing individual accountability have been much more successful in increasing student achievement than those that do not.

Some of the features of cooperative learning methods other than cooperation itself are directed not at solving the problems inherent in cooperation, but at solving other general problems of instruction. For example, STAD uses a reward-for-improvement system (see Slavin, 1980) designed to give all students a chance to be rewarded if and only if they do better than they have done in the past. The deleterious effects on motivation of evaluation/incentive systems, in which some individuals have little chance of success, whereas others find success easy, have been known for some time (see Atkinson, 1958), and traditional grading systems have been criticized on the basis that they create just such an inappropriate motivational system (e.g., Slavin, 1978a).

The Problem of Student Heterogeneity

This paper describes research on a new cooperative learning method designed to confront one of the most difficult and long-standing problems inherent in all education involving fewer teachers than students: the problem of student heterogeneity in level of preparation for or ability in the subject being taught. Carroll (1963) and later Bloom (1976) pointed out that because students differ in their rates of learning, instruction at a single pace is bound to leave some students behind and to hold back students who could progress at a much more rapid rate. In an instructional method in which there is a single pace of instruction, we may mistakenly conclude that some students are "unteachable," when, in fact, virtually all students are teachable if the rate and the level of instruction are appropriate to their needs (Bloom, 1976).

The problem of student heterogeneity is becoming even more important because of three trends. First, reductions in school populations often mean that tracking can no longer be as effective in creating homogeneous groups; a school with only one or two fourth grades can hardly obtain homogeneous class groups by this means. Second, tracking itself is often being abolished, especially at the elementary- and junior-high-school level. Tracking has not generally been found to have positive effects on student achievement (e.g., Esposito, 1973), and in some desegregated schools, tracking may resegregate the school. Finally, the mainstreaming of academically handicapped students in academic classes has increased the heterogeneity of these classes. In general, heterogeneous placements are better both academically and socially for academically handicapped students (see Madden and Slavin, 1983b), and racially heterogeneous schools are better than homogeneous ones for the achievement of black students (see Crain & Mahard, 1978). However, there is no denying that the implementation of these policies, regardless of their general positive effects, creates new instructional problems revolving around the issue of teaching heterogeneous groups.

Heterogeneity is a particular problem in mathematics instruction, where, because each skill builds on previously taught skills, students who do not keep up with the class pace may get hopelessly behind because they missed out on prerequisite skills. For example, a student who did not master one-digit division is hardly likely to be able to learn two-digit division. To meet the needs of students who have difficulty with mathematics, teachers typically adopt a pace of instruction much slower than that which their more able students could maintain.

A COOPERATIVE LEARNING SOLUTION

Cooperative learning methods, as they are typically implemented, are at least a partial solution to the problems of achievement heterogeneity. Students who have trouble keeping up with the class pace may be helped by group mates who do understand the lessons. High achievers may gain from the opportunity to teach others, as has been repeatedly found in studies of peer tutoring (Devin-Sheehan, Feldman, & Allen, 1976). Cooperative learning methods have been found to be more successful than traditional methods in increasing student achievement in racially or ethnically heterogeneous classes (e.g., Edwards, DeVries, & Snyder, 1972; Lucker, Rosenfield, Sikes, & Aronson, 1976; Slavin & Oickle, 1981; Ziegler, 1981) and in classes containing academically handicapped and nonhandicapped students (Madden & Slavin, 1983a). The positive effects of cooperative learning methods on relationships across racial and ethnic-group lines (Slavin & Hansell, 1983) and between academically handicapped and nonhandicapped students (Madden & Slavin, 1983a; Johnson & Johnson, 1982) have also been well documented.

However, there may be limits on the ability of cooperative learning methods to confront problems of heterogeneity. Existing cooperative learning methods are group-paced. When very wide disparities in student achievement levels exist, it is asking a great deal to expect the more able students to bring the less able ones up to the level of the rest of the class. Further, cooperative learning methods are typically evaluated in classes that have already been subjected to some sort of tracking. If tracking is to be abandoned, or if the mainstreaming of academically handicapped students is to be extended on a broad scale to academic subjects such as mathematics, then methods that confront the problem of heterogeneity more directly will have to be developed.

TEAM-ASSISTED INDIVIDUALIZATION

This chapter describes a program of research and development on a method that combines cooperative learning and individualized instruction for mathematics instruction. This program is called *Team-Assisted Individualization,* or TAI.

TAI was developed for several reasons. First, it was hoped that TAI would provide a means of combining the motivational power of cooperative incentives with an individualized instructional program capable of giving all students materials appropriate to their level of skill in mathematics and of allowing them to proceed through these materials at their own rates. It was felt that such a program would motivate students to move more rapidly in mathematics than in traditional classes or in group-paced cooperative learning programs because low-achieving students would gain the prerequisite skills for each successive unit and would not be left behind by the pace of instruction, while average- and high-achieving students could move through mathematics at a rate limited only by their ability to understand mathematical concepts.

Second, TAI was developed as a means of producing the well-documented social effects characteristic of cooperative learning (Slavin, 1983a) while meeting diverse needs. The principal concern here was with mainstreaming. It was felt that the mainstreaming of academically handicapped students in mathematics was limited by a feeling on the part of regular-class teachers that they were unprepared to accommodate the instructional needs of these students (see Gickling & Theobald, 1975). Madden and Slavin (1983b) have argued that some form of structured individualization may be needed in the mainstreamed classroom to provide the teacher with a methodology for meeting diverse needs. However, studies of attitudes toward academically handicapped students consistently find that these students are not well accepted by their nonhandicapped classmates (see Gottlieb & Leyser, 1981). Because cooperative learning methods have had positive effects on social relations of all kinds, and specifically on relationships between handicapped and nonhandicapped students (Ballard, Corman, Gottlieb, & Kaufman, 1977; Cooper, Johnson, Johnson, & Wilderson, 1980; Johnson & Johnson, 1982; Madden & Slavin, 1983a), it was felt that the best possible mathematics program for the mainstreamed classroom, or indeed for any classroom containing a heterogeneous group of students, would be one that combined cooperative learning with individualized instruction.

Finally, TAI was developed to solve many of the problems of programmed instruction. In the 1960s, programmed instruction and related methods were expected to revolutionize instruction, especially in mathematics. However, reviews of the research on programmed instruction methods in mathematics have consistently concluded that these methods are no more effective than traditional instruction (e.g., Miller, 1976; Schoen, 1976). Several problems inherent in programmed instruction have been cited as contributing to these disappointing findings (see Kepler & Randall, 1977; Schoen, 1976). Among these are too much time spent on management rather than teaching, too little incentive for students to progress rapidly through the programmed materials, and an excessive reliance on written instruction rather than instruction from a teacher. It was felt that by combining programmed instruction with cooperative learning and turning most of the management functions (e.g., scoring answers, locating and filing materials, keeping records, and assigning new work) over to the students themselves, these problems could be solved. If the students could handle most of the checking and management, the teacher would be free to teach individuals and small, homogeneous teaching groups. Students working in learning teams toward a cooperative goal could help one another study, could provide instant feedback to one another, and could encourage one another to proceed rapidly and accurately through the materials.

PRINCIPAL FEATURES OF TAI

The principal features of the TAI program are described below.

TEAMS

Students are assigned to four- to five-member teams. Each team consists of a mix of high, average, and low achievers, boys and girls, and students of any ethnic groups in the class, represented in the proportion that they make up of the entire class. Students identified as receiving resource help for a learning problem are also evenly distributed among the teams. Every four weeks, students are reassigned to new teams.

PLACEMENT TEST

Students are pretested at the beginning of the project on mathematics operations. They are placed at the appropriate point in the individualized program based on their performance on the placement test.

CURRICULUM MATERIALS

For most of their mathematics instruction, students work on individualized curriculum materials covering addition, subtraction, multiplication, division, numeration, decimals, fractions, word problems, and algebra. These materials have the following subparts:

- An instruction sheet explaining the skill to be mastered and giving a step-by-step method of solving the problems
- Several skill sheets, each consisting of 20 problems. Each skill sheet introduces a subskill that leads to a final mastery of the entire skill.
- A checkout, which consists of two parallel sets of 10 items
- A final test
- Answer sheets for the skill sheets, the checkouts, and the final tests

Team Study Method

Following the placement test, the students are given a starting place in the individualized mathematics units. They work on their units in their teams, using the following steps:

1. The students form into pairs or triads within their teams. They locate the unit that they are working on and bring it to the team area. Each unit consists of the instruction sheet, the skill sheets, and the checkouts stapled together, as well as the skill sheet answer sheets and the checkout answer sheets stapled together.

2. In pairs, the students exchange answer sheets with their partners. In triads, they give their answer sheets to the student on their left.

3. Each student reads his or her instruction sheet, asking teammates or the teacher for help if necessary. Then, the students begin with the first skill sheet in their units.

4. Each student works the first four problems on his or her own skill sheet and then has his or her partner check the answers against the answer sheet. If all four are correct, the student may go on to the next skill sheet. If any are wrong, the student must try the next four problems, and so on, until he or she gets one block of four problems correct. If they run into difficulties at this stage, the students are encouraged to ask for help within their teams before asking the teacher for help.

5. When a student gets four in a row on the last skill sheet, he or she takes Checkout A, a 10-item quiz that resembles the last skill sheet. On the checkout, the students work alone until they are finished. A teammate scores the checkout. If the student gets 8 or more of the 10 problems correct, the teammate signs the checkout to indicate that the student is certified by the team to take the final test. If the student does *not* get 8 correct, the teacher is called in to explain any problems that the student is having. The teacher might ask the student to work again on certain skill sheet items. The student then takes Checkout B, a second 10-item test comparable in content and difficulty to Checkout A. Otherwise, the students skip Checkout B and go straight to the final test. No student may take the final test until he or she has been passed by a teammate on a checkout.

6. When a student has "checked out," he or she takes the checkout to a student monitor from a different team to get the appropriate final test. The student then completes the final test, and the monitor scores it. Three different students serve as monitors each day.

Team Scores and Team Recognition

At the end of each week, the teacher computes a team score. This score is based on the average number of units covered by each team member and the accuracy of the final tests. Criteria are established for team performance. A high criterion is set for a team to be a "superteam," a moderate criterion is established for a team to be a "greatteam," and a minimum criterion is set for a team to be a "goodteam." The teams meeting the "superteam" and "greatteam" criteria receive attractive certificates.

TEACHING GROUPS

Every day, the teacher works for 5–15 minutes with small groups of students who are at about the same point in the curriculum. The purpose of these sessions is to introduce major concepts to the students. In general, the students have concepts introduced to them in the teaching groups before they work on them in their individualized units. While the teacher works with a teaching group, the other students continue to work in their teams on their individualized units.

HOMEWORK

Every day except Friday, the students are given brief homework assignments based on the teaching group they are in.

FACTS TESTS

Twice each week, the students are given three-minute facts tests (usually multiplication or division facts). The students are given fact sheets to study at home to prepare for these tests.

GROUP-PACED UNITS

Every fourth week, the teacher stops the individualized program and teaches a lesson to the entire class covering such skills as geometry, measurement, and sets (which are not included in the individualized units).

RESEARCH ON TAI

Seven field experiments have been conducted to evaluate TAI. In each of these, classes using TAI were compared to similar, untreated control classes on a variety of dependent measures. In Experiment 1 (Slavin, Leavey, & Madden, 1984; Slavin, Madden, & Leavey, 1984), the full TAI program was also compared to a program that included all the components of TAI except the teams. Experiment 1 was conducted as an initial evaluation of the effects of TAI on student achievement, attitudes, and behaviors, and on relationships between mainstreamed academically handicapped students and their nonhandicapped classmates. Experiment 2 (Slavin, Leavey, & Madden, 1984) was a replication of Experiment 1, involving a comparison between the full TAI program and untreated control classes on student achievement, attitudes, and behaviors. Experiments 1 and 2 were relatively brief (10 and 8 weeks, respectively). Experiment 3 (Slavin, Leavey, & Madden, in press) was conducted to evaluate the achievement effects of TAI on academically handicapped and nonhandicapped students in a much longer implementation (24 weeks). Experiment 4 (Oishi, Slavin, & Madden, 1983) and Experiment 5 (Oishi, 1983) were conducted both to attempt to replicate the TAI findings in Baltimore city schools (earlier studies had taken place in suburban schools) and to investigate the effects of TAI on relationships between black and white students and between boys and girls. Finally, Experiment 6 and Experiment 7 (Slavin & Karweit, in press-b) compared TAI to Good, Grouws, and Ebmeier's Missouri Mathematics Effectiveness Program (MMEP—1983), considered the best of whole-class instruction, and to an ability-grouped version of the MMEP.

The designs, methods, and results of the seven TAI studies are summarized in Table 1 and are described in detail in the following sections.

EXPERIMENT 1

Experiment 1 (Slavin, Leavey, & Madden, 1984; Slavin, Madden, & Leavey, 1984) was the first full-scale evaluation of TAI. It was conducted to evaluate the effects of TAI on the achievement, the attitudes, and the behaviors of students in general, and on the behavior and the peer acceptance of mainstreamed academically handicapped students.

SUBJECTS AND DESIGN

The subjects in Experiment 1 were 504 students in Grades 3, 4, and 5 in a middle-class suburban Maryland school district. Of these students, 80% were white, 15% were black, and 5% were Asian-American. Also, 6% of the students were receiving special-education services for a serious learning problem at least one hour per day, and an additional 17% of the students were receiving other educational services, such as special reading or speech instruction. The students were in 18 classes in six schools. The schools were randomly assigned to one of three conditions: Team-

TABLE 1. Summary of Research on Team-Assisted Individualization

Study and major reports	Setting and design characteristics					Measures and results[a]		
	No. of students	Grade levels	Duration (weeks)	Kinds of schools	Experimental design	Mathematics achievement	Attitudes	Behavior ratings
Experiment 1: Full sample (Slavin, Leavey, & Madden, 1984)	506	3–5	8	Suburban	Randomly assigned schools	+ CTBS Computations	+ Liking of math class Self-concept in math	+ Classroom behavior + Self-confidence + Friendships + Neg. Peer Behavior
Experiment 1: Academically handicapped students (Slavin, Madden, & Leavey, 1984)	117	3–5	8	Suburban	Randomly assigned schools	0 CTBS Computations	0 Liking of math class Self-concept in math "Best friend" choices "Rejection" choices	(+) Classroom Behavior 0 Self-confidence + Friendships + Neg. Peer Behavior
Experiment 2 (Slavin, Leavey, & Madden, 1984)	320	4–6	10	Suburban	Matched schools	+ CTBS Computations	+ Liking of math class Self-concept in math	0 Classroom Behavior + Self-confidence + Friendships 0 Neg. Peer Behavior
Experiment 3: Full sample (Slavin, Madden, & Leavey, in press)	1,371	3–5	24	Suburban	Matched schools	+ CTBS Computations + CTBS Concepts & Applications		

Experiment	N	Grades	Setting	Design	Measure	Effect[a]
Experiment 3: Academically handicapped students (Slavin, Madden, & Leavey, in press)	113	3–5	Suburban	Matched schools	CTBS Computations	+
					CTBS Concepts & Applications	+
Experiment 4 (Oishi, Slavin, & Madden, 1983)	160	4–6	Urban	Randomly assigned classes	CAT Computations	0
					CAT Concepts & Applications	0
					Cross-race:	
					Friends	+
					Rejects	+
					Nice	0
					Not nice	+
					Smart	0
					Not smart	(+)
Experiment 5 (Oishi, 1983)	120	4–6	Urban	Randomly assigned classes	Cross-Race:	
					Friends	0
					Playmates	+
					Nice	0
					Not nice	+
					Smart	+
					Not smart	0
Experiment 6 (Slavin & Karweit, in press b)	354	4–6	Urban	Randomly assigned classes	CTBS Computations	+
					CTBS Concepts & Applications	+
					Liking of math class	+
					Self-concept in math	0
Experiment 7 (Slavin & Karweit, in press b)	480	3–5	Rural	Randomly assigned classes	CTBS Computations	+
					CTBS Concepts & Applications	0
					Liking of math class	+
					Self-concept in math	0

[a] + = TAI students scores significantly higher than control students on the indicated measure, $p < .05$ or better.
(+) = Same as above, but $p < .10$.

Assisted Individualization (TAI), individualized instruction (II) without student teams, or control. These treatments are described below. One third, fourth, and fifth grade class was then selected to participate in the study in each school. The three treatments were implemented for eight weeks in Spring 1981.

TREATMENTS

TEAM-ASSISTED INDIVIDUALIZATION (TAI).   TAI was implemented as described above.

INDIVIDUALIZED INSTRUCTION (II).   The II group used the same curriculum materials and procedures as the TAI group with the following exceptions:
1. The students worked individually, not in teams. They checked their own answer sheets for all skill sheets and checkouts. The criteria for going on (i.e., 4 correct for skill sheets and 8 out of 10 for checkouts) were the same as for TAI.
2. The students did not receive team scores or certificates.

In all other respects, including curriculum organization, student monitors, teaching groups, and record keeping, the II treatment was identical to TAI.

CONTROL.   The control group used traditional methods for teaching mathematics, which consisted in every case of traditional texts and group-paced instruction, supplemented by small homogeneous teacher-directed math groups.

MEASURES

MATHEMATICS ACHIEVEMENT.   The Mathematics Computations subscale of the Comprehensive Test of Basic Skills (CTBS), Level 2, Form S, was administered as a pre- and posttest of student mathematics achievement. The CTBS (rather than a curriculum-specific test) was used to guarantee that the experimental and control classes would have equal opportunities to register their learning on the test. No efforts were made to design the curriculum materials to correspond to the CTBS items.

ATTITUDES.   Two eight-item attitude scales were given as pre- and posttests. The scales were Liking of Math Class (e.g., "This math class is the best part of my school day") and Self-Concept in Math (e.g., "I'm proud of my math work in this class"; "I worry a lot when I have to take a math test"). For each item, the students marked either "YES!", "yes," "no," or "NO!" The scores of the negatively scored items were reversed, so that high-scale scores indicated more positive attitudes.

BEHAVIOR RATINGS.   The teachers rated a sample of their students at pre- and posttesting on the School Social Behavior Rating Scale, or SSBRS. The subsamples consisted of all students receiving some form of special service for a learning problem (e.g., reading or math resource, speech, or special education), plus a random selection of six other students. The SSBRS consists of four scales designed to elicit teacher ratings of student behavioral and interpersonal problems. Students receiving special services were oversampled because they were seen as being the most likely to have behavioral and interpersonal problems that might be remedied by a cooperative-individualized treatment (see Slavin, Madden, & Leavey, 1984). The four scales were Classroom Behavior (e.g., "Does not attend to work"); Self-Confidence (e.g., "Becomes easily upset by failures"); Friendships (e.g., "Has few or no friends"); and Negative Peer Behavior (e.g., "Fights with other students"). There were six items on the Negative Peer Behavior Scale, and eight in the other three scales. A factor analysis using varimax rotation produced factor loadings consistent with the *a priori* scales.

PEER RATING.   A peer-rating form was given at pre- and posttesting to assess the acceptance and the rejection of mainstreamed students. Each student was given a class list and was asked to mark each classmate as "a best friend" or "okay." Two measures were derived from this form. The first was the number of nominations as "best friend" received by mainstreamed students. The second was the number of times mainstreamed students were listed neither as "best friends" nor as "okay," taken to be an indication of rejection. Only within-sex choices for boys were analyzed, as there were very few mainstreamed girls in the sample.

EXPERIMENT 1: RESULTS

The data were analyzed by means of multiple regressions, where for each dependent variable (posttest), the R^2 for a full model including pretest, grade, and treatment was tested against the R^2 for prestest and grade.

FULL SAMPLE

The Comprehensive Test of Basic Skills (CTBS) for all students indicated a marginally significant ($p < .07$) overall treatment effect, controlling for pretest and grade. The TAI group gained significantly more in achievement than the control group and the II group gained marginally ($p < .09$) more than the control group. However, there were no significant differences between the TAI and the II groups.

The results on the Liking of Math scale indicated a significant overall treatment effect, as well as significant differences between TAI and control and between II and control, with both experimental groups scoring higher than the control group, when pretest and grade were controlled for. There were no differences between TAI and II. Overall treatment effects were also found for Self-Concept in Math. TAI significantly exceeded control on this variable, and II marginally ($p < .08$) exceeded the control group.

Statistically significant overall treatment effects beyond the .001 level were found for all four behavioral rating scales. For Class Behavior, TAI students were rated as having significantly fewer problems, when pretest and grade were controlled for, than either the control students or the II students, but there were no differences between II and control. On Self-Confidence, the control group was rated as having more problems than either the TAI students or the II students. The TAI group had fewer problems reported than the II group. The control classes were also scored as having more friendship problems than either the TAI classes or the II classes, but there were no differences between TAI and II. The same pattern of effects was seen for ratings of Negative Peer Behavior: more problems were reported in the control classes than in the TAI or the II classes, but there were no differences between TAI and II.

Analyses of covariance for the academically handicapped subsample (Slavin, Madden, & Leavey, 1984) indicated that the TAI students exceeded the control students on both sociometric measures (i.e., they gained more "best friends" nominations and were less often rejected). The TAI students were also reported to have fewer problems than the control students on all four behavior-rating scales and were higher on the Liking of Math scale. Interestingly, the same pattern of results was found for the comparison of II and control treatments, with the exception of the Classroom Behavior scale, on which there were no differences. The TAI students exceeded the II students only on the Classroom Behavior and the Self-Confidence ratings, and on the Self-Concept in Math questionnaire scale.

Experiment 2

Experiment 2 (Slavin, Leavey, & Madden, 1984) was conducted primarily as a replication of the TAI–control comparison studied in Experiment 1.

Experiment 2: Methods

SUBJECTS AND DESIGN

The subjects in Experiment 2 were 375 students in Grades 4, 5, and 6 in a suburban Maryland school district different from the one involved in Experiment 1. Of these students, 55% were white, 43% were black, and 2% were Asian. Also, 4% of the students were receiving special-education services for a serious learning problem at least one hour per day, and an additional 23% of the students were receiving other special educational services, such as special reading or speech instruction. Four schools were involved in the study: Two TAI schools were matched with two control schools. One TAI and one control school were primarily middle- to lower-class in student population; one TAI and one control school were primarily lower-class. A total of 10 TAI and 6 control classes participated in the study.

TREATMENTS

Experiment 2 compared TAI to control methods (as described for Experiment 1) for 10 weeks in Spring 1981.

MEASURES

The achievement, attitude, and behavioral rating measures were the same as in Experiment 1.

Experiment 2: Results

The data were analyzed exactly as in Experiment 1.

The results for the CTBS closely mirror the comparison of TAI and control in Experiment 1. The TAI students scored significantly higher than the control students, when pretest and grade were controlled for. However, there were no significant differences on the Liking of Math or Self-Concept in Math scales. Controlling for pretests and grade, the TAI teachers reported significantly fewer problems than the control teachers with regard to Self-Confidence and Friendships, but there were no differences seen on Classroom Behavior or Negative Peer Behavior.

Thus, although the achievement results of Experiment 2 confirm the comparison of TAI and control in Experiment 1, the strong attitude effects were not replicated, and the behavioral rating results of Experiment 1 were replicated only for Self-Confidence and Friendship Behaviors.

Experiment 3

Experiment 3 (Slavin, Madden, & Leavey, in press) was conducted to assess the achievement effects of TAI over a longer period than in Experiments 1 and 2, to rule out the possibility that the positive effects found in the earlier experiments were due to short-lasting Hawthorne effects, and to establish the usefulness of TAI as the primary means of delivering mathematics instruction. Experiment 3 was also conducted to further investigate the achievement effects of TAI for academically handicapped students, and to study the effects of TAI on the Mathematics Concepts and Applications scale of the CTBS as well as on the Mathematics Computations scale used in the earlier studies.

Experiment 3: Methods

subjects and design

The subjects in Experiment 3 were 1,371 students in Grades 3, 4, and 5 in the same middle-class suburban school district that participated in Experiment 1. Students in 31 classes in four schools were assigned to use TAI, and students in 30 classes in three similar schools, matched on grade level, district-administered California Achievement Test scores, and type of neighborhood, served as the control group. Of these students, 113 (8%) were classified by the school district as being in need of special education for a serious learning problem at least one hour per day. The treatments were administered over a 24-week period from December 1981 to May 1982.

measures

The only measures used were the Mathematics Computations and the Mathematics Concepts and Applications scales of the CTBS. Students in Grades 3–4 took Level 2, Form S, of the CTBS, and those in Grade 5 took Level H, Form U. Scores from the corresponding scales of the California Achievement Test (CAT), given by the district in the fall of the third and the fifth grades, served as covariates to adjust for any initial differences in achievement level (none were statistically significant) and to increase statistical power. Thus, for the third- and the fifth-graders, the CAT scores were recent, but for the fourth-graders, the fall third-grade scores had to be used.

Experiment 3: Results

To deal with the problem of different pre- and posttests for different parts of the sample, all test scores were changed to grade equivalents.

Analyses of covariance, using CAT scores as covariates for the respective CTBS scores, were then computed. Overall, the TAI students achieved significantly more than the control students on both CTBS subscales, when CAT scores were controlled for. Statistically significant differences in the same direction were found for handicapped as well as nonhandicapped students. The effects of TAI were quite large for an intervention lasting less than a school year, especially for the academically handicapped students, who exceeded their control counterparts by .52 grade equivalents in Computations and .47 grade equivalents in Concepts and Applications. For nonhandicapped students, the differences were .42 and .23 grade equivalents, respectively. However, there were no handicap-by-treatment interactions on either measure.

Experiment 4

Experiment 4 (Oishi et al. 1983) was conducted primarily to assess the effects of TAI on relationships between black and white students. Earlier research on cooperative learning has clearly established that cooperative learning methods have positive effects on sociometric measures of cross-racial friendship and acceptance (see, for example, Slavin, 1983a; Slavin & Hansell, 1983). However, TAI is different from group-paced cooperative learning methods in ways that may be important in intergroup relations. In TAI, students primarily engage in structured interaction (checking) within their teams, in contrast to the less structured group study characteristic of such group-paced cooperative-learning methods as STAD. Further, the use of individualized materials in TAI could make ability differences more salient, perhaps exacerbating majority–minority prejudices. On the other hand, the reward-for-progress aspect of the individualized program might focus students on one another's efforts and cooperativeness, perhaps reducing majority–minority prejudices.

Experiment 4 also assessed cross-sex relationships as a possible outcome of TAI and examined the achievement effects of the program in a Baltimore city school (earlier implementations had been in suburban settings).

Experiment 4: Methods

Subjects and Design

The subjects in Experiment 4 were 160 fourth-, fifth-, and sixth-grade students in seven classes in a Baltimore city magnet school that serves a highly diverse population primarily composed of middle-class white and black students and lower-class black students. Overall, 106 students

(66%) were black, and 54 (34%) were white. The classes were randomly assigned to treatments counterbalancing grade levels and student ability levels. The treatments were implemented for 16 weeks in the spring semester of 1982.

MEASURES

CROSS-RACE AND CROSS-SEX RELATIONS. Two sociometric instruments and two rating scales were used at pre- and posttests to derive measures of cross-race and cross-sex relationships. The sociometric questions were "Who are your friends in this class?" (in-class friendships) and "Who would you rather *not* sit at a table with?" (rejections). The number of choices for each criterion from students of another race (cross-race) or sex (cross-sex) were divided by the number of cross-race or cross-sex choices possible. Scales were presented in the form of class rosters. Students were asked to rate each classmate on two scales: "How *smart* is this student?" ("very smart, a little smart, not at all smart") and "How *nice* is this student?" ("very nice, a little nice, not at all nice"). The variables computed from these scales were the number of very nice, not nice, very smart, and not smart ratings received from classmates of another race, or sex, divided by the number of choices possible.

ACHIEVEMENT. The achievement measures were the Mathematics Computations and Concepts and Applications scales of the California Achievement Test (CAT), given in fall and spring as part of the Baltimore city public schools' regular testing program.

EXPERIMENT 4: RESULTS

The data were analyzed by means of analyses of covariance, with pretests as covariates for their respective pretests. The students in the TAI classes significantly exceeded the control students (when pretests were controlled for) on cross-race in-class friendships. The control students received more cross-race rejection choices and ratings as "not nice" than did the TAI students; the effects of TAI on reducing negative choices were quite strong. There was a marginally significant effect ($p < .10$) on the "not smart" measure, indicating more cross-race "not smart" choices in the control group than in the TAI group, when pretest was controlled for. The only statistically significant effect on cross-sex ratings was a strong effect of TAI on "not nice" ratings, on which the TAI students declined and the control students increased over the course of the study. However, a marginally significant ($p < .10$) effect in the same direction was found for in-class rejections across sex lines. There were no treatment effects on student achievement. The implementation of TAI was judged to be quite poor in most classes; for example, none of the TAI teachers used teaching groups, or assigned homework or gave facts tests regularly.

Experiment 5

Experiment 5 (Oishi, 1983) was conducted to replicate and extend the findings of Experiment 4 regarding cross-race and cross-sex relationships. In the school that participated in Experiment 4, the students came from all over Baltimore and thus had little opportunity for out-of-school contacts. One of the purposes of Experiment 5 was to investigate the effects of TAI on out-of-school cross-racial friendships. The school used was in a lower-class, inner-city Baltimore neighborhood in which blacks and whites had lived in close proximity (though rarely on the same blocks) for generations. Students in the school could, at least in theory, easily visit one another's houses and play together after school.

Experiment 5 was also initially intended to extend the research on TAI and achievement by attempting to improve implementation in a Baltimore city school. However, after the assignment of classes to an experimental design counterbalanced on grade level and average achievement, one teacher (and her one experimental and one control class) dropped out of the study, destroying the counterbalancing, and leaving the control group significantly older and higher in achievement than the experimental group. For this reason, achievement analyses were not attempted.

Experiment 5: Methods

SUBJECTS AND DESIGN

As noted above, the classes involved in Experiment 5 were randomly assigned to treatments so that each teacher taught one TAI and one control class. Initially, the classes were counterbalanced on mean class achievement level, but the dropping out of one teacher left the TAI and control groups unequal. The remaining sample consisted of 119 students in Grades 4, 5, and 6 in an inner-city Baltimore elementary school. In the TAI classes, 24% of the students were black and 42% were male compared to 28% blacks and 56% males in the control classes. The average California Achievement Test grade-equivalent scores were 4.53 for TAI group and 5.08 for the control group.

MEASURES

CROSS-RACE AND CROSS-SEX RELATIONS. The sociometric and ratings scales listed in Experiment 4 were also used in Experiment 5, except that the "rejections" sociometric measure was not used. The students in Experiment 5 were also given one additional sociometric question: "Who in this school do you usually play with at lunch and recess?" They were also individually interviewed to determine with whom they played at home and were asked to list whom they would invite to their next birthday party. As in Experiment 4, all cross-race and cross-sex measures, except for the lunch/recess and interview measures, were divided by the number of other-race or other-sex students in the class, respectively.

EXPERIMENT 5: RESULTS

The data were analyzed as in Experiment 4. Analyses of covariance with pretests were used as covariates for their respective posttests. TAI students significantly exceeded control students in cross-race ratings as "very smart" and in lunch/recess playmates named (when pretests were controlled for), and the TAI students named significantly fewer classmates of another race as "not nice." Parallel analyses for cross-sex ratings indicated fewer cross-sex ratings as "not smart" and "not nice" in the TAI classes, as well as more cross-sex choices as lunch/recess playmates. The TAI students also declined in cross-sex "very nice" ratings marginally less ($p < .10$) than did the control students.

EXPERIMENT 6 AND EXPERIMENT 7

The principal purpose of Experiments 6 and 7 (Slavin & Karweit, in press b) was to compare the achievement effects of TAI to those of treatments representing (at least in theory) the best of whole-class instruction and the best of ability-grouped instruction. Previous studies had compared TAI to untreated control groups, leaving open the possibility that the positive effects of the program were due to Hawthorne effects, or that any well-structured program would be superior to standard practice.

The whole-class instructional method chosen was Good and Grouws's Missouri Mathematics Effectiveness Program (MMEP), a program that has been found in several field experiments to increase student achievement more than traditional methods (Good et al., 1983). The MMEP is designed to put into practice the main principles of direct instruction drawn from many process–product studies that compared the teaching practices of more and less effective teachers (see Brophy, 1979). The most important features of the Missouri Mathematics Effectiveness Program include a high ratio of direct instruction to seatwork, controlled practice before seatwork, frequent assessment, rapid pace, and several class-management strategies directed at increasing time on task. The MMEP program specifies whole-class instruction with few provisions for individual differences.

For ability-grouped instruction, a new program based on the MMEP was developed. This program was called *Ability-Grouped Active Teaching* (AGAT) (Slavin & Karweit, in press b). In AGAT, approximately 60% of the students in each class were assigned to a high-ability group, and 40% to a low-ability group. While the teacher taught one group, the other worked on seatwork activities. Several class-management strategies were used to help ensure smooth transitions between groups and high time on task in the group not working with the teacher. The teachers were encouraged to differentiate the pace and the materials in the two groups to meet their different needs. Otherwise, the AGAT program employed most of the principles embodied in the MMEP, including a high ratio of direct instruction to seatwork, rapid pace, and frequent assessment.

Experiments 6 and 7 were conducted at the same time and used the same designs, procedures, and measures, with one principal exception: Experiment 6 compared TAI, AGAT, and MMEP, but no untreated control group was used. Experiment 7 did include an untreated control group. Also, Experiment 6 took place in an urban school district under strict court orders to maintain racially balanced, heterogeneous classrooms, one of four districts that encompass Wilmington, Delaware, and its suburbs. Experiment 7 took place in a rural Maryland town and its largely agricultural environs. The schools in Experiment 7 represented a broad range of socioeconomic levels, but there was relatively little heterogeneity within the schools and, as the classes were tracked, even less within the classes. Thus, the two districts differed on an attribute likely to be of consequence in the interventions evaluated in these studies: classroom heterogeneity.

EXPERIMENT 6: METHODS

SUBJECTS AND DESIGN

The subjects in Experiment 6 were 354 students in 16 Grade 4–6 classes in the Wilmington, Delaware, public school district discussed above. Approximately 71% of the students were white, 26% were black, and 3% were Asian-American. The classes and their teachers were randomly assigned to experimental treatments, stratifying on grade level. The treatments were in effect for 18 weeks in Spring 1983.

TREATMENTS

TEAM-ASSISTED INDIVIDUALIZATION (TAI).   TAI was implemented as described earlier, although between Experiment 5 and Experiment 6, the materials were substantially revised, and new procedures were devised to increase the use of the teaching groups, to incorporate homework into the program, and to make other minor improvements.

ABILITY-GROUPED ACTIVE TEACHING (AGAT).   AGAT was a revision of the MMEP designed to partially address problems of the heterogeneous classroom by teaching students in two ability-homogeneous math groups, as described above.

MISSOURI MATHEMATICS EFFECTIVENESS PROGRAM (MMEP).   As described above, the MMEP (Good et al., 1983) is a group-paced instructional program that emphasizes many of the features found in process–product studies to be associated with effective instruction: high ratio of direct instruction to seatwork, frequent assessment, rapid pace, and management practices designed to increase time on task. Thomas Good, the principal author of the MMEP, was kind enough to conduct the training for the MMEP teachers.

MEASURES

MATHEMATICS ACHIEVEMENT.   The posttest achievement measures were the CTBS scales for Mathematics Computations and for Concepts and Applications. Recent California Achievement Test scores from district records were used as covariates to control for initial student ability.

ATTITUDES.   The Liking of Math Class and Self-Concept in Math scales described for Experiment 1 were also used in Experiment 6.

EXPERIMENT 6: RESULTS

Because different achievement tests were used at different grade levels, all achievement test scores were transformed to T scores (mean = 50, standard deviation = 10). These transformations were made separately for each grade, so that, in the resulting pooled analyses, the effects of grade level are completely removed. The CTBS scores were then adjusted for their respective CAT scores to remove the effects of prior knowledge and ability. These adjustments were made by means of separate linear regressions for each grade. The adjusted scores were then used in analyses of variance. For the attitude scales, analyses of covariance were used, with pretests serving as covariates for their respective posttests.

The results of Experiment 6 indicated strong overall differences between the three treatments on Computations and on both attitude variables. The difference between TAI and MMEP was statistically significant ($p < .001$) on all four variables and was quite large for achievement. The adjusted achievement mean differences between TAI and MMEP were 74% of a standard deviation in Computations. However, these differences are probably overestimates of the effect size; despite random assignment, there were statistically significant pretest differences on both achievement pretests, on which the TAI scores were higher than the AGAT scores, which were higher than the MMEP scores. There were no treatment effects on Concepts and Applications, and TAI and AGAT did not differ on either achievement measure.

On the Liking of Math Class and Self-Concept in Math scales, the TAI students scored significantly higher than either the MMEP or the AGAT students, who did not differ from each other.

Thus, Experiment 6 provided strong evidence of the positive effects of TAI on student achievement, as compared to an effective whole-class instructional program. However, TAI did not differ from within-class ability grouping (AGAT), so that once again, we must ask the question raised in Experiment 1: To what degree are the positive achievement effects of TAI due to its individualized nature rather than to its use of cooperative teams? However, for affective outcomes, TAI was clearly superior to the other two treatments, supporting an assertion that the cooperative teams are necessary, at least for effective gains.

EXPERIMENT 7: METHODS

SUBJECTS AND DESIGN

The subjects in Experiment 7 were 480 students in 23 Grade 3–5 classrooms in and around Hagerstown, Maryland, a town in western Maryland. Almost all the students were white. The classes and their teachers were randomly assigned to the experimental treatments, stratifying on grade level. The treatments were implemented over a 16-week period in Spring 1983.

TREATMENTS

The treatments were the same as in Experiment 6, with the addition of an untreated control group that was simply pre- and posttested.

MEASURES

The measures were the same as in Experiment 6.

EXPERIMENT 7: RESULTS

The data from Experiment 7 were analyzed as in Experiment 6. The results indicated statistically significant overall effects for both achievement measures and for "Liking of Class" (all $p < .001$), but no differences were found for Self-Concept in Math. As in Experiment 6, the achievement effects were large. On Computations, TAI exceeded MMEP by 35% of a standard deviation and exceeded the control classes by 64% of a standard deviation. However, there were no differences between TAI and AGAT on Computations, and no differences between TAI, MMEP, and control on Concepts and Applications; the AGAT students scored significantly higher on this variable than the students in the other three conditions. MMEP exceeded control students in Computations, but not Concepts and Applications.

On the Liking-of-Class measure, the TAI students scored significantly higher that the AGAT or the control students but did not differ from the MMEP students.

Particularly with respect to Computations, there is a remarkable degree of correspondence between Experiment 7 and Experiment 6, despite the quite different settings. In both studies, the TAI and the AGAT students performed much better than the MMEP or the control students in Computations but did not systematically differ from each other. In both studies, TAI produced the most positive attitudes toward the math class.

SUMMARY OF RESULTS

ACADEMIC ACHIEVEMENT

In five of the six studies that assessed student achievement, achievement in the TAI classes was significantly higher than in the control classes. The one exception was Experiment 4, in which the implementation of many of the components of TAI was poor. The results of Experiments

3, 6, and 7 showed that the effects of TAI on achievement are not limited to brief implementations. However, the results of Experiment 1 make it unclear whether the positive effects of TAI on achievement are due to the combination of cooperative learning and individualized instruction. An individualized instruction program without cooperative teams increased achievement almost as much as the full TAI program. In Experiments 6 and 7, within-class ability grouping, another form of individualization, was also found to be as effective as TAI. Further research is currently being conducted on the importance of the cooperative reward structure to the effects of TAI on student achievement.

In many of the TAI studies, the effects of the program on student Computation skills were quite large. In the relatively brief Experiments 1 and 2, the TAI students gained about twice as many grade equivalents in Mathematics Computations as the control students. The difference between the experimental and the control classes in Experiment 3 was more than 40% of a grade equivalent in Computations in only 24 weeks, and more than half a grade equivalent for academically handicapped students. In Experiment 6, the TAI students exceeded those who had experienced the Missouri Mathematics Effectiveness Program (MMEP) by 74% of a standard deviation in adjusted Computations scores, and in Experiment 7, the difference was 34% of a standard deviation between TAI and MMEP and 64% of a standard deviation between TAI and an untreated control group. These are hardly trivial effects.

The principle practical drawback to the use of TAI, in comparison with STAD or TGT, is that it is much more expensive, because it requires the purchase of individualized curriculum materials. However, in addition to the larger achievement effects, there are two important advantages of TAI over STAD or TGT. The most obvious is that TAI allows for the accommodation of a very wide range of academic abilities, facilitating mainstreaming, desegregation, and the abolition of tracking. To the extent that these policies are desirable in themselves, TAI makes a particularly important contribution. Another important advantage of TAI is its pattern of use. STAD and TGT tend to be used as supplements to traditional instruction. Teachers typically choose several four- to-eight-week units to teach using STAD or TGT; very few teachers use these methods all year, although a recent year-long evaluation of STAD in mathematics (Slavin & Karweit, in press a) showed that year-long use was possible and effective. On the other hand, TAI is always used as the primary means of teaching mathematics. Most of the teachers who participated in Experiments 1, 2, 3, 6, and 7 (including teachers who were originally in the individualized instruction treatment in Experiment 1) have continued to use TAI as their principal means of teaching mathematics for two years or longer and expect to continue indefinitely, and scores of other teachers not in these studies have also used TAI as their primary mathematics program for extended periods.

The achievement results of Experiment 4 and informal observations of program implementation in Experiment 5 would justify caution in applying TAI to urban schools, such as the Baltimore city schools in which these studies took place. In both cases, the teachers experienced difficulties implementing TAI that were never seen in the suburban schools in which Experiments 1, 2, and 3 were conducted. However, Experiment 6, conducted in inner-city Wilmington, Delaware, showed that TAI can be implemented very effectively in inner-city locations, but because of an extensive metropolitan busing plan in Wilmington, these schools do not have the concentrations of lower-class students typical of Baltimore city schools. TAI requires a good deal from students in terms of their ability to take responsibility and to work independently. Current work is being directed at helping students to learn to operate more effectively within the TAI program, but in Experiments 4 and 5, it was clear that many students lacked the self-organizational skills necessary to make TAI maximally effective. At present, it is most prudent to suggest that if TAI is to be used in lower-class urban settings, an aide or resource teacher should be added to each class to help the regular teacher, or perhaps, two teachers should team so that one can work with the teaching groups while the other helps with the individualized work. STAD and TGT, which have frequently been found to be effective in increasing mathematics achievement in inner-city settings, might be better choices than TAI at this point for low-achieving inner-city classes without aides or other help.

One effect of TAI on student achievement that is not apparent from the data presented here is that average and above-average students in TAI typically cover content to which they would not normally be exposed in elementary school. Many fifth-graders and a few fourth-graders completed the introduction-to-algebra units in TAI, which include such skills as solving simultaneous equations. Some students could have gone further but ran out of TAI units (they were then given enrichment activities). These students were quite solid in these advanced skills and did well on the many difficult word-problems units designed to force students to apply their skills in ambiguous situations. That is, the experience with TAI indicates that able students can progress much more rapidly in mathematics than they do now. This possibility creates a curious problem for schools; few schools are prepared to offer algebra to sixth-graders, yet, after a year of TAI in the fifth grade, many students are clearly ready for a full algebra course in the sixth grade, if not earlier. So far, the schools have dealt with this problem by assigning these students to gifted classes and by reducing the pace of the TAI program by decreasing the time in TAI and increasing enrichment activities for able classes. But if it turns out that a large body of students are really ready for advanced mathematics at an earlier age, the schools will ultimately have to respond.

Another observation worth noting is that the students greatly enjoyed TAI. Many teachers reported difficulty in getting students to go to the next class; many students asked to do math all day! This reaction is typical of cooperative learning in general but seems especialy pronounced in TAI.

Mainstreaming

The results of Experiment 1 concerning the behavior and the social acceptance of mainstreamed academically handicapped students are very positive. By the time of the posttest, the behavior of the mainstreamed TAI subsample was not significantly different from that of nonhandicapped students in the control group, as rated by their teachers. In marked contrast, at pretest the mainstreamed students were rated much lower than nonhandicapped students. Mainstreamed TAI students also gained significantly more than the control students in ratings as "best friends" and received fewer "rejection" choices than did their counterparts in the control group. On these measures, the mainstreamed students in the individualized instruction groups scored at a point between the TAI and the control groups.

The sociometric results indicated that, when academically handicapped students worked in small groups with nonhandicapped classmates, they were better accepted than were students who did not work in such groups. This outcome replicates findings in studies of STAD (Madden & Slavin, 1983a) and other cooperative learning methods (e.g., Ballard et al., 1977; Cooper et al., 1980; Johnson & Johnson, 1982). Allport's (1954) contact theory, originally developed to explain when the improved race relations result from interracial contact, can be easily extended to predict that when academically handicapped and nonhandicapped students engage in nonsuperficial, cooperative activities, they learn to like and respect one another (see Gottlieb & Leyser, 1981; Madden & Slavin, 1983b). However, it is interesting that the individualized instruction treatment without teams also had a positive effect on the acceptance of academically handicapped students. This finding suggests that individualization itself makes an important contribution to the acceptance of academically handicapped students. Other research on individualized instruction (e.g., Meece & Wang, 1982) bears this suggestion out: mainstreamed students are better accepted in individualized instructional programs than in traditional classrooms. One reason is probably that, in individualized programs, academically handicapped students do not stand out from the rest of the class, as all students are working in the same ways on the same types of materials, and all students are experiencing about the same level of success (at their own levels). A similar explanation would apply to effects on student behavior. However, more research on the effects of individualized instruction on the social acceptance and the behavior of academically handicapped classmates is needed before these results can be understood.

The effects of TAI on the achievement of academically handicapped students appear to be positive. No differences were found in Experiment 1, but in the larger and longer Experiment 3, the academically handicapped students learned significantly more in TAI than in the control classes.

The success of TAI in improving the social acceptance, the behavior, and the achievement of academically handicapped students has major implications for mainstreaming. It suggests that the academic needs of low-achieving handicapped students can be met in the regular classroom, in a context that improves the social acceptance and the behavior of these students. Achievement, social acceptance, and behavior are the principal problems faced by academically handicapped students (Madden & Slavin, 1983b) and, in fact, define them as academically handicapped in the first place.

Madden and Slavin (1983b) have noted that when mainstreaming has been found to improve the achievement, the behavior, and the self-concepts of academically handicapped students, it is almost always the case that the classroom in which these students are mainstreamed is using individualized instruction in some form. Neither individualized instruction in special classes nor mainstreaming without individualized instruction is as effective as this combination for either social or academic outcomes. The research on TAI further substantiates this observation. A logical next step in research on mainstreaming would be to investigate the effects of moving the resource teacher and his or her mildly handicapped students into regular classes, using individualized instruction, such as TAI, to meet the individual needs of these students in the context most conducive to social-emotional and academic growth: the regular class.

INTERGROUP RELATIONS

The results of Experiments 4 and 5 provide partial support for the expectation that TAI would have positive effects on intergroup relations similar to those of other cooperative learning methods (see, for example, Cooper *et al.*, 1980; Slavin, 1979; Slavin & Hansell, 1983; Slavin & Oickle, 1981; Ziegler, 1981). It is interesting, however, that the effects were more consistent and stronger in reducing negative attitudes than in increasing positive ones. Because earlier studies have not measured negative attitudes, it is unclear whether this pattern is unique to TAI or would apply to cooperative learning methods in general.

One particularly interesting and important result of Experiments 4 and 5 concerns the "smart" ratings in both studies. In Experiment 4, a marginally significant effect was found in the "not smart" ratings, and in Experiment 5, a significant effect was found in the "very smart" ratings. In both studies, the effects indicated improved cross-race "smartness" ratings for TAI as compared to the control classes, due primarily to the increased positive ratings and the decreased negative ratings of black students by white classmates.

These findings bring important information to bear on a criticism of cooperative learning often made by Elizabeth Cohen (e.g., Cohen, 1975). This criticism essentially predicts that as black and white students work together on tasks that clearly involve academic or reading ability, these attributes will take on increased importance in these students' social perceptions. Because black students often achieve less well than their white classmates, Cohen predicted that experience in cooperative learning activities in academic tasks will lead to an increased perception of blacks as academically incompetent. If anything, TAI might be expected to make relative performance levels even more salient, as students can plainly see where each of their classmates is performing in mathematics.

However, the results of Experiments 4 and 5 were just the opposite of what Cohen might have predicted. The whites gained in respect for the academic ability of their black classmates in both studies. Actually, it is more accurate to say that TAI checked the decrease in cross-racial evaluations characteristic of the control groups in both studies. It may be that in traditional classes, students do not receive much accurate information on one another's true performance levels, so racial stereotypes determine perceptions to a substantial degree. In TAI, students may discover that their classmates of different ethnic backgrounds are more able than they had thought.

CROSS-SEX RELATIONSHIPS

The results of Experiments 4 and 5 also indicated TAI's positive effects on cross-sex relationships. Even more than was the case for race relations, the effects of TAI on cross-sex relationships were mostly to reduce negative attitudes rather than to increase positive ones. The two exceptions were a significant effect on lunch and recess playmates and a marginally significant effect on the "very nice" ratings in Experiment 5.

As the effects of cooperative learning on cross-sex relationships have rarely been studied, these effects are important in establishing that a cooperative learning program can reduce negative attitudes and (in the case of Experiment 5) can increase positive ones across sex lines.

CONCLUSIONS

In summary, seven field experiments evaluating TAI have shown the following:

1. TAI has been consistently effective in increasing student mathematics achievement in lower-middle- to middle-class suburban, urban, and rural schools. These effects were not found in Baltimore city schools, probably because of poor implementation.

2. TAI improves the acceptance of academically handicapped students by their nonhandicapped classmates and improves the classroom behavior, the social behavior, and the self-confidence behavior of these students (as rated by their teachers). In the longer of the two studies that assessed the achievement effects on academically handicapped students, TAI was found to have significantly positive effects on these students' mathematics achievement.

3. TAI improves intergroup relations among black and white students. These effects are greater in reducing negative attitudes than in increasing positive ones. TAI increases cross-racial ratings of "smartness"; in particular, whites rate blacks as "smarter" in TAI classes than in control classes.

4. TAI improves relationships across sex lines. Again, these effects are greater in reducing negative attitudes than in increasing positive ones.

5. Teachers' and students' reactions to TAI have been quite positive, and most teachers who have used TAI have continued to do so in the years following their initial training.

TAI has achieved most of its cognitive and affective objectives. However, there are several important issues yet to be resolved. As noted earlier, it is unclear to what degree the cooperative teams used in TAI contribute to the various effects. Also, the use of regular teaching groups seems critical to the achievement effects of TAI, but direct evidence is lacking. Several practical problems of integrating the teaching-group lessons and the individualized work are yet to be completely solved, and more work is needed to make TAI more effective in inner-city schools. Further research and development are necessary both to improve teachers' lessons on the principal concepts of mathematics and to use the learning teams to explore higher order skills and applications of mathematics. Finally, more research is needed to investigate the effects of TAI on mainstreamed, academically handicapped students and on intergroup relations.

Though much work remains to be done, the research to date on TAI had demonstrated that principles of cooperative learning can be applied to individualized instruction in mathematics, and that the combination enhances the effects of each on cognitive and affective outcomes.

Acknowledgments

I would like to thank Marshall Leavey, Nancy Madden, Sabine Oishi, Reva Bryant, and Kathy Glyshaw for their help with this research.

REFERENCES

Allport, G. *The nature of prejudice.* Cambridge, Mass.: Addison-Wesley, 1954.

Aronson, E. *The Jigsaw classroom.* Beverly Hills, Calif.: Sage, 1978.

Atkinson, J. W. Towards experimental analysis of human motivation in terms of motives, expectancies, and incentives. In J. W. Atkinson (Ed.), *Motives in fantasy, action, and society.* Princeton, N.J.: Van Nostrand, 1958.

Ballard, M., Corman, L., Gottlieb, J., & Kaufman, M. Improving the social status of mainstreamed retarded children. *Journal of Educational Psychology,* 1977, 69, 605–611.

Bloom, B. S. *Human characteristics and school learning.* New York: McGraw-Hill, 1976.

Brophy, J. Teacher behavior and its effects. *Journal of Educational Psychology,* 1979, 71, 733–750.

Carroll, J. B. A model for school learning. *Teachers College Record,* 1963, 64, 723–733.

Cohen, E. G. The effects of desegregation on race relations. *Law and Contemporary Problems,* 1975, 39, 271–299.

Cooper, L., Johnson, D. W., Johnson, R., & Wilderson, F. Effects of cooperative, competitive and individualistic experiences on interpersonal attraction among heterogeneous peers. *Journal of Social Psychology,* 1980, 111, 243–252.

Crain, R., & Mahard, R. Desegregation and black achievement: A review of the research. *Law and Contemporary Problems,* 1978, 42, 17–56.

Devin-Sheehan, L., Feldman, R. S., & Allen, V. L. Research on children tutoring children: A critical review. *Review of Educational Research,* 1976, 46(3), 355–385.

DeVries, D. L., & Slavin, R. E. Teams-Games-Tournament (TGT): Review of ten classroom experiments. *Journal of Research and Development in Education,* 1978, 12, 28–38.

Edwards, J. J., DeVries, D. L., & Snyder, J. P. Games and teams: A winning combination. *Simulation and Games,* 1972, 3, 247–269.

Esposito, D. Homogeneous and heterogeneous ability grouping: Principal findings and implications for evaluating and designing more effective educational environments. *Review of Educational Research,* 1973, 43, 163–179.

Gickling, E., & Theobald, J. Mainstreaming: Affect or effect. *Journal of Special Education*, 1975, *9*, 317–328.

Good, T., Grouws, D., & Ebmeier, H. *Active mathematics teaching*. New York: Longman, 1983.

Gottlieb, J. & Leyser, Y. Friendship between mentally retarded and nonretarded children. In S. Asher & J. Gottman, *The development of children's friendships*. Cambridge: Cambridge University Press, 1981.

Johnson, D. W., & Johnson, R. T. Instructional goal structure: Cooperative, competitive, or individualistic. *Review of Educational Research*, 1974, *44*, 213–240.

Johnson, D. W., & Johnson, R. T. *Learning together and alone*. Englewood Cliffs, N. J.: Prentice-Hall, 1975.

Johnson, D. W., & Johnson, R. T. Effects of cooperative and individualistic instruction on handicapped and non-handicapped students. *Journal of Social Psychology*, 1982, *118*, 257–268.

Kepler, K., and Randall, J. Individualization: Subversion of elementary schooling. *The Elementary School Journal*, 1977, *70*, 358–363.

Lucker, G. W., Rosenfield, D., Sikes, J., & Aronson, E. Performance in the interdependent classroom: A field study. *American Educational Research Journal*, 1976, *13*, 115–123.

Madden, N. A., & Slavin, R. E. Cooperative learning and social acceptance of mainstreamed academically handicapped students. *Journal of Special Education*, 1983, *17*, 171–182. (a)

Madden, N. A., & Slavin, R. E. Mainstreaming students with mild academic handicaps: Academic and social outcomes. *Review of Educational Research*, 1983, *53*, 519–569. (b)

Meece, J., & Wang, M. *A comparative study of social attitudes and behaviors of mildly handicapped children in two mainstreaming programs*. Paper presented at the Annual Convention of the American Educational Association, New York, April 1982.

Miller R. L. Individualized instruction in mathematics: A review of research. *Mathematics Teacher*, 1976, *69*, 345–351.

Oishi, S. *Effects of Team Assisted Individualization in mathematics on the cross-race and cross-sex interactions of elementary school students*. Unpublished doctoral dissertation, University of Maryland, 1983.

Oishi, S., Slavin, R., & Madden, N. *Effects of student teams and individualized instruction on cross-race and cross-sex friendships*. Paper presented at the annual convention of the American Educational Research Association, Montreal, 1983.

Schoen, H. L. Self-paced mathematics instruction: How effective has it been? *Arithmetic Teacher*, 1976, *23*, 90–96.

Sharan, S., & Sharan, Y. *Small-group teaching*. Englewood Cliffs, N. J.: Educational Technology Publications, 1976.

Slavin, R. E. Classroom reward structure: An analytic and practical review. *Review of Educational Research*, 1977, *47*(4), 633–650.

Slavin, R. E. Separating incentives, feedback, and evaluation: Toward a more effective classroom system. *Educational Psychologist*, 1978, *13*, 97–100. (a)

Slavin, R. E. Student teams and achievement divisions. *Journal of Research and Development in Education*, 1978, *12*, 39–49. (b)

Slavin, R. E. Effects of biracial learning teams on cross-racial friendships. *Journal of Educational Psychology*, 1979, *71*, 381–387.

Slavin, R. E. Effects of individual learning expectations on student achievement. *Journal of Educational Psychology*, 1980, *72*, 520–524.

Slavin, R. E. *Cooperative Learning*. New York: Longman, 1983. (a)

Slavin, R. E. When does cooperative learning increase student achievement? *Psychological Bulletin*, 1983, *94*, 429–445. (b)

Slavin, R. E., & Hansell, S. Cooperative learning and intergroup relations: Contact theory in the classroom. In J. Epstein & N. Karweit (Eds.), *Friends in school*. New York: Academic Press, 1983.

Slavin, R. E., & Karweit, N. L. Student teams and mastery learning: A factorial experiment in urban Math Nine classes. *American Educational Research Journal*, in press. (a)

Slavin, R. E., & Karweit, N. L. Effects of whole class, ability grouped, and individualized instruction on mathematics achievement. *American Educational Research Journal*, in press. (b)

Slavin, R. E., & Oickle, E. Effects of cooperative learning teams on student achievement and race relations: Treatment by race interactions. *Sociology of Education*, 1981, *54*, 174–180.

Slavin, R. E., Leavey, M., & Madden, N. A. Combining cooperative learning and individualized instruction: Effects on student mathematics achievement, attitudes, and behaviors. *Elementary School Journal*, 1984, *84*, 409–422.

Slavin, R. E., Madden, N. A., & Leavey, M. Effects of cooperative learning and individualized instruction on the social acceptance, achievement, and behavior of mainstreamed students. *Exceptional Children*, 1984, *50*, 434–443.

Slavin, R. E., Madden, N. A., & Leavey, M. Effects of Team Assisted Individualization on the mathematics achievement of academically handicapped and non-handicapped students. *Journal of Educational Psychology*, in press.

Ziegler, S. The effectiveness of cooperative learning teams for increasing cross-racial friendship: Additional evidence. *Human Organization*, 1981, *40*, 264–268.

8

Small-Group Learning and Teaching in Mathematics

A Selective Review of the Research

NEIL DAVIDSON

Since the late 1960s, a variety of types of cooperative learning procedures have been used in teaching many different mathematics courses, ranging from elementary school through graduate school. The procedures include small-group interaction in which students work together in groups of three to six members, partner learning taking place in dyads, and a peer-tutoring variation of partner learning in which one student is assigned to tutor another. Peer tutoring includes both same-age tutoring and cross-age tutoring, in which an older student tutors a younger one.

At present, there is a substantial body of research on small-group learning and teaching of mathematics. This chapter presents a selected sample, as opposed to a comprehensive review, of that research. Studies of peer tutoring are not included in this review, as that body of research can be found in other places (e.g., Devin-Sheehan, Feldman, & Allen, 1976).

The various small-group learning procedures have in common the following basic notions. First, the class is divided into small groups, of two to six members apiece. Each group has its own working space, which may or may not include a section of the blackboard. Each group is involved in discussing mathematical concepts and principles, in practicing mathematical techniques, and in solving problems. The teacher moves from group to group, checks the students' work, and provides assistance in varying degrees. The groups sometimes gather outside class to work on projects.

In each type of small-group teaching, there are certain basic leadership and management functions that must be performed—many of them by the teacher. How these functions are performed varies consid-

NEIL DAVIDSON • Curriculum and Instruction Department, College of Education, University of Maryland, College Park, Maryland 20742.

erably, depending on the model of small-group instruction that is used. The basic set of functions is as follows:

Initiate group work
Present guidelines for small-group operation
Form groups
Prepare and introduce new material in some form
    Orally to entire class
    Orally to separate groups
    Via written materials
        Worksheets, activity packages, text materials, special texts designed for groups
Interact with small groups in various possible ways:
    Observe groups, check solutions, give hints, clarify notations, ask and answer questions, point out errors, provide encouragement, help groups to function, furnish overall classroom management
Tie ideas together
Make assignments of homework or in-class work
Evaluate students' performance

As stated earlier, each of these functions can be performed in various ways and to varying degrees, depending on the model of small-group instruction in effect.

Several texts have been designed for small-group learning in mathematics. There are texts in elementary algebra (Stein & Crabill, 1972), plane geometry (Chakerian, Crabill, & Stein, 1972), abstract algebra (Davidson & Gulick, 1976), and mathematics for elementary-education or liberal-arts majors (University of Maryland Mathematics Project, 1978; Weissglass, 1979).

Main Effects of Small-Group Methods

Small-Group Discovery Method

Davidson (1971a, b, 1979) developed and tested a small-group discovery method in a year-long course in elementary calculus. The method was based on the educational philosophy of Dewey (1916/1966, 1938/1963) with supporting practices from social psychology (Deutsch, 1960; White & Lippitt, 1960).

The instructor introduced new material with brief lectures at the beginning of class, during which he posed problems and questions for investigation. For most of the class time, the students worked together cooperatively at the blackboard in four-member groups. The students discussed mathematical concepts, proved theorems, made conjectures, constructed examples and counterexamples, and developed techniques for problem solving. The instructor provided guidance and support for the small groups, employing all the practices described earlier for interaction with small groups.

The instructor stated the following guidelines for group behavior: (1) Work together in groups of four; (2) cooperate with other group members; (3) achieve a group solution for each problem; (4) make sure that everyone understands that solution before the group goes on; (5) listen carefully to others, trying whenever possible to build on their ideas; (6) share the leadership of the group; (7) make sure that everyone participates and no one dominates; and (8) take turns writing problem solutions on the board.

In the initial study, the students chose their own groups and switched the membership after each unit. The students were evaluated by means of take-home exams and an in-class final. There was no significant difference in performance on the final between the students in the experimental class and those in the control classes taught by the lecture method. A questionnaire showed highly positive attitudes in the experimental class.

Two other investigations examined the effects of the small-group discovery method in elementary calculus. Loomer (1976) modified the method by including some of the Polya (1965) heuristic strategies for problem solving. He compared achievement in this modified method with that in a lecture control class. On five of six measures, there was no significant difference. However, in a delayed retest of problem solving, the control class scored marginally significantly higher ($p < .10$) than the small-group class. Unfortunately, one cannot separate the effects of the small groups from those of the heuristics.

Brechting and Hirsch (1977) employed modifications of the small-group discovery method and of Davidson's calculus course notes. The students in their small-group treatment scored significantly higher than those taught by traditional methods on a test of manipulative skills. There was no significant difference on a concept measure.

LABORATORY AND DATA COLLECTION

A second category of cooperative learning involves the use of data collection, manipulative materials, and laboratory equipment in small groups. Weissglass (1977, 1979) used a small-group laboratory method in a course in mathematics for elementary teaching. His approach was based on the theory of reevaluation counseling (Jackins, 1978). The course involved a sophisticated treatment of the mathematical concepts taught in elementary or junior high school and used a variety of study guides and laboratory activities. The groups investigated mathematical concepts with equipment including attribute blocks, Cuisenaire rods, geoboards, tangrams, geoblocks, and dice. In a comparison of the laboratory class with a lecture class, there was no significant difference on an achievement test. There was evidence indicating that the laboratory approach was more successful in "motivating those students with more mathematical knowledge and skills" (Weissglass, 1977, p. 382).

COMPUTER-ASSISTED INSTRUCTION

Group work can be used in conjunction with computers. Golton (1975) studied the use of computer-assisted instruction (CAI) in probability and statistics at the sixth-grade level. In the experimental group, the students worked in pairs selected by free choice; in the control group, the students used the equipment alone. No significant differences were found between treatment and control on an achievement and retention test. Golton concluded that the cost of CAI can be halved by pairing students.

REMEDIAL MATHEMATICS

Small groups can be used in remedial courses. Chang (1977a, b) worked with remedial students in arithmetic and algebra in community colleges. In the experimental section, the students discussed mathematics in small groups with three or four members. The control section used the lecture–demonstration approach. The treatment group scored significantly higher than the control group on tests of arithmetic and algebra and on a combined test. Of the experimental students, 75% received a mark of C or better in the next math course, compared to only 47% of the control students.

Gilmer (1978) experimented with a developmental algebra course in a technical college. The experimental class used small-group discussions; the control class used an individual self-pacing approach. There were no significant differences in achievement or intellectual involvement. Pacing was faster in the control group. The experimental group had significantly higher course interest and attitude, as well as a trend toward a lower withdrawal rate, than the control group ($p < .07$).

REVIEW

Pence (1974) compared the effects of small-group versus individual review on subsequent individual performance. Sixth-grade students were assigned to different treatments for the review of topics that they had failed on diagnostic tests. Three types of small-group review were contrasted with individual review. There were nonsignificant trends in achievement scores in favor of small-group review over individual review. Additionally, small-group review required more time.

GOAL STRUCTURES

Johnson and Johnson (1974, 1975) have differentiated among cooperative, competitive, and individualistic goal structures and have developed "learning-together" methods for the cooperative goal structure. They have conducted a number of studies in diverse subject areas comparing the effects of the three goal structures.

In one such study in mathematics, Johnson, Johnson, and Scott (1978) compared cooperative and individualistic methods involving high-achieving fifth- and sixth-grade students in an advanced math class, studying one hour per day for 50 days. In the cooperative condition, the students were told to work together as a group of four and to complete one assignment pamphlet and record slip for their entire group, with all students contributing ideas and seeking assistance from each other, not from the teacher. The teacher "praised and rewarded" the group as a whole. In the individualized condition, the students were told to work on their own and to complete individual assignment pamphlets and record slips, to avoid interaction with other students, and to seek help and clarification from the teacher. The teacher praised and rewarded each student individually.

The students in the cooperative groups, in comparison with the students working individually, had more positive attitudes toward heterogeneity among their peers, believed that they were doing a better job of learning in school, and performed their daily tasks faster and more accurately. When the students in the cooperative treatment were tested in their groups and could help one another with their tests, they scored significantly higher than did the individualized students tested individually, on two of three final unit tests and on a retention test two months later. However, when all the students were tested individually, the students in the individualized treatment scored significantly higher than the students in the cooperative treatment in about 50% of the comparisons.

Robertson (1982) evaluated the Johnsons' methods in second- and third-grade mathematics courses and found no significant differences in mathematics achievement between the experimental and the control groups.

GROUP REWARDS FOR INDIVIDUAL LEARNING

Slavin (1980a, 1983a, b) has presented and reviewed an extensive body of research dealing with three methods of cooperative learning in which there is both group study and a group reward for individual learning. These are Teams-Games-Tournaments (TGT), Student Teams-Achievement Divisions (STAD), and Team-Assisted Individualization (TAI). STAD and TGT are described as follows:

> These methods typically involve students working in small groups to master worksheets or other information initially presented by the teacher. Following the group study time, the students are individually assessed, and the group members' scores are summed to form group scores. These are recognized in class newsletters, or qualify the groups for certificates, grades, or other rewards. . . In STAD, the teacher presents a lesson, and then students study worksheets in four-member teams that are heterogeneous on student ability, sex, and ethnicity. Following this, students take individual quizzes, and team scores are computed based on the degree to which each student improved over his or her own past record. The team scores are recognized in class newsletters. TGT is the same as STAD, except that instead of taking quizzes, students compete against members of other teams who are similar in past performance to add points to their team scores. (Slavin, 1983b, p. 432)

In TAI, the students work in heterogeneous teams and form pairs or triads within their teams. They work on individualized curriculum materials at their own levels and rates. The students exchange answer sheets with their partners within the teams; the partners check each other's answers after solving four problems on a skill sheet. The team members help one another with problems. The students must solve a block of four problems correctly before they can go on to the next skill sheet, and eventually, they take various tests. The teams receive certificates based on the number of units completed and on the members' performance on the final tests. TAI is an individualized program that can be managed by a single teacher without an aide, as the students themselves manage the routine checking and procedures of the program. The TAI program and research on it are described in more detail in the preceding chapter.

The four studies of TGT in mathematics have been conducted with seventh-grade students by Edwards and DeVries (1972, 1974); Edwards, DeVries, and Snyder (1972); and Hulten and DeVries (1976). In three of the four studies, there was a significant difference in achievement gains favoring the TGT group over the control group taught by traditional large-group instruction. In the three studies involving integrated schools, effects on race relations were measured by asking the students to name their friends of the opposite race. In two of these three studies, the TGT students gained significantly more on the race relations criteria than did the control students. A measure of mutual concern examined the students' liking of their classmates and feelings of being liked by them. In both studies measuring this variable, there was a significant difference in mutual concern in favor of the TGT treatment over the control treatment.

The three studies of STAD in mathematics were carried out by Madden and Slavin (1983), Slavin and Karweit (1982), and Huber, Bogatzki, and Winter (1982). The grade levels were 3–6, 9, and 7, respectively. In all three studies, the student gains in achievement were significantly higher in STAD than in the traditionally taught control group.

One combined program employed three cooperative learning methods with the same fourth- and fifth-grade students in three different subject areas (Slavin & Karweit, 1981). TGT was used in mathematics. There was no significant difference in mathematics achievement scores between the TGT students and the controls. However, the TGT mutual concern scores were significantly higher than those of the controls.

Six studies of TAI in mathematics were conducted. These are reviewed in the preceding chapter. In five of these studies, the gains in achievement scores in the TAI approach were significantly higher than in the large-group control approach on the mathematics portion of the Comprehensive Test of Basic Skills (CBTS). However, the TAI students' scores were not significantly higher than the scores of students working individually with the TAI materials (Slavin, Leavey, & Madden, 1984). Several studies showed positive effects of TAI on affective variables, as described in the preceding chapter.

One of the TAI studies (Slavin, Madden, & Leavey, 1984a) compared the effects of TAI, an individualized program using TAI materials, and a traditional control method on the social acceptance, the behavior, and the achievement of mainstreamed, mildly academically handicapped children. The use of TAI and of the individualized program with TAI materials significantly improved the social acceptance of the mainstreamed students; this improvement was indicated by the increased numbers of choices that they received as "best friends" and by the decreased numbers of received "rejections." The TAI mainstreamed students were rated as having significantly fewer behavioral problems than the mainstreamed students in the control class. This finding did not hold for the individualized students using TAI materials. No significant differences in the achievement of the mainstreamed students were found among the treatments; however, achievement data from a later study (Slavin, Madden, & Leavey, 1984b) with a larger sample of mainstreamed students showed gains in achievement that were significantly higher in TAI than in the control treatment.

In summary, throughout the set of studies comparing TGT, STAD, or TAI with traditional total-class instruction, significant differences in gains in student achievement in favor of the small-group treatment occurred in 11 out of 14 studies. For the most part, these were obtained on measures of basic skill learning and on simple application problems.

Reviews of team learning usually include an additional method: Aronson's Jigsaw (1978) and its variation, Jigsaw II (Slavin, 1980b). In these approaches, the material to be learned in each group is divided into several parts, each of which is assigned to one group member. The group members learn their own parts of the material by studying them with others who are also to become "experts" on the same topic. The experts then return to their own groups and teach the material to the other group members. As the Jigsaw methods have not been used in mathematics instruction, their results are not described here.

RESEARCH ON INTERNAL DYNAMICS IN COOPERATIVE LEARNING

GROUP FORMATION PROCEDURES

The research on internal dynamics in cooperative learning includes several studies investigating different procedures in forming small groups. Stam (1973) compared sociometric choice grouping with random grouping in fifth-grade classes. The outcome measures were tasks requiring convergent thinking and divergent thinking. On the divergent-thinking tasks, the sociometric groups performed significantly better than the random groups. There were no significant differences on the convergent-thinking tasks.

Grant (1975) compared three grouping procedures in a course for prospective elementary teachers taught by the small-group discovery method. The first procedure used sociometric choice in conjunction with group dynamics exercises for two weeks. The second was based on interpersonality compatibility as measured by the Fundamental Interpersonal Relations Orientation-Behavior (FIRO-B) (Schutz, 1966). The third involved students' choosing their groups in class. The groups using sociometric choice with group dynamics exercises scored significantly higher than the groups formed by in-class choice on a composite measure of achievement, mathematical attitude, and small-group attitude. There was no significant difference between the groups formed with the FIRO-B and those formed by means of the other procedures.

Webb (1977) compared the effects of problem practice on complex tasks performed in mixed-ability groups, in uniform-ability groups, or by individuals. Eleventh-grade students worked in four-person groups. Overall, the results on individual tests showed the following order from best to worst conditions: mixed-ability grouping, individual learning, and uniform-ability grouping. Webb found an aptitude–treatment interaction. The above order held for low-ability students but was reversed for medium-ability students. High-ability students performed less well in uniform-ability groups than in the other conditions.

GROUP–PROCESS AND APTITUDE–TREATMENT INTERACTIONS

Webb (1980a, b, c, 1982a) has conducted a number of correlational studies relating group process to student achievement in mathematics. Much of this work is summarized elsewhere in this volume. Webb's presentation (1982b) summarized the results of four of these studies. One of them involved eleventh-grade students learning material on probability, algebra, and geometry. The other three studies involved seventh-, eighth-, or ninth-grade students learning general mathematics. In three of the four studies, all group work was tape-recorded, and interaction was coded from the tape transcripts. This procedure yielded much more useful information than a process of coding the interaction directly from observations of the students in class.

Webb (1982b) distinguished among all instances of help, explanations, and terminal responses. Explanations generally consisted of step-by-step descriptions or detailed accounts of problem solutions or error corrections. Terminal responses were forms of "help" that did not include these detailed descriptions, for example, giving an answer without an explanation or simply pointing out an error.

Webb's studies consistently showed that giving explanations was positively related to achievement, that is, that explaining to others helped one's own learning. However, giving terminal responses was not related to achievement. Receiving terminal responses was negatively related to achievement, as was receiving no response to a request for help. The results for receiving explanations were not completely consistent but did suggest that receiving explanations tended to benefit achievement.

Janicki (1979) compared the effects of individual and small-group instruction. The students were fourth- and fifth-graders learning a two-week unit on fractions. In one treatment, the students worked on seatwork individually and were given a homework assignment at the end of class. In the other treatment, the students did seatwork in mixed-ability groups of four students; those who completed the seatwork could choose to do their homework or to play math games in their small group. No main effects of the treatments were found, but there was an aptitude–treatment interaction. The students who had a positive attitude and an internal locus of control performed better on the achievement and retention tests in the small-group approach. The students who had a less positive attitude and an external locus of control performed better in the individual approach.

Peterson and Janicki (1979) investigated aptitude–treatment interactions with students learning in large-group and mixed-ability small-group approaches. Fourth-, fifth-, and sixth-grade classes studied fractions for two weeks; each class used only one of the two instructional approaches.

Again, no main effects of treatment on achievement were found, but aptitude–treatment interactions did occur. Students of high ability retained more in the small-group approach than in the large-group approach. Students of low ability retained more in the large-group approach. Students who initially preferred one of the approaches (small-group or large-group) did better on the retention test in the other, nonpreferred approach. High-ability students had a more positive attitude toward mathematics in the small-group approach, and low-ability students had a more positive attitude in the large-group approach. Both high-ability and low-ability students had a more positive attitude toward the instructional approach in the small-group treatment, but medium-ability students had a more positive attitude toward instruction in the large-group treatment. Overall, the attitudes toward instruction were more positive in the large-group approach.

The aptitude–treatment interactions were explained through observations of group process as follows: The high-ability students probably liked math better and retained more in the small-group approach "because they were actively involved in explaining the math problems and helping others." The low-ability students probably liked math better and retained more in the large group "because the teacher provided direction and help" (Peterson & Janicki, 1979, p. 686).

Peterson, Janicki, and Swing (1981) investigated aptitude–treatment interactions with students learning in large-group and mixed-ability small-group approaches. Fifth- and sixth-grade classes studied a two-week unit on geometry, using one of the two instructional approaches in each class. There were no significant differences on achievement and retention tests between the two treatments. However, both high-ability and low-ability students performed better in the small-group approach than in the large-group approach. Medium-ability students tended to do slightly better, but not significantly so, in the large-group approach. These results were explained on the basis of classroom observations. The high-ability students spent more time giving explanations than the low-ability students; both spent more time explaining than the medium-ability students. The more time spent explaining to others, the better the student's performance; that is, the students learned by teaching. This finding was consistent with the prior results of Peterson and Janicki (1979) and Webb (1980a, b, c, 1982a).

Students had a more positive attitude toward instruction overall in the large-group approach. Students with better-than-average ability had a more positive attitude toward the instructional method in the large-group approach than in the small-group approach. This interaction, which was inconsistent with the prior result of Peterson and Janicki (1979), was explained by a group-process observation that the high-ability students "worked much harder" in the small-group approach by giving explanations to other group members.

In all the studies reviewed in this section, there was a consistent positive relationship between giving help and achievement. However, in two of the studies (Peterson & Janicki, 1979; Peterson et al., 1981), there was no significant relationship between receiving help and achievement. Webb (1982b) commented that the help received may have included both explanations and terminal responses, the effects of which canceled each other out.

In two studies (Peterson & Janicki, 1979; Peterson et al., 1981), overall student attitudes toward instruction were more positive in the large-group than in the small-group approach. However, the interactions involving student attitudes were not consistent across the studies.

GROUP TESTING, BRAINSTORMING, AND COGNITIVE DEVELOPMENT

Klingbeil (1974) examined the effects of group testing in a mathematics course for prospective elementary teachers. All sections learned by the small-group discovery method. Klingbeil stated the following guidelines for small-group examinations:

1. *All* group members must contribute in some way to the mathematical solution of each problem on the exam.
2. All problems should be worked out on the blackboard.
3. Each group must do its own work and cannot use information obtained from other groups.
4. The task of writing down the group solution must be rotated within the group for each exam.
5. All copies of the exam sheet including a copy with the group solutions (which is the only one that will be graded) must be handed in at the end of the hour. (p. 29)

There were three examination treatments: In one section, the students took all exams individually. In a second section, the students took all exams together in their small groups. In the third, the students alternated between individual and group exams for the six exams. There were no significant differences among the treatments on an individual final exam and on attitude measures. Strong but nonsignificant tendencies were found for the alternating individual–group exam procedure to result in lower test anxiety than the other treatments. On each test, the group exam scores were dramatically higher than the individual exam scores, presumably because the students could work together. Klingbeil recommended the limited use of group tests as part of an evaluation system.

BRAINSTORMING

Gallicchio (1976) investigated the effects of brainstorming in mathematics classes for elementary education majors taught by the small-group discovery method. In the experimental group, there were 11 problem-solving sessions in which small groups used brainstorming. In the control section, small groups solved the same problems without brainstorming. The following guidelines were stated for group brainstorming:

1. List all ideas, such as facts given or possible strategies, on the chalkboard using the following brainstorming rules:
   a. Quantity is wanted. The more ideas you have, the higher chance you have of solving the problem.
   b. Wild ideas are acceptable.
   c. Combination and improvement of ideas are sought.
   d. No criticism is permitted of your own or other group members' ideas.
2. No idea may be evaluated until the brainstorming list is completed.
3. Each person in the group participates and no one dominates.
4. Each group should do its own work and should not use information obtained from other groups.
5. The group will be asked to hand in the brainstorming list as well as the solution(s) to the problem at the end of the session. (pp. 43–44)

Brainstorming did not significantly enhance mathematical creativity, achievement, or attitude or reduce test anxiety. However, the data obtained by observations and questionnaires indicated that brainstorming encouraged small-group interaction and helped the students to become more confident in their problem-solving ability.

Cognitive Development

Shearn (1982) examined the effects of small-group learning on students' cognitive development, as measured by the Perry (1970) sequence of stages. In Perry's scheme, students in Positions 1 and 2 (dualism) believe that all questions have right or wrong answers, that authority figures possess knowledge and answers, and that the opinions of peers in learning are not to be taken seriously. In Positions 3 and 4 (multiplicity), students become more accepting of a diversity of viewpoints, move toward less dependence on authorities, and have more respect for the views of their peers. In Position 5 (contextual relativism), students reason within different contexts, view the instructor more as a colleague than as an authority, and have respect for the opinions of their peers when supported by logic or by evidence. The later positions in Perry's scheme deal with ethical issues related to commitments. Although most research to date on Perry's scheme has dealt with college students (Widick, Knefelkamp, & Parker, 1975), it is clear that the stages are also pertinent to younger students.

Shearn's study (1982) involved the use of two forms of the small-group discovery method in a one-semester course in mathematics for prospective elementary teachers; most of the students were college sophomores. Although the study had several aspects, the finding pertinent to this review is that the students in small-group learning progressed significantly in cognitive development, as measured by ratings of Perry's stages before and after the course. Such a developmental movement would not typically occur without an instructional intervention. Some future studies assessing cognitive development in small groups need to include a traditional control treatment for comparison.

Summary and Recommendations for Research

Summary of Findings

Considerable progress in the development of small-group teaching procedures in mathematics has occurred since the late 1960s. Small-group interaction has been used in conjunction with discovery learning, laboratory and data collection methods, computer-assisted instruction, peer tutoring, remedial work, review, group testing, and brainstorming. Instructional materials have been developed for several courses, as have programs to train teachers to use small-group instructional procedures. A summary of findings based on the research in small-group teaching of mathematics follows:

1. Considering all the studies comparing student achievement in small-group instruction and traditional methods in mathematics, the majority showed no significant difference. When significant differences were found, they almost always favored the small-group procedure. Only two studies (Loomer, 1976; Johnson et al., 1978) provided limited partial support for the superiority of the control procedure. No evidence showed that either small-group instruction or the control procedure was superior in fostering the learning of higher order concepts and principles or the solution of nonroutine problems.

If the term *achievement* refers to computational skills, simple concepts, and simple application problems, the studies at the elementary and secondary levels in mathematics support Slavin's (1983b) conclusions: (a) "Cooperative learning methods that use group rewards and individual accountability consistently increase student achievement more than control methods in . . . elementary and secondary classrooms" and (b); "Cooperative learning methods that use group study but not group rewards for individual learning do not increase student achievement more than control methods" (p. 443).

Although Conclusions (a) and (b) hold for the main effects of treatment, the situation is more complex when aptitude–treatment interactions are taken into account. In studies that did *not* involve group rewards for individual learning, Peterson and Janicki (1979) and Peterson *et al.* (1981) found that students of high ability in mathematics achieved significantly more in small-group than in large-group approaches.

Slavin did not extend his conclusions to the college level, as he did not review that literature. Indeed, Conclusion (a) has not been tested at the college level in mathematics; the studies have not examined the effects of group rewards on individual learning. Conclusion (b) cannot be completely extrapolated to the college level in mathematics, as shown by the studies of Chang (1977) and Brechting and Hirsch (1977), which obtained significant differences in achievement without using group rewards.

2. The issue of student attitudes toward the subject matter and the method of instruction is rather clouded. In some studies (e.g., Gilmer, 1978), students preferred a small-group treatment, and in others (e.g., Peterson & Janicki, 1979), they preferred a large-group treatment. The

interactions between student ability level and attitudes toward instruction were not consistent across the studies. In one study (Peterson & Janicki, 1979), the students learned less in the method that was their initial preference.

3. There is evidence that the use of TGT in mathematics has positive effects on measures of mutual concern and on race relations in integrated schools. The evidence of these effects of TGT and also STAD has been gathered more extensively in subject areas other than mathematics.

4. In terms of group formation procedures, two studies (Stam, 1973; Grant, 1975) showed some positive effects on learning when groups were formed by sociometric choice procedures. In one study (Webb, 1977), the use of mixed-ability groups led to higher achievement than the use of uniform-ability groups; however, the effects of the group formation procedure interacted with the ability level of the students. Forming groups heterogeneously by ability, sex, and ethnicity led to increased mutual concern and race relations in several studies reviewed by Slavin (1980a, 1983a).

5. In several studies summarized by Webb (1982b), students' giving explanations in small groups was positively related to their achievement, whereas giving terminal responses was not so related. Receiving terminal responses or no responses to requests for help was negatively related to student achievement.

6. In two studies (Klingbeil, 1974; Johnson *et al.*, 1978), the scores on small-group exams were significantly higher than the scores on the same exams taken individually. There is considerable controversy about the desirability of allowing group exam scores for evaluation.

7. None of the following practices led to significant differences in individual student achievement: laboratory work, group review, group testing, and group brainstorming. However, for each practice, only one or two studies were available for consideration.

RECOMMENDATIONS FOR RESEARCH

Not surprisingly, this review of research has led to a number of further issues for investigation. Each of the following appears to offer a promising line of inquiry:

1. Attempting to extend the range of TGT, STAD, and TAI methods upward to geometry, algebra II and trigonometry, calculus, and perhaps other college-level courses. This extension may require modifications of the methods to handle material that is more complex and less skill-oriented.

2. Directly contrasting TAI with individualized programs that do not use group interaction or student management of learning.
3. Implementing the Jigsaw or Jigsaw II model in mathematical problem-solving.
4. Assessing the outcomes of methods such as TGT, STAD, and TAI in skills-oriented courses, which might prepare students better for various state-required functional math tests.
5. Examining the results of various small-group procedures used in conjunction with microcomputers.
6. a. Searching further for aptitude–treatment interactions related to small-group learning.
   b. Seeking limited generalizations that give specific outcomes of particular combinations of characteristics related to the student, the type of task and content, the method of instruction, and the environment. Such studies seem especially pertinent to seeking conditions under which discovery or laboratory procedures enhance student learning; they do not do so across the board.
7. Studying the group-process variables, for example, students' giving explanations, which may be predictors of student learning or may help explain aptitude–treatment interactions.
8. Looking more closely at the effects of different procedures for small-group formation, including, for example, an instrument such as the Myers-Briggs Type Indicator (Briggs & Briggs Myers, 1977), which has not been previously used for this purpose in mathematics.
9. Examining the cognitive, affective, and behavioral outcomes of training students to cooperate more effectively in groups, in contrast to promoting intragroup cooperation by means of intergroup competition.
10. Implementing curriculum development models that allow for the identification of stylistic differences in learning mathematics and the incorporation of student-generated learning sequences.
11. Designing small-group instruction to enhance student ability to solve nonroutine problems and to learn higher order concepts and principles, and testing the extent to which these goals are achieved.
12. Assessing the effects of various forms of small-group teaching on cognitive development, using progression through the Perry (1970) cognitive development stages as an outcome variable.

In conclusion, professionals involved in the research and development of small-group teaching in mathematics have included mathematics educators, mathematicians, classroom teachers, social psychologists, and educational psychologists. Although many of the workers in the field have been unaware of the efforts of others, a number of instances of collaborative efforts are found, often involving professionals within the same general category. One may hope that this review will lead to a greater degree of mutual awareness and cooperation in directing future efforts in the field. Indeed, many of the proposed questions cannot be addressed without such cooperation.

REFERENCES

Aronson, E. *The Jigsaw classroom.* Beverly Hills, Calif.: Sage, 1978.

Brechting, Sister M. C., & Hirsch, C. R. The effects of small-group discovery learning on student achievement and attitudes in calculus. *American Mathematics Association of Two-Year Colleges Journal,* 1977, 2, 77–82.

Briggs, K. & Briggs Myers, I. *Myers-Briggs Type Indicator.* Palo Alto, Calif.: Consulting Psychologists Press, 1977.

Chakerian, G. D., Crabill, C. D., & Stein, S. K. *Geometry: A guided inquiry.* Boston: Houghton Mifflin, 1972.

Chang, P-T. *On relationships among academic performance, sex difference, attitude and persistence of small groups in developmental college level mathematics courses.* Doctoral dissertation, Georgia State University, School of Education, Atlanta, Georgia, 1977. (a)

Chang, P-T. Small group instruction: A study in remedial mathematics. *American Mathematics Association of Two-Year Colleges Journal,* 1977, 2, 72–76. (b)

Davidson, N. The small-group discovery method as applied in calculus instruction. *American Mathematical Monthly,* August–September 1971, 789–91. (a)

Davidson, N. *The small-group discovery method of mathematics instruction as applied in calculus.* Doctoral dissertation, University of Wisconsin, 1970. Technical Report No. 168. Wisconsin Research and Development Center for Cognitive Learning, Madison, 1971. (b)

Davidson, N. The small-group discovery method: 1967–77. In *Problem Solving Studies in Mathematics.* J. Harvey & T. Romberg (Eds.),Wisconsin Research and Development Center for Individualized Schooling, University of Wisconsin, Madison, 1979.

Davidson, N., & Gulick, F. *Abstract algebra: An active learning approach.* Boston: Houghton Mifflin, 1976.

Davidson, N., McKeen, R. & Eisenberg, T. Curriculum construction with student input. *The Mathematics Teacher,* 1973, 66(3), 271-275.

Deutsch, M. The effects of cooperation and competition upon group process. In D. Cartwright & A. Zander (Eds.), *Group Dynamics: Research and theory* (2nd ed.). New York: Harper & Row, 1960.

Devin-Sheehan, L., Feldman, R., & Allen V. L. Research on children tutoring children: A critical review. *Review of Educational Research,* 1976, 46, 335–385.

Dewey, John. *Democracy and education.* New York: Free Press, 1966. (Originally published, 1916.)

Dewey, John. *Experience and education.* New York: Collier, 1963. (Originally published, 1938.)

Edwards, K. J., & DeVries, D. L. *Learning games and student teams: Their effects on student attitudes and achievement.* Center for Social Organization of Schools, The Johns Hopkins University, 1972, Report No. 147.

Edwards, K. J., & DeVries, D. L. *The effects of Teams-Games-Tournaments and two structural variations on classroom process, student attitudes, and student achievement.* Center for Social Organization of Schools, The Johns Hopkins University, 1974, Report No. 172.

Edwards, K. J., DeVries, D. L., & Snyder, J. P. Games and teams: A Winning combination. *Simulation and Games* 1972, 3 247–269.

Gallicchio, A. *The effects of brainstorming in small group mathematics classes.* Doctoral dissertation, University of Maryland, College Park, 1976.

Gilmer, G. F. *Effects of small discussion groups on self-paced instruction in a developmental algebra course.* Doctoral dissertation, Marquette University, Milwaukee, Wis., 1978.

Golton, R. F. *The effect of student interaction on computer-assisted instruction in mathematics at the sixth grade level.* Doctoral dissertation, University of California, Berkeley, Calif., 1975.

Grant, S. *The effects of three kinds of group formation using FIRO-B compatibility, sociometric choice with group dynamics exercises, and in-class choice on mathematics classes taught by the small-group discovery method.* Doctoral dissertation, University of Maryland, College Park, 1975.

Huber, G., Bogatzki, W., & Winter, M. *Cooperation: Condition and goal of teaching and learning in classrooms.* Unpublished manuscript, University of Tübingen, West Germany, 1982.

Hulten, B. H., & DeVries, D. L. *Team competition and group practice: Effects on student achievement and attitudes.* Center for Social Organization of Schools, Johns Hopkins University, 1976, Report No. 212.

Jackins, H. *The human side of human beings* (2nd ed.). Seattle: Rational Island Publishers, 1978.

Janicki, T. C. *Aptitude-treatment interaction effects of variations in direct instruction.* Unpublished doctoral dissertation, University of Wisconsin, Madison, 1979.

Johnson, D. W., & Johnson, R. T. Instructional goal structure: Cooperative, competitive, or individualistic. *Review of Educational Research*, 1974, 44, 213–240.

Johnson, D. W., & Johnson. R. T. *Learning together and alone.* Englewood Cliffs, N.J.: Prentice-Hall, 1975.

Johnson, D. W., Johnson, R. T., & Scott, L. The effects of cooperative and individualized instruction on student attitudes and achievement. *Journal of Social Psychology*, 1978, 104, 207–216.

Klingbeil, D. *An examination of the effects of group testing in mathematics courses taught by the small-group discovery method.* Doctoral dissertation, University of Maryland, College Park, 1974.

Loomer, N. J. *A multidimensional exploratory investigation of small-group heuristic and expository learning in calculus.* Doctoral dissertation, University of Wisconsin, Madison, 1976.

Madden, N. A., & Slavin, R. E. Effects of cooperative learning on the social acceptance of mainstreamed academically handicapped students. *Journal of Special Education*, 1983, 17, 171–182.

Pence, B. M. J. *Small group review of mathematics: A function of the review organization, structure, and task format.* Doctoral dissertation, Stanford University, Stanford, Calif., 1974.

Perry, W. G. *Forms of intellectual and ethical development in the college years: A scheme.* New York: Holt, Rinehart and Winston, 1970.

Peterson, P. L., & Janicki, T. C. Individual characteristics and children's learning in large-group and small-group approaches. *Journal of Educational Psychology*, 1979, 71, 677–687.

Peterson, P. L., Janicki, T. C., & Swing, S. R. Ability × treatment interaction effects on children's learning in large-group and small-group approaches. *American Educational Research Journal*, 1981, *18*, 453–473.

Polya, G. *Mathematical discovery*, Vol. 2. New York: Wiley, 1965.

Robertson, L. *Integrated goal structuring in the elementary school: Cognitive growth in mathematics*. Unpublished doctoral dissertation, Rutgers University, New Brunswick, N.J., 1982.

Schutz, W. C. *The interpersonal underworld*. Palo Alto, Calif.: Science and Behavioral Books, 1966.

Shearn, E. L. *Adapting the developmental instruction model, based on Perry's theory, to a mathematics content course for preservice elementary teachers to enhance attitudes toward mathematics, cognitive development, and achievement*. Unpublished doctoral dissertation, University of Maryland, College Park, 1982.

Slavin, R. E. Cooperative learning. *Review of Educational Research*, 1980, *50*, 315–342 (a).

Slavin, R. E. *Using student team learning (rev. ed.)*, Baltimore, Md.: Center for Social Organization of Schools, The Johns Hopkins University, 1980. (b)

Slavin, R. E. *Cooperative learning*. New York: Longman, 1983. (a)

Slavin, R. E. When does cooperative learning increase student achievement? *Psychological Bulletin*, 1983, *94*, 429–445. (b)

Slavin, R. E., & Karweit, N. L. Cognitive and affective outcomes of an intensive student team learning experience. *Journal of Experimental Education*, 1981, *50*, 29–35.

Slavin, R. E., & Karweit, N. L. *Student teams and mastery learning: An experiment in urban Math 9 classes*. Paper presented at the Annual Convention of the American Educational Research Association, New York, March 1982.

Slavin, R. E., Leavey, M., & Madden, N. A. *Combining student teams and individualized instruction in mathematics: An extended evaluation*. Paper presented at the Annual Convention of the American Educational Research Association, Montreal, April 1983.

Slavin, R. E., Leavey, M., & Madden, Nancy A. Combining cooperative learning and individualized instruction: Effects on student mathematics achievement, attitudes, and behaviors. *Elementary School Journal*, 1984, *84*, 409–422.

Slavin, R. E., Madden, N. A., & Leavey, M. Effects of cooperative learning and individualized instruction on mainstreamed students. *Exceptional Children*, 1984, *50*, 434–443. (a)

Slavin, R. E., Madden, N. A., & Leavey, M. Effects of Team Assisted Individualization on the mathematics achievement of academically handicapped and non-handicapped students. *Journal of Educational Psychology*, *76*, 813–819, 1984 (b).

Stam, P. J. *The effect of sociometric grouping on task performance in the elementary classroom*. Doctoral dissertation, Stanford University, Stanford, Calif. 1973.

Stein, S., & Crabill, C. *Elementary algebra: A guided inquiry*, Boston: Houghton Mifflin, 1972.

University of Maryland Mathematics Project (UMMaP). *Unifying concepts and processes in elementary mathematics*. Boston: Allyn and Bacon, 1978.

Webb, N. M. *Learning in individual and small-group settings*. Technical Report No. 7. Stanford, Calif.: Aptitude Research Project, School of Education, Stanford University, 1977.

Webb, N. M. An analysis of group interaction and mathematical errors in heterogeneous ability groups. *British Journal of Educational Psychology*, 1980, *50*, 1–11. (a)

Webb, N. M. Group process: The key to learning in groups. *New Directions for Methodology of Social and Behavioral Science: Issues in Aggregation*, 1980, *6*, 77–87. (b)

Webb, N. M. A process-outcome analysis of learning in group and individual settings. *Educational Psychologist*, 1980, *15*, 69–83. (c)

Webb, N. M. Group composition, group interaction and achievement in cooperative small groups. *Journal of Educational Psychology*, 1982, *74*, 475–484. (a)

Webb, N. M. *Student interaction and learning in small groups: Research summary*. Paper presented at the Meeting of the International Association for the Study of Cooperation in Education, Provo, Utah, 1982. (b)

Weissglass, J. Mathematics for elementary teaching: A small-group laboratory approach. *American Mathematical Monthly*, May 1977, 377–382.

Weissglass, J. *Exploring elementary mathematics: A small-group approach for teaching*. San Francisco: W. H. Freeman, 1979.

White, R., & Lippitt, R. Leader behavior and member reaction in three "Social Climates". In D. Cartwright & A. Zander (Eds.), *Group dynamics: Research and theory*. New York: Harper & Row, 1960.

Widick, C., Knefelkamp, L., & Parker, C. The counselor as a developmental instructor. *Counselor Education and Supervision*, 1975, *14*, 286–296.

9

The Effects of Modified Jigsaw on Achievement, Classroom Social Climate, and Self-Esteem in High-School Science Classes

REUVEN LAZAROWITZ, J. HUGH BAIRD,
RACHEL HERTZ-LAZAROWITZ,
AND
JAMES JENKINS

Cooperative learning in schools is not a new idea. Deutsch's theorizing, published in 1949, about cooperation and competition has become a foundation for much of the development and research on cooperation in education (Sharan, Hare, Webb, & Hertz-Lazarowitz, 1980; Slavin, 1983).

In secondary science classes, teams for laboratory investigation and students working in groups on special projects have been an accepted practice for more than four decades. More recently, specific directions on grouping students for classroom study were given by Washton (1967):

> The problem-solving method, the project method, the field trip, the case study and, in some instances, the laboratory, may permit effective learning experiences through group work. Science activities should, of course, encourage students to participate as individuals as well as in groups; but in learning scientific information, attitudes, and skills, the students should learn how to work with fellow students in seeking solutions to common problems. . . .
>
> Group work in science may have great significance for the future scientist. Research in science is more often team research than individual research. Frequently, scientists with related specialties and skills are brought together to form a team for attacking a given problem. This is another reason for encouraging the formation of pupil committees to perform group activities in various methods and problems to be used. (p. 251)

REUVEN LAZAROWITZ • Department of Education in Technology and Science, Technion-Israel Institute of Technology, Haifa, Israel.   J. HUGH BAIRD AND JAMES JENKINS • Department of Secondary Education, Brigham Young University, Provo, Utah 84602.   RACHEL HERTZ-LAZAROWITZ • School of Education, Haifa University, Haifa, Israel.

Washton continued by citing Asch (1956) as evidence that "there are certain dangers in the group approach." Washton also suggested that students in groups might be pressured into conforming to the thinking and practices of the group. Montean (1961) emphasized that the test for all cooperative group work is the extent to which it contributes to the better learning of facts, attitudes, skills, habits, appreciation, and understanding.

During the early 1970s, considerable effort was expended in developing specific classroom cooperative methods: Teams-Games-Tournaments ((TGT)—DeVries & Slavin, 1978), Student Teams-Achievement Divisions,) ((STAD)—Slavin, 1978), and Jigsaw (Aronson, Blaney, Stephan, Sikes, & Snapp, 1978) are three of the more popular methods. All three were developed to facilitate positive interpersonal, interethnic relations among students, to increase self-esteem, and to increase academic achievement. The applications and rewards of these newer methods have occurred mainly in elementary and middle schools. For example, Slavin summarized 28 research studies and reported that 14 of them were done in Grades 1–6, 11 in Grades 7–9, and only 3 in Grades 10–12 (Slavin, 1980). In their review of research (1975), Johnson and Johnson cited few studies done with high-school students and no studies done in high-school science. We concluded that these newer cooperative methods are not yet being used in most high-school classrooms.

What, then, is the future for cooperation in high-school science? Could the rather consistent improvements in self-esteem and interpersonal skills occurring in elementary and middle schools under cooperative procedures also occur in high-school classrooms? How do high-school students—who may be more intent on learning subject matter—respond to methods that promote social interaction? Are older learners amenable to methods emphasizing cooperation rather than competition or independent study? We believe that it is both theoretically and practically important to investigate all of the above questions about learning methods in high-school science classrooms.

This paper will report three separate investigations in which a Modified Jigsaw (MJ) method was used to teach high-school science. Jigsaw, as developed by Aronson *et al.* (1978), is a method in which the class is divided into groups of four to six persons (Jigsaw groups) and the lesson is divided into enough parts so that each student has a section of the lesson to learn. All students in the class with the same part to learn study together in groups known as *counterpart groups*. In the counterpart groups, the students read their part of the lesson, discuss it and clarify its meaning, and plan how they will teach it to other students.

When prepared, the students go back to their Jigsaw groups, and each student teaches his or her part of the lesson to the others.

The students understand that each of them will be tested on the entire lesson. They come to understand that they can learn only through cooperating with the other students in their groups: paying attention to their peers, asking good questions, learning and teaching their assigned material, and helping each other to teach. The results of this method at the elementary level are consistent and positive (Aronson *et al.* 1978):

1. Children in the Jigsaw classrooms grew to like their groupmates more than they liked others in their classrooms.
2. Both Anglo and black children in the Jigsaw classrooms started to like school better than the Anglo and black children in competitive classrooms.
3. The self-esteem of the children in the Jigsaw classrooms increased more than that of children in competitive classrooms.
4. In terms of the mastery of classroom material, children in the Jigsaw classrooms performed as well or better than children in competitive classrooms.
5. Children in the Jigsaw classrooms cooperated more and saw their classmates as learning resources more often than children in competitive classrooms did. (pp. 30–31)

Similar findings have been reported by Sharan (1980). In a study comparing TGT, STAD, and Jigsaw among junior-high social-studies students (Carlson & Stuple, 1982), the Jigsaw students gained in self-esteem. They also shifted toward a more internal locus of control over a six-week period. Fewer social isolates were noticed: "Individuals who before had little or no contact with isolates began to understand and accept others not previously included in their social group" (p. 154). However, in this junior-high study, some negative effects also appeared: After six weeks of Jigsaw, the students expressed a less favorable attitude toward working with other students on projects, discussions, and class presentations, and activities involving teacher–student interactions (with the teacher in the dominant role) gained in popularity.

Studies in which the cooperative method was implemented at junior high school level reported greater mastery and retention of the subject and positive attitudes toward the method both in physical science (Humphreys, Johnson, & Johnson, 1982) and, in Israel, in social studies (Sharan, Kussell, Hertz-Lazarowitz, Bejarano, Raviv, & Sharan, 1984), although in the latter study difficulties in implementing the method at the junior high school level are mentioned.

The three studies described herein focus on cooperative learning in high-school sciences and thus add data to the implementation and use of this method.

During the academic year of 1981–82, we implemented a Modified Jigsaw (MJ) method in three experimental projects in secondary science classes, Grades 10–12 (Lazarowitz, Baird, & Hertz-Lazarowitz, 1982; Lazarowitz, Baird, Hertz-Lazarowitz, & Jenkins, 1982; Lazarowitz, Hertz-Lazarowitz, & Baird, 1982).

Experiment 1 was conducted to determine the following:

1. *Academic growth.* Will Modified Jigsaw result in the same amount of gain in academic learning as individualized mastery learning in high-school science classes?
2. *Student response to cooperation.* How will students who are used to studying independently of other students respond to activities requiring them to teach each other and learn from each other?
3. *Self-esteem.* Will using Modified Jigsaw with older high-school students result in the same gains in self-esteem as those reported for younger students?
4. *On-task behavior.* How does Modified Jigsaw affect the on-task behavior of high-school students? (Not reported in this study.)
5. *Social growth.* How do high-school science students and teachers who are inclined to learn and teach subject matter respond to an equal emphasis on social learning—esteem, cooperation, and so on?

In Experiment 2, we attempted to control for the teacher variable identified in Experiment 1; we tried to replicate our study in another science subject; we also wanted to collect data on the effects of cooperation, such as number of friends.

Experiment 3 was designed to investigate the following additional questions:

1. *Classroom norms.* How will high-school science students who are used to learning from a teacher respond to learning from each other?
2. *Student roles.* Can students in high-school science be taught and persuaded to help each other as teachers and learners?
3. *Preparing students.* Can the Jigsaw method itself be used instead of a series of cooperative games to teach students the value of cooperation?
4. *Time.* Does Modified Jigsaw take more or less time to teach a given amount of "science" than the usual lecture–demonstration method?

Table 1 presents a summary of the characteristics of our three studies. In the first project, two experimental biology classes studied for five

TABLE 1. Characteristics of Three Studies in Cooperation in High-School Science Classes

		Experiment	
	1	2	3
1. Cooperation method	Modified Jigsaw	Modified Jigsaw	Modified Jigsaw
Control method	Individualized Mastery	Individualized Mastery	Traditional Mastery
2. Sample sizes			
a. Cooperation	52 in 2 classes	50 in 3 classes	51 in 3 classes
b. Control	61 in 2 classes	33 in 2 classes	18 in 1 class
3. Subject matter	Biology Cell and plant morphology	Geology Energy sources	Genetics Biochemistry of cells
4. Duration	6 weeks	3 weeks	2 weeks[a]
5. Students prepared with team-building activities?	Yes	Yes	No
6. Students' previous experience with Jigsaw	None	None	Two previous units over 4 weeks[a]
7. Rewards	Criterion-referenced, individualized grades	Criterion-referenced, individualized grades	Criterion-referenced, individualized grades

[a]Students had prepared for Experiment 3 by using Jigsaw in two previous science units.

weeks in a Modified Jigsaw system while two control classes studied in an individual method. The second experiment was a replication of Experiment 1 under slightly different conditions. In the same school, three earth-science classes studied in the cooperative method, while two control classes studied in an individualized method. In all five of these classes, we included less able students who were being mainstreamed. The third experiment was conducted by use of the same procedures for student cooperation in a more traditional high-school science class. The three projects enabled the researchers and the public-school science teachers to examine carefully the effects of one approach to cooperative learning, Modified Jigsaw, on a secondary science classroom. In addition to studying data on academic achievement, self-esteem, and classroom climate, the research team directly observed the students and obtained feedback from them about their feelings and experiences in cooperative classrooms.

Settings for the Three Experiments

Individualized-Mastery Learning

The high school in which the first two experiments were conducted, the Bingham High School near Salt Lake City, Utah, taught all science classes using an Individualized-Mastery Learning (IML) approach based on principles suggested by Keller and Bloom (Block, 1974). Science subjects such as biology, chemistry, earth science, and physics are taught using IML. The school had achieved a nationwide reputation for its program. The instruction process has the following characteristics:

1. All learning tasks are given to students as handouts and assignment sheets that are grouped into curriculum units.
2. The students follow a sequence of learning tasks and learning activities at their own rate. Sometimes, the students work together on prescribed labs, but most of the time, they work independently.
3. The IML program is highly systematized, and pupil performance on pre- and posttests is monitored daily by computer.
4. Prior to beginning a unit of study, the students take a unit pretest. Those scoring 80% or higher are exempt from studying the unit.
5. When a student finishes the learning materials of the unit, he or she is eligible to take a criterion-referenced posttest for the unit.
6. Students who do not pass a unit posttest (usually at the 80% level) continue to study or restudy the materials and, within a few days, take a similar test.
7. The teacher's role is to guide the students, to help them when necessary, and to keep track of their activities, encouraging them to pursue work on the units.

Modified Jigsaw

The cooperative method tested in all three experiments was identical. For all three experimental groups, the science units were written in Jigsaw form (Aronson *et al.*, 1978). Each unit was rewritten so that each pupil received one section of the unit to learn in his or her counterpart group. The students worked on their sections in their counterpart groups for three or four entire class periods. They saw films, read from texts, observed demonstrations, performed laboratory experiments, interviewed resource experts, and completed worksheets. After sufficient preparation, they returned and taught their Jigsaw group members, using the same materials that they had studied. The procedure modified Aronson's original Jigsaw method in four ways:

1. The students in counterpart groups were learning a large quantity of material with many interrelated concepts and facts. Aronson's children worked in counterpart groups for only a short period to learn a simple idea.

2. The students learned by using an inquiry approach, seeking information and knowledge.

3. The Jigsaw method was the students' only experience in the science class for at least two weeks.

4. Although the students in Experiments 1 and 2 were accustomed to studying without teacher domination, in the Modified Jigsaw, the teachers removed themselves almost completely from the student activities. This action forced the students to rely completely on each other and the instructional materials. In Experiment 3, the teacher attempted to work as an available resource person without interfering with group or individual activities.

SAMPLE

Table 1 gives the sample size for each experiment. We worked with a total of 153 students in eight experimental classes and 112 students in five control classes. In Experiments 1 and 2, we were working with students who were poorly motivated to study science. They were fulfilling a requirement for high-school graduation. On the General Aptitude Test Battery (GATB), the experimental groups had a mean percentage of 46.36 in "general learning" aptitudes, 44.06 in "verbal" aptitudes, 50.93 in "numerical" aptitudes, and 59.95 in "spatial" aptitudes. The control group had a mean percentage of 57.41 in "general learning" aptitudes, 54.05 in "verbal" aptitudes, 55.78 in "numerical" aptitudes, and 69.69 in "spatial" aptitudes. We noticed from these scores that the entry aptitudes of the experimental group were lower than those of the control groups in all four areas measured by the test.

The students in Experiment 3 were also fulfilling a high-school graduation requirement, and many expressed a dislike of science, though these students were more heterogeneous in their interest in science and in academic ability than the students in Experiments 1 and 2.

The Jigsaw students in Experiment 1 and 2 were prepared for cooperative learning in two ways. First, their usual mode of study (IML) had helped to establish an expectation of studying written materials alone or in small groups without constant assistance from the teacher.

Additionally, the students were trained in cooperation activities. In Experiment 3, the students were not given specific, separate training in cooperation; rather, we trained them by introducing them to Modified Jigsaw and by teaching them how to do it as they studied a science unit just prior to our experiment.

SUBJECT MATTER

The unit learning materials for the Modified Jigsaw group in all three experiments were divided into six different, but approximately equal, packets. Each packet contained (1) a specific set of directions for the student, (2) an instructional goal to be learned and taught, (3) a learning guide directing the students to sources of information about the goal, (4) a copy of essential handouts referred to in the learning guide, and (5) a list of suggestions for the student to use in teaching this goal to his or her Jigsaw group members (see Appendix A). Each student was allowed to work individually long enough to preview his or her assignment and then joined the counterpart group.

The unit learning materials for the control group were arranged in identical packets. Each student in the control group received one of these packets. The assignments in the packet were completed by the class as directed by the teacher.

For Experiment 1, three texts were used as learning materials for both groups. The first, Biological Sciences Curriculum Study (BSCS), *Green Version* (1978), stresses ecological concepts. It is based on inquiry learning methods and is written at about a tenth-grade level. The second text, *Biology of Living Systems,* by Oram, Hummer, and Smoot (1979), is written in a traditional style for biology study at about a ninth- or tenth-grade level. The third book, *Modern Biology,* by Otto, Otto, Towle, and Weaver, (1977), is also written in a traditional style, but at a twelfth-grade level.

For Experiment 2, a learning unit on energy was developed that focused on the kinds of natural and artificial energy sources, their production, and their advantages and disadvantages. Each unit was divided into subunits for groups of five students. The learning tasks required of the students a greater variety of activities, such as observations, conducting experiments, interviewing people, and reading books and magazines.

The material for Experiment 3 was packaged for experimental classes similarly to that for Experiments 1 and 2. The text *Modern Biology* was used for Experiment 3, but much of the material came from other written sources. The control class used the same text, but because they studied in a predominantly teacher-controlled situation, they were given no packets. They were, however, given the same unit goals and handouts, saw the same films, and did the same tasks.

The Modified Jigsaw classes in Experiments 1 and 2 received four hours of introduction to cooperation (e.g., Broken Squares, Clue, and Up with People). The experimental students in Experiment 3 had been prepared for cooperation by doing Modified Jigsaw in two previous biology units. As they studied those units, we discussed with them, the reasons for cooperation with peers and ways of studying and teaching more effectively.

MEASURES OF PUPIL GROWTH

The following kinds of pupil growth were measured and were regarded as dependent variables:

1. *Academic growth* was measured in all three studies on criterion-referenced pre- and posttests. Test content validity was judged by a group of high-school biology teachers. All tests contained 20–25 multiple-choice questions. The posttests used the same questions with either the alternatives or the questions rearranged.

2. *Self-esteem* was measured in all three studies. The instrument developed contained items from two separate measures: Aronson *et al.* (1978) and Offer (1969). Some of the items were personal items (e.g., "How much do you like being yourself?"), and some were school-related items (e.g., "When you are in class how important do you feel?"). The same instrument was given as a pretest and as a posttest (see Appendix B).

3. *Classroom social climate* was measured in Experiments 1 and 2. The questionnaire was based on the Learning Environment Inventory developed by Walberg (1974), further adapted by Hertz-Lazarowitz, Sapir, and Sharan (1981). It includes 42 items in five subscales: involvement in class, cohesiveness, cooperation and equality, competition, and attitude toward the subject matter (see Appendix C).

4. *Sociometric friendship* was determined by asking each student in both the experimental and the control classes in Experiment 2 to list the names of the classmates with whom he or she would feel comfortable working in the class. A student was free to list as many names as he or she wished to list. This measure was given as both a pre- and a posttest.

5. As part of the posttest in all three studies, the students were asked to evaluate their experience by answering one or two open ques-

tions. Experimental students in 1 and 2 were asked, "Which do you like better, Jigsaw (MJ) or Individualized Learning (IML)? Explain why." In Experiment 3, the Jigsaw students were asked which they liked better, Jigsaw (MJ) or their teacher's usual method. The control students were not asked to evaluate their experience.

THE RESEARCH DESIGN

The research design for all three studies followed the Campbell and Stanley (1963) Nonequivalent Control Group Design, with the following modifications. In Experiment 1, the biology classes of two teachers were used. One teacher taught both Jigsaw classes; the other, the IML classes. For Experiments 2 and 3, classes taught by the same teachers were randomly assigned to experimental and control treatments. All outcomes were pre- and posttested except the student evaluations of Modified Jigsaw.

RESULTS

In all three studies, academic growth was measured with curriculum-specific objective tests. In neither Experiment 1 nor Experiment 2 were the gains in mean scores significant, although they favored Modified Jigsaw. In Experiment 3, there was a significant difference in mean gains favoring the control group ($p = .05$).

Changes in self-esteem were measured in all three studies (Table 2). The students in Experiments 1 and 2, using Modified Jigsaw, gained significantly over their peers in the control classes. Experiment 3 produced no significant differences in gains. However, the pre- and posttest mean gain scores for both experimental and control students were negative (-1.1).

The students in Experiment 2 were asked to list the persons in the class with whom they would like to study. Table 3 shows a significant

TABLE 2. Comparison of Pre- and Post Mean Gains in Self-Esteem in Three Experiments with Modified Jigsaw Learning

Experiment		Mean gain score	F	p
1	Experimental (MJ)	.04		
	Control	− .22	3.63	.05
2	Experimental	.24		
	Control	.10	5.66	.01
3	Experimental	−1.09		
	Control	−1.10	—	NS

TABLE 3. A Comparison of Pre- and Post-Mean Number of Friends in Modified Jigsaw and Individualized-Mastery Learning Classrooms[a]

Treatment	Pre		Post				
	Mean	SD	Mean	SD	Difference	F	p
Experimental (MJ)	5.01	3.06	6.70	3.51	1.69		
Control (IML)	5.22	2.54	4.58	2.38	−1.36	3.99	.05

[a]Data came from Experiment 2 only.

difference, with the gain in friends favoring the Modified Jigsaw classes. The number of friends was not measured in the other two experiments.

We administered a "classroom-social-climate" measure in Experiments 1 and 2. Table 4 shows that, in Experiment 1, the Modified Jigsaw students made significantly more gain than the control students on the measures "Involvement in learning," "Cooperation," and "Attitude toward the subject." There were no differences between the scores for the

TABLE 4. Pre- and Post Mean Gains in Classroom Social Climate[a] between ModifiedJigsaw and Individualized-Mastery Learning Classrooms[b]

Measure	Experiment	Treatment	Mean gain score[c]	F	p
Involvement in learning	1	Experimental[d]	.06		
		Control	−.07	4.21	.04
	2	Experimental	.06		
		Control	.02		NS
Cohesiveness	1	Experimental	−.001		
		Control	−.10		NS
		Experimental	.01		
		Control	−.03		
Cooperation	1	Experimental	.09		
		Control	−.06	8.94	.003
	2	Experimental	.01		
		Control	.02		NS
Competition	1	Experimental	.09		
		Control	.003		NS
	2	Experimental	.10		
		Control	.10		
Attitude toward the subject	1	Experimental	.05		
		Control	−.06	5.03	.02
	2	Experimental	.08		
		Control	.05		NS

[a]See Appendix C.
[b]Data come from Experiments 1 and 2.
[c]Mean gain scores = pretest mean score minus posttest mean score.
 Scale was 1 = strongly agree; 4 = strongly disagree.
[d]All experimental groups used Modified Jigsaw.

experimental and the control students on the other subscales, and there were no differences on any subscales for Experiment 2.

One of the questions that we raised as we conducted the experiments concerned the amount of time required by Modified Jigsaw compared to either Individualized-Mastery Learning (the control method for Experiments 1 and 2) or the more traditional lecture–demonstration method used as a control in Experiment 3. Even though the teachers tried to have the experimental and the control classes finish the units of study at the same time, the Modified Jigsaw classes took two days (20%) longer in Experiments 1 and 2 and three days (30%) more in Experiment 3.

At the conclusion of each experiment, the students were given an open-ended question in which they could tell what they liked or did not like about the instructional methods being tested. Table 5 lists their most common responses in rank order.

Seven of the ten reasons given (1, 2, 6, 7, 8, 9, and 10) appear to relate to students' social needs. These students valued knowing and working with other students, needing others, and being needed. The students also listed their reasons for liking Modified Jigsaw that related to learning science. They said that the method helped them to learn more with less personal reading.

When the students were asked to list their reasons for disliking Modified Jigsaw, (see Table 6), they again displayed their antisocial needs (2, 4, 6, 8, 10, and 15) by naming preferences for students not in their group and listing a need to study alone. The majority of the students (9 of 15) seemed to blame Modified Jigsaw for their inability to perform well in the subject matter being studied. Though the attitude is not reflected adequately in the tables, most Jigsaw students in Experiment 3 were frustrated and angry before the study was finished. They acknowledged their inability or their irresponsibility in applying the Jigsaw pro-

TABLE 5. Major Reasons Given by High School Students for Liking Modified Jigsaw[a]

1. I got to know more classmates and make friends.
2. I felt important helping others to learn.
3. It helps me understand the materials better.
4. I don't have to study (read) all the materials.
5. I learn more.
6. We learned to cooperate and why it is important to cooperate.
7. It makes me feel needed.
8. It causes me to be dependable and do my assignment.
9. I like to study in a group with other students.
10. It was fun.

[a]The same 10 major reasons were listed by the students in all three experiments.

TABLE 6. Major Reasons Given by High School Students for Disliking Modified Jigsaw[a]

Experiment 1

1. Jigsaw is slower than studying by myself. (Faster students were bored.)
2. In our groups, we visited and got off the subject.
3. If one person doesn't prepare, the whole group suffers.
4. I don't like being separated from my friends.
5. Others don't care and don't cooperate.

Experiment 2

6. I can go at my own speed in the individualized method.
7. I got more done working by myself.
8. I like to work alone.
9. I learn more in the individualized method.
10. I can depend on myself in the individualized method.

Experiment 3

11. I didn't learn as much.
12. Others didn't learn their material and cooperate.
13. We were not given enough time to learn.
14. I didn't understand others' teaching.
15. I don't like to rely on others.

[a]We have listed the top five reasons by each group in rank order.

cedures, and they blamed the method for their poor scores on the posttest.

We found one other difficulty with the Modified Jigsaw: Students who had not prepared well tended to miss class on the day that they were scheduled to teach—a situation that would not have existed if the complete Jigsaw lesson had been studied and taught in one class period.

DISCUSSION

We conducted three experiments to determine if a modified version of Aronson's Jigsaw method could be used successfully in high-school science classes. Changing the independent variables and measuring different effects, we sought answers to the following questions:

What happens to achievement and interest when instead of Jigsaw lessons intermingled with other methods, students learn in Jigsaw classrooms where this is the only method available to the students for two or three weeks? The students did learn science in Jigsaw units that covered many days. However, we tend to disagree with Aronson et al. (1978) when he suggests that "the kinds of positive effects of cooperation reported in this volume are a linear function of the amount of cooperation—that is, as jigsawing increases, so do the benefits" (p. 131). There were problems. We observed in all three experiments that some students scheduled to teach their material at the end of the unit, sometimes five or six days after studying it, did not remember the material as well as those who taught their Jigsaw group first. A large unit of material (one chapter or more) seemed to be too much for one Jigsaw assignment.

Though our high-school science students in all three experiments listed benefits of Jigsaw, they also expressed a need for variety, for more interaction with their teacher, and for a chance to study alone sometimes. Eventually, it may be determined that Jigsaw is more helpful for some kinds of students than for others, a finding reported in studies by Kenney (1975), Ross and Harrigan (1980), and Webb (1980).

Will Modified Jigsaw result in the same gain in academic learning as an Individualized-Mastery Learning program in high-school science? How important is academic learning to teachers and students? We found that both methods were equally effective and that they were both good. We found that previously unencountered science material can be learned by use of the Modified Jigsaw material. The experimental students, many of whom were poor readers and below average in ability, learned higher level concepts and science process skills as well as recall information.

The teachers with whom we were working placed top priority on pupil growth in knowledge of science rather than on the acquiring of social skills such as cooperation. Methods that cannot produce significant subject-matter gains in students are likely to be rejected by high-school science teachers, no matter how effective they are in increasing self-esteem or interpersonal skills. There appeared to be an inverse relationship between the students' ability to succeed in learning science and their willingness to work with other students—studying together, teaching each other, sharing learning tasks, and so on. The more able they were, the more emphasis they placed on independent study and academic achievement. It was as if the more able students were more intent on learning science information than on learing social skills. They seemed to be saying that science classrooms were not appropriate places to learn to cooperate. The teachers who expressed opinions tended to agree. However, the majority of the students, including the less able, were much more willing to include cooperation as part of their curriculum.

In all of the experiments, the science classes were required for high-school graduation. One wonders what the effects of Jigsaw would be in elective science classes, such as those adapted for the less able student and also those, such as physics and advanced-placement courses, offered for the more able pupil.

Will using Modified Jigsaw with high-school students result in the same gains in self-esteem as with younger students? Probably so. We found significant results favoring Modified Jigsaw in two experiments. In the third experiment, self-esteem, as we measured it, decreased in both the experimental and the control groups. Where the Modified Jigsaw was successful, the students made such comments as "I made more friends," "I felt important when helping others," "I learned more," and "It makes me feel needed." To the degree that a method causes these kinds of feelings in students, it will undoubtedly increase students' self-esteem (Offer, 1969).

Even though we believe that Modified Jigsaw produced significant positive feelings in the students, we are compelled to be cautious in our conclusions. Coopersmith and Feldman (1974), Purkey (1970), and others have reminded us that permanent changes in self-esteem are usually slow in developing—they certainly require more than two or three weeks in one 50-minute high-school class. We may have captured strong feelings about self with our measure of self-esteem rather than permanent changes in self-concept. To determine the latter, readers may need to test Jigsaw over long periods of time with more sophisticated measures.

How will high-school science students, used to learning from a teacher who plays the dominant role in the class, respond to learning from each other? This was the major question of our third experiment. Our findings completely agree with Joyce and Harootunian (1967): "If students . . . are to participate actively in education themselves, then they must be clear about [and accept, we might add] their roles and the role of those who teach them" (p. 170). The students in Experiment 3 were so used to being taught by the teacher that we found it impossible in the six weeks we worked with them to cause them to redefine their role or the teacher's. High-school students can be taught how to cooperate. Our Jigsaw students in all three experiments knew *what* to do. The students who had learned to accept responsibility for their learning performed well in cooperative learning activities, but for students who had been taught for several years in school that theirs was a passive learning role, our brief introduction to Modified Jigsaw failed. In situations like this, we strongly encourage more team building and cooperation games combined with brief Jigsaw lessons. We recommend that students be helped to see how effective the Jigsaw lessons are in helping them to attain their goals, and we recommend building in some kind of competitive reward structure between Jigsaw groups.

Does Modified Jigsaw require more time to teach a given amount of science? Our experiments lead us to believe that it does. Student absenteeism and the extra time needed to set up and use films and labs and demonstrations more than once (once for the counterpart group and again in each Jigsaw group) complicated and extended the schedule in the Jigsaw science classes. Also, experienced teachers can be more efficient in their use of time than students who have never taught the subject matter before.

We conducted our experiments to investigate the power and the effects of cooperative learning activities, specifically Jigsaw learning in high-school science classes. We wanted to know about achievement, interest in science, and self-esteem. We wondered if we could modify Jigsaw to accommodate whole units of instruction as the only type of learning to be employed over an extended time without sacrificing the social and academic growth reported in other studies of Jigsaw teaching. We wondered how high-school science teachers and students with a strong orientation to, and focus on, subject-matter learning, would respond to an instructional approach that also emphasizes growth in social skills. Finally, we wondered how students and teachers who saw the teacher's main role as that of information giver and who saw the student in a more passive role would respond to Modified Jigsaw.

We have begun to collect data in answer to our questions. Our data support this use of Jigsaw methods in high-school science classes. We are convinced that students need to be taught how to cooperate. Both they and teachers will need help in thinking through their roles in the classroom. Although we are excited about the use of Jigsaw in high-school science classes, we are even more convinced than before that a variety of methods—cooperative and competitive—is essential to optimum student growth.

REFERENCES

Aronson, E., Blaney, N., Stephan, C., Sikes, J., & Snapp, M. *The Jigsaw classroom*. Beverly Hills, Calif.: Sage Publication, 1978.

Asch, S. Studies of independence and conformity. *Psychological Monographs*, 1956, 9, Whole No. 416.

Biological Sciences Curriculum Study. *An Ecological Approach, Green Version* (4th ed.). Chicago: Rand McNally, 1978.

Block, H. *Schools, society, and mastery learning*. New York: Holt, Rinehart and Winston, 1974.

Campbell, D. T., & Stanley, J. E. *Experimental and quasi-experimental designs for research*. Chicago: Rand McNally College Publishing, 1963.

Carlson, M., & Stuple, S. J. *Cooperative small-group learning methods: A comparative study of*

Student Teams-Achievement Division (STAD), Teams-Games-Tournaments (TGT), and the Jigsaw classroom. Unpublished thesis, Reed College, Oregon, 1982.

Coopersmith, S., & Feldman, R. Fostering a positive self-concept and high self-esteem in the classroom. In R. H. Cox & K. White (Eds.), *Psychological concepts in the classroom.* New York: Harper & Row, 1974.

Deutsch, M. A Theory of Cooperation and Competition. *Human Relations*, 1949, 2, 129–151.

DeVries, D. L., & Slavin, R. E. Teams-Games-Tournaments: A research review. *Journal of Research and Development in Education*, 1978, 12, 28–38.

Hertz-Lazarowitz, R., Sapir, C., & Sharan, S. *Academic and social effects of two cooperative learning methods in desegregated classrooms.* Master's thesis, Haifa University, Israel, 1981.

Humphreys, B., Johnson, T. R., & Johnson, W. D. Effects of cooperative, competitive, and individualistic learning on students' achievement in science class. *Journal of Research in Science Teaching*, 1982, 19 (5), 351–356.

Johnson, D. W., & Johnson, R. T. *Learning together and alone.* Englewood Cliffs, N.J.: Prentice-Hall, 1975.

Joyce, B. R., & Harootunian, B. *The structure of teaching.* Chicago: Science Research Associates, 1967.

Kenney, P. F. *Effects of group interaction stimulated by competition between groups as a motivating technique in a ninth-grade mathematics classroom.* Report NIE-P-0321. Washington, D.C.: National Institute of Education, 1975.

Lazarowitz, R., Baird, H., & Hertz-Lazarowitz, R. *Academic achievements, learning environment, self-esteem and inquiry skills of high school students in biology taught in cooperative-investigative small groups.* Paper presented at the National Association of Research in Science Teaching (NARST) Annual Meeting, The Abbey, April 5–7, 1982.

Lazarowitz, R., Baird, H., Hertz-Lazarowitz, R., & Jenkins, J. *Cooperative learning comes to science classes in the high school: Academic and non-academic measures in two instructional methods: Individualized mastery learning vs. group mastery learning.* Paper presented at the Second International Conference for the Study of Cooperation in Education. Brigham Young University, Provo, Utah, July 6–9, 1982.

Lazarowitz, R., Hertz-Lazarowitz, R., & Baird, H. *Cooperative learning comes to the high school: Content analysis of students' responses.* Paper presented at the Annual Convention of the American Education Research Association, New York, 1982.

Montean, J. The discussion group method in science education. *Science Education*, 1961, 45, 227–230.

Offer, D. *The psychological world of the teenager.* New York: Basic Books, 1969.

Oram, R., Hummer, P., Jr., & Smoot, R. *Biology of living systems.* Columbus, Ohio: Merrill Publishing, 1979.

Otto, J., Otto, D., Towle, A., & Weaver, R. *Modern biology.* New York: Holt, Rinehart and Winston, 1977.

Purkey, W. W. *Self concept and school achievement.* Englewood Cliffs, N.J.: Prentice-Hall, 1970.

Ross, H. G., & Harrigan, J. Small group learning climate and achievement styles. *Journal of Experimental Education*, 1980, 48 (4), 307–315.

Sharan, S. Cooperative learning in small groups: Recent methods and effects on achievement, attitudes and ethnic relations. *Review of Educational Research.* 1980, 2, 241–271.

Sharan, S., Hare, P., Webb, C. D. & Hertz-Lazarowitz, R. (Eds.). *Cooperation in Education.* Provo, Utah: Brigham Young University Press, 1980.

Sharan, S., Kussel, P., Hertz-Lazarowitz, R., Bejarano, Y., Raviv, S., & Sharan, Y.

Cooperative learning in the classroom: Research in desegregated schools. Hillsdale, N.J.: Erlbaum, 1984.

Slavin, R. E. Student teams and achievement divisions. *Journal of Research and Development in Education,* 1978, *12,* 39–49.

Slavin, R. E. Cooperative learning. *Review of Educational Research,* 1980, *50* (2), 315–342.

Slavin, R. E. *Cooperative learning.* New York: Longman, 1983.

Walberg, H. J. *Evaluating educational performance.* Berkeley, Calif.: McCutchan Publishing, 1974.

Washton, N. *Teaching science creatively in the secondary schools.* Philadelphia: W. B. Saunders, 1967.

Webb, N. M. An analysis of group interaction and mathematical errors in heterogeneous ability groups. *British Journal of Educational Psychology,* 1980, *50,* 266–276.

A MODIFIED JIGSAW LEARNING MATERIAL PACKET

Course _____ Biology I _____   TRACE Number 211-211

Unit Title _____ You and the Cell _____   Name _____

Directions: Before beginning please make sure everyone in this counterpart group is learning goal #3.

Each student, while in your counterpart group, should learn the following goal by doing those things which are listed on the learning guide and be prepared to teach this goal following the suggestions listed below when you return to your Jigsaw group. Those items which have an asterisk (*) by them must be used to teach the material.

You should work with each other in your counterpart group, but please make sure you are well prepared to teach this goal by yourself when you return to your Jigsaw group.

3. Goal: You are able to predict from given diagrams the direction selected substances (water, iodine, and starch) will flow through a cell membrane.

Learning Guide: Read: *Green Version*, pp. 367–369
                    Living Systems, pp. 70–74
                    Modern Biology, pp. 75–82
          Word List: Write a definition for each work in the *material movement* section of the word list.
          Lab: *Green Version*, p. 370, Investigation 11.2

Suggestions for teaching the material when you return to your Jigsaw group:

*A. Have group read the pages listed above and make reading notes.
*B. Have group write definitions of terms.
*C. Have group do laboratory investigation.
*D. Discuss the movement of water, iodine, and starch, using diagrams of beakers and cell membrane.
*E. Discuss why the movement of materials is important for the cells in your body.
*F. Develop a five-question quiz to test knowledge of the goal.

SELF-ESTEEM TEST

1. Indicate if this test is a pretest or a posttest.

2. Directions: Each of the 10 questions for this test will be read aloud twice. You should indicate your answer for each question by marking one of the seven boxes which best describes your feelings about the question. Under each box is a verbal description of the meaning of that box.

3. Questions:
   1. How much do you like being yourself?

   2. When you are in the classroom, how important do you feel?

   3. When you are in class, how often do you feel you can learn whatever you try to learn?

   4. How much do you like school this year?

   5. When you are in the classroom, how bored do you feel?

   6. When you are in the classroom, how relaxed do you feel?

   7. When you are in the classroom, how easy is it for you to make friends?

   8. When you are with other students in the classroom, how happy do you feel?

   9. When you are in the classroom do you mind being corrected by others?

   10. How often do you think that other people do not like you?

CLASSROOM ENVIRONMENT CHECKLIST

Dear Student:

This checklist contains different statements describing possible situations in your class.

Please read each one and mark with a circle on the right side whether you strongly agree (1), agree (2), disagree (3), or strongly disagree (4) that it actually represents the situation *in your class.*

Since there is no right or wrong answer, please mark the column that exactly describes the situation to your best knowledge. Do not sign your name. Your answers will not be available to the school and will not be used for grading or any kind of evaluation. They will be used *only* for research study purposes.

Thank you very much for your cooperation.

R. Lazarowitz
J. H. Baird

1.	Certain groups of students like to sit next to each other.	1	2	3	4
2.	Students are very interested in the class's learning progress.	1	2	3	4
3.	Class is composed of students who do not know one another.	1	2	3	4
4.	The students are satisfied with the biology lessons.	1	2	3	4
5.	In the classroom, the students get along well together.	1	2	3	4
6.	Students are not interested in what is going on in the lessons.	1	2	3	4
7.	Students in the class very rarely compete.	1	2	3	4
8.	Special projects are given to only good students.	1	2	3	4
9.	There is friction among classmates.	1	2	3	4
10.	It is important to study biology in order to understand nature.	1	2	3	4
11.	Some students are preferred over other students.	1	2	3	4
12.	Most of the students do not care if their classmates fail.	1	2	3	4
13.	Students found biology studies to be difficult.	1	2	3	4

251

14. There is not enough interaction among students for
    sympathy or nonsympathyrelations to develop.   1   2   3   4
15. I would take biology even if it were only an elective
    course.   1   2   3   4
16. In biology, we discuss a variety of problems that are
    related to daily issues.   1   2   3   4
17. Students do not care about the friendship situation
    in the classroom.   1   2   3   4
18. There is great competition among students for high
    achievement.   1   2   3   4
19. During a biology lesson, the teacher progresses ac-
    cording to the good students' rate of understand-
    ing.   1   2   3   4
20. I like to study biology.   1   2   3   4
21. The better students in the class get special privi-
    leges.   1   2   3   4
22. The classroom is well organized and the teaching
    techniques are effective.   1   2   3   4
23. I prefer not to study biology.   1   2   3   4
24. In a biology period, most of the students cooperate
    and do not compete with one another.   1   2   3   4
25. Learning about biology is worthwhile for my future
    goals.   1   2   3   4
26. There is mutual help in learning among the stu-
    dents.   1   2   3   4
27. In biology lessons, some students always try to be
    more successful than their friends.   1   2   3   4
28. Students show a willingness to cooperate with each
    of their friends in the class.   1   2   3   4
29. Most of the students in the class know each other. 1   2   3   4
30. The rate of instruction in the class is too fast.   1   2   3   4
31. Most of the students cooperate with each other
    without discrimination.   1   2   3   4
32. There is competition among students as to who can
    do a better job in biology.   1   2   3   4
33. Tension in the classroom contributes to separation
    among classmates.   1   2   3   4
34. What happens in a biology period is determined by
    a small number of students who are the teacher's fa-
    vorites.   1   2   3   4
35. The students care if the class does not succeed.   1   2   3   4
36. Some students do not honor others.   1   2   3   4
37. In biology lessons, students have difficulty keeping
    up with the learning materials.   1   2   3   4
38. Each person in the class has an opportunity to get to
    know the other students.   1   2   3   4

39. There are students who are not willing to listen to what their friends are saying during a classroom discussion.   1   2   3   4
40. Some students tend to raise different problems that relate to the topic under discussion.   1   2   3   4
41. Most of the students want their work to be better than others.   1   2   3   4
42. Biology is the most important subject studied in school.   1   2   3   4

IV

Cooperative Learning and the Multiethnic Classroom

SHLOMO SHARAN

Almost since their inception, cooperative learning methods have been applied in desegregated, multigroup educational settings. Underlying all these efforts has been the fundamental principle, demonstrated years earlier by Sherif and Sherif (1956), that people who help each other and who join forces to achieve a common goal will generally grow to feel more positively about each other and will be willing and able to interact constructively when performing a collective task. Cooperative learning methods have brought this principle to bear on the design of normative classroom pursuits instead of continuing to view learning and social relations as separate domains requiring different programs and settings. Learning in school has transpired within a social context replete with complex social processes and relationships (Schmuck & Schmuck, 1982). When the class is comprised of pupils from different ethnic, racial, or cultural backgrounds, these processes and relationships suddenly assume for teachers a degree of salience that they may not have had when all of the students were of the same social group. Teachers report that the multiethnic class presents a far greater instructional challenge than the so-called homogeneous class (Amir & Sharan, 1984). Teachers, when confronted by this challenge, may become more open to a possible change in their style of classroom management and teaching, provided there is some prospect of developing positive intergroup relations and collaboration in the learning effort.

The first chapter in this section poses some fundamental questions about the social ideology directing the desegregation enterprise in general, and the application of cooperative learning techniques to multiethnic classrooms in particular. Shelagh Towson's chapter is thought-provoking on several accounts, not the least of which is the fact that it relates cooperative learning to a wider social context. Clearly, investigators of interethnic cooperation in desegregated settings do not necessarily share the same social ideology. Some may subscribe to an

SHLOMO SHARAN • School of Education, Tel Aviv University, Tel Aviv, Israel.

assimilationist position. They would construe cooperation as a vehicle for promoting the eventual absorption of the minority group and culture, perceived as relatively primitive, by the more advanced and "progressive" majority-group culture. Other educators concerned with intergroup cooperation may subscribe to a pluralistic ideology that views cooperation as a form of social exchange where the contributions of all social subgroups play a role in building the social order, but where the integrity of each group is safeguarded and supported by society. The latter position is doubtless more difficult to sustain in a competitive and individualistic society. Assimilationist ideology has a long tradition in human social history, and many subgroups have embraced this ideology in the hope that eliminating their separate identity will lead to total acceptance by the majority and to sharing in the material benefits of the larger society. Many minorities hover on the brink of self-negation because they have lost any conscious sense of their self-worth. Pluralism seems to have been far less prevalent as a form of social organization, at least in the Western world.

It is of interest to note that the assimilationist ideology itself is not monolithic in its goals or motives. Some spokespersons for this outlook maintain that their primary concern is for social stability and cohesiveness. They argue that, if education promotes subgroup identities, it will actually be encouraging social divisiveness and atomization. The more subgroups see themselves as separate and unique, the less they will identify with the society as a whole. Other assimilationists take a position more akin to the "white man's burden" ideology, that, by having minority-group children cooperating with majority-group children in the same classroom, the lower status pupils will imitate or adopt the values and strivings of the higher status pupils. Both versions of the assimilationist position could advocate employing cooperative learning methods in desegregated classrooms as the preferred means of fostering ethnic integration, but each approach would support cooperative learning for distinctly different reasons.

Educators favoring pluralism in the sense of supporting ethnic identity would advocate interethnic cooperation in schools directed at cultivating equal coexistence and mutual respect among pupils from different ethnic groups. Concurrently, they would argue that fostering subgroup integrity need not undermine the cohesion of the social order. Quite the contrary: A deepened sense of group identity is fertile soil for a sense of connectedness with others and an ability to perceive other groups without threat to one's own integrity. Groups secure in their own sense of self and survival may be prepared to assume heightened responsibility for the fate and progress of the larger society (Sharan,

Amir, & Ben-Ari, 1984). Failing to cultivate this sense of group identity can be a potential source of great social unrest: "Ignored differences assert themselves, and in the end rise against efforts to ride over them in favor of an assumed, or desired, uniformity" (Berlin, 1982, p. 353). In sum, the techniques of cooperative learning can be employed to promote uniformity or diversity. What these methods will achieve probably depends, to some extent at least, on how they are implemented and under what circumstances and in what context. We are in Towson's debt for drawing our attention to these ideologies as they may impinge on the use of cooperative learning and the subtle implications of these different orientations.

The second and third chapters in this section describe two extensive experiments conducted at the same time 9,000 miles apart—in California and in Israel. Both studies were quite complex, comparing the effects of three instructional methods that the investigators implemented and evaluated in multiethnic classrooms. In California, the groups involved were white, black, and Mexican-American children, and in Israel, the groups were Jewish children from Middle Eastern and Western backgrounds. Both studies encompassed a wide range of measures to assess the effects on academic achievement and on social relations and attitudes within and between the ethnic groups in these mixed-ethnic classes. These features alone set these studies apart from most other work, which has concentrated on a small set of dependent variables and on the direct comparison of one cooperative method versus whole-class instruction. This is the first time that two cooperative methods, albeit different ones in each of the two experiments, are compared to each other. These are the main similarities between the two studies.

Among the more important differences between the two experiments are these: the experiment of Spencer Kagan, G. Lawrence Zahn, Keith F. Widaman, Joseph Schwarzwald, and Gary Tyrrell compared TGT and STAD with whole-class teaching; both of the former methods are peer-tutoring approaches (Sharan, 1980); and the study by Shlomo Sharan, Peter Kussell, Yael Bejarano, Shulamit Raviv, Rachel Hertz-Lazarowitz, and Yael Sharan compared STAD and the Group Investigation method, as well as comparing them to whole-class teaching. Hypothetically, these four methods could be placed on a continuum representing varying degrees of cooperation involved in the procedures of the different methods:

Low cooperation			High cooperation
1	2	3	4
WC	TGT	STAD	GI

Except for TGT (see Kagan *et al.*'s chapter), the degree of cooperation inherent in these methods also reflected the degree of competition in inverse order; that is, GI was least competitive and WC most competitive. Thus, Kagan *et al.*'s study included the three methods placed on the left side of the continuum, omitting the most cooperative Group-Investigation method, whereas Sharan *et al.*'s study selected the two more cooperative methods on the right of the continuum to compare to the most competitive method.

Both these experiments introduce concepts into the field of cooperative learning research that have not figured prominently in the studies available thus far. Kagan *et al.*'s thesis regarding structural bias in classroom instruction, to the effect that some teaching methods exert negative effects on pupils from certain ethnic groups, can be heuristically fruitful not only for cooperative learning but for a wide range of research in education. This concept emerged organically from Kagan's entire research career on the cooperative-competitive behavior of children as a function of their cultural history (Kagan, 1980). As Mexican-American children display a more cooperative orientation than their Anglo-American peers, it was reasonable to anticipate that traditional whole-class instruction, with its competitive orientation and its liberal use of social comparison as a major strategy for arousing pupils' motivation to learn, would exert a wide range of negative effects on the behavior of Mexican-American children in school settings.

Kagan places his research in the context of person-by-situation interaction studies. Cooperative learning provides a set of methods for designing educational procedures that are more consistent with the social orientation of various cultural subgroups in society. However, person-by-environment research focuses largely on the individual's aptitudes or inclinations. This school remains in the tradition of the psychology of individual differences typical of American psychological research. For all its similarity to this approach, Kagan's work concentrates squarely on the social values and orientations shared by many of the members of historically, culturally, and ethnically identifiable groups. Thus, this research is a genuinely social-psychological approach to evaluating educational phenomena because the reality of the group's value systems and social history is its fundamental premise. Kagan's work is unequivocally on the side of pluralism, in terms of the issues raised by Towson. Kagan views the social order as comprised of groups, not of disconnected individuals, and consequently, this approach is not "culture-blind," nor does it assume, or preach, that everyone is, or should be, alike. Treating the social orientation of an ethnic group toward cooperation and competition as a factor that should influence the design of the children's educational experience is an important way of acknowledging and supporting the integrity of that group. Obviously, there are many equally important educational techniques for accomplishing this goal. Kagan's work occupies what may be a unique place in psychoeducational research because of its social and behavioral approach to ethnicity and schooling, which differs from the individualistic and content-oriented methods of recognizing ethnic identity and integrity.

Empirical investigation of the structural bias concept will require a long research effort. If we agree that many Western societies explicitly or implicitly embrace an assimilationist ideology in their educational institutions, it is unlikely that the educational establishment in various nations will wish to allocate the resources needed to pursue this topic. Yet, failing to do so runs counter to several urgent goals of these societies to provide effective schooling for multiethnic populations in desegregated classrooms. Hence, the concept of structural bias, once empirically substantiated—and Kagan et al.'s work reported here takes a big step in that direction—will prove to be a politically unpopular notion with considerable potential for understanding and improving educational practice. Is that not the position in which many important innovative ideas in education have found themselves? Perhaps this time, the cost of ignoring this message will be seen to be too great to incur.

One is tempted to compare the results of the research conducted in Israel by Sharan and colleagues with those reported by Kagan et al. in California. However, these introductory comments do not presume to integrate or evaluate the results of these studies, a task that the editors must leave in large part to the reader. Such a comparison would actually require a chapter all is own. One point, however, deserves special mention to ensure that it will not be overlooked. Only limited findings indicating the differential effects of cooperative learning methods on pupils from Middle Eastern and Western ethnic background in Israel appeared in the Sharan et al. study. Hence, at this time, we cannot draw crosscultural analogies in terms of the concept of structural bias proposed by Kagan, at least not for the cooperative learning methods. No evidence was generated in the Israel study supporting the notion that cooperative learning affected children differently as a function of their ethnic identity. The pupils from both major ethnic groups responded similarly to the cooperative learning methods, in the academic as well as in the social domains evaluated in the study reported here. Results concerning achievement are not independent of the subject matter involved or of the manner in which pupil learning is evaluated, and the differences between the two studies presented here might be a function, in part, of those factors.

Interestingly, the traditional whole-class method exerted a negative effect on pupil's ethnic attitudes in the Israel study. Although the size of the effect was distinctly larger for Middle Eastern pupils, it was nevertheless significant in the attitudes expressed by Western-background pupils as well. Thus, the overall finding from the Sharan et al. study was that cooperative learning methods promoted better achievement and more positive social relations, within and between ethnic groups, for all pupils regardless of their ethnic background. Whole-class instruction was found to be less effective because it fostered a lower level of learning and less positive, more competitive social relations among peers, as well as negative ethnic attitudes. This outcome was not due to bias for or against any particular ethnic group.

We must not omit mention of the fact that, unlike Kagan et al.'s work, the Israel study had no data base for predicting the differential effects of any given instructional technique on pupils from either ethnic group. It is not known if one group typically displays more or less cooperation and/or competition than the other group. Consequently, the Sharan et al. study does not support the structural bias thesis as far as Israeli society is concerned. Of course, it may be that the Middle Eastern ethnic group, many of whom immigrated to Israel from the less urbanized and less industrialized nations of North Africa and Asia, already underwent a thorough process of acculturation into the competitive values of Israel as a Western technological society, similar to the process that has overtaken some ethnic groups in other parts of the world (Graves & Graves, 1978; Kagan, 1980). That interpretation remains to be documented. Another interpretation, with much empirical evidence, refers to the fact that the two ethnic groups in Israel affirm their common historical and religious heritage, perceive themselves as belonging to one historical nation now restoring its political sovereignty in its own land, and, despite the differences that have developed between various Jewish subgroups, are still more similar to each other than are the ethnic subgroups in countries like the United States, England, and Germany (Amir & Sharan, 1984). Hence, facile analogies between social conditions regarding ethnicity and its consequences in these different countries are often misleading.

The Sharan et al. study also stresses some new approaches and topics that have not been explored heretofore in the cooperative-learning research literature. These include an explicit theoretical framework to account for the relationship between cooperative interaction in small groups and the learning of given subject matter (in this case, the study of English as a second language); the introduction of behavioral measures to document interethnic cooperation as a function of having been exposed to particular classroom procedures, rather than employing self-report measures exclusively; and the evaluation of ethnic attitudes and stereotypes regarding particular ethnic groups as social entities, rather than inferring ethnic attitudes and relationships from measures of relationships with given individuals whose ethnicity is not identified explicitly (such as sociometric questions and peer evaluations). This latter emphasis is consistent with Towson's rejection of "colorblindness" as the criterion for tolerance implicit in much research on school desegregation and ethnic relations.

The final chapter in this section is directed toward the future. Geoffrey Maruyama provides a multidimensional perspective for investigating what surely must occupy center stage in future research on cooperative learning in general, and on its effects in desegregated classrooms in particular. That subject is the analysis of how classroom processes affect learning outcomes. Maruyama's model could sustain an entire research program concerned with specifying how social relations transpiring during cooperative learning influence pupils' academic achievement, with particular emphasis on how peer interactions occurring in the cooperative learning class induce changes in minority-group pupils' learning. Research thus far, including the work reported in this volume, has demonstrated repeatedly the relative effectiveness of cooperative learning methods in promoting academic achievement (Slavin, 1983). However, we know relatively little about how these effects come about. Webb's (1982) process–product research has begun to explore this issue from a cognitive perspective. Maruyama's thoughtful and provocative contribution to this subject will, we hope, lead the next generation of investigators to focus on the *relationship* between social and learning processes.

In the majority of research studies published thus far on the effects of cooperative learning, in all of its various manifestations, social and academic learning variables have been studied as parallel rather than as interrelated phenomena. Hence, the proposals made by Maruyama in his chapter not only suggest a new approach to data analysis but require revisions in the basic conception of how cooperative learning experiments should be conducted. The proposed model urges us to plan studies that have a far more integrative perspective than that employed heretofore, a perspective that is likely to encompass a wider scope of topics and variables perceived within a nexus of relationships. Maruyama has instructed us on how to analyze the data obtained from such studies. What remains to be explained in detail, and to be demonstrated, is a plan for carrying out experiments in real-life settings with the degree of complexity required by the theoretical model.

What must not be overlooked is the clear change in direction required by this model and by the process–product research now emerging from the school of investigators concerned with peer cooperation and learning in schools. Schooling almost universally occurs with relatively large classroom groups rather than with aggregates of individuals. The study of the relationship between peer interactions and influences and their relation to school learning appears, finally, to be receiving serious acknowledgment by educational researchers, enriching previous research focusing on individuals' traits and their interaction with educational treatments. The fact that Maruyama has produced this model at this time may suggest that the social interactional aspects of life in classrooms is finally attracting the attention that it deserves from theoreticians and students of the educational process.

Given the way in which peer cooperation in small learning groups can be linked with a wide range of theoretical positions about intergroup relations of various kinds, only some of which were touched on in the research reported here, we anticipate that cooperative learning will continue to be employed in many more studies dealing with intergroup contact in educational settings.

REFERENCES

Amir, Y., & Sharan, S. (Eds.). *School desegregation: Cross-cultural perspectives.* Hillsdale, N.J.: Erlbaum, 1984.

Berlin, I. *Against the current: Essays in the history of ideas.* New York: Penguin Books, 1982.

Graves, N., & Graves, T. The impact of modernization on the personality of a Polynesian people. *Human Organization,* 1978, *37,* 147–162.

Kagan, S. Cooperation-competition, culture, and structural bias in classrooms. In S. Sharan, P. Hare, C. Webb, & R. Hertz-Lazarowitz (Eds.), *Cooperation in education.* Provo, Utah: Brigham Young University Press, 1980.

Schmuck, R., & Schmuck, P. *Group processes in the classroom* (4th ed.). Dubuque, Iowa: Brown, 1982.

Sharan, S. Cooperative learning in small groups: Recent methods and effects on achievement, attitudes and ethnic relations. *Review of Educational Research,* 1980, *50,* 241–271.

Sharan, S., Amir, Y., & Ben-Ari, R. School desegregation: Some challenges ahead. In Y. Amir & S. Sharan (Eds.), *School desegregation: Cross-cultural perspectives.* Hillsdale, N.J.: Erlbaum, 1984.

Sherif, M., & Sherif, C. *An outline of social psychology.* New York: Harper & Brothers, 1956.

Slavin, R. *Cooperative learning.* New York: Longman, 1983.

Webb, N. Student interaction and learning in small groups. *Review of Educational Research,* 1982, *52,* 421–445.

10

Melting Pot or Mosaic
Cooperative Education and Interethnic Relations

SHELAGH TOWSON

Although, as human beings, we do not derive all our attitudes, beliefs, and values from empirical evidence, we do try, as social scientists, to conduct our research and interpret our results as objectively as we can. Despite our best efforts, however, I would like to suggest that some assumptions are so basic to a particular culture or subculture and so pervasive that we let them shape both theory and research, with only minimal acknowledgment or awareness of their influence. In this chapter, I would like to explore the notion that research on the use of cooperative classroom groups as a strategy to facilitate positive interethnic relations has been profoundly affected by the two ideologies that have dominated North American thought on this issue: the melting pot and the mosaic—or, more prosaically, assimilation and pluralism.

Berry's (1977) eight-cell scheme of modes of group relations in complex societies provides a good starting point for this discussion. Reference to Table 1 indicates that the scheme is based on dichotomous answers to three questions. First, is retention of ethnic identity regarded positively or negatively? Second, are positive relations among ethnic groups regarded as necessary and desirable? Third, are minority ethnic groups given a choice regarding the particular mode of group relations being proposed? The various possible combinations of "yes" and "no" answers to these three questions generate eight patterns of intergroup relations.

1. *Integration (democratic pluralism)*. Ethnic retention and positive intergroup relations are valued by ethnic group(s). Free and regular association of culturally distinct groups is motivated by some mutual (national) set of goals, sufficient to maintain positive relations. Because choice is free, an individual is not obliged to retain his or her own ethnicity and could theoretically move from one group to another (e.g., Switzerland).

SHELAGH TOWSON • Department of Psychology, Trent University, Peterborough, Ontario, K9J 7B8, Canada.

TABLE 1. Scheme of Modes of Group Relations in Complex Societies Based upon
Answers to Three Questions[a]

Question 1	Question 2	Question 3	Pattern	
Retention of identity?	Positive relations?	Choice by ethnic group?	Number/Name	
Yes	Yes	Yes	1. Integration (democratic pluralism)	
		No	2. Paternal integration (inclusive segregation)	
	No	Yes	3. Rejection (self-segregation)	
		No	4. Exclusive segregation	
No	Yes	Yes	5. Assimilation 1 (melting pot)	
		No	6. Assimilation 2 (pressure cooker)	
	No	Yes	7. Marginality	
		No	8. Deculturation	

[a]Adapted from Berry (1977).

2. *Paternal integration (inclusive segregation)*. Dominant society requires maintenance of ethnicity and positive intergroup relations. An
ethnic individual is not entitled to relinquish his or her own ethnicity or
to engage in negative relations with dominant society. The pattern usually requires an efficient set of social control agents (e.g., police, passes)
for its enforcement (e.g., South Africa).

3. *Rejection (self-segregation)*. Ethnic group(s) affirms culture and
identity but denies usefulness of positive intergroup relations. Among
higher acculturated ethnic groups, the pattern is often referred to as *reaf-
firmation* (e.g., red or black power movements in North America, Celtic
nationalists in Europe, negritude in Africa).

4. *Exclusive segregation*. This pattern was more common a few years
ago, when it was legally and economically possible in many countries to
forcefully exclude ethnic groups from major participation in society
(e.g., United States, prewar South Africa). Now, either the adoption of
more democratic values or the recognition of the economic value of ethnic groups has lessened the frequency of this pattern.

5. *Assimilation 1 (melting pot)*. Ethnic groups decide to merge identity
with the larger society in pursuit of pervasive, general goals. Although it
is no longer as widespread as it once was (e.g., Irish immigrants to
United States), this pattern still occurs in various countries whenever an
immigrant group accepts the goals of the new society, and is willing to
adopt patterns of the new society to attain the goals.

6. *Assimilation 2* (*pressure cooker*). This pattern differs from Pattern 5 because the decision to give up culture is forced on ethnic groups by the larger society. Ethnic groups are pressured to assimilate rather than allowed to decide for themselves whether to assimilate (e.g., Australia, white majority and aboriginal Australians).

7. *Marginality*. Ethnic groups, apparently without pressure, occupy a position between two cultural systems, belonging to neither, and having few positive intergroup contacts (e.g., part-Aborigines in Australia, Metis in Canada, Anglo-Indians in India); however, many are developing new culture and, if successful, move into Patterns 1 or 3 (integration or rejection).

8. *Deculturation*. All three questions are answered negatively: no ethnic retention, no positive intergroup relations, no choice. This pattern may come about when marginal groups (Pattern 7) cease to have hope or motivation, and apathy and withdrawal become dominant features.

The history of intergroup relations in the United States may be defined largely in terms of its early and consistent advocacy of Pattern 5—melting pot assimilation. Most immigrant groups were able to work themselves into the "melting pot" and the "American way of life" within a generation. Some groups, which were too visibly different, were excluded from the assimilation process. This situation was seen in dichotomous terms—the assimilationist ideal (Pattern 5 in Berry's model) or the exclusionist reality (Pattern 4), and in 1954, when the U.S. Supreme Court declared segregated education unconstitutional and Allport (1954) proposed the contact theory of intergroup relations on which subsequent cooperative education research would be based, the goal of these and other proposals for social change was to find the best way to fulfill that ideal for all minority groups.

With reference to Berry's model, the idea of retention of ethnic identity was not so much rejected as considered almost irrelevant:

> Those favoring cultural pluralism regard it as a great loss . . . when ethnic groups discard their distinctive and colorful ways: the cuisine of the Near East, the Italian love of opera. . . . Yet it is true that at least one large group against which there is prejudice, the American Negro, can scarcely be said to have a distinctive culture. (Allport, 1958, p. 479)

Similarly, it seemed that the question of ethnic group choice was never asked, as minority-group members would naturally want to develop the "greater confidence in the American Democratic Creed . . . and a fuller sense of sharing the American Dream" (Suchman, Dean, & Williams, 1958, p. 71) that resulted from assimilation.

Perhaps because of its longevity, the assimilationist ideology had by this point evolved into a complex belief system incorporating a number of related and usually implicit assumptions, including the following:

1. *Basic value similarity.* People belonging to different ethnic groups do not differ in any important ways:

> People are really alike—they want the same things, have the same values, share most beliefs. . . . If people of different races could be shown that they are really alike . . . we could break down a good deal of social discrimination. (Weissbach, 1976, p. 159)

2. *Tolerance as "color blindness."* The truly unprejudiced person should be "color-blind" regarding ethnic differences.

> The most tolerant people are those in whom ethnic attitudes have no salience at all. They have no interest in group distinctions. To them a person is a person. . . . As much as one might wish to treat a Negro simply as a human being, circumstances force an awareness of race. The prevalence of *social* discrimination tends to make ethnic attitudes salient. (Allport, 1958, p. 401)

3. *Interethnic awareness as hostility or prejudice.* Allport (1958) defined prejudice as "an antipathy based upon a faulty and inflexible generalization" (p. 10), and he stressed that not every generalization is a prejudice. However, adherence to the assimilationist ideology and the assumption that tolerance equals color blindness almost inevitably leads to the assumption that intolerance or prejudice equals awareness of ethnic differences, regardless of the affect associated with that awareness. If the awareness of ethnic differences is accompanied by negative feelings, the color-blind "set" almost precludes an objective examination of the basis for this antipathy. And if the antipathy proves to be based on an overgeneralization, little effort will be made to determine the extent to which it is faulty and/or inflexible.

4. *Intraethnic awareness as ethnocentrism.* The ethnocentric assumption, discussed by LeVine and Campbell (1972), posits a direct negative relationship between intraethnic and interethnic attitudes, so that the more positive one feels about one's own group, the more negative one will feel about other groups. Therefore, expressions of ethnic pride presumably indicate prejudice against other groups.

5. *Unidirectionality of effects.* Because minority groups are expected to adopt the values of the dominant society, an asymmetry exists between the predicted benefits of assimilation for minority and majority groups. In the case of school desegregation in the United States, for example, black students could expect myriad benefits from their contact with whites (e.g., Suchman *et al.*, 1958), but for whites, the virtue of sharing the American dream with others was presumably its own reward and the only one to be expected.

It is futile to speculate on what might have happened had the assimilationist dream become a reality in the United States. In any case, the possibility of its eventual fulfillment faded fast with the advent of another model of intergroup relations. By the early 1960s, ethnic minorities had begun to assert themselves, demanding legal, social, and economic equality without the sacrifice of their own cultural values. They reacted strongly against the ethnocentrism they saw as implicit in the assimilationist ideology, arguing that *integration* thus defined spelled cultural and ethnic genocide. In terms of Berry's model, the crucial questions, both answered in the affirmative, became retention of ethnic identity and recognition of ethnic group preferences. The question of whether these relations should or, indeed, could be positive became less important, with some groups opting for self-imposed segregation (Pattern 3). Although most minority-group members wanted positive intergroup relations and advocated cultural pluralism (Pattern 1), the implicit emphasis had definitely shifted from the assimilationist goal of positive affect—liking—to the pluralist goal of mutual *respect*, hopefully but not necessarily accompanied by friendly feelings.

In rejecting assimilation for pluralism, ethnic minorities also questioned its related assumptions. Regarding value similarity, it was argued that cultures may differ along value dimensions more substantial than those of diet or art. True tolerance was redefined as the recognition and the positive acceptance of ethnic diversity rather than the denial of ethnic differences. In place of the ethnocentric assumption, the "multicultural hypothesis" was proposed—the belief that the way to "break down disciminatory attitudes and cultural jealousies" is to create "confidence in one's own individual identity; out of this can grow respect for that of others and a willingness to share ideas, attitudes and assumptions" (Government of Canada, 1971, p. 2). And finally, genuine cultural exchange was advocated, with the expectation that both groups could benefit from intergroup contact.

In the intervening decade since the cultural pluralist perspective was first seriously proposed in the United States, it has gained increasing support among both minority- and majority-group members, and I believe few educators today would publicly subscribe to the idea that ethnic minorities have no culture worth preserving. With reference to cooperative educational strategies, however, I would like to suggest that the ideological climate in which an idea is first developed can affect its formation and its subsequent development long after the original ideological base has been eroded or replaced.

The cooperative learning strategies developed within the last decade (e.g., Aronson & Bridgeman, 1979; Aronson, Bridgeman, &

Geffner, 1978; Aronson, Blaney, Stephan, Sikes, & Snapp, 1978; Cook, 1978; DeVries & Edwards, 1974; Devries & Slavin, 1978; DeVries, Edwards, & Slavin, 1978; Johnson & Johnson, 1975, 1978; Johnson, Johnson, Johnson, & Anderson, 1976; Johnson, Johnson, & Scott, 1978; Slavin, 1977a, b, 1978, 1979; Weigel & Cook, 1975; Weigel, Wiser, & Cook, 1975) were designed as tests and applications of Allport's contact theory, a theory designed to facilitate the development of affectively positive intergroup contact through the fulfillment of three conditions: (1) strong institutional support for the intergroup contact; (2) equal status for both groups in the contact situation; and (3) a group task requiring mutual interdependence among the interacting group members.

Allport's own writings indicate quite clearly that he favored the ideology defined in Berry's terms as assimilationist, as "when groups completely fuse there is no longer any visible or psychological base for prejudice" (Allport, 1958, p. 479) or, even more explicitly, "People who talk in terms of the ultimate assimilation of all minority groups into one ethnic stock are speaking of a distant Utopia" (p. 469). Therefore, although it could be argued that contact theory itself is value-free, its interpretation in assimilationist terms was almost inevitable, given the historical context in which it was formulated. In particular, I would suggest that the influence of the assimilationist ideology on cooperative education research is evident in its emphasis on the mutual interdependence condition of contact theory as the key condition for its fulfillment.

The underlying rationale for cooperative education programs is that students' self-esteem and academic performance are strongly influenced by perceived peer and teacher expectations (Brookover, Paterson, & Thomas, 1964; Coopersmith, 1967). In the typical classroom, children compete with each other for teacher-dispensed rewards, a system that works well for academically proficient children. For children who are more often "losers" than "winners" in the ongoing classroom competition, failure to obtain tangible rewards is coupled with the perception of negative peer opinions to create a self-fulfilling cycle of academic failure and low self-esteem. If most of the "losers" are members of one ethnic group and most of the "winners" are members of another, negative interethnic attitudes and behaviors are the almost inevitable result. If the children are assigned to equal-status, mutually interdependent groups, however, they gradually learn to see each other as academically and socially competent—as colleagues rather than as competitors. The recognition of mutual interdependence promotes better interpersonal relations among the students, a valuable end in itself, which leads in turn to increased self-esteem and improved academic performance. The implicit underlying model posits the improvement of intergroup *liking* through the establishment of mutual interdependence as the key to other positive changes. As for the equal-status condition of contact theory, it is assumed to be fulfilled as a function of the equal and inter-dependent participation required of all group members.

Is this assumption a tenable one? Basing her arguments on expecta-tion states theory (Berger, Cohen, & Zelditch, 1966, 1972; Berger & Fisek, 1974), Cohen (1980) contended that the members of most cooperative groups do *not* have equal status and consequently do not evaluate each other as equally competent. Certain attributes like gender, ethnicity, and age function as *diffuse status characteristics*, differentially valued in our society, associated with a set of specific abilities, and arousing general expectations regarding the competence or incompe-tence of persons holding that status (Mercer, Iadicola, & Moore, 1980). People use this status information to make judgments regarding the rel-ative competencies of other group members in a mixed-status group. Therefore, expectations about the relative competence of minority- and majority-group members, based on each group's status in the larger so-ciety, are carried into an ostensibly equal-status contact situation. The stage is set for self-fulfilling prophecies, so that members of the higher status group probably will dominate lower ranked members, and, in fact, their performance on the group task may actually be superior.

Research conducted by Cohen and her colleagues (Cohen, 1972; Cohen & Roper, 1972; Cohen, Lockheed, & Lohman, 1976) indicates that the equal-status condition of contact theory is probably *not* fulfilled in many cooperative groups. How has Cohen explained the successful re-sults of so many cooperative intervention strategies? In part, she has ar-gued that the wrong attitudes and behaviors were assessed. If increased interethnic liking is assumed to mediate all other changes, dependent measures may focus on affect rather than on evaluations of competence, and a program may be judged successful almost solely on the basis of evidence that positive *affective* change has occurred. And Cohen has ar-gued that *liking* does not necessarily indicate *respect* or compensate for the lack of it. Referring to one study, for example (Weigel *et al.*, 1975), Cohen (1980) suggested that

> although there were no systematic observations of group interaction by the researchers, one can well imagine that much of it consisted of the superior students (middle-class Whites) helping out the Mexican-Americans on their English lessons. What attitude toward the disadvantaged minority group would that experience be likely to change? More likely, attitudes about Black and Brown intellectual incompetence so endemic to American society would be reinforced. (p. 254)

In contrast to the cooperative education strategies derived directly from contact theory, the multiability classroom interventions designed and tested by Cohen and her colleagues reflect an implicit model in which the establishment of equal status seems to be regarded as the critical contact-theory component, leading to changes in perceptions of intraethnic and interethnic *competence* that are assumed to mediate self-esteem and academic performance changes.[1]

Only empirical research can determine which of the two models is "correct" or whether some combination of both is preferable to either one alone (e.g., Gonzalez, 1980; Towson, 1982). The issue at this point, however, is whether the unconscious adherence to an assimilationist ideology perhaps prevented or at least postponed the exploration of alternatives not directly suggested by contact theory. Sexism has been described as a "nonconscious ideology" (Bem & Bem, 1970), and various researchers have pointed out ways in which this ideology has shaped and, in some cases, has distorted research in a number of areas. It could be argued that the assimilationist ideology has been the "nonconscious ideology" of ethnic relations and has had analogous effects.

Further, even if we are fully conscious of the cultural pluralist position, our theories, research, and behavior may continue to reflect assimilationist rather than pluralist assumptions simply because the belief system underlying the cultural pluralist ideology is not yet as well defined or elaborated as that of the assimilationist ideology that preceded it. In other words, although we may support the general principle of ethnic diversity wholeheartedly, we may be unsure of what that principle means in terms of specific attitudes and behaviors. Do ethnic jokes indicate a positive awareness of cultural diversity? Or just good old-fashioned prejudice? My guess is that, in many such ambiguous circumstances, even if we are conscious of inconsistency, we will behave as we did when we were assimilationists, just as the man who has had his feminist consciousness raised will often forget *not* to open the door for his female colleagues!

The possibility that unrecognized assimilationist assumptions may shape our cooperative learning research has implications not only for program structure and evaluation but also for program content. Although the positive effects of participation in cooperative groups seem

---

[1] To what extent did expectation states theory owe its development to the influence of a cultural pluralist ideology? Of course, it is impossible to say. But the pluralist perspective is clearly reflected in Cohen's call (1980) for "a reexamination of friendship as a goal for treatment of the desegregated situation. The desired end state of the school is not, after all, universal love and brotherhood. A more reasonable goal for the desegregation process is some social integration and a lack of overt conflict whereby different racial and ethnic group members given an objective important to both, can trust each other and listen to each other sufficiently well to complete the task at hand, whether it be a vocational task, an educational task, or a political task" (p. 259).

to persist over time (Slavin, 1979; Ziegler, 1981) and to generalize to some in-school out-of-classroom settings (Slavin, 1983), various investigators (Aronson, Blaney, Sikes, Stephan, & Snapp, 1975; Fruehling, 1977) have suggested that positive feelings about classmates belonging to other ethnic groups may not generalize very much to out-of-school relationships and have speculated that the lack of generalization, if it occurs, might be partially due to the low salience of ethnicity in cooperative groups. In order to make ethnicity more salient, Aronson *et al.* (1978) suggested the inclusion of social studies units on ethnicity as part of the Jigsaw curriculum, and Miller and Maruyama (1979) suggested that

> when racially mixed groups of children cooperatively work together, a teacher can structure the learning task so that the unique values, interests, and abilities of minority children can contribute to successful task completion as importantly as do those of white children. (p. 13)

Despite their recognition of cultural diversity, I do not believe that these programs would prove particularly successful, both because of the contexts in which they would be implemented and because of the presence of a certain "assumptional inconsistency." First, let us examine the probable context for an ethnic studies intervention. In many ways, Wexler Middle School was a model example of desegregation. Located in racially "neutral" territory, it had been integrated since its opening; it was a "magnet" school, attended voluntarily by black and white students from all over the city. The faculty was approximately 25% black, including a black vice-principal, and many of the teachers shared their principal's preference for individualized instruction, assigning work consistent with each student's skill and awarding A's on the basis of the fulfillment of weekly work contracts (Schofield & Sagar, 1979, p. 160).

Despite these factors working in its favor, however, a high degree of racial cleavage was apparent, accompanied by negative interethnic attitudes and behaviors. Black *and* white children regarded blacks as less intelligent and more aggressive than whites, and black students saw whites as "stuck up," condescending, and prejudiced (Schofield, 1980; Patchen, Hoffman, & Davidson, 1976).

After extensive observation, Schofield (1980) concluded that the students' negative intraethnic and interethnic attitudes were based not on prejudice, but on objectively valid perceptions of genuine behavioral and attitudinal differences between the black and white students. The white students at Wexler *did* perform much better academically on the average than the black students, and the black students *were* consistently more "physical" than the whites. Schofield argued that many of the differences between the black and white students at Wexler were due to social class differences rather than to ethnicity *per se*, but for the Wexler students, ethnicity was a much more salient characteristic than social class, and so the differences that they observed between themselves and their classmates were attributed almost entirely to ethnic differences.

What role did the teachers play in the development of the students' negative perceptions of themselves and others? Most of the staff tried very hard to live up to the color-blind philosophy espoused by the black vice-principal: "I try to treat youngsters . . . as youngsters and not as black, white, green or yellow . . . Children are children" (Schofield, 1980, p. 33). Equating acknowledgment of ethnicity with prejudice, the teachers deliberately avoided ethnicity as a topic of discussion and mentioned it only when telling students to ignore it (Schofield, 1977; Schofield & Sagar, 1979). As a result, the students were deprived of opportunities to discover and discuss the reasons for black and white differences; the ethnic component of the students' social identities went "underground" and assumed disproportional importance.

The Wexler School studies were conducted in the 1970s, and my guess is that the majority of teachers and students, if asked, would have subscribed to a cultural pluralist rather than to an assimilationist ideology. However, their behavior reflected an equation of ethnic tolerance with color blindness that is quite definitely an assimilationist assumption, the legacy of an assimilationist ideology.

Obviously, the program content suggested by cooperative education researchers, involving the discussion of ethnicity in positive terms, would be superior to a situation in which ethnicity is deliberately ignored. However, a close reading of the proposed solutions suggests an interpretation of cultural identity as largely artifactual and historical, a view much closer to an assimilationist than to a pluralist perspective.

It is interesting to contrast this perspective with the attributional approach of Feldman (1979). Feldman discussed several areas of cultural difference that impinge on interpersonal relations, including different norms, role expectations, values, and habits, and argued that interethnic hostility originates in misattributions due to unrecognized actual differences rather than to prejudice *per se*. For example, suppose

> one person says to another "That's a nice sweater. How much did you pay for it?" Such questions may be appropriate in the addressee's culture only to family or intimate friends. Thus, the questioner has violated a norm, an affectively negative action . . . . the behavior . . . implies that the questioner is "nosy" or "rude." . . . Further observation of this person may show similar behaviors enacted with respect to others over time, thus strengthening not only the inference of "rudeness" but associated traits as well. If the person is a member of an identifiable outgroup, the tendency to attribute dispositions

to the actor will be strengthened. Thus, the affective value of the original question, coupled with the trait inferences, produces a negative attitude and general tendency to avoid the person . . . . if other members of the same outgroup exhibit similar behavior, stereotype formation is likely, increasing the probability that a previously unknown member of the group will be seen in similar terms. (Feldman, 1979, p. 25)

This attributional analysis is a relatively accurate characterization of the Wexler School situation, and in such a context, it seems unlikely that learning about black contributions to America's musical heritage, for example, would have helped Wexler's black and white students to deal with each other in more constructive ways.

Programs *do* exist that, in combination with genuinely equal-status, mutually interdependent cooperative groups, could conceivably lead to significantly improved intraethnic and interethnic attitudes and behaviors. Triandis (1967, 1975, 1977) has developed attributional training programs for use with ethnically mixed work groups and Americans going to work and live overseas. In these groups, the probability of misattribution is reduced by teaching

each actor the attributional system of the other, and the norms, values, category systems, and so forth that influence the behavior of each. In short, teach each actor to explain behavior in the same terms as the other. By teaching each to conceive of behavior in the other's terms, a more differentiated view of the world is created, and the probability of misattribution is reduced. (Feldman, 1979, p. 30)

Again, as with our discussion of Cohen's expectation-states theory model, the point is not so much the value of the technique itself, but the fact that it illustrates the possibilities for program development that lie outside an implicitly assimilationist framework. In 1971, Metzger charged that

the convergence of liberal and sociological thought in the area of race relations is striking and raises serious questions about the 'value-free' character of sociological inquiry in this area. (p. 629)

I do not believe that cooperative education theory and research in the area of interethnic relations necessarily should or can be value-free, but as social scientists, we should at the very least know what our values are and where they are leading us.

REFERENCES

Allport, G. W. *The nature of prejudice*. Reading, Mass.: Addison-Wesley, 1954.
Allport, G. W. *The nature of prejudice* (abridged). Garden City, N.Y.: Doubleday, 1958.

Aronson, E., & Bridgeman, D. Jigsaw groups and the desegregated classroom: In pursuit of common goals. *Personality and Social Psychology Bulletin,* 1979, *5*(4), 438–446.

Aronson, E., Blaney, N., Sikes, J., Stephan, C., & Snapp, M. Busing and racial tension: The jigsaw route to learning and liking. *Psychology Today,* 1975, *8,* 43–59.

Aronson, E., Blaney, N., Stephan, C., Sikes, J., & Snapp, M. *The Jigsaw classroom.* Beverly Hills, Calif.: Sage, 1978.

Aronson, E., Bridgeman, D. L., & Geffner, R. The effects of a cooperative classroom structure on student behavior and attitudes. In D. Bar-Tal & L. Saxe (Eds.), *Social psychology of education: Theory and research.* New York: Wiley, 1978.

Bem, S. L., & Bem, D. J. Case study of a nonconscious ideology: Training the woman to know her place. In D. Bem (Ed.), *Beliefs, attitudes and human affairs.* Belmont, Calif.: Brooks/Cole, 1970.

Berger, J., & Fisek, M. A generalization of the theory of status characteristics and expectation states. In B. Berger *et al.* (Eds.), *Expectation status theory: A theoretical research program.* Cambridge, Mass.: Winthrop, 1974.

Berger, J., Cohen, E., & Zelditch, M. Status characteristics and expectation states. In J. Berger, M. Zelditch, & E. Anderson (Eds.), *Sociological theories in progress.* Boston: Houghton Mifflin, 1966.

Berger, J., Cohen, E., & Zelditch, M. Status conceptions and social interaction. *American Sociological Review,* 1972, *37,* 241–255.

Berry, J. W. Psychological aspects of cultural pluralism: Unity and identity reconsidered. In R. W. Brislin (Ed.), *Culture learning: Concepts, applications, and research.* East-West Culture Learning Institute. Honolulu: University Press of Hawaii, 1977.

Brookover, W. B., Paterson, A., & Thomas, S. Self-concept of ability and school achievement. *Sociology of Education,* 1964, *37,* 271–278.

Cohen, E. Interracial interaction disability. *Human Relations,* 1972, *25,* 9–24.

Cohen, E. G. Design and redesign of the desegregated school: Problems of status, power, and conflict. In W. G. Stephan & J. R. Feagin (Eds.), *School desegregation: Past, present, and future.* New York: Plenum Press, 1980.

Cohen, E., & Roper, S. Modification of interracial interaction disability: An application of status characteristics theory. *American Sociological Review,* 1972, *37,* 643–657.

Cohen, E., Lockheed, M., & Lohman, M. The center for interracial cooperation: A field experiment. *Sociology of Education,* 1976, *49,* 47–58.

Cook, S. W. Interpersonal and attitudinal outcomes in cooperating interracial groups. *Journal of Research and Development in Education,* 1978, *12*(1), 97–113.

Coopersmith, S. *The antecedents of self-esteem.* San Francisco: W. H. Freeman, 1967.

DeVries, D. L., & Edwards, K. J. Student teams and learning games: Their effects on cross-race and cross-sex interaction. *Journal of Educational Psychology,* 1974, *66,* 741–749.

DeVries, D. L., & Slavin, R. E. Teams-Games-Tournaments (TGT): Review of ten classroom experiments. *Journal of Research and Development in Education,* 1978, *12*(1), 28–38.

DeVries, D. L., Edwards, K. J., & Slavin, R. E. Biracial learning teams and race relations in the classroom: Four field experiments in Teams-Games-Tournament. *Journal of Educational Psychology,* 1978, *70,* 356–362.

Feldman, J. M. The case for cultural training in elementary and secondary schools. Ms. 1903. Abstracted in the *JSAS Catalog of Selected Documents in Psychology,* 1979, *9*(3), 63.

Fruehling, R. T. Multicultural education as social exchange. *Phi Delta Kappan,* 1977 (January), 398–400.

Gonzalez, A. *Classroom cooperation and ethnic balance.* Unpublished doctoral dissertation, University of California, Santa Cruz, 1980.

Government of Canada. Statement by the Prime Minister (Response to the Report of the Royal Commission on Bilingualism and Biculturalism, Book 4, House of Commons). Ottawa: Press release, October 8, 1971.

Johnson, D. W., & Johnson, R. T. *Learning together and alone: Cooperation, competition, and individualization.* Englewood Cliffs, N.J.: Prentice-Hall, 1975.

Johnson, D. W., & Johnson, R. T. The instructional use of cooperative, competitive, and individualistic goal structures. In H. Walberg (Ed.), *Educational environments and effects.* Berkeley, Calif.: McCutchan, 1978.

Johnson, D. W., Johnson, R., Johnson, J., & Anderson, D. The effects of cooperative vs. individualized instruction on student prosocial behavior: Attitudes toward learning, and achievement. *Journal of Educational Psychology*, 1976, *68*, 446–452.

Johnson, D. W., Johnson, R., & Scott, L. The effects of cooperative and individualistic instruction on student attitudes and achievement. *Journal of Social Psychology*, 1978, *104*, 207–216.

LeVine, R. A., & Campbell, D. T. *Ethnocentrism: Theories of conflict, ethnic attitudes, and group behavior.* New York: Wiley, 1972.

Mercer, J. R., Iadicola, P., & Moore, H. Building effective multiethnic schools: Evolving models and paradigms. In W. G. Stephan, & J. R. Feagin (Eds.), *School desegregation: Past, present, and future.* New York: Plenum Press, 1980.

Metzger, L. P. American sociology and Black assimilation: Conflicting perspectives. *American Journal of Sociology*, 1971, *76*, 627–647.

Miller, N., & Maruyama, G. *Normative influence in desegregated classrooms.* Paper presented at the American Psychological Association meetings, New York, 1979.

Patchen, M., Hoffman, G., & Davidson, J. Interracial perceptions among high school students. *Sociometry*, 1976, *39*(4), 341–354.

Schofield, J. W. *Social process and peer relations in a "nearly integrated" middle school.* (Contract No. 400-76-0011, 1977.) Final project report, 1977.

Schofield, J. W. Complementary and conflicting identities: Images and interaction in an interracial school. In S. Asher, & J. Gottman (Eds.), *The development of friendship: Description and intervention.* Cambridge: Cambridge University Press, 1980.

Schofield, J. W., & Sagar, H. A. The social context of learning in an interracial school. In R. C. Rist (Ed.), *Desegregated schools: Appraisals of an American experiment.* New York: Academic Press, 1979.

Slavin, R. E. Classroom reward structure: An analytic and practical review. *Review of Educational Research*, 1977, *47*(4), 633–650. (a)

Slavin, R. E. Using student learning teams to integrate the desegregated classroom. *Integrated Education*, 1977, *15*(6), 56–58. (b)

Slavin, R. E. Student teams and comparison among equals: Effects on academic performance and student attitudes. *Journal of Educational Psychology*, 1978, *70*, 532–538.

Slavin, R. E. Effects of biracial learning teams on cross-racial friendships. *Journal of Educational Psychology*, 1979, *71*(3), 381–387.

Slavin, R. E. Personal communication, April 1983.

Suchman, E. A., Dean, J. P., & Williams, R. M., Jr. *Desegregation: Some propositions and research suggestions.* New York: Anti-Defamation League of B'nai B'rith, 1958.

Towson, S. M. J. *Cooperative intervention strategies, perceived status and student self-esteem.* Paper presented at the American Educational Research Association meetings, New York, March 1982.

Triandis, H. C. Interpersonal relations in international organizations. *Organizational Behavior and Human Performance*, 1967, *2*, 26–55.

Triandis, H. C. Culture training, cognitive complexity and interpersonal attitudes. In R. W. Brislin, S. Bochner, & W. J. Lonner (Eds.), *Cross-cultural perspectives on learning*. New York: Wiley, 1975.

Triandis, H. C. *Interpersonal behavior*. Monterey, Calif.: Brooks/Cole Publishing, 1977.

Weigel, R. H., & Cook, S. W. Participation in decision-making: A determinant of interpersonal attraction in cooperating interracial groups. *International Journal of Group Tensions*, 1975, 5(4), 179–195.

Weigel, R. H., Wiser, P. L., & Cook, S. W. The impact of cooperative learning experiences on cross-ethnic relations and attitudes. *Journal of Social Issues*, 1975, 31(1), 219–244.

Weissbach, T. A. Laboratory controlled studies of change of racial attitudes. In P. A. Katz (Ed.), *Towards the elimination of racism*. New York: Pergamon Press, 1976.

Ziegler, S. The effectiveness of cooperative learning teams for increasing cross-ethnic friendship: Additional evidence. *Human Organization*, 1981, 40(3), 264–268.

11

Classroom Structural Bias

Impact of Cooperative and Competitive Classroom Structures on Cooperative and Competitive Individuals and Groups

SPENCER KAGAN, G. LAWRENCE ZAHN,
KEITH F. WIDAMAN, JOSEPH SCHWARZWALD,
AND
GARY TYRRELL

There is now considerable theoretical support for the claim that classroom structures common in the U.S. public schools discriminate against the achievement, the cultural values, and the well-being of Mexican-American and black students (Kagan, 1980, 1983). The purpose of the present chapter is to present empirical evidence that bears on that hypothesis, called the *structural bias hypothesis.* Although some of the evidence to be presented comes from published research, much of the evidence was generated by a large-scale investigation of the structural bias hypothesis conducted as part of a cooperative project by the School of Education and the Psychology Department at the University of California, Riverside. Before describing and discussing the empirical data relevant to the evaluation of the structural bias hypothesis, theoretical support for the hypothesis is reviewed, and the Riverside Cooperative Learning Project is described.

THE THEORY OF STRUCTURAL BIAS

DEFINITION OF STRUCTURAL BIAS

Structural bias is the bias against an individual or a group that occurs as a consequence of the task and/or reward structure of a classroom. Numerous types of task and reward structures are possible in a classroom.

SPENCER KAGAN, G. LAWRENCE ZAHN, KEITH F. WIDAMAN, AND GARY TYRRELL Department of Psychology, University of California, Riverside, California 92521. • JOSEPH SCHWARZWALD Department of Psychology, Bar-Ilan University, Ramat Gan, Israel.

For example, students may be required to work alone at their desks at a learning task and may be rewarded (e. g., graded) based on how well they achieve in relation to other students. In such a classroom, there is an individualistic task structure and a competitive reward structure. Or students may be asked to work in a small group, using peer-tutoring techniques to master the learning task, and may be rewarded on the basis of how well their team does compared to other teams. In such a classroom, there is a cooperative task structure, a cooperative within-team reward structure, and a competitive between-team reward structure. A detailed discussion of various possible cooperative, competitive, and individualistic task and reward structures is presented elsewhere in this volume (see Chapter 3).

The choice of task and reward structures has the potential for either positive or negative academic and social outcomes for various individuals and cultural groups, and reliance on a single type of classroom structure can bias educational outcomes in favor of or against certain individuals and groups. Just as a psychological test can be biased in favor of the performance of some groups over others, an instructional program, because of its reward and/or task structure, can be biased to favor the outcomes desired by certain groups more than by others. Various types of negative effects can occur as a result of structural bias; these include lower academic achievement, poorer interethnic relations, and greater self-deprecation and the erosion of important cultural values.

ACHIEVEMENT BIAS

Different rewards for achievement are associated with different types of classroom structures. Some of these rewards are extrinsic, including teacher praise, peer approval, and points or rewards that are given for superior performance. Depending on the classroom structure, various kinds of cooperative and competitive outcomes are also associated with achievement. For example, in a competitive class structure, achievement may be associated with advancing to the highest achievement group in the class or with having one's name at the top of a performance list. In a cooperative classroom structure, achievement may be associated with helping one's teammates to learn, and to receive good grades or class recognition. Because various individuals and ethnic groups place a different value on these various rewards, different classroom structures are differentially rewarding of achievement for various individuals and groups. Thus, a given classroom structure can be biased for or against the academic achievement of certain individuals and groups.

Obviously, it would be unfair to give pink bracelets to all students, boys and girls, who do well on their spelling tests each week. With that type of reward, the girls probably would be more motivated to learn spelling than would the boys, even though the reward and the standards for achieving it are ostensibly equal. Given that some individuals and groups come to school with a high value on competitive rewards and others with a high value on cooperative rewards, it is unfair to set up a class structure that provides exclusively or even primarily competitive rewards. When achievement is equivalent to "winning" in a competitive social-comparison situation, individuals and groups who place a high value on winning will be more motivated to achieve than those who do not value, or who negatively value, obtaining more than others.

Structural bias against the achievement of cooperatively oriented students is not always as easy to recognize as would be the use of only pink bracelets as rewards. Competitive rewards are imbedded within the context of classroom structures that have been accepted, unquestioningly, for years. Often, these competitive rewards are not overt and tangible; they are part of an implicit social-comparison process that occurs among students as a function of classroom reward and task structures. A relatively common reward structure is to make public the achievement of students. For example, a chart may be posted indicating the names of the students who have reached criterion on some academic task. Colorful rocket ships with students' names on them may indicate how "high" the students have advanced in the math or spelling tasks; a bar graph or posted exams may indicate how many perfect tests the students have obtained. Given such rewards, competitive students will find it rewarding to learn because they value "besting" others. When such rewards are used, however, the students who come to school with a value on equality rather than superiority will find the rewards for achievement of little or even of negative value. Similarly, even if the competitive rewards in a classroom are covert, involving a competitive social-comparison process that results from the classroom structure, competitively oriented students will find the rewards for achievement more worth working for than will cooperatively oriented individuals and groups. Because minority students have been found to be more cooperatively oriented than are majority students, it is plausible that the lower academic achievement of cooperative minority groups in public schools may be attributed in part to classroom structural bias.

ETHNIC-RELATIONS BIAS

A classroom structure can create a social climate or a pattern of social relations in which the members of a group are either accepted and valued by their peers or disparaged and alienated. Thus, classroom structures can be said to have either a positive or a negative ethnic-relations bias. It is likely that minority students will suffer most from classroom structures that have a negative ethnic-relations bias.

The U.S. courts have indicated that separate schools are by their essence not equal and have demanded desegregation in our public-school systems. By mandating desegregation, the courts cast on the schools the racial problem of the larger society. Unfortunately, the schools were ill prepared to deal with this problem; they maintained traditional, competitive, and individualistic classroom structures that re-created society's segregation within the classroom. We now know that if desegregated students had been sent to classrooms in which cooperative, racially integrated classroom structures had been used, the results of the desegregation movement would habe been radically different. Court-mandated desegregation has failed to produce positive race relations largely because the schools did not apply long-established principles of social science research that make it possible to create *integration* in the classroom, rather than a nominal *desegregation.*

It was well established at the time of the initial court-mandated desegregation that the nature of the contact between the members of the different racial groups would determine how desegregation would proceed (Cook, 1979; Slavin, 1981). In the famous "Social Science Statement" (*Minnesota Law Review,* 1953), leading social scientists of the time warned that successful desegregation would depend on "the absence of competition for a limited number of facilities or benefits . . . and the possibility of equivalence of positions and functions among all of the participants within the desegregated situation" (p. 438). By failing to heed this warning, teachers and school administrators have re-created in the classroom the outgroup status for minority students that had been accorded them in the larger society. Researchers have noted that desegregation into classrooms that employ traditional, whole-class structures has not led to improved ethnic relations. For example, in their analysis of ethnic relations in the desegregated Riverside public schools, Gerard, Jackson, and Conolley (1975) concluded,

> The unprecedented amount of data we have examined points unmistakably to the conclusion that, with the exception of playground interaction, little or no real integration occurred during the relatively long-term contact situation represented by Riverside's desegration program. If anything, we found some evidence that ethnic cleavage became somewhat more pronounced over time. (p. 237)

Broad reviews of school desegregation have been negative with regard to its impact on race relations (St. John, 1975; Stephen, 1978). Exclusive reliance on competitive classroom structures is almost certain to foster a negative ethnic-relations bias in which minority students are seen as members of different and inferior outgroups.

Evidence indicates that the adoption of cooperative class structures can radically change the entire social climate of a classroom so that minority children do not suffer the negative consequences of within-class segregation (Slavin, 1980, 1983). Traditional, competitive classroom structures, in contrast, lead students to segregate along racial lines, causing the creation of a minority outgroup. This negative ethnic-relations bias is probably associated with alienation, lower self-esteem, and lower academic achievement among minority students.

CULTURAL VALUE BIAS

A classroom structure may be more or less in synchrony with the cultural values of a group. When a desegregated classroom relies exclusively on certain classroom structures, it will create value conflicts for groups that do not share those values. For example, if minority students come to school with cooperative values and the classroom structure provides a strong press for competitive and individualistic behaviors, then a value conflict is created for the minority students. Serious value conflicts create identity confusion and can interfere with the learning of academic material. Students can resolve home–culture/school–society value conflicts only by suffering negative consequences: They become alienated from the school and the society, alienated from their home and their culture, or alienated from both. Thus, the exclusive reliance within the public schools on certain kinds of classroom structures can have the effect of systematically undermining core cultural values and the psychological stability of certain minority students. Internal conflict, alienation, and dropping out are some of the probable consequences of cultural value bias.

PROBABLE CAUSES OF STRUCTURAL BIAS

There are at least two plausible explanations of the way in which bias against cooperative individuals and minority groups is fostered by traditional, competitive classroom structures: (1) They foster the formation of lower status minority outgroups; and (2) they create a mismatch between the social structure of the classroom and the social orientation of cooperative individuals and groups.

THE OUTGROUP HYPOTHESIS

The exclusive use of competitive classroom reward and task structures creates an extremely strong press for students to form identities along racial lines, with minority racial groups filling lower status, outgroup positions. In a classic study, Allport (1954) provided evidence that racial relations could be damaged or improved, depending on the nature of the contact between racial groups. Competitive contact and contact between individuals of different status damaged race relations, whereas cooperative contact and contact between equal-status groups improved race relations. The social psychological literature supports the conclusion that the use of competitive reward structures fosters the formation of ingroups and outgroups. When competitive reward structures are used, the success of one individual is dependent on the relative failure of another. Thus, competitive reward structures are inherently alienating; they provide a strong press for individuals to disidentify with each other, to see others as a "they" rather than as part of a "we" (Brewer, 1979; Hornstein, 1976; Kagan & Madsen, 1971; Sherif, 1956).

Individuals will look for differences between themselves and others as a basis for disidentifying with others in situations in which there is a strong press for doing so. Among the most obvious differences between the students in a desegregated classroom are racial differences, and competitive reward structures are therefore likely to foster segregation along race lines within the classroom. Another set of obvious differences among students in most classrooms is differences in achievement levels, and because minority students tend to be lower than majority students in achievment levels, segregation along achievement lines also fosters racial segregation. Traditional and competitive instructional formats limit interpersonal relations, and this limitation, together with placing minority groups in the lower rank, serves to strengthen racial and ethnic stereotypes instead of disspelling them.

The likely consequences of this negative ethnic-relations bias are several: First, minority students probably adopt the majority view of themselves to some extent, with negative effects on their self-esteem and their cultural identity, producing a sense of alienation from their classmates and their family. Further, outgroup members have less opportunity or desire to maintain positive contact with the ingroup, so there is a lower likelihood that minority-group members will adopt the achievement values held by majority-group members. And, of course, rather than giving and receiving support for achievement, students in a competitive classroom structure, because they are placed in a negative interdependence situation, actively begin to hope for the failure of their peers, especially their outgroup peers.

THE MISMATCH HYPOTHESIS

There is a mismatch between the social orientation of cooperative and minority students and the social structure of most public-school classrooms. Traditional classroom structures provide a press for and a reward for competitive behaviors among students; achievement leads to competitive rewards in a competitive social-comparison process. Whereas competitive rewards are valued by competitive students, cooperative and minority students value competitive rewards less and are therefore alienated in the traditional classroom. Thus, traditional classroom structures provide a poor "fit" or "match" for the needs of cooperative and minority-group students.

The prediction of negative effects of a mismatch between classroom structure and individual social orientation obtains general support from a broad literature indicating the importance of person–situation interactions for predicting behavior (Cronbach, 1957; Magnusson & Endler, 1977). A number of studies have indicated important interactions between student characteristics and classroom and/or teacher characteristics (Cronbach & Snow, 1977). For example, in an experimental study, students low in need for structure were found to achieve better if a teacher adopted a teaching style low in structure; in contrast, more highly dependent students performed better in a more highly structured classroom (Amidon & Flanders, 1961). In a study directly related to cooperative, small-group teaching, a topic in physiology was taught by either live presentations, which included social interaction, or taped lectures. The students who were more sociable responded better to the live, small-group procedures (Doty, 1970). It appears likely that more cooperative students, like the more sociable students, would perform better in cooperative classroom structures that use small, interactive groups as the basis of the classroom social organization. Evidence indicates a link between cooperativeness and need for affiliation (Kagan & Knight, 1981), suggesting that cooperative, small-group teaching methods would best fill the needs of cooperative students. In a small, but direct, test of the relation of social orientation to class structure, Wheeler (1977) found that very cooperatively oriented students learned more in a cooperative than in a competitive instructional format, whereas competitively oriented students learned more in a competitive format.

There is pervasive reliance on competitive and individualistic task and reward structures in the U.S. public schools. Most of the class day is spent in a whole-class structure in which students work at their seats independently (Gump, 1967). Teachers spend most of their time as emitters and directors, rarely as targets of student communication or as resource persons (Adams & Biddle, 1970; Perkins, 1964). The use of groups or teams is extremely rare, occurring almost exclusively in physical education and elementary reading instruction, and even in the rare cases where grouping or teams are used, there is very little systematic use of cooperative reward and task structures.

In a cooperative reward structure, achievement is associated with equal outcomes among cooperating peers; performing well helps others and one's group. Because a cooperative individual values equality, altruism, and group enhancement (see Kagan, 1977), a cooperative individual in a cooperative reward structure will find achievement rewarding. By achieving academically, valued outcomes are obtained. The same cooperative individual, however, in the typical competitive or individualistic classroom structure, will not find academic achievement rewarding. Whereas competitive students may find obtaining more than others or lowering the outcomes of others to be rewarding, these are outcomes that are not valued or that may be negatively valued by cooperators. Thus, different class structures will be differentially rewarding of achievement for individuals differing in cooperative-competitive social orientation.

Applying the match–mismatch hypothesis to the achievement of minority students provides a basis for predicting that traditional, competitive classroom structures create bias against the academic achievement and the cultural values of minority students. There is extremely strong evidence that Hispanic students generally are more cooperative in their social orientation than are majority students (Kagan, 1977, 1984). Further, there is evidence that black students are also more cooperative than majority students (DeVoe, 1977; Richmond & Weiner, 1973; Sampson & Kardush, 1965). Hence, it appears that traditional, competitive classroom structures are in an important way inconsistent with the values and the needs of the two largest minority populations in the U.S. public schools.

THE RIVERSIDE COOPERATIVE LEARNING PROJECT

On the basis of the theoretical support for the structural bias hypothesis, as well as the generally positive results of cooperative learning studies, a large-scale training and evaluation project on cooperative learning was carried out at the University of California at Riverside. The Riverside Cooperative Learning Project involved training student teachers in the theories and techniques of cooperative learning and assessing the impact of that training on the student teachers and their pupils.

As part of the Riverside Cooperative Learning Project, data were collected that bear on the evaluation of the structural bias hypothesis. The Riverside Cooperative Learning Project has involved thousands of pupils over the last several years. Assessments have been made of the effects of cooperative and traditional classroom structures on a wide range of variables, including academic achievement, cross-race and cross-sex social relations, classroom climate, self-esteem, empathy, prosocial development, and attitudes toward cooperative, competitive, and individualistic work. A consistent finding across analyses in these various domains has been that classroom structures impact differently on major ethnic groups, generally in ways consistent with the structural bias hypothesis. The choice of a classroom structure necessarily results in more favorable results for some cultural groups than for others. It is beyond the scope of the present chapter to present a detailed description of all of the measures and methods of the Riverside Cooperative Learning Project. Nevertheless, we will survey a number of the results from the first year of the project that bear on the evaluation of the structural bias hypothesis. Those results at both the elementary and high-school levels indicate strong support for the structural bias hypothesis, with important implications for educational theory and practice.

The Elementary-School Study

In the first year of the Riverside Cooperative Learning Project, at the elementary-school level 35 student teachers were randomly assigned to one of three classroom structure conditions: (1) Traditional, whole-class; (2) Student Teams-Achievement Divisions; or (3) Teams-Games-Tournaments. Because of other aspects of the design, there were more students in the traditional, whole-class condition than in the other treatment groups. The students of the student teachers were approximately 66% white, 20% Mexican-American, and 13% black, with fairly proportional ethnic representation in each treatment group. The exact number of pupils involved in each analysis differed, but approximately 900 students were involved in the comparisons to be reported. The content area for the study was spelling, which was taught for slightly less than one hour a day over a six-week period. The details of the procedures involved in Conditions 2 and 3, Student Teams-Achievement Division (STAD) and Teams-Games-Tournaments (TGT), have been presented elsewhere (Slavin, 1980).

The two critical points for interpreting the results of the elementary-school study are that (1) the two cooperative learning conditions differ from the traditional condition by inclusion of cooperative student teams, which create cooperative within-team reward and task structures; and (2) the two cooperation conditions are virtually identical, with one very important exception: In STAD, the students are assessed by a weekly quiz, and there is no direct interpersonal competition; in TGT, in contrast, each week the students are assigned in triads to tournament tables, at which they actively compete against students at similar ability levels from other teams. Competition at the tournament tables is very intense; the students challenge each other and win extra points if other students fail following a challenge. The tournament tables are a negative interdependence situation: Students maximize their points not by improving over their own past performance, as in STAD, but by outperforming the other students at the tournament table. Whereas STAD has an individual evaluative task structure, TGT emphasizes an intensely competitive evaluative task structure. Thus, the first-year elementary study allows inferences regarding (1) the impact of cooperative teams (comparison of Condition 1, the traditional, whole-class condition, with Conditions 2 and 3, the student-team learning conditions); and (2) the impact of a competitive versus individualistic evaluative task structure (comparison of Condition 2, STAD, the "no-tournament" condition, with Condition 3, TGT, the competitive tournament condition).

THE HIGH-SCHOOL STUDY

At the secondary level, the high-school teachers taught two similar classes for eight weeks; one class was randomly assigned to a traditional, whole-class instructional format, and the other was taught with Co-op Co-op. Thus, the high-school study differed from the elementary-school study in design: The teachers at the high-school level served as their own control. Co-op Co-op, like STAD and TGT, uses small student teams that are heterogeneous with regard to achievement level, racial background, and sex. Unlike STAD and TGT, however, the students work together to produce a product that they share with the whole class, so between-team competition is minimized or eliminated, and the students have more control of what and how to learn. The details of Co-op Co-op are presented elsewhere (see Chapter 16).

At the time of the preparation of the present chapter, a preliminary analysis of the high school study data was available for classroom climate and cooperativeness. The high school study involved approximately 250 students in 10 classrooms. The students were approximately 60% Anglo-American; 25% black, and 15% Mexican-American, roughly proportionally divided among the traditional and the Co-op Co-op treatment groups.

EMPIRICAL EVIDENCE OF STRUCTURAL BIAS

The evidence that traditional, whole-class instructional formats are biased against the achievement and the well-being of cooperative and minority students comes from several sources. In the following empirical review, evidence from previous studies and the Riverside Cooperative Learning Project is summarized regarding the impact of traditional and cooperative classroom structures on cooperative and competitive minority and majority students. The dependent variables in these studies were academic achievement, two types of classroom climate, two types of self-concept, cooperativeness, and interpersonal relations. Both the cooperativeness and the interpersonal relations measures allowed intensive examination of the effect of cooperative and traditional classroom structures on ethnic relations. Across all of the studies, there was an overriding consistency: Classroom structures impacted differently on cooperative versus competitive individuals and on minority versus majority groups; that is, the choice of competitive classroom structures produced academic and social outcomes for cooperative individuals and minority groups that were unfavorable compared to those produced by a more exclusively cooperative social organization of the classroom.

As is revealed in the presentation of the empirical evidence for structural bias, two general expectations were held at the onset of the study that were not met when the data from the Riverside Cooperative Learning Project were analyzed. First, from the literature that has built up around STAD and TGT, at the onset of the study the two techniques were conceptualized as being similar cooperative learning methods that include a theoretically important but relatively minor difference in the evaluative task structure. As can be seen in the results, however, what was thought to be a minor difference, the inclusion of competitive tournaments in TGT as opposed to individual quizzes in STAD, turned out to be a very important difference: Our results thus support a reconceptualization of TGT as a class structure that is both cooperative and competitive rather than primarily cooperative.

The second unmet expectation was the nature of the cooperation–competition differences among the cultural groups sampled in the Riverside Cooperative Learning Project. From the large cross-cultural literature regarding Mexican-American–Anglo-American social orientation differences (see Kagan, 1977, 1984), we assumed that the Mexican-American students would be more cooperative than the Anglo-American students in the Riverside Cooperative Learning project. Our results, though, were a surprise: Pretest measures of social orientation indicated that the black students were significantly more cooperative than the other two groups, which did not differ significantly, $F(2,625) = 3.08$, $p < .05$. Although the lack of a significant cooperation–competition difference between Mexican-American and Anglo-American students is interpretable in terms of the highly acculturated nature of the Mexican-American sample in the Riverside Cooperative Learning Project (see Knight & Kagan, 1977), the finding means that the sample provided a very poor population with which to test some aspects of the structural bias hypothesis. The expectation of poorer performance by the Mexican-American students in traditional classrooms was based on the assumption of a more cooperative social orientation among those students. Although Mexican-Americans generally are more cooperative, that characteristic did not hold for the population sampled by the Riverside Cooperative Learning Project. Thus, although the Riverside Cooperative Learning Project can provide a good test of the hypothesis that traditional and competitive classroom structures create structural bias against pupils with a cooperative social orientation, it cannot provide a representative test of the structural bias hypothesis as it applies to Mexican-American pupils.

The analyses of data from the Riverside Cooperative Learning Project were performed by means of techniques based on the general linear model. Some analyses utilized complete least-squares analyses of variance, others general regression models in which only main and two-way interaction effects were estimated. In all analyses, main effects of ethnicity, sex, grade, social orientation, and classroom structure were included, as were appropriate interactions among these variables. In analyses of race relations, the ethnicity of the target person was an additional main and interactive effect. In all analyses, the significance of the effects among all three classroom structures was estimated initially. In the cases in which STAD and TGT produced significantly different results, the differences among all three conditions are presented here; however, when STAD and TGT did not differ significantly, they were collapsed so that we could analyze and present the differences between traditional and cooperative class structures. Similarly, in the cases in which blacks and Mexican-Americans differed significantly, the distinctions among all three ethnic groups were retained; but in the cases in which the two minority groups did not differ significantly, the majority-versus-minority contrast is presented to provide a parsimonious picture of the results. The results reported in the following empirical review do not include all of the evidence of structural bias from the Riverside Cooperative Learning Project. Instead, representative instances within each behavioral domain are presented to illustrate the nature and the extent of structural bias.

Academic Achievement

ETHNICITY AND ACHIEVEMENT

Three major published studies have produced remarkably similar results indicating that minority students suffer academically from traditional, whole-class instructional formats when compared to cooperative classroom methods (Aronson, Blaney, Stephan, Sikes, & Snapp, 1978; Slavin, 1977; Slavin & Oickle, 1981). In each of these studies, the Anglo-Americans showed equal or somewhat greater academic gains in cooperative classrooms compared to traditional classrooms, but the minority students showed dramatically greater gains in the cooperative compared to the traditional formats. What stands out in these studies is not the main effect of classroom structure, but the interaction of classroom structure and ethnicity as the determinant of achievement.

As stated by Slavin (1977), "Further analysis showed that the treatment effect on achievement was largely due to a race × treatment interaction. Black students did much better in STAD than in control" (p. 57). Similarly, Aronson *et al.* (1978) indicated that, "specifically, the data show that in integrated schools Anglos learned equally well in both jigsaw and competitive classes, but blacks and Mexican Americans learned much more in jigsaw than in competitive classes" (p. 117). What is particularly striking about these initial studies demonstrating that cooperative class structures produce more positive effects on minority students is that the studies used very different cooperative learning methods, suggesting that the finding has generality.

The results of the most recently published study (Slavin & Oickle, 1981) indicating the differential impact of coperative and traditional structures on minority and majority pupils are the most dramatic; they are plotted in Figure 1. As pictured in Figure 1, the research demonstrated only slightly greater gains among white students in cooperative classrooms than in traditional classrooms, but the black students in cooperative classrooms showed dramatic improvements over their counterparts in traditional classrooms. In fact, the black students in traditional classrooms showed almost no gain, whereas the black students in cooperative classes gained more than twice as much as any other group. It was as if the black students were not motivated to learn in the traditional competitive-individualistic classrooms but were highly motivated to learn when learning was associated with cooperative group rewards.

The very dramatic "catch-up" effect for minority students that occurred in these cooperative learning studies has profound implica-

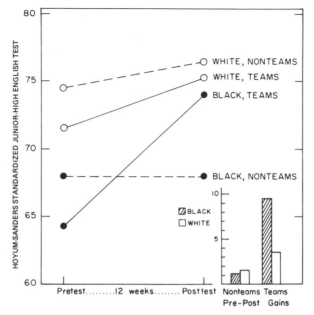

FIGURE 1.   Language achievement gains of black and white students in cooperative and traditional junior-high English classes (Slavin & Oickle, 1981).

tions for educational practice and theory. Traditionally, the achievement gap between minority and majority students has been attributed to deficits among minority students, usually in either intelligence or motivation. These attributions now appear to be context-bound. That is, minority students may lack motivation to learn, but only when they are placed in traditional, competitive-individualistic classroom structures. As demonstrated so clearly by the results plotted in Figure 1, in a relatively short time what appears to be a long-term minority student deficiency in basic language skills can be overcome by transforming the social organization of the classroom. It appears that it is better to attribute the majority–minority achievement gap not to personal deficiencies of minority students, but to the relatively exclusive reliance in public schools on traditional classroom structures, structures that appear to be ineffective in producing achievement among minority students.

   With regard to achievement, the Riverside Cooperative Learning Project produced results that are supportive of a general form of the structural bias hypothesis, but that do not support the conclusion that cooperative learning is always the best classroom structure for minority students. Overall, as revealed by a significant pretest main effect of ethnic group on teacher-constructed spelling tests, $F(2,484) = 10.26$, p <.0001, prior to the experiment the Anglo-American students spelled correctly more words than did the black ($p < .01$) and the Mexican-American ($p < .005$) students. The gains that the students made, however, depended on the interaction of ethnic group and class structure. The spelling gains for Anglo-American, black, and Mexican-American students in the traditional, STAD, and TGT classrooms are plotted in Figure 2. There was an optimal classroom structure for each cultural group: The Anglo-American students learned the most in TGT, which includes direct intense interpersonal competition; the black students, who were the most cooperative group sampled, learned the most in STAD, the most purely cooperative technique; and the Mexican-American students learned the most in the traditional treatment. This technique × race interaction was significant, $F(4,484) = 5.53$, p <.001. Clearly, the choice of any one classroom structure amounts to the choice of higher achievement for some groups and lower achievement for others. Thus, the results support the structural bias hypothesis: Class structures are biased in favor of some groups and against others. Most important, the most purely cooperative classroom structure, STAD, produced the best results for the black students, who, in the present sample, were significantly more cooperative than were the other two groups.

The inconsistency of the form of structural bias observed in the Riverside Cooperative Learning Project and that observed in the three prior published studies revealing interactions between culture and classroom structure is interpretable in terms of population differences in cooperation and competition. Contrary to what is usually the case, the Mexican-American students of the Riverside Cooperative Learning Pro-

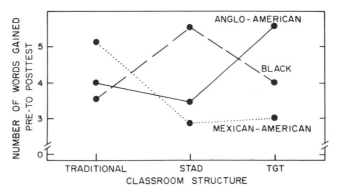

FIGURE 2. Spelling achievement gains of Anglo-American, black, and Mexican-American elementary pupils in traditional, STAD, and TGT classrooms (Riverside Cooperative Learning Project).

ject were not more cooperative than the Anglo-American students, as measured by cooperation–competition choice cards. The social orientation of minority students, at least Mexican-American students, is strongly a function of acculturation; as they acculturate, Mexican-American children adopt the competitve norms of the majority group (Knight & Kagan, 1977). The Mexican-American students of the Riverside Cooperative Learning Project were highly acculturated; most were third-generation, with little knowledge of Spanish. Thus, the Mexican-American population of the Riverside Cooperative Learning Project provides a poor test of some aspects of the structural bias hypothesis; it may be unreasonable to expect cooperative learning structures to provide greater gains for minority populations that do not differ in social orientation from majority populations.

COOPERATIVENESS AND SPELLING ACHIEVEMENT

Within the Riverside Cooperative Learning Project, there is strong evidence that had the minority and the majority students differed in social orientation, as they often do, the minority students would have shown greater achievement gains in the most cooperative classroom structure. When the achievement of the students was plotted as a function of their cooperativeness, a significant cooperativeness × technique interaction emerged, $F(2,484) = 5.83$, $p < .005$: In TGT, the structure with the most intense direct interpersonal competition, the competitive students gained far more than the cooperative students, as might be expected. In STAD, the most purely cooperative technique, there was a tendency toward the opposite pattern: The cooperative students gained somewhat more than the competitive students. The traditional technique favored competitive over cooperative students, but only slightly (See Figure 3).

Interestingly, it appears that the inclusion of a competitive evaluative task structure, the tournament, had more impact on achievement gains than did the inclusion of cooperative teams. With regard to the achievement of the cooperators and the competitors, TGT and STAD differed more from each other than either did from the traditional treatment, as seen in Figure 3. The relationship was most dramatic for the most competitive students (indicated in Figure 3 as "Low cooperativeness"). As the only difference between the TGT and the STAD treatments is the inclusion in TGT of competitive tournaments, we can conclude that tournaments are tremendously important for competitive students, increasing their gains substantially.

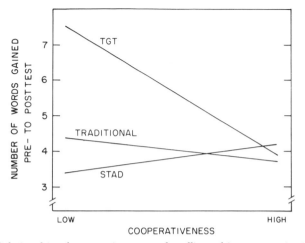

FIGURE 3. Relationship of cooperativeness and spelling achievement gains in traditional, STAD, and TGT elementary classrooms.

COOPERATIVENESS AND STANDARDIZED ACHIEVEMENT TEST SCORES

For the elementary students, scores on several scales of the Stanford Achievement Test (SAT) were obtained and analyzed. The students' scores on the following SAT scales were available: Listening Vocabulary, Listening Comprehension, and Listening Total (which was a composite of the preceding two scales); Reading Comprehension, Word Study Skills, and Reading Total (a composite of the preceding two scales); and Mathematics Concepts, Mathematics Computations, and Mathematics Total (once again, a composite of the preceding two scales). The SAT was administered to all students in the school district in June of each year; the SAT scores from the June testing preceding the cooperative learning experiment by about nine months were used as pretest measures, a .d the SAT scores from the June testing following the experiment by about two months were used as posttest measures.

Structural bias against cooperative students would be supported if the relationship beween the students' cooperativeness and their gain in achievement differed as a function of classroom structure. Specifically, cooperativeness should have been negatively related to achievement gains in the traditional, competitively structured classrooms and positively related to achievement gains in the classrooms using cooperative learning. To test this hypothesis, the pre- to posttest gain in achievement on each of the nine SAT scales was regressed on the five main effects of (1) student ethnic status, (2) sex, (3) grade, (4) class structure, and (5) student cooperative social orientation, and the 10 two-way interactions among these factors. When we restrict our attention to the three total scores, the cooperative-competitive by class structure interaction was significant, as predicted, for two of the three total scores—Listening Total: $F(2,368) = 5.06$, $p < .01$, and Mathematics Total: $F(2,372) = 5.76$, $p < .005$—but was nonsignificant for the third, Reading Total: $F(2,381) = 1.00$. Of greater importance were the regression weights relating cooperative social orientation to gain in achievement. As shown in Figure 4, the regression slopes relating cooperativeness to achievement gains were negative for all three total scores for the students in the traditional classroom, but they were positive in all six instances for the students in the classrooms using the cooperative learning methods, STAD and TGT.

It may seem somewhat anomalous that the results were the weakest for the Reading Total, when the cooperative learning of spelling words is a learning task presumably related to reading. It should be noted in this regard that even though the predicted interaction was not significant for the Reading Total, the regression weights were in the hypothesized direction. Further, the Listening Total, which was composed of the Listening Vocabulary and the Listening Comprehension tests, was the measure of achievement most similar to the behavior in which the students engaged in their cooperative study groups, and the Listening Total showed effects of the cooperativeness × class structure interaction as great as those shown on the Mathematics Total. Of most importance,

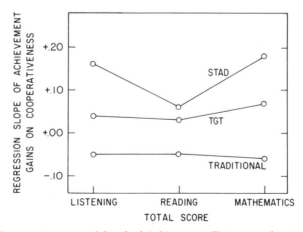

FIGURE 4. Cooperativeness and Stanford Achievement Test scores for students in traditional, STAD, and TGT classrooms (Riverside Cooperative Learning Project).

the results across type of class structure were consistent theoretically: The most purely cooperative structure, STAD, showed the strongest positive relationship between cooperativeness and achievement gain, whereas TGT, which has significant competitive elements, fell between the STAD and the traditional class structures.

CLASSROOM CLIMATE

Academic achievement is only one of the desired outcomes of the school experience. Classroom processes have a profound impact on students' attitudes toward academic content areas, class, and school. Similarly, classrooms impact on student feelings of being liked and supported, their liking for others, and their feeling supportive of the achievement of others.

In order to test how the traditional and the cooperative class structures affect the classroom climate for majority and minority students, a 32-item questionnaire was administered to the students in the traditional, STAD, and TGT conditions of the first-year elementary-school study of the Riverside Cooperative Learning Project. Sixteen pairs of positively and negatively worded items were presented to the students, who indicated agreement or disagreement. There were two pairs for each of eight climate variables: (1) own liking for others; (2) feeling liked by others; (3) own support of others' achievement; (4) feeling that others support one's own achievement; (5) liking for group work; (6) liking for spelling; (7) liking for class; and (8) liking for school. Through factor-analytic techniques, seven primary and two second-order factors emerged. The second-order factors were (1) a social relations factor, including the mutual concern measures, concern about absences, and liking for cooperative work; and (2) an achievement or schoolwork factor, including liking for spelling, liking for class, and liking for school.

ELEMENTARY-SCHOOL CLASS CLIMATE

The percentage agreement with the items of these factors for the minority and the majority students in the traditional, STAD, and TGT conditions of the elementary-school study are plotted in Figure 5. For both factors, a very similar pattern emerged: The classroom climate tended to be more positive in the cooperative classrooms than in the traditional classrooms for both minority and majority students, but STAD and TGT had a different impact on minority and majority students. The ethnic group × technique interaction comparing STAD with TGT was significant for schoolwork attitudes, $F(1,314) = 9.13$, $p < .01$, and social atti-

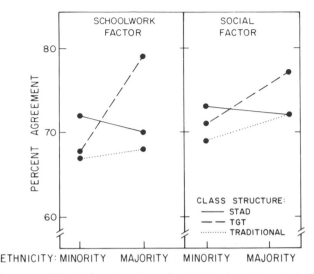

FIGURE 5. Classroom Climate for minority and majority elementary students in traditional, STAD, and TGT classrooms (Riverside Cooperative Learning Project).

tudes, $F(1,314) = 4.96$, $p < .03$. Apparently, the inclusion of the competitive tournament of TGT had a very favorable impact on the classroom climate for the majority students, but for the minority students, it provided a classroom climate that was unfavorable compared to the more purely cooperative structure of STAD.

The use of cooperative teams (STAD and TGT) produces a more favorable climate for all students than the use of traditional, whole-class structures. The traditional approach is not best for any group. Thus, the overall comparison of cooperative and traditional class structures with regard to classroom climate provides no evidence for structural bias. Rather, it presents a case of one approach (the inclusion of cooperative teams) providing a superior outcome for all students compared to the use of another approach (the whole-class format). Evidence for structural bias does appear, however, with regard to the *type* of cooperative learning method chosen: When a cooperative class structure that includes intense direct interpersonal competition is chosen, as in the "mixed" structure represented by TGT, there is structural bias in favor of a positive climate for majority students at the relative expense of minority students. If, on the other hand, a more purely cooperative class structure is chosen, as represented by STAD, minority students experience the class climate as more favorable than do majority students.

Importantly, with regard to achievement climate, minority students experience little difference between the traditional and the TGT structures; it is only in the absence of competitive tournaments that they experience a more favorable class climate for achievement. Probably because of their emphasis on competitive task and reward structures, traditional and TGT classroom structures diminish liking for content areas, as well as liking for class and school for minority students. Given that traditional class structures are pervasive, and that there is a general absence of relatively pure cooperative class structures like those represented by STAD, we can conclude that the public schools have settled on forms of structuring classrooms that, compared to more cooperative structures, are damaging to the classroom climate for minority students.

HIGH-SCHOOL CLASS CLIMATE

The structural bias hypothesis was supported at the high-school level for the social relations factor, but not for the schoolwork factor. A significant ethnic group $\times$ treatment interaction, $F(2,176) = 3.75$, $p < .05$, indicated that the social relations in the Co-op Co-op classrooms differed little from those in the traditional classrooms for the Anglo-American students (Co-op = 15.02, traditional = 14.58); and the black students (Co-op = 13.60, traditional = 14.28); but class structure had a relatively large impact on class climate for the Mexican-American students (Co-op = 16.11, traditional = 13.58). Thus, at the high-school level, as at the elementary level, the choice of a classroom structure biased important educational outcomes in favor of some groups, but at the expense of other groups. The large favorable impact of the Co-op Co-op method for the Mexican-American but not for the other students at the high-school level remains unexplained.

SELF-CONCEPT

As indicated by the structural bias theory, both the outgroup hypothesis and the mismatch hypothesis predict that minority and cooperative students are likely to have lower self-concepts in classes that contain competitive structures. As an outgroup member, a student may internalize the majority view of herself or himself. Further, if the classroom structure is out of synchrony with the core values of the student, the student may feel less worthy.

To test the impact of class structure on the self-concept of Anglo-American, Mexican-American, and black students, the Piers-Harris Self-Concept Scale was administered to the elementary students of the Riverside Cooperative Learning Project. In addition to an overall measure of self-concept, the Piers-Harris Self-Concept Scale provides six factors of self-concept (Behavior, Intellectual and School Status, Physical Status,

Anxiety, Popularity, and Happiness). The tests for structural bias were significant on the Intellectual and School Status Factor and on the Behavior Factor.

ETHNICITY AND INTELLECTUAL SELF-CONCEPT

Classroom structures had a different impact on the intellectual self-concept of the three ethnic groups. The Intellectual and School Status Factor of the Piers-Harris contains items such as "I am good in school work" and "I am smart." On that factor, structural bias emerged for the ethnic groups in very clear form, as plotted in Figure 6. This ethnic group × technique interaction was significant, $F(4,437) = 2.84$, $p < .03$.

As with classroom climate, for self-concept among the elementary-school students it was not the cooperative–traditional comparison that produced evidence of structural bias, but the STAD–TGT comparison. The inclusion of competitive tournaments in TGT appeared to have very negative consequences for the self-concept of the minority but not the majority students. Apparently, the inclusion of competitive tournaments leaves minority students feeling intellectually inadequate; TGT was associated with a low Intellectual and School Status concept for both Mexican-American and black students. Face-to-face competition in a negative interdependence situation can have quite adverse effects on the self-concept of minority students, perhaps because of the lower overall achievement levels of the minority students.

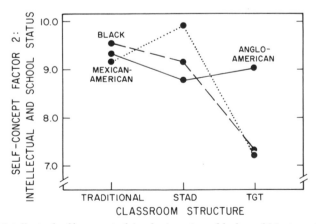

FIGURE 6.   Intellectual self-concept of Anglo-American, black, and Mexican-American elementary students in traditional, STAD, and TGT classrooms (Riverside Cooperative Learning Project).

There was a suggestion that a purely cooperative team experience had a positive impact on feelings of intellectual competence for the Mexican-American students: STAD produced the highest self-concept scores for the Mexican-American students. In contrast, the traditional class structure worked best for the Anglo-American and the black students. Again, the choice of one structure was associated with superior outcomes for one cultural group, but at the relative expense of other groups.

COOPERATIVENESS AND BEHAVIORAL SELF-CONCEPT

Theoretically, the cooperative student placed in a competitive class structure should feel little motivation to learn, which, in turn, might lower his or her feelings of competence or self-concept. To test that hypothesis, self-concept was analyzed as a function of student cooperativeness, which was obtained prior to the introduction of the treatments. Structural bias emerged for the behavioral self-concept factor, as presented in Figure 7. The cooperativeness × technique interaction was significant, $F(2,437) = 3.71$, $p < .03$.

The Behavior factor of the Piers-Harris Self-Concept Scale reflects a generalized feeling about one's goodness. High scores are obtained by affirmative answers to questions like "I am a good person" and "I am well behaved." Apparently, the cooperative students placed in a class that emphasized competitive tournaments lost their general feeling of worth, as reflected by lower scores on the behavioral self-concept factor for the cooperative students in the TGT classrooms. Conversely, the

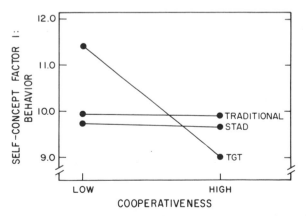

FIGURE 7.   Behavioral self-concept of high and low cooperators in traditional, STAD, and TGT elementary classrooms (Riverside Cooperative Learning Project).

competitive students felt enhanced worth after a series of competitive tournaments. Interestingly, there was little difference between the traditional and the STAD classrooms for cooperative and competitive students, indicating that competitive tournaments were a more important variable than cooperative teams for the behavioral self-concept of cooperative and competitive students. The inclusion of cooperative teams did not raise the behavioral self-concept of the cooperative students, but the inclusion of competitive tournaments did raise the behavioral self-concept of the competitive students. The most important point, however, is that the inclusion of competitive tournaments had a positive impact on the competitive students *at the expense of* the cooperative students. Thus, producing weekly winners at the expense of weekly losers in a very explicit social-comparison process biased the self-concept outcomes of the classroom in favor of the competitive over the cooperative students.

COOPERATIVENESS

A prosocial orientation is a desirable educational outcome. Society will be better served when our schools influence the development of students so that they prefer to maximize the outcomes of others rather than minimizing the outcomes of others. Although a cooperative social orientation is a desirable educational outcome for both majority and minority students, it is possible that traditional and cooperative classroom structures have a different impact on those groups with regard to fostering cooperativeness. If so, this different impact would be yet another form of structural bias. That is, if traditional or competitive classroom structures are best for fostering prosocial development among majority students, but cooperative classroom structures are best for fostering prosocial development among minority students, the choice of a traditional classroom structure would amount to the choice of a class structure that favors the development of desired traits more among majority than among minority students.

Because measures of cooperativeness were included in both the elementary and the secondary studies of the Riverside Cooperative Learning Project, it is possible to test for structural bias with regard to prosocial development at both the elementary and the secondary levels. The prosocial development measure used in both studies was the Social Behavior Scale, administered in the sociometric version, as pictured in Figure 8.

The students were presented with the names of their classmates and the four-alternative Social Behavior Scale. Their task was to choose

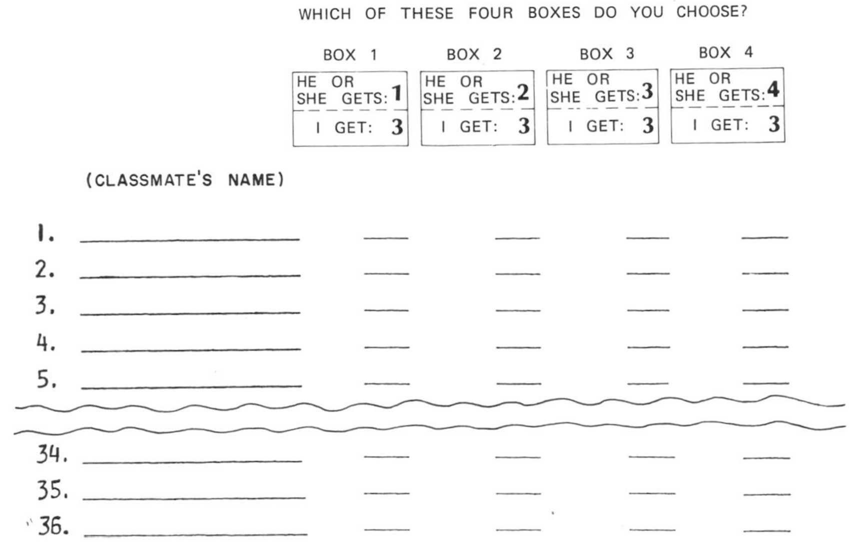

WHICH OF THESE FOUR BOXES DO YOU CHOOSE?

BOX 1	BOX 2	BOX 3	BOX 4
HE OR SHE GETS: **1**	HE OR SHE GETS: **2**	HE OR SHE GETS: **3**	HE OR SHE GETS: **4**
I GET: **3**	I GET: **3**	I GET: **3**	I GET: **3**

(CLASSMATE'S NAME)

I. _____   ____   ____   ____   ____

2. _____   ____   ____   ____   ____

3. _____   ____   ____   ____   ____

4. _____   ____   ____   ____   ____

5. _____   ____   ____   ____   ____

~~~~~~

34. _____   ____   ____   ____   ____

35. _____   ____   ____   ____   ____

36. _____   ____   ____   ____   ____

FIGURE 8.   The Sociometric Social Behavior Scale.

one of the four alternatives for each of their classmates. The alternatives all result in the same number (3) of valued rewards for the chooser, but they differ in the rewards that they provide for the classmates, ranging from 1 to 4. Details of the administration format, the reliability, and the validity of the Sociometric Social Behavior Scale have been presented elsewhere (Kagan, 1984).

ELEMENTARY-SCHOOL COOPERATIVENESS

At the elementary-school level, the cooperative treatments produced more cooperativeness among the students than the traditional treatment in Grades 5 and 6, for both minority and majority students. In Grades 2–4, the cooperative treatments produced more cooperativeness than the traditional class structure for the minority students but, unexplicably, not for the majority students. The interaction of class structure × grade × ethnic group × ethnicity of the other was significant, $F(1,512) = 12.91$, $p < .001$, and is plotted in Figure 9.

Interestingly, the minority students in Grades 2–4 were only slightly more cooperative than the majority students in the traditional classrooms, but in the cooperative classrooms, they were far more cooperative. It was as if the traditional classroom structure suppressed the cooperativeness of young minority students, which was released in the classrooms that used cooperative teams. Alternatively, it could be

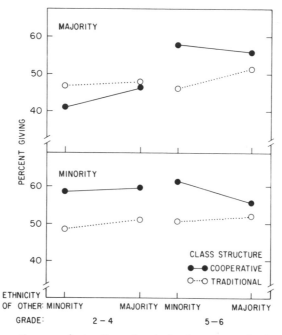

FIGURE 9. Cooperativeness of minority and majority elementary-school students toward minority and majority students in traditional and cooperative classroom (Riverside Cooperative Learning Project).

that young minority students are more sensitive to the press toward cooperativeness and competitiveness provided by the cooperative and competitive classroom structures. In any case—for the young students, at least—there appears to be some structural bias: The choice of traditional classroom structures suppresses the prosocial development of minority students considerably, whereas it does not appear to do so for the majority students. At the higher elementary-school grade levels, however, the traditional classroom structures seem to lower the prosocial choices of the minority and the majority students about equally.

An interaction with regard to race relations emerged in the upper grades: In the traditional class structure, both minority and majority students were more cooperative to majority than to minority students, giving them more. In contrast, when cooperative student teams were employed, both minority and majority students were more cooperative toward the minority students. It appears that older minority students are given higher social status in cooperative than in traditional class structures.

HIGH-SCHOOL COOPERATIVENESS

At the high-school level, there was also evidence of a different impact of the cooperative and traditional classroom structures on minority and majority students. For the minority but not the majority students, the cooperative classroom structure Co-op Co-op led to higher levels of cooperativeness than did the traditional structure. The interaction of ethnicity × technique × ethnicity of the other was significant, $F(1,190) = 5.63$, $p < .02$, and is pictured in Figure 10. In the traditional classrooms, a pronounced asymmetry emerged, indicating that both groups revealed a preference for majority-group classmates; the cooperative method produced more balanced relations. This pattern parallels the preference for majority students observed in the traditional but not the cooperative classrooms in the upper-grade elementary-school data.

The structural bias hypothesis received support at the high-school level. The two types of class structure had a different impact on the minority and the majority students: A desired educational outcome, prosocial development, was for some reason somewhat higher in the traditional class structure among the Anglo-American students, but it was fostered considerably more by a cooperative class structure among the Mexican-American and the black students. This finding is noteworthy because it was obtained among high-school students using Co-op Co-op, a cooperative learning technique quite distinct from STAD and TGT, which were used at the elementary-school level. It appears, then, that the more favorable impact of the cooperative structures on minority students has some generality across the developmental age span, across cooperative learning techniques, and across various desired educational outcomes.

As in the elementary study, important interactions emerged in the high-school cooperativeness data with regard to race relations. As shown in Figure 10, the minority students manifested very little giving toward the majority students in the traditional classrooms but were quite cooperative toward the majority students in the classrooms that used cooperative learning. Apparently, the minority students responded to being part of a cooperative team by becoming more cooperative. Because almost all of the teammates of the minority students were majority students, the increased cooperativeness of the minority students was directed mostly toward majority students. The majority students, in contrast, typically had both majority and minority students as teammates, and they did not discriminate along racial lines in their cooperativeness. The most important point with regard to race relations revealed by the high-school cooperativeness data is the very

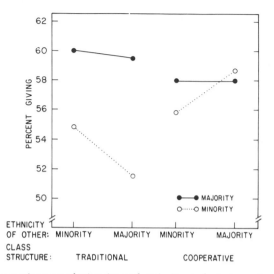

FIGURE 10. Cooperativeness of minority and majority students toward minority and majority high-school students in traditional and Co-op Co-op classrooms (Riverside Cooperative Learning Project).

dramatic improvement of attitudes of minority students toward majority students created by the cooperative class structures.

INTERPERSONAL RELATIONS

Class structures can operate either to promote harmonious social relations among students of different racial and cultural backgrounds or to create self-segregation among the students along racial lines. If the class structure fosters segregation along racial lines, generally there is a formation of a majority ingroup (which is perceived as academically and socially superior) and a minority outgroup (which is perceived as academically and socially inferior).

Although considerable evidence indicates that cooperative classroom structures promote positive race relations more than do traditional classroom structures (Sharan, 1980; Slavin, 1980, 1983), much of that evidence is based on weak measures of race relations. For example, having students simply nominate their friends in a classroom can lead to an artificially positive picture of the impact of cooperative teams on race relations. Students are unlikely to write down the names of others if they cannot spell their names. Thus, if the use of racially mixed student teams leads only to learning how to spell the names of one's teammates, this process can lead to an apparent increase in friendship on a typical friendship measure that involves the listing of names. Measures that involve listing the names of others are weak in other ways: If a student is absent on the test day, he or she is rather less likely to be listed. Also, name-listing measures give very little information with regard to the quality of friendship; listing someone as a friend may have quite different meanings for different students, especially students of different cultural backgrounds.

The Interpersonal Relations Assessment Technique (IRAT), developed by Schwarzwald and Cohen (1982), is not subject to many of the problems common to sociometric friendship measures. The IRAT provides each student with a list of all of his or her classmates and a set of behaviors that differ in the degree of friendship that they indicate, as pictured in Figure 11. Students respond by answering yes or no to each of the behavioral friendship items with regard to each other student in the class. A student might respond to someone with whom there is little

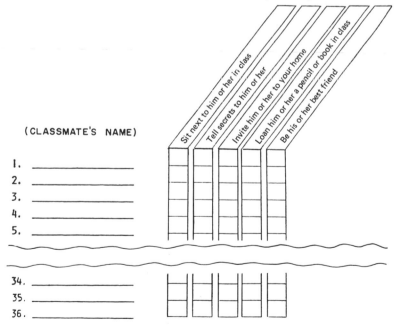

FIGURE 11. The Interpersonal Relations Assessment Technique (IRAT).

friendship by indicating only a willingness to loan a pencil or a book in class; the same student would respond to a close friend by indicating a willingness to engage in all of the behaviors listed on the IRAT, including a willingness to invite him or her home and to share personal secrets with him or her. The IRAT has been validated on thousands of students; it is a unidimensional scale with high coefficients of reproducibility and scalability.

The race-relations data from the IRAT are the most dramatic and important of the Riverside Cooperative Learning Project. In the traditional classrooms, with increased grade level, there was a radical movement toward increased segregation among the students along race lines, a phenomenon commonly encountered in public schools. This progressive racism did not occur in the cooperative classrooms. As can be seen in Figure 12, in Grades 2–4, in the traditional classes, there was a slight tendency for the minority and the majority students to manifest more friendliness toward others of their own group. By Grades 5 and 6, this slight ethnic cleavage became an enormous chasm: Being of the same ethnicity became almost a prerequisite for friendship. In marked con-

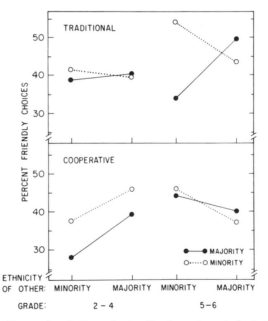

FIGURE 12. Friendliness of majority and minority elementary students toward majority and minority students in cooperative and traditional classrooms (Riverside Cooperative Learning Project).

trast, there was no significant ethnic cleavage at either grade level in the classrooms that included cooperative student teams. This interaction of technique $\times$ grade $\times$ ethnicity $\times$ ethnicity of the other was extremely highly significant, $F(1,495) = 18.62$, $p < .0001$.

As pictured in Figure 12, in the cooperative classrooms, there was some tendency for the students to be more friendly toward majority students at the lower grade levels and more friendly toward minority students at the higher grade levels. The critical point, however, is that same-ethnicity dropped out as a significant predictor of friendship in the cooperative classrooms at both grade levels. It seems that in traditional classrooms, at least at the higher grade levels, the students were looking for some basis to form in- and outgroup friendship patterns, and they settled on ethnicity as a basis for doing so. In contrast, in classrooms that included mixed-ethnic cooperative teams, there was no formation of in- and outgroup friendship patterns along ethnic lines. Traditional classroom structures lead to self-segregation and racism in the classroom; cooperative classroom structures lead to integration.

Importantly, a different pattern of findings emerged with regard to cooperativeness and friendship. The two variables did not correlate highly overall and were influenced in different ways by the cooperative and the traditional treatments. The cooperative classroom structures appeared to increase cooperativeness for most students, but they did not increase friendliness overall. The impact of class structure on friendliness was primarily on the pattern of friendliness within the classroom, not on the absolute level of friendliness observed. Whereas the students in the cooperative classrooms were not becoming more friendly overall, they were becoming more democratic in their friendship choices, or at least, they were not reserving friendliness only for those of their own cultural background. Having worked together cooperatively with others of different ethnic backgrounds, the students began choosing whether or not to be friendly with others on the basis of the personal qualities of the person, not on the basis of his or her color or culture.

CONCLUSION

The evidence reviewed in this chapter demonstrates that structural bias exists. The use of traditional, whole-class structures and mixed classroom structures that contain intensely competitive elements can have very damaging effects on achievement, classroom climate, self-concept, prosocial development, and race relations for cooperative individuals and minority groups. Across a variety of outcome domains, representing a sample of the most important educational outcomes, a similar pattern emerges: A purely cooperative class structure produces more desired outcomes for cooperative individuals and minority groups than do traditional and mixed class structures. This pattern of findings has implications for educational theory and practice.

Because there is an almost exclusive reliance in the United States on traditional classroom structures that produce academic, social, and emotional outcomes for cooperative and minority students less favorable than those that would be produced by purely cooperative classroom structures, a commitment to the democratic principle of maximizing the opportunity for positive educational outcomes for all individuals and cultural groups demands that the classrooms common in public schools be restructured. The direction of restructuring suggested by the empirical data reviewed here is not toward the exclusive use of cooperative classroom structures. Rather, if educational opportunities are to be maximized for all individuals and groups, the use of a variety of classroom structures is needed. Because students come to school with a variety of social values, they should be taught within a variety of classroom reward and task structures: There is need for competitive, individualistic, *and* cooperative structures. The American educational system should be faulted not for the inclusion of highly competitive and individualistic class structures, but for its failure to include cooperative class structures as well.

It is important to note that the beneficial effects for cooperative and minority students of cooperative classroom structures in the Riverside Cooperative Learning Project occurred as a result of adopting student teams for less than one hour a day in one academic content area, for relatively few weeks. If such profoundly positive consequences can occur for cooperative individuals and minority groups following such a limited exposure to student teams, the use of student teams should be considered for inclusion as part of the educational experience in all classrooms.

In turning to some of the more mundane implications of the present empirical review, it should be noted that the results support a reinterpretation of the effects of the competitive tournaments of TGT. Apparently, the tournaments are a positive experience for majority and competitive students, but a negative experience for minority and cooperative students. TGT and STAD can no longer be viewed as relatively interchangeable cooperative-learning structures: The pattern of results indicates that great caution should be used before TGT is adopted, especially in classrooms with high concentrations of cooperative and minority students. TGT probably should be reconceptualized as a mixed cooperative-competitive class structure rather than as one among several cooperative learning methods.

Another implication of the study is that because the results of cooperative learning interact with social orientation and are to some extent domain-specific, some of the sweeping generalizations that have appeared in the cooperative learning literature must be questioned. Reviews of cooperative learning (Johnson, Maruyama, Johnson, Nelson, & Skon, 1981; Slavin, 1980) have conveyed the impression that cooperative methods are superior for all students in all domains. In contrast, the present study indicates that social orientation interacts with class structure so that no single class structure is best for all students. In some domains, competitive students profit most from TGT, the class structure that contains the most direct, intense competitive experiences. Not only do competitive students achieve better in classrooms that contain competitive tournaments, they also feel better about themselves, their class, their school, and their classmates. The same competitive class structure, however, can be quite damaging to educational and social outcomes for cooperative and minority students. Cooperative small-group techniques, when compared as a group to traditional class structures, were superior for producing positive race relations, prosocial development, and classroom climate for all students. In contrast, in the present sample, the cooperative techniques did not produce superior overall outcomes with regard to achievement and self-concept. Thus, conclusions about the effects of cooperative learning must be population and domain-specific.

Although there is much in the present review to suggest the superiority of cooperative over traditional class structures in some domains, especially prosocial development and ethnic relations, the review supports an interactionist view with respect to other domains. There is a need for educational researchers to reconceptualize the effects of cooperative as opposed to traditional classroom structures, providing a more differentiated, domain-specific picture that accounts for the interaction of class structure with social orientation and with ethnic status. At the level of educational practice, the review indicates a need for educators to provide more cooperative learning experiences in order to maximize positive educational outcomes for cooperative individuals and minority groups.

A benefit of including a diversity of classroom structures within the educational experience of all students would be that such diverse experiences would better prepare students for the rapidly changing world that they will encounter as adults. Our world is changing at a rapid rate, and as concerned educators, we no longer can predict with confidence the kind of social ecology that our students will encounter as mature individuals. Our only adaptive recourse, therefore, is to prepare pupils not to be rigidly cooperative, competitive, or individualistic, but to be adaptively flexible—to recognize a broad range of social situations and the kinds of behaviors appropriate to each. There are situations in which competition is an adaptive strategy; there are other situations in which cooperation is adaptive; and there are yet other situations in which an individualistic approach is most successful. By including a variety of task and reward structures within the classroom, teachers can prepare their students to recognize a fuller range of environmental contingencies and to be able to adjust their behavior accordingly.

Given the relatively exclusive reliance on competitive and individualistic classroom structures that has occurred for the past several generations, as well as the importance of those structures in the socialization process, it is not surprising that we are faced with so many examples of individuals and groups persisting in competitive and/or individualistic behaviors in situations in which cooperative behaviors would be more likely to produce the outcomes that they desire (Edney, 1980; Hardin, 1968; Kagan & Madsen, 1971). By exclusive reliance on competitive and individualistic classroom structures, we have blinded individuals to adaptive cooperative possibilities. The ill effects of this imbalance in our educational system are observable in many domains, extending from interpersonal to international relations.

Acknowledgments

The Riverside Cooperative Learning Project was initiated at the suggestion of Irving Balow, Dean, School of Education; his vision and support made the project possible. Financial support for the project has come from The Center of Social and Behavioral Sciences, University of California, Riverside, initially under the direction of David Warren and then Robert Singer. The work of training and supervising student teachers in cooperative learning has been masterfully carried out at the elementary level by Sarah E. Blaker, Beverly M. Guidero, Pauline S. Tingey, and Mary H. Williamson, and at the secondary level by Sylvia Andreatta, Pam Klute, and James Reardon, Supervisors of Teacher Education. The authors gratefully acknowledge the support of Patricia M. Dahms, Director of Student Teacher Supervision, University of California, Riverside; Dr. Clark Cox, Superintendent, Riverside Unified School District; and Starrett Dalton, Administrator, Department of Research and Evaluation, Riverside Unified School District.

REFERENCES

Adams, R. S., & Biddle, B. J. *Realities of teaching: Explorations with video tape.* New York: Holt, 1970.

Allport, G. *The nature of prejudice.* Cambridge, Mass.: Addison-Wesley, 1954.

Amidon, E., & Flanders, N. A. The effect of direct and indirect teacher influence on dependent-prone students learning geometry. *Journal of Educational Psychology,* 1961, *52,* 286–291.

Aronson, E., Blaney, N., Stephan, C., Sikes, J., & Snapp, M. *The Jigsaw classroom.* Beverly Hills, Calif.: Sage, 1978.

Brewer, H. B. In-group bias in the minimal intergroup situation: A cognitive-motivational analysis. *Psychological Bulletin,* 1979, *8,* 307–324.

Cook, S. W. Social science and school desegregation: Did we mislead the Supreme court. *Personality and Social Psychology Bulletin,* 1979, *5,* 420–437.

Cronbach, L. J. The two disciplines of scientific psychology. *American Psychologist,* 1957, *12,* 671–684.

Cronbach, L. J., & Snow, R. E. *Aptitudes and instructional methods: A handbook for research on interactions.* New York: Irvington, 1977.

DeVoe, M. W. Cooperation as a function of self-concept, sex, and race. *Educational Research Quarterly,* 1977, *2,* 3–8.

Doty, B. A. Teaching method effectiveness in relation to certain student characteristics. *Journal of Educational Research,* 1970, *60,* 363–365.

Edney, J. J. The commons problem: Alternative perspectives. *American Psychologist,* 1980, *35,* 131–150.

Gerard, H. B., Jackson, T. D., & Conolley, E. S. Social contact in the desegregated classroom. In H. B. Gerard & N. Miller (Eds.), *School desegregation: A long-term study.* New York: Plenum Press, 1975.

Gump, P. V. The classroom behavior setting: Its nature and relation to student behavior. Final Report, Contract No. CE-4-10-107, United States Bureau of Research, HEW, 1967. Described in Dunkin, M. J. & Biddle, B. J. *The study of teaching.* New York: Holt, 1974.

Hardin, G. The tragedy of the commons. *Science,* 1968, *62,* 1243–1248.

Hornstein, H. A. *Cruelty and kindness: A new look at aggression and altruism.* Englewood Cliffs, N.J.: Prentice-Hall, 1976.

Johnson, D. W., Maruyama, G., Johnson, R. T., Nelson, D., & Skon, L. Effects of competitive, and individualistic goal structures on achievement: A meta-analysis. *Psychological Bulletin,* 1981, *89,* 47–62.

Kagan, S. Social motives and behaviors of Mexican American and Anglo American children. In J. L. Martinez (Ed.), *Chicano psychology.* New York: Academic Press, 1977.

Kagan, S. Cooperation-competition, culture, and structural bias in classrooms. In S. Sharan, P. Hare, C. D. Webb, & R. Hertz-Lazarowitz (Eds.), *Cooperation in education.* Provo, Utah: Brigham Young University Press, 1980.

Kagan, S. Social orientation among Mexican American children: A challenge to traditional classroom structures. In E. E. Garcia (Ed.), *The Mexican American child: Language, cognition, and social development.* Tempe, Ariz.: Center for Bilingual Education, 1983.

Kagan, S. Interpreting Chicano cooperativeness: Methodological and theoretical considerations. In J. L. Martinez, Jr., & R. H. Mendoza (Eds.), *Chicano psychology (2nd ed.).* New York: Academic Press, 1984.

Kagan, S., & Knight, G. P. Social motives among Anglo American and Mexican American children: Experimental and projective measures. *Journal of Research in Personality,* 1981, *15,* 93–106.

Kagan, S., & Madsen, M. C. Cooperation and competition of Mexican, Mexican-American, and Anglo-American children of two ages under four instructional sets. *Developmental Psychology*, 1971, 5, 32–39.

Knight, G. P., & Kagan, S. Acculturation of prosocial and competitive behaviors among second- and third-generation Mexican American children. *Journal of Cross-Cultural Psychology*, 1977, 8, 273–284.

Magnusson, D., & Endler, N. S. *Personality at the crossroads: Current issues in interactional psychology*. New York: Wiley, 1977.

Minnesota Law Review. The effects of segregation and the consequences of desegregation: A social science statement. Appendix to appellant's briefs of *Brown vs. Board of Education of Topeka, Kansas*. 1953, 37, 427–439.

Perkins, H. V. A procedure for assessing the classroom behavior of students and teachers. *American Educational Research Journal*, 1964, 1(4), 249–260.

Richmond, B. O., & Weiner, G. P. Cooperation and competition among young children as a function of ethnic grouping, grade, sex and reward condition. *Journal of Educational Psychology*, 1973, 64, 329–334.

St. John, N. H. *School desegregation: Outcomes for children*. New York: Wiley, 1975.

Sampson, E., & Kardush, M. Age, sex, class, and race differences in response to a two-person non-zero-sum game. *Conflict Resolution*, 1965, 9, 212–220.

Schwarzwald, J., & Cohen, S. Relationship between academic tracking and the degree of interethnic acceptance. *Journal of Educational Psychology*, 1982, 74(4), 588–597.

Sharan, S. Cooperative learning in small groups: Recent methods and effects on achievement, attitudes, and ethnic relations. *Review of Educational Research*, 1980, 50, 241–271.

Sherif, M. Experiments in group conflict. *Scientific American*, 1956, 195(5), 54–58.

Slavin, R. E. How student learning teams can integrate the desegregated classroom. *Integrated Education*, 1977, 15, 56–58.

Slavin, R. E. Cooperative learning. *Review of Educational Research*, 1980, 50, 315–342.

Slavin, R. E. Cooperative learning and desegregation. *Journal of Educational Equity and Leadership*, 1981, 1, 145–161.

Slavin, R. E. *Cooperative learning*. New York: Longman, 1983.

Slavin, R. E., & Oickle, E. Effects of learning teams on student achievement and race relations: Treatment by race interactions. *Sociology of Education*, 1981, 54, 174–180.

Stephen, W. G. School desegregation: An evaluation of predictions made in *Brown v. Board of Education*. *Psychological Bulletin*, 1978, 85, 217–238.

Wheeler, R. *Predisposition toward cooperation and competition: Cooperative and competitive classroom effects*. Paper presented at the meeting of the American Psychological Association, San Francisco, August 1977.

12

Cooperative Learning Effects on Ethnic Relations and Achievement in Israeli Junior-High-School Classrooms

SHLOMO SHARAN, PETER KUSSELL,
RACHEL HERTZ-LAZAROWITZ, YAEL BEJARANO,
SHULAMIT RAVIV,
AND
YAEL SHARAN

Israel is a country of immigrants whose ethnic ties are roughly divided into two groups: Jews who emmigrated to Israel from the Muslim countries of the Middle East, Asia, and North Africa (referred to as *Middle Eastern*), and those who came from Europe, the Americas, and South Africa (referred to as *Western*). The integration of these two major ethnic groups is acknowledged to be one of the central problems confronting Israel's educational system. The population of the country is roughly equally divided at present between the two groups. Research on various aspects of school desegregation in Israel has been extensively summarized in a recent volume (Amir & Sharan, 1984).

This chapter describes a field experiment conducted in desegregated junior high schools in Israel. The experiment compared the effects of three teaching methods on the pupils' academic learning, cooperative behavior, and attitudes toward peers of their own and of the other ethnic group. The three methods were Group-Investigation (GI—Sharan & Hertz-Lazarowitz, 1980; Sharan & Sharan, 1976; Thelen, 1960); Student Teams-Achievement Divisions: (STAD—Slavin, 1980b); and traditional whole-class (WC) instruction. The first two are cooperative learning methods utilizing small groups of students within the typical classroom (up to 40 pupils). Within these groups, pupils collaborate with one another in various ways according to the operational guidelines of the particular method.

SHLOMO SHARAN • School of Education, Tel Aviv University, Tel Aviv, Israel.   PETER KUSSELL AND YAEL SHARAN • Israel Educational Television Center, Ramat Aviv, Tel Aviv, Israel.   YAEL BEJARANO • Everyman's University, Tel Aviv, Israel.   SHULAMIT RAVIV • Wingate Institute for Physical Education and Sport, Netanya, Israel.   RACHEL HERTZ-LAZAROWITZ • School of Education, Haifa University, Haifa, Israel.

It should be noted that this is one of the few experiments reported to date that compared cooperative learning methods with each other as well as with whole-class instruction (see Chapter 11, which reports another experiment with a similar design). Also, no research has been done thus far to assess the effects of the Group-Investigation method on interethnic behavior and attitudes. Finally, this study employed a wide range of outcome measures, including behavioral observations to evaluate effects in diverse psychoeducational domains of the pupils' functioning. Most studies to date have limited themselves to a narrow range of measures in assessing outcomes and have relied almost exclusively on self-report measures (Sharan, 1980; Slavin, 1983). The limited design, as well as the small number of measures used to evaluate the outcomes, contributed to the interpretation of the results from a correspondingly restricted perspective. A diversity of measures, such as in the present study, naturally extends the ability to examine treatment effects over a broadened base. Yet, however significant such practical gains may be, they inevitably introduce other difficult problems, such as how the various measures may be related theoretically.

Applying cooperative learning methods to multiethnic classrooms as a means of promoting ethnic integration was one of the initial goals of cooperative learning theory and investigation (see reviews by Johnson, Johnson, & Maruyama, 1983; Sharan, 1980; Slavin, 1983). Either implicitly or explicitly, research on cooperative learning effects on ethnic integration have often taken as their point of departure Allport's (1954) three principles for the design of intergroup contact in social settings for reducing prejudice. These principles assert that it is possible to reduce intergroup prejudice in multiethnic settings if certain conditions are maintained: (1) if the members of the different groups experience direct and unmediated contact; (2) if the contact occurs under conditions of equal status and cooperative interaction; and (3) if the contact receives clear sanction by the people in authority.

Studies of desegregation outcomes have employed percentages of group representation in the multiethnic classroom as an index of cross-ethnic contact (Amir, 1976; Stephan, 1978; St. John, 1975). A common assumption of these studies is that the exposure to one another of pupils assigned to the same classroom constitutes direct, unmediated contact.

Cooperative learning theorists have argued that traditionally organized classrooms, where the presentation–recitation approach to instruction prevails, do not promote direct, unmediated contact among pupils. Although sharing the same classroom environment may be a necessary condition, it has been maintained that it is hardly a sufficient one for guaranteeing direct and unmediated contact. Indeed, classroom observation studies in the past have documented the relative paucity of interpupil communication (Amidon & Hough, 1967). Furthermore, when direct communication among peers has occurred, self-selecting factors, fixed seating plans, friendship patterns and other social factors have inevitably limited the amount and the quality of cross-ethnic exchanges.

Any reasonably frequent implementation of direct cross-ethnic contact among pupils in a multiethnic classroom could be achieved only be restructuring the patterns of interpersonal communication in the classroom. Small groups are ideally suited to this purpose because they provide the social setting for interpersonal contacts that are direct, frequent, and intimate. Communications in small groups are not anonymously addressed to an entire class of pupils, many of whom are not tuned in to what the reciting pupil has to say (Sommer, 1967). Indeed, "direct contact," in Allport's theory, clearly implies a relatively high frequency of face-to-face interaction, as well as a relatively intimate quality in the interaction. It is the frequency and quality of the interactions that allow the participants to become acquainted with one another and to experience genuine exchange.

Any serious plan for incorporating these interactional features into the process of classroom learning requires an organizational structure wherein direct peer interaction is the norm, not the exception, directed at achieving learning goals, and not just another extracurricular activity. These considerations have formed part of the background for the design of several cooperative-learning systems and for the design of classroom-based experiments intended to evaluate the effects of these methods.

THREE TEACHING METHODS: THE INDEPENDENT VARIABLE

Several considerations led to the inclusion in this experiment of two cooperative-learning methods. Typically, one cooperative-learning method is considered the experimental method, and whole-class instruction serves as the control method. The two methods employed here represent distinct approaches both theoretically and procedurally. (A list of the topics on which the procedures of the two methods may be seen to differ has been published elsewhere; see Sharan, 1980.) Theoretically, the Group-Investigation method is grounded in a Deweyan orientation toward school learning as inquiry in a social context, whereas STAD is a peer-tutoring approach based on motivation theory. The clear conceptual and practical distinctions between the two methods provide a basis for comparing their effects. On the other hand, other cooperative methods found in the current literature do not differ in essential ways from one or the other of these two methods. In some instances, a given method incorporates procedures from both these prototypes, reflecting a mixture of models.

The whole-class method still remains standard instructional fare in a majority of schools in the Western world. Hence, the inclusion of this method in experiments evaluating the effects of instructional variation retains a high social priority. This is particularly true for the presentation of the research data to teachers, who almost invariably want to know what the standard method of instruction would accomplish under the same conditions as the "new" method.

TEACHERS AND PUPILS

The project staff was directed to three schools near Tel Aviv, Israel, by the national supervisor of junior high schools. His criterion for selecting these schools was that each had a student body with a close to equal representation of Israel's two major Jewish ethnic groups.

All teachers of English as a foreign language and of literature in these three schools elected to participate in this experiment after receiving detailed explanations of the project's methods, goals, and requirements. There were a total of 18 English teachers, who taught a total of 33 classes, and 15 literature teachers, who taught 21 classes. English classes in Israel are typically composed by ability grouping, perhaps because achievement in English is one of the chief academic yardsticks by which Israeli students are measured. Literature, on the other hand, is seen as less important in Israel's achievement-oriented educational system, and literature classes have never been grouped by ability level. English classes are also typically smaller than literature classes.

The teachers were told that a primary requirement of this study was that ability grouping be abandoned because it results in a marked degree of *de facto* ethnic segregation within classes, despite desegregation in the school as a whole. The relatively smaller size of the English classes had to be retained, however, because we could not change the total number of teaching hours assigned to each teacher. We did insist nonetheless that the percentage of ethnic-group representation found in the school as a whole be retained in each classroom. The school guidance counselors agreed to assume the responsibility for composing the classrooms with the specified percentage of ethnic representation by selecting pupils at random—according to ethnic background—from the large group of pupils entering the seventh-grade junior-high level from the surrounding elementary neighborhood schools. Despite these instructions, the ethnic composition of the homeroom classes, which were identical to the literature classes, ranged from a low of 31% to a high of 66% of Western pupils in the three different schools. In only 1 of the total of 22 classes did the percentage of Western pupils drop below this level. Thus, in all but this one case (with a reported 20% Western representation), a 30% representation of one of the two ethnic groups was maintained.

In addition, the teachers of both English and literature were randomly assigned by the project staff to one of the three teaching methods investigated. Everything possible was done to assure that self-selective mechanisms, such as the teachers' experience, abilities, preferences, or prior knowledge, would not become factors in teachers' assignment to a particular method.

SOURCES OF TEACHERS' RESISTANCE

Although the subjects of this experiment were pupils, the teaching methods were implemented exclusively by regular classroom teachers, not by members of the project staff or specially trained personnel. Thus, the teachers of the two cooperative-learning methods had to be retrained. Moreover, most of the English teachers were being asked to cope with two major innovations simultaneously: the abolition of ability grouping, plus the acquisition of new teaching skills for those who were assigned to the Group-Investigation or STAD conditions. None of the teachers in these schools had ever learned how to conduct classrooms with any but the traditional presentation–recitation method.

In addition to the fact that the English teachers faced a more complex change than the literature teachers, many of the former were also convinced that their pupils could not acquire new language skills unless they told the pupils directly everything—or almost everything—that they had to learn. Learning within small groups, it was claimed, would mislead the pupils. The English teachers expressed objections to cooperative learning for clearly professional considerations as well. The most salient source of resistance to learning and implementing the cooperative methods was the absence of prepared curricular materials appropriate for group-centered learning. All the curricular materials supplied—and required by the Ministry of Education—were designed for use in the traditional classroom. Each pupil was to study the same material at the same pace, set by the classroom teacher. Because the classes were allegedly unilevel in academic achievement, owing to the tracking policies sanctioned by the ministry, the English textbook publishers had sought to arrive at the "solution" by producing one or more alternate versions of the same English textbook. It was thus hoped that almost all the students at a given academic level, as well a their teacher, could be accommodated and would progress apace.

Restoring pupil homogeneity to the classroom was the school system's way of coping with academic heterogeneity. Ironically, this solution for coping with academic heterogeneity only impeded progress toward the achievement of one of the major goals of the institution itself: promoting ethnic integration. The junior-high-school system was instituted both in order to cope with the need for higher quality instruction and in order to deal with ethnic heterogeneity. These two major institutional goals were unfortunately at odds with each other within the system's solution to academic heterogeneity.

TEACHER TRAINING AND IMPLEMENTATION

Three separate series of workshops were set up to provide in-service training for all of the teachers. A separate series of workshops was devoted to each of the three teaching methods, including the whole-class method.

The workshops were begun in late August, with 12 hours of sessions spread over three days. During these sessions, in addition to the training experiences, the teachers participated in a series of decisions regarding subject-matter and textbook selection. Following the summer meetings, there were 12 additional evening sessions held weekly from September through December, each session lasting about 2 1/2 hours.

The training sessions in both of the cooperative learning methods were planned in light of the principles of experiential learning (Kolb & Fry, 1975). The teachers were to experience the very methods that they were being trained to use in their classrooms by collaborating in small groups working on various relevant tasks. In the Group-Investigation workshops, the teachers determined a great many of the activities that they were to carry out. We had at our disposal a series of closed-circuit videotapes demonstrating a variety of the classroom situations that typically arise during the implementation of the Group-Investigation method. These tapes served as stimuli for analyses and discussions within the small groups (Sharan, Hertz-Lazarowitz, & Reiner, 1978). During these sessions, the teachers learned about various cooperative learning skills, including classroom organization with small groups, communication skills, group planning procedures, and the various phases of development in the unfolding of the group's progress in carrying out its task (Sharan & Hertz-Lazarowitz, 1980; Sharan & Sharan, 1976). A total of 14 teachers (7 teachers of English and 7 teachers of literature) were assigned to the Group Investigation condition.

In addition, 11 teachers (6 of English and 5 of literature) were assigned to the STAD method. A translation and adaptation of a manual for conducting STAD classes (Slavin, 1980a) was distributed to the teachers, and a filmstrip demonstrating team learning and implementation was employed. Sample instructional units were prepared and discussed, and subject-matter consultants attended the workshop sessions to assist the teachers in preparing curricular materials in the format required by STAD.

Training in the whole-class method was conducted through techniques typical of this approach, for example, lecture demonstrations, the use of audiovisual aids, and questioning techniques. The emphasis was on the "fine tuning" of existent or latent skills (Joyce & Showers, 1981). The agenda followed in the whole-class workshops included (1) the application of Bloom's taxonomy to the formulation of teacher questions; (2) the use of a variety of teaching aids to increase pupil involvement in learning; (3) discussions of the relationship between teacher and student behavior; and (4) the preparation and analysis of learning units.

From the onset of the August workshops, it was evident that the teachers in the two cooperative-learning conditions were experiencing a great deal of stress, which they expressed openly, at times even angrily. The lack of preplanned lessons and group-oriented curricular materials meant that they would bear the burden of preparing such materials. This anxiety increased after the opening of the school year when teachers tried to apply what they had learned in their new, multilevel classes. Because they had just begun to learn how the cooperative methods functioned, their early experiences aroused considerable anxiety. The workshop trainers urged the teachers to try the group methods for 10 minutes at a time, beginning with pairs of pupils. They were advised against attempting all implementation of group work with groups of four or five, at least in the early stages of training.

The full story of our teacher-training efforts in this study is related elsewhere (Sharan, 1984). Suffice it to say that the literature teachers gradually acquired the skills needed to employ the cooperative methods and were able to begin the experimental period for measures of achievement at the end of January. The English teachers received much more extensive consultation in their classrooms to help them cope with the multilevel population through a rich variety of group teaching techniques. With it all, they continued to be very unhappy with the conditions created by the cancellation of ability grouping and by the need to invent group-centered teaching materials. Progress in the English teachers' actual implementation of the cooperative methods proceeded at such a slow pace that the official onset of the experimental period for studying achievement effects was postponed until the end of February to allow for additional practice and the cultivation of more confidence. Without this delay, it was clear that we would not be able to measure the effects of the cooperative methods as they had been envisioned by their authors.

A full analysis of why the English teachers reacted as they did requires extensive research. Promising findings that may shed further light on this phenomenon are emerging from some studies now in progress (Yaakobi & Sharan, in preparation). Our data suggest that language teachers tend to believe that the details of a new language must be transmitted intact as a theoretical body of knowledge, the learning of which cannot benefit from the pupils' life experiences. Hence, peer-group interaction in small groups is not perceived as making a positive contribution to the learning of a new language (Barnes, 1976).

DEPENDENT VARIABLES

As noted, the independent variable in this study consisted of three conditions: the Group-Investigation approach to cooperative learning, the STAD method for cooperative learning, and the whole-class method of instruction. These three methods were implemented in 22 mixed-ethnic seventh-grade classrooms in three junior high schools ($N = 848$).

The effects on the pupils were measured in three domains:

1. Academic achievement in English as a second language and in literature
2. Cooperative and competitive behavior among peers in small task-oriented groups
3. Social relations among pupils, divided into three subtopics:
   a. Peer evaluations
   b. Classroom social climate
   c. Ethnic attitudes

We shall present the background for the study of these variables as effects of the teaching methods, followed by an overview of the results of the study. The three sets of variables studied constitute a general progression from the individual cognitive level (achievement), to interpersonal interaction (cooperative behavior), to perceptions of classroom-level relationships (classroom social climate), and, finally, to the evaluation of change in the pupils' attitudes toward the other ethnic group in general—as a group—and toward the Middle Eastern group in particular. Evaluating the effects of the three methods on each of these dependent variables posed its own set of problems and required a different conceptual framework for each domain. We present first the background, the method, and the results relevant to each of these categories of measures. A general discussion of the results and their implications appears afterward.

The schedule of procedures as actually carried out in this project was as follows:

1.	August 1980–January 1981	Teacher training in workshops and consultations in schools
2.	October 1980	Social relations questionnaire administered to all pupils
3.	January 1981	Literature pretest examination administered to all pupils
4.	February–June 10	Literature experiment carried out
5.	End of February	First classroom observations in literature classes.
6.	March 1–6, 1981	English pretest administered
7.	March 8–June 10	English experiment carried out
8.	End of March	First classroom observations in English classes
9.	End of April	Second classroom observations in literature classes
10.	End of May	Second classroom observations in English classes
11.	June 1–June 14	Evaluation of pupils' cooperative behavior performed
12.	June 11–June 21	English, literature, and social relations posttests administered

ACADEMIC ACHIEVEMENT: ENGLISH AND LITERATURE

English language and literature were selected for this study because they allegedly require the pupils to learn different kinds of information. Foreign-language learning appears to require the acquisition of discrete component skills, whereas the study of literature appears to afford opportunities for pupils to conduct discussions intended to clarify ideas and themes, in which the acquisition of discrete bits of information plays only a supportive role. Peer tutoring in small groups, such as in the STAD method, was designed in part to facilitate the learning of basic skills by having pupils concentrate on the review and rehearsal of teacher-taught materials. Hence, it was conjectured that STAD might prove more effective than the other methods in teaching skill-oriented material (Slavin, 1980a). The Group-Investigation method, on the other hand, is based on inquiry, discussion, and a collective synthesis of products, and thus, it promised greater effectiveness than the other two methods in teaching literature. We had made the distinction between low-level knowledge (e.g., recall and basic skills) and high-level knowledge (e.g., evaluation and synthesis) in the evaluation of the effects of cooperative learning on pupils' achievement in earlier research with elementary-school children, and we found more consistent positive effects of this method on high-level than on low-level skills in comparison with traditional methods (Sharan, Hertz-Lazarowitz, & Ackerman, 1980).

These considerations, however, do not explain why the cooperative methods should prove more productive than the whole-class method for these subjects. To answer this question, we must discuss some current conceptions about foreign language instruction and its relationship to cooperative learning. Recently, the study of a foreign language has been conceptualized as a process of acquiring communicative competence rather than the rote learning of grammar and vocabulary. Communicative competence is developed through repeated interaction between persons employing the target language. To be natural, the interaction must be concerned with the content of the speech, with the message that the speakers wish to convey to one another, and with their understanding of the message, not with the grammatical form of the utterance or the rule that it exemplifies (Breen & Candlin, 1979; Brumfit, 1980; Krashen, 1981; Littlewood, 1981). Using language for communication entails, first and foremost, activation of the pupils' life experience and existing communicative ability, not only the use of school knowledge (Widdowson, 1979). It has been shown that pupils prefer to interact with peers more than with adults. Social settings that promote peer interactions succeed in exchanging the pupils' traditional role in school as receivers of messages for the more active role of transmitters of messages previously reserved for the teacher (Barnes, 1976; Barnes, Britton, & Rosen, 1971; Krashen, 1981). These theoretical principles provide a rationale for making the study of a foreign language appropriate for cooperative learning in small groups in an essential way, not only in light of a general orientation to classroom instruction. Indeed, two bodies of theory—namely, the concepts underlying the psychosocial process of small-group interaction and the communicative theory of foreign-language teaching—cohered in a genuinely complementary fashion when we formulated the principles of foreign-language teaching in small groups.

The complementary use of these two theoretical orientations assisted in the preparation of an entire series of learning tasks embodying these principles. The teachers in both the Group-Investigation and the STAD conditions were taught some of the same group-centered procedures, whereas other techniques were more appropriate for one or the other group methods.

There was no specific instructional theory available for the teaching of literature that was compatible with group-centered processes. The design of the study tasks was directed by the principles of small-group learning, such as division of labor, group discussion, and the synthesis of group products through mutual assistance (Sharan & Sharan, 1976).

MEASURES

Special achievement tests in English and in literature were constructed for use in this experiment. Two tests were necessary for literature because the posttest evaluated the students' understanding of specific literary works that they had studied in groups over a period of some 4 1/2 months after the administration of the pretest. The pretest evaluated the pupils' knowledge of the material studied during the first semester. Posttest consisted of the same number of items in similar categories of knowledge but referred to different works of literature. Each of the two tests in literature was comprised of 20 items: 10 questions requesting responses of information or simple understanding (low level) and 10 questions requiring synthesis or application of ideas (high-level).

Despite constant consultations with the teachers, some teachers presented different literary selections from the curriculum. Also, the sequence of works taught varied from class to class, as a function of the teachers' daily classroom needs regardless of what had been agreed on in advance. The net result was that about half of the pupils were found to have studied one set of materials, and the other half of the population a somewhat different set, so that the number of subjects whose responses could be compared statistically was limited.

The achievement test in English was used twice, as the pretest and as the posttest. Ninety-one items were divided into four subtests:

1. *Listening comprehension (57 items)*. This subtest evaluated the pupils' ability to comprehend spoken English. A tape recorder with a

large loudspeaker was brought to each classroom, and a standard tape was played on which the speaker read a passage and asked a series of questions. The pupils were asked to mark the correct answer from a four-item multiple-choice format.

2. *Reading comprehension (19 items).* The pupils were asked to match sentences with pictures appearing in their test booklet.

3. *A cloze test (10 items).* The pupils read a paragraph with missing word items and selected the correct word for each missing word from a four-item multiple-choice format.

4. *Asking questions (5 items).* The pupils were required to reformulate direct statements in the appropriate question pattern, choosing once again from a four-item multiple-choice format.

RESULTS: ACHIEVEMENT[1]

Analyses of variance with repeated measures were performed on the data from each scale separately, as well as on the scores from the English test as a whole. These analyses revealed a significant difference in the extent of the improvement in the pupils' scores from the pretest to the posttest as a function of teaching method. The significant difference in the change occurred on the total score, $F(2,662) = 3.75$, $p < .05$, as well as on the listening-comprehension subtest, $F(2,662) = 6.88$, $p < .005$, but not on any of the other three subtests. Separate analyses were performed comparing data from each pair of teaching methods (Group-Investigation vs. STAD; STAD vs. whole-class; Group-Investigation vs. whole-class) to determine which methods promoted this difference in the change over the course of the four-month period. These analyses showed that Group-Investigation and STAD promoted greater improvement on the total score and on the listening-comprehension subtest compared to the whole-class method, but that Group-Investigation and STAD did not differ in terms of how they affected achievement in English.

No other effects for achievement in English were found in this study. That is to say:

1. There were no effects for ethnicity: The pupils from the two ethnic groups made similar progress within each instructional method.

2. There were no interaction effects for initial academic level: The pupils who scored low, medium, or high on the pretest were not affected differently by any of the three teaching methods. There was a main effect for achievement level: The pupils with the initially highest

[1]The data themselves appear in Sharan (1984).

scores registered less progress on the achievement test than did the pupils with medium or low-level scores, regardless of method. This finding was not due to a ceiling effect of the exam itself.

3. There was no effect for classroom ethnic composition. A separate analysis of covariance was performed using the percentage of Western background pupils in the class as a covariant. There were no differences in the achievement change scores as a function of teaching method when classroom ethnic composition served as a covariant.

An analysis of the literature data revealed an effect for method over time, indicating that the pupils in the Group-Investigation method made more progress in their ability to respond to the high-level questions than did their peers in the STAD and whole-class methods, $F(2,447) = 8.30$, $p < .01$. On the low-level questions, the opposite result emerged. The pupils in both the STAD and the whole-class methods yielded higher achievement scores than did the pupils in the Group-Investigation method, $F(2,447) = 9.54$, $p < .01$. Again, there was no effect for ethnic group in any of the results obtained here in the evaluation of achievement in literature.

COOPERATIVE BEHAVIOR

Only a handful of studies have been reported thus far about the effects of schooling on cooperation among children. Yet, this topic should be of central concern to investigators of ethnic desegregation in the schools. Do children in desegregated settings actually cooperate with each other? Are different instructional methods able to promote cross-ethnic cooperation *in practice,* and not only to affect children's verbal choices of friends or verbal peer evaluations? It is imperative to ascertain if, in fact, the behavioral norms cultivated by particular styles of classroom learning are consistent with the social policies that we strive to implement. There are theoretical and practical bases for asserting that this is not necessarily the case.

The marked effects of different social-cultural environments on children's cooperative behavior have been studied extensively (Kagan, 1980; Kagan & Madsen, 1972; Madsen, 1971; Madsen & Shapira, 1970; Shapira, 1976). How schooling affects cooperative behavior is less well known, but the available evidence strongly suggests that different kinds of classroom experience do exert differential effects on children's cooperative behavior both in and out of the classroom (Hertz-Lazarowitz, Sharan, & Steinberg, 1980; Ryan & Wheeler, 1977). Cohen and colleagues (Cohen & Roper, 1972; Cohen & Sharan, 1980) performed several studies of cross-ethnic behavior in groups but they did not focus on cooperation *per se,* nor did they study ethnic relations as a function of classroom instructional methods. To the best of our knowledge, no other research has been reported thus far that employed behavioral measures to study pupils' interethnic cooperation as a function of variation in instructional style. Recent research with cooperative learning methods in mixed-ethnic classrooms did reveal salutory effects on cross-ethnic friendship selections and other attitudes. These studies will be considered later in the chapter in connection with the study of other aspects of cross-ethnic social relations. The focus of the present study was to assess children's cooperative behavior both within and between ethnic groups as a function of their participation in one of the three teaching methods implemented here.

SUBJECTS, MEASURES, AND PROCEDURES

Several six-person groups, each composed of three Western and three Middle Eastern children, were selected at random from each classroom. All groups were given an identical task to perform of constructing a human figure from pieces of Lego. Each group was seated around a table in a large, empty room in the school during school hours. The experimenter in charge of this portion of the research was completely unknown to the pupils and could not be identified as a member of the project team. (As this study was carried out by regular classroom teachers, members of the project team were rarely seen by the pupils, in any case.) Nor were the pupils given any information that might have led them to associate this exprience with their classroom learning method. Each team received 48 pieces of Lego and was shown a model and two pictures of the figure that they were asked to construct. After hearing detailed instructions, the group was told that they had 15 minutes to plan *how* to carry out their joint task, and another 15 minutes to actually construct the figure.

At the table with each group sat two trained observers, both of whom had been kept scrupulously "blind" about the instructional method to which any given group of pupils had been exposed prior to their participation in this criterion task. Each observer recorded pupil behaviors: Each pupil wore a large placard with a number on it for ease of identification. The data were recorded to identify who addressed what kind of act or communication to whom. Two recordings were entered for each child every five minutes; the result was 12 recordings per child for the 30-minute period, or 72 recordings per group. A total of 390 children—close to 50% of the total population in this study—were included in 65 groups: 21 groups from Group-Investigation classrooms, 26 groups from STAD classes, and 18 groups from whole-class classes. Except for one classroom, from which there were two such groups selected, three 6-person groups were selected from all classrooms (21) in this study. This study was carried out in June at the conclusion of the experiment.

RESULTS: COOPERATIVE BEHAVIOR

The pupils from the three teaching methods behaved quite differently on the Lego-man task in three categories of observed behavior: verbal cooperation, nonverbal cooperation, and competition. The pupils in the Group-Investigation classrooms produced more cross-ethnic cooperation, both verbal and nonverbal, than did the pupils from the other two methods. Competitive behavior was displayed more frequently by the pupils from the whole-class method than by those from either STAD or Group-Investigation classrooms. In the whole-class method, competitive and cooperative acts appeared with equal frequency, whereas cooperative acts were far more frequent (2 1/2 times more in STAD; 5 times more in Group-Investigation) in the behavior of the pupils from the two cooperative learning methods than in the behavior of the pupils from the whole-class method. All of these findings are for cross-ethnic acts. There were no differences in the overall number of cross-ethnic versus same-ethnic acts. Cross-ethnic interaction occurred in mixed-ethnic groups whatever may have been the children's classroom learning method. However, the quality of that interaction was markedly affected by instructional style, with the traditional whole-class method promoting twice or three times the amount of competition promoted by the cooperative methods.

Furthermore, it was learned that pupils from both the Western and the Middle Eastern groups who studied in the Group-Investigation method behaved more cooperatively and less competitively toward peers from the other ethnic group than did peers from both groups who studied in the whole-class classes. Group-Investigation pupils from both groups were more cooperative than those from STAD classes, but the Group-Investigation and STAD methods did not differ on competition: Both methods limited the amount of competition considerably. These results are summarized in Table 1.

The following comments are intended to facilitate the reading of Table 1: In the left-hand column, the data rows are divided into the three categories of observed behavior: verbal cooperation, nonverbal cooperation, and competition. In each of these three sections, the letters

TABLE 1. Means, SDs, F, and t Statistics of Cross-Ethnic and Same-Ethnic Acts of Cooperation and Competition Displayed by Pupils of Western and Middle Ea stern Background in Each of Three Instructional Methods

Category		GI (N = 21)	STAD (N = 26)	WC (N = 18)	F	GI vs. WC	t-tests STAD vs. WC	GI vs. STAD
Verbal cooperation								
W to ME	M	7.29	3.88	3.56	13.10**	4.44	0.41	4.44
	SD	2.94	2.55	2.81				
ME to W	M	8.14	6.34	5.50	3.26*	2.46**	−.83	1.83
	SD	2.99	3.00	4.12				
W to W	M	6.92	6.28	6.50	.099	0.27	−.14	0.44
	SD	4.12	5.89	4.21				
ME to ME	M	6.07	4.26	2.67	2.71*	2.31*	1.14	1.34
	SD	5.14	4.79	3.36				
Nonverbal cooperation								
W to ME	M	7.71	3.96	3.33	14.51***	4.81***	0.72	4.51***
	SD	2.45	2.62	3.48				
ME to W	M	8.47	6.27	4.06	7.13***	3.77***	1.98*	2.06*
	SD	4.73	3.41	2.26				
W to W	M	7.57	5.71	5.33	1.40	1.51	.027	1.38
	SD	4.18	5.26	3.96				
ME to ME	M	6.28	5.08	3.00	2.34	2.15*	1.42	0.87
	SD	4.52	5.71	3.25				
Competition								
W to ME	M	1.19	2.08	3.55	4.76**	3.07**	2.00*	1.26
	SD	1.21	2.99	2.48				
ME to W	M	2.19	2.23	6.00	12.81***	4.39***	4.55***	0.05
	SD	2.98	2.05	3.15				
W to W	M	1.14	1.96	6.66	11.74***	4.50***	4.01**	0.73
	SD	2.22	2.02	6.43				
ME to ME	M	.71	1.38	2.08	2.17	2.08*	1.11	1.12
	SD	.90	1.58	3.26				

$*p < .05. **p < .01. ***p < .001.$

ters W and ME identify the ethnic group (Western or Middle Eastern) of the pupil initiating the act and of the pupil to whom it was directed. The first three columns of data on the left-hand side are the mean number of acts (or standard deviations of the mean acts) in each of the three instructional methods. Note that the number in the uppermost row under the title of the teaching method represents the number of 6-person groups that participated in the criterion task for that method. The fourth column is the F values for the analyses of variance, which compared the data obtained from the criterion groups chosen from the classrooms conducted with the three teaching methods (GI, STAD, and WC). The three columns on the right-hand side of the table present the *t* values of the contrasts performed between each pair of teaching methods. These analyses were performed to identify the precise source of the differences between the three methods.

In the Group-Investigation method, cooperative and competitive acts initiated by pupils from both ethnic groups toward the other group were of close to equal frequency, so that the behavior in these groups appears to have been reciprocal.

In the STAD method, the Middle Eastern pupils expressed more cooperative acts toward their Western group mates than the latter expressed toward the Middle Eastern pupils. STAD appears to have affected the behavior of the lower status group more than that of the higher status group. This pattern is similar to that occurring in the whole-class classes.

In the whole-class method, the lack of cross-ethnic reciprocity is obvious. The Middle Eastern pupils address more cooperative statements to the Western pupils than the latter address to the Middle Eastern students, and the Western pupils addressed more verbal-cooperative statements to their same-ethnic peers than did the Middle Eastern students to their ethnic peers.

SOCIAL RELATIONS: PEER EVALUATIONS, CLASSROOM CLIMATE, AND ETHNIC ATTITUDES

PEER EVALUATIONS

The social-psychological implications of peer friendships in school and classrooms have been reviewed in detail by Schmuck and Schmuck (1982). Social isolation in the classroom is acknowledged to be a most undesirable and potentially negative condition for schoolchildren. Vulnerability to being a social reject or a member of an "outgroup" increases when one belongs to a lower status subgroup in the class, such as an ethnic minority group. Investigators of cooperative learning methods have focused on the effects of classroom learning style on pupils' peer relations. Theoretically, one would expect that conducting classroom learning—even for part of the time—through the medium of task-oriented peer interaction and cooperation would substantially increase positive peer contacts and would result in improved peer friendships and evaluations. Social investigators have conjectured that the same logic would hold for cross-ethnic perceptions and friendships as for same-ethnic relations in desegregated classrooms.

Introducing peer-tutoring techniques in racially desegregated classrooms has been found to generate more positive peer relationships cross-racially than traditional instruction (DeVries, Edwards, & Slavin, 1978; Slavin, 1978a, b; Hansell & Slavin, 1981). In several of these latter studies, the pupils were simply asked to name their friends in the class. Slavin and Oickle (1981) found significant gains in white children's friendships toward black children following their participation in classrooms conducted with the STAD method. However, no comparable finding emerged in the friendship selection by black children of their white classmates. Cooper, Johnson, Johnson, and Wilderson (1980) reported improved cross-racial friendship choices in one study of cooperative learning, and a study by Cook and associates (Weigel, Wiser, & Cook, 1975) found that white and Mexican-American children increased their cross-group friendship selections, though no comparable effects emerged for black–white or black–Mexican-American relations.

Earlier research with the Group-Investigation method did not employ peer evaluations, and none of the previous studies of this method involved multiethnic classes. Thus, we decided to include a peer evaluation measure in the present study, albeit a relatively complex measure not subject to the limitations of the one-item format of "Who are your friends?" We will return to this topic later in this section when we discuss the nature of the measures employed here.

CLASSROOM SOCIAL CLIMATE

Very little is known about peer relations in classrooms in general, and far less about how these relations are affected by alternative designs of classroom social structures (Jackson, 1968; Johnson, 1981). Recent research on school learning climate has studied the relationship between social contextual factors and pupils' academic achievement (Brookover, Beady, Flood, Schweitzer, & Weisenbaker, 1979; Crain, Mahard, & Narot, 1982). These process variables, characteristic of schools as social systems, have been found to exert distinct and significant effects on racial integration and/or on learning outcomes.

The present study evaluated pupils' perceptions of classwide social relations as a function of the specific social environments created by the different teaching methods. Did the variation in the design of classroom social conditions exert differential effects on the social climate in desegregated classrooms? That is the problem posed in this portion of the study. Desegregation in Israel seeks to consolidate the body politic and to promote the building of the social order (Amir, Sharan, & Ben-Ari, 1984). How do pupils perceive the "social order" on the level of the social microcosm that is their classroom environment?

Some data are available indicating that pupils' perceptions of the classroom *social* climate—not only of school *learning* climate—are related to academic outcomes (Walberg, 1969; Walberg & Anderson, 1968). Research in Israel found that pupils become increasingly disenchanted with classroom social relations as they progress through the grades (fourth through eighth) of elementary school (Hertz-Lazarowitz & Sharan, 1979).

Cooperative learning experiments, involving most of the current cooperative-learning methods, have produced positive effects on pupils' perceptions of classroom social relations (Blaney, Stephan, Rosenfield, Aronson, & Sikes, 1977; Cooper, Johnson, Johnson, & Wilderson, 1980; Johnson et al., 1983; Sharan, 1980; Slavin, 1980a). In a study involving hundreds of elementary-school pupils over an 18-month period in Israel, the classroom climate was found to remain stable in cooperative learning classrooms and to decline significantly in traditional control classes (Sharan & Hertz-Lazarowitz, 1981). Research with peer-tutoring methods also yielded positive effects on measures of classroom social relations (DeVries & Slavin, 1978).

ETHNIC ATTITUDES

Would perceptions of and attitudes toward members of the other group—*as a group*, rather than as individuals—be affected by the different styles of classroom instruction? That was the research question posed in this portion of the cooperative learning experiment. Hitherto, the research effort in this study had focused on individual or interpersonal variables, as well as on perceptions of such relationships in the classroom. This question is addressed to *intergroup* attitudes and perceptions. Along with other investigators of intergroup relations (Tajfel, 1981; Tajfel & Turner, 1979), we assumed that interpersonal and intergroup attitudes are not necessarily related and must be investigated separately. Indeed, experiments on the effects of teaching methods in desegregated settings have generally concentrated on interpersonal relations of various kinds but have rarely examined intergroup attitudes.

Earlier research in Israel on ethnic attitudes as a function of desegregation, albeit without any change in classroom teaching styles, found the following: Over the course of the first year in desegregated classes, pupils from Western backgrounds expressed greater acceptance of their Middle Eastern peers and less of an ingroup orientation than they had had at the beginning of the year. The Middle Eastern pupils registered enhanced perceptions of their own group without changing their initially high-level evaluations of the Western group. Thus, desegregation apparently showed some sign of closing, however slightly, the gap in ethnic attitudes prevailing prior to these pupils' entry into desegregated ninth-grade classrooms (Amir, Sharan, Bizman, Ben-Ari, & Rivner, 1978; Amir, Sharan, Bizman, Rivner, & Ben-Ari, 1978). The main point of interest is that the lower status Middle Eastern group improved its attitudes toward itself, and the higher status Western group improved its attitudes toward the Middle Eastern group, so that some change occurred to compensate for the initial asymmetry in these groups' ethnic attitudes. Research from desegregation studies in the United States did not find such mutual adjustment (Gerard & Miller, 1975; Schofield, 1980). Would this initial asymmetry in attitudes be rectified to some degree by the cooperative learning methods?

MEASURES

A three-part questionnaire was administered twice to all pupils, once at the beginning of the year and again on conclusion of the experiment at the end of the academic year. Each of the three parts of the questionnaire evaluated one of the three subtopics of social relations, as follows:

1. *Classroom climate*: Twenty-four items, each placed on a 4-point scale (where 4 was the most positive reply), assessed pupils' perceptions of classroom social relations. Statistical analysis of the pretest data ($N = 799$), including factor analysis and correlational analysis, led to the recognition of four subscales: (a) friendship in classrooms; (b) cooperation in classrooms; (c) classroom cohesiveness; and (d) attraction to the class. A score for the total scale of 24 items was also calculated.

2. *Peer evaluations*: Seven questions made up the peer evaluation scale. Every pupil was asked to evaluate every other pupil in the class on each of the seven questions. Again, the evaluations were made on a 4-point scale. A list of all the pupils in each class was attached to the questionnaire so that each name appeared next to the row where the evaluations of that person were to be registered. Thus, in a class of 38 pupils, each one had to make 266 separate evaluations. Three questions dealt with the pupil's willingness to maintain contact with the person being evaluated (sit next to him or her, meet during recess, or do homework together); two items described personal traits (a good sport, a smart student); one item dealt with helping behavior (helps others in the class); and one item assessed the extent to which the person was consid-

ered deviant (causes problems in the class). The first two factors were identified by a factor analysis of the pretest data. The scores were evaluated by identifying the ethnic group of the pupil making the evaluation and whether the pupil being evaluated was from the same or the other group. In this fashion, four scores for pretest and four for posttest measures were generated: Western to Western, Western to Middle Eastern, Middle Eastern to Middle Eastern, and Middle Eastern to Western.

3. *Ethnic attitudes*: The pupils responded to six questions, placed on a 4-point scale, assessing their ethnic attitudes and perceptions. A correlational analysis of the pretest data led to the formation of two subscales of three items each. The first subscale consisted of statements about the Middle Eastern and Western groups (children from Middle Eastern background are better friends, are better students, than those from Western background). The second scale included negative statements about the "other" group (I don't like to be friendly with pupils from a different ethnic group).

The correlations between the three scales evaluating social relations, based on the pretest data, were as follows: Classroom climate correlated .03 with ethnic attitudes and .24 with peer evaluations, and the latter correlated .14 with ethnic attitudes.

Results: Social Relations

The data from the social relations questionnaire were analyzed by a series of analyses of variance with repeated measures, where treatments (3) and ethnic groups (2) were between-subjects factors, and time (pre- and posttest) was the within-subject repeated measure.

A capsule statement of the findings to emerge from the social relations data would be that:

1. The classroom climate declined in all classrooms regardless of teaching method.

2. Peer evaluations improved in all classes, again unaffected by any particular style of classroom teaching.

3. Ethnic attitudes were significantly affected by the teaching methods. There was a marked decline in attitudes expressed by pupils from both ethnic groups who had studied with the whole-class method, whereas the ethnic attitudes of pupils in the two cooperative-learning methods remained largely unchanged over the course of the year.

The latter finding emerged on each of the two subscales, Scale I: $F(2,722) = 6.08$, $p < .01$; Scale II: $F = 4.26$, $p < .01$, as well as on the total scale, $F = 18.68$, $p < .001$. Separate analyses of variance performed on data from pupils in each pair of methods revealed that both the Group-

TABLE 2. Means and *SD*s of Western and Middle Eastern Pupils' Perceptions of Ethnic Attitudes in Three Instructional Methods (*N* = 725)

Scale	Time	GI (*N* = 242)		STAD (*N* = 303)		WC (*N* = 180)	
		Western	Middle Eastern	Western	Middle Eastern	Western	Middle Eastern
1	Pre *M*	4.80	6.04	4.68	6.02	4.78	6.20
Range = 3–12	*SD*	1.88	2.60	2.00	2.72	1.94	2.61
	Post *M*	4.58	5.69	4.31	5.91	4.06	4.61
	SD	2.21	2.98	1.96	3.29	2.69	3.23
	Diff.	−.22	−.35	−.37	−.11	−.72	−1.59
2	Pre *M*	4.32	4.64	4.08	5.04	4.45	4.73
Range = 3–12	*SD*	1.78	2.02	1.55	2.19	1.68	1.90
	Post *M*	3.67	4.36	3.71	4.50	3.39	3.66
	SD	1.46	2.25	1.63	2.30	2.26	2.40
	Diff.	−.65	−.28	−.37	−.54	−.06	−1.07
Total scale							
range = 6–24	Pre *M*	15.22	15.99	15.41	15.74	15.33	16.54
	SD	2.95	3.76	3.01	3.46	2.16	2.82
	Post *M*	15.39	15.79	14.75	15.47	13.51	13.13
	SD	3.62	4.10	4.06	4.83	6.02	6.69
	Diff.	+.17	−.20	−.66	−.27	−1.82	−3.41

Investigation and the STAD methods differed from the whole-class method (Group-Investigation vs. whole-class: $F(1,420) = 30.76, p < .001$; STAD vs. whole-class: $F(1,481) = 25.76, p < .001$) but not from each other. There was no effect for the ethnic group of the pupils making the evaluations. The ethnic attitude data appear in Table 2. (For more details about results on peer evaluations and classroom climate, see Sharan, 1984.)

DISCUSSION

Different styles of classroom instruction, involving variation in pupil interactive patterns and communication patterns, yield different outcomes in pupil learning, social behavior, and attitudes in a wide range of psychoeducational domains. Moreover, some of these outcomes affect interethnic relations positively, thereby contributing to social integration in multiethnic classrooms while improving academic achievement for all pupils. The present study is consistent with the claim made often in recent years not only that desegregation alone, without specific programs to promote social integration, is inadequate to meet the challenge of the multiethnic classroom, but that *failure* to implement well-considered changes in the kind of instruction transpiring in desegregated classes results in undesirable consequences for many pupils. The net outcome of desegregation without planned methods of coping with its consequences for teachers is a lack of community support for desegregation. In addition, many pupils experience academic and social losses of other kinds. These issues, in terms of their relevance to conditions in Israel and the United States, have been discussed in another publication (Amir & Sharan, 1984).

We turn now to examining the findings of this study in some detail and to considering their implications. Table 3 presents a convenient overview of the results pertaining to all of the variables evaluated here.

TABLE 3. Relative Effects of the Three Teaching Methods on All Dependent Variables in This Study[a]

		GI	STAD	WC
I.	*Academic achievement*			
	1. English as a second language			
	(total test)	1	1	2
	Subtests:			
	Listening comprehension	1	1	2
	Reading	1	1	1
	Asking questions	1	1	1
	Cloze	1	1	1
	2. Literature			
	Low-level (information)	2	1	1
	High-level (ideas)	1	2	3
II.	*Cooperative behavior*			
	1. Cooperation (for all pupils)	1	2	3
	Within ethnic groups	3	2	1
	Between ethnic groups	2	2	1
III.	*Social attitudes*			
	1. Classroom climate	Declined	Declined	Declined
	2. Peer evaluations			
	Of all pupils	Improved	Improved	Improved
	Of Western pupils	2[b]	2[b]	2[b]
	Of Middle Eastern pupils	1[b]	1[b]	1[b]
	3. Ethnic attitudes	1	2	3

[a]1 = highest or most positive score; 2 = lower or less positive score; 3 = lowest or least positive score.
[b]Ranks 1 and 2 here refer to the comparison of Western and Middle Eastern pupils' peer evaluations.

ACADEMIC ACHIEVEMENT

The two cooperative methods proved equally effective for teaching English as a second language, whereas the whole-class method was less effective. This result emerged on the listening-comprehension subtest and on the total test. On the three other subtests, all the methods produced the same results. As predicted, the pupils in the Group-Investigation method achieved higher scores on the high-level questions than the pupils in the other two methods. On the low-level questions, the STAD and whole-class methods were more effective than Group-Investigation.

Before pursuing the question of how or why the cooperative methods produced these results, let us survey the findings about the other variables evaluated here. As predicted, the cooperative learning methods did, in fact, foster more cooperative behavior, within and between ethnic groups, than the whole-class method, whereas the latter—again, predictably—fostered more competition. In the realm of cooperation, the Group-Investigation method yielded more cooperation and less competition on the criterion task than STAD, whereas the STAD method limited competition but fostered less cooperation among pupils than did the Group-Investigation method. Exactly the same pattern emerged in the data obtained about pupils' ethnic attitudes: No change occurred over the year in these attitudes among pupils in the Group-Investigation and STAD methods, but there was a significant decline in ethnic attitudes toward both ethnic groups among pupils in the whole-class method.

The findings that emerged in this study support the fundamental premise and hypothesis of cooperative learning in small groups: Mutual assistance among peers organized into small, manageable social units oriented toward achieving specified learning goals can exert salutary effects on pupils' learning progress as well as on their relationships. Why this should be so is explained differently by the theorists from the various disciplines. Educators and linguists concerned with second-language acquisition in schools, or with adult education, have recently formulated a communicative theory of language learning as distinct from the more didactic lecture approach. The communicative theory asserts that language is best learned when pupils have many opportunities for using the language to establish contact with others in social encounters (Dulay, Burt, & Krashen, 1982; Krashen, 1981; Littlewood, 1981; Oller, 1979; Winitz, 1981). Discourse processing is central to many kinds of learning, but it is particularly crucial for language learning. Learners engaging in natural communication are concerned less with the form of their utterances than with the message that they are trying to convey. When communicating, a person brings to bear not only school knowledge, but his or her general life experience as well. New language skills are not just a set of isolated rules and bits of information, and by utilizing them in communicative acts, students integrate such skills with other portions of their life experience and knowledge (Widdowson, 1979).

The cooperative learning methods employed an entire set of group-centered learning activities designed to embody these theoretical principles. These activities fostered mutual exchange among peers in the new language. In the small-group settings, the pupils were released from the pressure typically found in whole-class instruction to employ terse, "final draft" forms of speech free from grammatical or syntactic errors (Barnes, 1976). They could talk with one another rather than recite in front of one another. In this way, the theory and the procedures of small-group learning were adapted and applied in ways consistent with the theoretical principles of the communicative approach to language instruction. The fact that cooperative learning fostered improved comprehension of English as a spoken language reflects the specific contribution of communicative exchange among pupils to the learning of the new language, whereas there were no differences in achievement on the other subtests of the achievement test in English.

The achievement outcomes in literature were also as predicted. The pupils from the Group-Investigation classrooms displayed scores on high-level questions in comparison superior to those of the pupils from both the STAD and the whole-class classes, although the latter groups surpassed their peers from the Group-Investigation classes on the low-level questions. These results generally coincide with those from previous studies that have demonstrated high-level learning in small groups (Sharan et al., 1980). It seems that the opportunity afforded for mutual assistance and discussion of ideas in the Group-Investigation method allows pupils to reach integrated levels of understanding. Both the STAD and the whole-class methods allowed for a more structured review by pupils of teacher-taught information. Such reviews led to higher scores on the low-level items for those pupils than for their peers in Group-Investigation classes. But as both the STAD and the whole-class pupils did equally well on these items, it appears that group rehearsal, as practiced in STAD, neither helped nor hindered the low-level learning of literature beyond what traditional teaching accomplishes.

CROSS-ETHNIC COOPERATION

This study also provides support for the prediction that cooperative learning experiences in small, multiethnic groups will promote cooperative cross-ethnic behavior among pupils in multiethnic classrooms. Cooperative interaction, both within and between ethnic groups, occurred most frequently among the pupils from the Group-Investigation method, which emphasized egalitarian procedures for peer interactions within groups rather than peer tutoring, which may foster a tutor–tutee relationship among peers. Also, the Group-Investigation method includes the distribution of labor and tasks among group members. This procedure appears to preclude social comparison processes based on similar task assignments, as noted by Pepitone (1980). When everyone is occupied with a different task, the basis for comparisons become highly attenuated, and the opportunity for collaboration in pursuit of a superordinate goal is utilized.

The fact that the whole-class style of instruction does promote competitive patterns of interaction among peers from the same as well as the other ethnic group is amply documented in this study. This finding is consistent with claims by several investigators (Johnson & Johnson, 1975; Pepitone, 1980). The data reported here reflect children's actual behavior in a mixed-ethnic-group setting. They all performed a task (constructing the Lego-man) that served as a measure of how the children would transfer behavioral patterns from their classroom experience to another kind of group task outside the classroom. The results support Allport's theory that direct interaction between members of different groups under conditions of cooperation and equal status sanctioned by the authorities improves intergroup relations. Here, we tried to evaluate the effects on peer cooperation and competition caused by the style in which the pupils experienced their regular classroom learning activities. It is important to recall that the effects reported here did not stem from extracurricular programs of any kind: They are attributable only to the nature of the classroom learning procedures. Transforming the normative process of schooling to allow for cooperative interaction among pupils during the pursuit of learning goals does promote positive interethnic behavior. Moreover, failing to transform the classroom teaching style, and allowing traditional, whole-class instruction to continue unchanged in multiethnic classes, promotes competition among pupils from the same ethnic group. These findings also support the conclusion reached from a reanalysis of the data from a wide range of studies aimed at improving race relations in multiracial classrooms, to the effect that the most effective vehicle for promoting positive cross-racial behavior is face-to-face cooperative groups (Slavin & Madden, 1979). The cross-method comparison performed in this experiment further emphasizes the importance of incorporating all three of Allport's conditions into the ethnic contact setting, that is, equal-status contact along with cooperation and a supportive climate. Limiting competition alone does not necessarily promote greater cooperation!

ETHNIC ATTITUDES, CLASSROOM CLIMATE, AND PEER EVALUATIONS

The third and last category of measures in this study shown to be affected differently by the three teaching methods was ethnic attitudes. We conjecture that the competitive atmosphere created by the whole-class method, along with the social comparisons that accompany the competition, serve to emphasize ethnic stereotypes and negative group evaluations (Worchel, 1979). By contrast, the more supportive relationships and the relative absence of social comparisons typical of the cooperative learning classrooms played down ethnic stereotypes. In this environment, the pupils related to each other on a personal basis, and their ethnic membership receded into the background. This explanation coincides with Tajfel's theory of intergroup relations (Tajfel, 1981; Tajfel & Turner, 1979). He argued that social attitudes and behavior can be placed on a continuum with respect to the degree to which they are influenced by one's group membership. Events that magnify the salience of group membership in a given social setting can cause interactions to be affected largely by prevailing group stereotypes regardless of how the people involved may relate to each other as individuals. Thus, individual relationships and the prevalence of group stereotypes are not necessarily related, and they can and do appear with different values within the same social setting. In the whole-class classroom, a poor recitation or the failure of a pupil's response to a teacher's questions becomes a public display of incompetence. His or her own classroom status suffers, and so does the status of his or her entire ethnic group because performance "on the classroom stage" arouses many levels of social comparisons. Pupils from the lower status ethnic group in these conditions are particularly vulnerable to becoming the objects of negative group attitudes and stereotypes. In point of fact, the decline in the whole-class classes in attitudes toward the Middle Eastern group was distinctly larger than the decline registered in attitudes toward the Western group.

Of course, one obvious question still remains unanswered: How can we account for the lack of results in the two areas of classroom climate, which declined over the year, and peer evaluations, which improved over the year? Also, how can one explain the apparent contradiction between these two sets of findings, where one variable declined and the other improved, and where instructional method had no special influence? Cooperative learning should have prompted improvement on both these variables. How, then, can we explain that the same pupils, exposed to the same experiences, responded so differently to these two measures?

In our view of this experiment and its effects, the results obtained on the two measures of classroom climate and peer evaluations stem from very different social units and relationships. Pupils at a given grade level are exposed to the same peers over and over again in different settings in the school, and they come to know each other fairly well. The membership of the peer group remains quite stable over the course of the year, and perhaps for many years. Peer evaluations reflect this stability and the relative intimacy among the pupils in the same class. The results obtained here suggest that, regardless of the nature of the learning process, pupils gradually develop more friendly relationships with one another over the course of the school year. Even if some classes are more cooperative and others more competitive, personal relationships are apparently not affected.

Pupil evaluations of classroom climate are influenced by very different facts. As we will note, these factors can account for the decline in pupils' perceptions of classroom climate even though they evaluate their peers more favorably over the year. The present experiment encompassed only two subjects, which met for a total of six sessions per week, out of a total of eight or more subjects, which met for over 24 hours a week. Findings from earlier research in Israel documented the fact that pupils' perceptions of classroom climate tend to decline over the course of the years (the available data cover Grades 4–8 in elementary schools, but not in junior high schools). Even if cooperative learning methods succeeded in reversing this trend for the specific classes in which they were conducted, we surmise that pupils cannot separate their perceptions of relationships in these particular classes from those formed on the basis of their experiences in school as a whole. The classroom climate measured here could not restrict the pupils' responses to their experience in cooperative learning classes *alone*, to the exclusion of all other classes and activities. Hence, the pupils' general perception of peer relations in classrooms, of attraction to the class, and of classroom social cohesiveness declined during the year in this study because that was how the pupils felt about school in general, and not about cooperative learning classes in particular.

If this interpretation is valid, it means that the effect of cooperative learning on classroom climate has yet to be evaluated. The studies conducted thus far have not been satisfactory. In part, this is true because of the problems encountered in reliably measuring the effects of an educational treatment embedded in a school context that exposes pupils to a variety of learning environments, some of which differ radically from the cooperative classroom. One obvious solution to this problem is to introduce cooperative learning into a large number of classrooms in a given school so that the pupils will experience a greater degree of consistency in learning style as they move from one teacher to the next. Indeed, changing the instructional methods in an entire school may even prove less difficult than trying to change the behavior of a small group of teachers (Sharan & Hertz-Lazarowitz, 1982). The latter strategy has proved effective in elementary schools, but junior high schools are far more complex organizations and pose a far greater challenge to agents of change than do elementary schools (Berman & McLaughlin, 1978). Another solution is to evaluate classroom climate with specific teachers and subjects, focusing the pupils' attention on those classes only. At this time, we do not place much confidence in that approach because pupils' relations cannot help but be deeply influenced by their experiences in other than the target classrooms. Hence, treatments limited to 25% of pupils' school time—as in this study—still cannot effect the changes in classroom life that are required in order to reverse the trend toward increasingly greater disaffection with school over the course of time.

CONCLUSION

In sum, cooperative learning in small groups exerted a wide range of effects on pupils. We interpreted these effects in light of different theories, each relevant to a different domain of the pupils' psychoeducational experience. Moreover, each theory explained the effects generated by cooperative learning in small groups in its own terms. Nevertheless, all of the effects were produced simultaneously, as part of the same set of social-educational experiences. Language learning drew on the communicative theory; interethnic cooperation while coping with a group task drew on Allport's contact theory; ethnic attitudes were explained in light of Tajfel's theory of intergroup relations. All of these theories were instrumental in providing the groundwork for interpretations of the effects generated by cooperative learning methods. Yet, we must not forget that the results obtained here as a whole ultimately contribute to the development of the theory and practice of cooperative learning as a distinct domain of educational practice and research. The results should not be construed solely as supporting the various theories invoked here to explain the data relevant to particular dependent variables. It is the design and the implementation of school learning processes that lie at the heart of this research effort. Our central concern must remain how to make children's school learning most effective on all levels of their experience.

REFERENCES

Allport, G. *The nature of prejudice.* Cambridge, Mass.: Addison-Wesley, 1954.

Amidon, E., & Hough, J. (Eds.). *Interaction analysis: Theory, research and application.* Reading, Mass.: Addison-Wesley, 1967.

Amir, Y. The role of intergroup contact in change of prejudice and ethnic relations. In P. Katz (Ed.), *Toward the elimination of racism.* New York: Pergamon Press, 1976.

Amir, Y., & Sharan, S. (Eds.), *School desegregation: Cross-cultural perspectives.* Hillsdale, N.J.: Lawrence Erlbaum, 1984.

Amir, Y., Sharan, S., Bizman, A., Ben-Ari, R., & Rivner, M. Asymmetry, academic status, differentiation and the ethnic perceptions and preferences of Israeli youth. *Human Relations,* 1978, *31,* 99–116.

Amir, Y., Sharan, S., Bizman, A., Rivner, M., & Ben-Ari, R. Attitude change in desegregated Israel high-schools. *Journal of Educational Psychology,* 1978, *70,* 63–70.

Amir, Y., Sharan, S., & Ben-Ari, R. Why integration? In Y. Amir & S. Sharan (Eds.), *School desegregation: Cross-cultural perspectives.* Hillsdale, N.J.: Lawrence Erlbaum, 1984.

Barnes, D. *From communication to curriculum.* Middlesex, England: Penguin Books, 1976.

Barnes, D., Britton, J., & Rosen, H. *Language, the learner and the school* (rev. ed.). Harmondsworth, England: Penguin, 1971.

Berman, P. & McLauglin, M. *Federal programs supporting educational change, Vol. VIII: Implementing and sustaining innovations.* Santa Monica, Calif.: Rand Corporation, 1978.

Blaney, N., Stephan, C., Rosenfield, D., Aronson, E., & Sikes, J. Interdependence in the classroom: A field study. *Journal of Educational Psychology,* 1977, *69,* 121–128.

Breen, M., & Candlin, C. The essentials of a communicative curriculum in language teaching. *Applied Linguistics,* 1980, *1,* 89–111.

Brookover, W., Beady, C., Flood, P., Schweitzer, J., & Wisenbaker, J. *School social systems and student achievement.* New York: Praeger, 1979.

Brumfit, C. *Problems and principles in English teaching.* New York: Pergamon Press, 1980.

Cohen, E., & Roper, S. Modification of interracial interaction disability: An application of status characteristics theory. *American Sociological Review,* 1972, *37,* 643–657.

Cohen, E., & Sharan, S. Modifying status relations in Israeli youth. *Journal of Cross-Cultural Psychology,* 1980, *11,* 364–384.

Cooper, L., Johnson, D., Johnson, R., & Wilderson, F. The effects of cooperative, competitive, and individualistic experiences on interpersonal attraction among heterogeneous peers. *The Journal of Social Psychology,* 1980, *111,* 243–252.

Crain, R., Mahard, R., & Narot, R. *Making desegregation work.* Cambridge, Mass.: Ballinger, 1982.

DeVries, D., & Slavin, R. Teams-Games-Tournaments: A research review. *Journal of Research and Development in Education,* 1978, *12,* 28–38.

DeVries, D., Edwards, K., & Slavin, R. Biracial learning teams and race relations in the classroom: Four field experiments using Teams-Games-Tournaments. *Journal of Educational Psychology,* 1978, *70,* 356–362.

Dulay, H., Burt, M., & Krashen, S. *Language two.* New York–Oxford: Oxford University Press, 1982.

Gerard, H., & Miller, N. *School desegregation.* New York: Plenum Press, 1975.

Hansell, S., & Slavin, R. Cooperative learning and the structure of interracial friendships. *Sociology of Education,* 1981, *54,* 98–106.

Hertz-Lazarowitz, R., & Sharan, S. Self-esteem, locus of control and children's perception of classroom social climate: A developmental perspective. *Contemporary Educational Psychology,* 1979, *4,* 154–161.

Hertz-Lazarowitz, R., Sharan, S., & Steinberg, R. Classroom learning style and cooperative behavior of elementary school children. *Journal of Educational Psychology*, 1980, 72, 97–104.

Jackson, P. *Life in classrooms*. New York: Holt, Rinehart and Winston, 1968.

Johnson, D. Student–student interaction: The neglected variable in education. *Educational Researcher*, 1981, 10, 5–10.

Johnson, D., & Johnson, R. *Learning together and alone*. Englewood Cliffs, N.J.: Prentice-Hall, 1975.

Johnson, D., Johnson, R., & Maruyama, G. Interdependence and interpersonal attraction among heterogeneous and homogeneous individuals: A theoretical formulation and a meta-analysis of the research. *Review of Educational Research*, 1983, 53, 5–54.

Joyce, B., & Showers, B. *Teacher training research: Working hypothesis for program design and directions for further study*. Paper presented to the annual meeting of the American Educational Research Association, Los Angeles, April 1981.

Kagan, S. Cooperation-competition, culture, and structural bias in classrooms. In S. Sharan, P. Hare, C. Webb, & R. Hertz-Lazarowitz (Eds.), *Cooperation in education*. Provo, Utah: Brigham Young University Press, 1980.

Kagan, S., & Madsen, M. Experimental analyses of cooperation and competition of Anglo-American and Mexican children. *Developmental Psychology*, 1972, 6, 49–59.

Kolb, D., & Fry, R. Towards an applied theory of experiential learning. In C. Cooper (Ed.), *Theories of group processes*. London: Wiley, 1975.

Krashen, S. *Second language acquisition and second language learning*. New York: Pergamon Press, 1981.

Littlewood, W. *Communicative language teaching: An introduction*. New York: Cambridge University Press, 1981.

Madsen, M. Development and cross-cultural differences in the cooperative and competitive behavior of young children. *Journal of Cross-Cultural Psychology*, 1971, 2, 365–571.

Madsen, M., & Shapira, A. Cooperative and competitive behavior of urban Afro-American, Anglo-American, Mexican American and Mexican village children. *Developmental Psychology*, 1970, 3, 16–20.

Oller, J. *Language tests at school*. London, England: Longman Group, 1979.

Pepitone, E. *Children in cooperation and competition*. Lexington, Mass.: Lexington Books, 1980.

Ryan, F., & Wheeler, R. The effects of cooperative and competitive background experiences of students on the play of a simulation game. *Journal of Educational Research*, 1977, 70, 295–299.

St. John, N. *School desegregation: Outcomes for children*. New York: Wiley, 1975.

Schmuck, R., & Schmuck, P. *Group processes in the classroom* (4th ed.). Dubuque, Iowa: Wm. Brown, 1982.

Schofield, J. Cooperation as social exchange: Resource gaps and reciprocity in academic work. In S. Sharan, P. Hare, C. Webb, & R. Hertz-Lazarowitz (Eds.), *Cooperation in education*. Provo, Utah: Brigham Young University Press, 1980.

Shapira, A. Developmental differences in competitive behavior of kibbutz and city children in Israel. *Journal of Social Psychology*, 1976, 98, 19–26.

Sharan, S. Cooperative learning in small groups: Recent methods and effects on achievement, attitudes and ethnic relations. *Review of Educational Research*, 1980, 50, 241–271.

Sharan, S. *Cooperative learning in the classroom: Research in desegregated schools*. Hillsdale, N.J.: Lawrence Erlbaum, 1984.

Sharan, S., & Hertz-Lazarowitz, R. A group-investigation method of cooperative learning in the classroom. In S. Sharan, P. Hare, C. Webb, & R. Hertz-Lazarowitz (Eds.), *Cooperation in education*. Provo, Utah: Brigham Young University Press, 1980.

Sharan, S., & Hertz-Lazarowitz, R. Classroom social climate, self-esteem and locus of control. In S. Sharan & R. Hertz-Lazarowitz, *Changing schools: The small-group teaching project in Israel*. Tel Aviv: Ramot, Tel Aviv University, 1981. (in Hebrew)

Sharan, S., & Hertz-Lazarowitz, R. Effects of an instructional change program on teachers' behavior, attitudes and perceptions. *Journal of Applied Behavioral Science*, 1982, *18*, 185–201.

Sharan, S., & Sharan, Y. *Small-group teaching*. Englewood Cliffs, N.J.: Educational Technology Publications, 1976.

Sharan, S., Hertz-Lazarowitz, R., & Reiner, T. Television for changing teacher behavior. *Journal of Educational Technology Systems*, 1978, *7*, 119–131.

Sharan, S., Hertz-Lazarowitz, R., & Ackerman, Z. Academic achievement of elementary school children in small group versus whole class instruction. *Journal of Experimental Education*, 1980, *48*, 125–129.

Slavin, R. Student teams and achievement division. *Journal of Research and Development in Education*, 1978, *12*, 39–49. (a)

Slavin, R. Student teams and comparison among equals: Effects on academic performance and student attitudes. *Journal of Educational Psychology*, 1978, *70*, 532–538. (b)

Slavin, R. Cooperative learning. *Review of Educational Research*, 1980, *50*, 315–342. (a)

Slavin, R. *Using Student Team Learning*. Baltimore, Md.: Johns Hopkins University, 1980. (b)

Slavin, R. *Cooperative learning*. New York: Longman, 1983.

Slavin, R., & Madden, N. School practices that improve race relations. *American Educational Research Journal*, 1979, *16*, 169–180.

Slavin, R., & Oickle, E. Effects of cooperative learning teams on student achievement and race relations: Treatment by race interactions. *Sociology of Education*, 1981, *54*, 174–180.

Sommer, R. Classroom ecology. *Journal of Applied Behavioral Science*, 1967, *3*, 489–503.

Stephan, W. School desegregation: An evaluation of predictions made in *Brown* v. *Board of Education. Psychological Bulletin*, 1978, *85*, 217–238.

Tajfel, H. Social stereotypes and social groups. In J. Turner & H. Giles (Eds.), *Intergroup behavior*. Chicago: The University of Chicago Press, 1981.

Tajfel, H., & Turner, J. An integrative theory of intergroup conflict. In W. Austin & S. Worchel (Eds.). *The social psychology of intergroup relations*. Monterey, Calif.: Brooks/Cole, 1979.

Thelen, H. *Education and the human quest*. New York: Harper & Row, 1960.

Walberg, E. Social environment as a mediator of classroom learning. *Journal of Educational Psychology*, 1969, *60*, 443–448.

Walberg, H., & Anderson, C. Classroom climate and individual learning. *Journal of Educational Psychology*, 1968, *59*, 414–419.

Weigel, R., Wiser, P., & Cook, S. The impact of cooperative learning experiences on cross-ethnic relations and attitudes. *Journal of Social Issues*, 1975, *31*(1), 219–245.

Widdowson, H. *Explorations in applied linguistics*. London: Oxford University Press, 1979.

Winitz, H. (Ed.). *The comprehension approach to foreign language learning*. Rowley, Mass.: Newbury House, 1981.

Worchel, S. Cooperation and the reduction of intergroup conflict: Some determining factors. In W. Austin & S. Worchel (Eds.), *The social psychology of intergroup relations*. Monterey, Calif.: Brooks/Cole, 1979.

Yaakobi, D. & Sharan, S. *Teachers' theories of knowledge, attitudes toward instruction and classroom instructional behavior*. In preparation.

13

Relating Goal Structures to Other Classroom Processes

GEOFFREY MARUYAMA

This chapter describes one way in which future research might increase our understanding of how goal-structuring interventions are related to basic classroom achievement and classroom social interaction processes in heterogeneous classrooms. It proposes a merging of nonexperimental data-analysis techniques with experimental or quasi-experimental treatments. By merging the two approaches and collecting the data necessary for each, researchers should be able to examine the ways in which cooperative learning interventions impact basic educational processes. For example, goal-structuring interventions could possibly affect outcomes by mediating the effects of variables that are part of achievement processes, enhancing the impact of variables already present in the classroom, or injecting new sources of influence into the classroom. Of these alternatives, the middle one might be viewed as the most interesting, for it is intriguing to think of cooperative learning as a catalyst that triggers a reaction from variables that are commonly present in contact situations. Least interesting is the notion of cooperative learning interventions' acting as mediating variables, for if such interventions merely mediate effects already present, their impact on classroom processes could not be very great.

Viewed from a somewhat different perspective, the approach described in this chapter can potentially provide insights into achievement and social interaction processes in the classroom in which cooperative learning comprises a regular and enduring part of the curriculum. That is, the shortcoming of most studies of cooperative learning techniques is that they have lsted for a short time—in some instances as short a time as two weeks (e.g., see Slavin, 1980). Consequently, it is difficult to know what the effects of longer and more varied interventions might be.

GEOFFREY MARUYAMA • Department of Educational Psychology, University of Minnesota, Minneapolis, Minnesota 55455. Support for this project was provided by Department of Education Grant G-007902006 (David Johnson, Principal Investigator), by a Spencer Foundation Fellowship awarded by the National Academy of Education to the author, and by National Science Foundation Grant BNS-8211171.

Interestingly, if data testing the approach described in this paper argue for a specific conceptual view of how cooperation affects classroom processes, that view can be extrapolated to anticipate and predict the long-term effects of the use of cooperative techniques.

In order to provide a context for the approach to be proposed, I first provide a broader framework that describes three different theoretical views of how school achievement processes operate in heterogeneous classrooms. The three views have been chosen because they represent the three most influential orientations to issues of schooling and heterogeneity. In addition, the approach described in this paper can potentially examine the predictions of all three views while interrelating them. Second, the patterns of causal sequencing of variables implied by the three conceptual views are delineated. As part of this discussion, the role of cooperative learning techniques within the classroom processes defined by each theoretical view is briefly examined. Third, a model is presented for examining how cooperative learning experiences affect school processes. Finally, the concluding discussion links the model back to the three theoretical views of school achievement processes and suggests other possible applications to the study of cooperative learning of the approach described here.

THEORIES OF GROUP CONTACT IN HETEROGENEOUS CLASSROOMS

Research on desegregation has reflected the diversity of interests, disciplinary orientations, and beliefs of social science researchers. Yet within this diverse body of research, a small number of orientations have exerted a primary influence on the type of research that has been done. For example, one orientation that shaped much of the early research on desegregation viewed desegregation as a variable that could be manipulated. It was basically atheoretical and led to numerous studies focusing on student achievement in segregated and desegregated schools. The basic purpose of such studies was to determine whether desegregation was successful. Over the years, this somewhat simplistic and atheoretical view has been replaced by a number of other views. Three other views, drawn directly or indirectly from social science theories, have provided the major foci for research on intergroup contact in schools. These views, which are examined in this paper, are the social-influence or "lateral-transmission-of-values" hypothesis (e.g., Lewis & St. John, 1974); contact theory (e.g., Allport, 1954; Cook, 1970); and expectation states (e.g., Cohen, 1980).

LATERAL TRANSMISSION OF VALUES

As was true of the research that considered desegregation a variable, each of the three theoretical views listed above has implicitly or explicitly provided approaches for studying the effects of desegregation. The "transmission-of-values" view assumes that minority children in desegregated schools can and will be assimilated into the mainstream culture, and that their changes during assimilation can be tapped by studying social interaction, personality (e.g., achievement motivation), and school outcome variables. Thus, research examining the "transmission of values" has focused on school-related and general values that children have prior to desegregation and how those values change in desegregated schools. Because the view argues for the "transmission of values," peer relationships have provided a second focus for this research; unless friendship patterns develop, value transmission should be greatly inhibited. Finally, this perspective links value and peer relation variables to classroom outcomes.

The lateral-transmission-of-values hypothesis seems to have provided the most widely accepted (if implicitly theoretical) model for explaining how school desegregation produces academic benefits for minority children. It assumes that (1) school desegregation generates intergroup contact, which (2) enables the achievement-related values and motives of high-achieving (white) children to be transmitted to low-achieving (minority) children, which (3) facilitates the academic achievement of the low-achieving children. The internalization of achievement norms and values is either the result of peer acceptance or occurs in anticipation of receiving it. Thus, desegregation should result in the assimilation of minority children as they internalize the values that facilitate achievement.

From a multicultural or pluralistic perspective, the transmission of values may appear to be only a small modification of the atheoretical perspective described earlier, for it seems to suggest that the transmission of values would be a naturally occurring part of intergroup contact. Thus, it may appear to reflect a poorly developed theoretical perspective. I would argue, however, that the theoretical perspective is poorly translated rather than poorly developed. The theory underlying the transmission-of-values hypothesis is deeply rooted in the social-psychological literature on normative influence, which shows that certain sets of values seem to facilitate achievement, that such values have been found to be more prevalent among white than among minority children, and that social influence flows predominantly from the majority to the minority (e.g., Jones & Gerard, 1967).

Social influence processes can be subdivided into two components, each of which may occur in desegregated classrooms. First, using terminology taken from Deutsch and Gerard (1955), *informational social influence* can occur simply as a result of being in the presence of others. For example, observing the behavior of a professional tennis player may help a novice, for the novice can see what types of behaviors are successful and how those behaviors are performed. Second, *normative social influence* requires one to attempt to conform to another's positive expectations. Thus, attempts to gain peer acceptance provide the impetus for normative social influence. One adopts patterns of behavior and values in order to be accepted. If the novice wants to become friendly with the "tennis crowd," his or her dress, mannerisms, and behavior patterns increasingly conform to those of the "tennis crowd." Given widespread ancedotal evidence for the impacts on children of peer norms about appropriate dress (e.g., the importance of wearing "designer" jeans), it seems difficult to trivialize the effects of social influence processes.

Cognitive consistency theories provide an alternative perspective for arriving at the view that the transmission of values should occur. At first, many children will be faced with conflicting sets of cognitions, such as "These children seem different, and I don't think I will like them," and "These new children will be my classmates throughout my years of schooling." Consistency theorists have suggested that these inconsistencies are most easily resolved through the development of positive peer relations, which should facilitate the development of achievement-oriented values. This view has been called the *psychology of inevitability* (see Aronson, 1976).

In addition to the findings and the theories described above, there are reasons to believe that the transmission of values might occur in desegregated classrooms. First, the circumstances in which school desegregation has been implemented often assure that the numerical majority of students will be both white and high-achieving. Second, the classroom reward structure typically supports the norms and behaviors of high-achieving children via institutional sanctions, grades, teacher praise, and so on.

To summarize, the transmission-of-values perspective relies on social influence processes to lead to positive intergroup contact, to a merging of value orientations, and to a general sense of coorientation among classmates. These factors should result in achievement gains and assimilation. Yet, what seems to be a major shortcoming of this perspective is that it doesn't explicitly hypothesize any set of conditions that must be met in order for the positive outcome to occur. Not surprisingly, research has not provided support for this view (e.g., Maruyama, 1983).

The next theoretical perspective, contact theory, specifies a number of necessary conditions for positive intergroup contact. According to contact theory, only under such conditions should social influence processes operate.

CONTACT THEORY

Of the three views described in this paper, contact theory was the first to be developed (for a review, see Johnson, Johnson, & Maruyama, 1983). According to contact theory, increased contact with others provides accurate information about them, which can lead to decreased prejudice and tension and improved intergroup relations. Alternatively, contact can increase prejudice, threat, and tension and can harm intergroup relations. The benefits of the heterogeneous mixing of children depend on the nature of the contact situation. Among the limiting conditions for positive contact are (1) equal status contact, (2) mutual interdependence (cooperation), (3) a social climate with norms favoring egalitarian intergroup contact, (4) attributes of group members that contradict prevailing stereotypes, and (5) contact that promotes personal or intimate association (e.g., Cook, 1970; Watson, 1947). Another possible condition is the presence of goals that all share and that require joint effort, namely, superordinate goals.

Because contact theory explicitly delineates a number of limiting conditions that shape classroom processes, student interactions, and student outcomes, it suggests that implementing specific strategies should result in beneficial outcomes for students, and that without such strategies, the outcomes could be unfavorable. Thus, the research on contact theory has attempted either to meet the limiting conditions and show that beneficial outcomes accrue or to contrast the settings in which limiting conditions are met with other settings in which they are not met. It is perhaps surprising that even though contact theory was developed well before the *Brown* and *Dunn* decisions, which led to the increased heterogeneity of classrooms, contact theory has not occupied a central position in strategies related to heterogeneity. In fact, only recently has much research in schools examined the contact theory predictions. Although this research is very promising, it is by no means definitive. Further, there are basic conceptual inconsistencies between contact theory and the third perspective, expectation states, which also offers promise.

EXPECTATION STATES

Even though contact theory can be viewed as a restrictive variant of the transmission of values that defines the conditions under which value transmission might occur, the third perspective, expectation states, is even more restrictive. It argues that shaping contact may not be sufficient for producing equal educational opportunities for all children. The theory of expectation states focuses on cultural boundaries that impact on the school environment. It suggests that, in order to be beneficial, approaches must alter fundamental assumptions of students and teachers that can shape interaction patterns. For example, Cohen (1980) has argued that the status order of society produces expectations (which need not be conscious) in both white and minority (alternatively, in middle- and lower-class or nonhandicapped and handicapped) students that white (or middle-class or nonhandicapped) students are more competent. Further, Cohen argues that there is a self-fulfilling effect, so that expectations are confirmed in actual contact situations. Her empirical studies have shown that white children dominate mixed work groups both when the children are matched for ability on the task and when the minority children are more expert. Her view argues that unequal status contact is virtually guaranteed when white and minority children interact.

The research testing expectation states has been of two types. First, there have been studies demonstrating that general expectation states seem to affect classroom interaction in predictable ways. Second, other studies have attempted (often successfully) to alter expectation states in order to create more egalitarian classrooms.

IMPLIED CAUSAL SEQUENCING OF THEORIES
OF GROUP CONTACT

Now that the conceptual bases of the three theoretical views have been summarized, their implicit views about classroom social and achievement processes will be explored. Such views are examined within the perspective of other work on school achievement processes. Social-psychological models of school achievement processes explicitly include social interaction variables; therefore, the social processes of the classroom will be included as part of classroom achievement processes.

First, it is well known that family background variables, exemplified by social class and academic ability, are major determinants of school outcomes. Yet, the background-to-achievement link runs counter to American values of equal opportunity, for it implies that certain students have "unfair" advantages stemming from their background. In order to provide equality of educational opportunity, the schools need to provide all students with the opportunity to overcome disadvantages resulting from their family background. Thus, there must be variables within the school setting that shape students and provide opportunity. Although there may be other types of important variables (e.g., structural ones such as class size or time spent on instruction), the variables addressed by the transmission-of-values hypothesis are of two types: social influence, tapping the effects of significant others (e.g., teachers, family, and peers), and personal adjustment, tapping attitudes, values, and personality characteristics. Unlike structural variables, whose impact tends to occur at a classroom level, the social and adjustment variables tend to affect individual children within the classroom. The ordering implied by the transmission-of-values hypothesis places social influence variables causally prior to adjustment variables. Therefore, as specified by the transmission-of-values hypothesis, the achievement process should be causally sequenced as follows: background variables to social influence variables to personal adjustment to school achievement. (A variation of this model omits personal adjustment, arguing that social influence variables directly affect achievement.) Equality of opportunity could occur if the background variables primarily affect the social influence variables. In such instances, changing social-influence patterns could potentially overcome background differences.[1]

Cross-sectional correlational studies of the effects of school desegregation (e.g., Coleman, Campbell, Hobson, McPartland, Mood, Weinfeld, & York, 1966; Crain & Weisman, 1972; U.S. Commission on Civil Rights, 1967) have reported results that are consistent with the notion that the transmission of values is an important if not a necessary part of the improved academic performance of minority students in desegregated schools. These findings emphasize the importance for minority children of having achievement-oriented values as well as having

---

[1]Note, however, that even if the achievement process appeared to match the process posited by the transmission-of-values–social-influence model, there would be no guarantee that interventions at various points in the model would, in fact, produce equality of opportunity. In the absence of random assignment to background variables, there may be selection variables that are responsible for differences, that is, other variables on which children differ that prevent social influence processes from acting on some children as they do on other children.

white friends. In addition, a longitudinal study by Lewis and St. John (1974), which employed causal modeling techniques to examine the influence of peer acceptance on academic achievement, provides findings consistent with the transmission-of-values hypothesis. According to Lewis and St. John, peer acceptance positively affected grades, and normative social influence accounted for the positive effect.

More recently, however, a study of school desegregation by Gerard and Miller (1975) focusing on the transmission-of-values hypothesis presented evidence contrary to transmission of values. Although acceptance by whites was related to the achievement of the minority children, Gerard and Miller did not find any evidence that the minority children were adopting achievement-oriented values. Further analyses of the Gerard and Miller data provide, at best, minimal evidence for the transmission-of-values hypothesis (Maruyama, 1977; Maruyama & Miller, 1980; McGarvey, 1978). These studies are especially relevant because they applied structural equation techniques that improved causal modeling methodologies (e.g., Jöreskog & Sörböm, 1978; Maruyama & McGarvey, 1980). (It is these methodologies that provide the approach for examining the plausibility of the model that is developed later in this paper.) Examining a cross-sectional model that assumed the validity of the lateral-transmission-of-values hypothesis by specifying peer acceptance as "causally" prior to achievement, Maruyama (1977) found some support for the transmission-of-values model. Longitudinal analyses of data from the same sample, however, which test the hypothesis more directly, argue that achievement causes peer acceptance rather than the reverse (Maruyama & Miller, 1980; McGarvey, 1978). Thus, Maruyama's initial support (1977) probably reflects an error in the specification of the model to be tested.

In an attempt to understand the inconsistency between the findings from the Gerard and Miller (1975) study and those of Lewis and St. John (1974), the Lewis and St. John data were reanalyzed by means of structural equation techniques (Maruyama & Miller, 1979). These analyses contradicted the findings of Lewis and St. John; achievement appeared to exert a causal influence on popularity, but popularity did not appear to influence achievement.

Given the above findings, it appears that the model generated by the transmission-of-values hypothesis does not adequately explain school achievement. Achievement was found to be highly stable over time, that is, to be a cause rather than an effect. The adjustment variables were not strongly related to achievement, and they often changed in unanticipated ways in desegregated classrooms. Nevertheless, the model has not received a strong test, for the causal modeling studies examined classrooms in which beneficial outcomes for minority students were the exception rather than the rule. Further, based on prior research, it seems unlikely that social influence processes are unimportant; numerous studies illustrate the effects of influence exerted by significant others (e.g., Jones & Gerard, 1967). Certainly, the transitions experienced by college freshmen as they move from home to college environments stands as easily observable evidence of the effects of social influence processes; such transitions have been found to continue throughout the college years (e.g., Newcomb, 1943). Behavior changes in response to social influence are even more dramatic than attitudinal or value shifts (e.g., Asch, 1952); thus, it is possible that peer pressure may force children to achieve positive school outcomes that they would not pursue on their own.[2]

Because social influence processes are well documented and seem to have the potential for enhancing student outcomes, this paper focuses on the situations in which social influence processes seem most likely to occur. Thus, one direction in which to extend the work described above is to examine classrooms in which more beneficial outcomes occurred; a second is to examine other theoretical views to see when social influence variables are most likely to be influential. Both of these extensions lead to an examination of contact theory and of cooperative learning interventions.

Given the variability in the findings of studies of desegregation, it is not surprisng that researchers have explored the logical consequences of contact theory's assertions. It seems that contact theory holds much promise and has led to several avenues of productive research. One could examine the consequences of meeting each of contact theory's "necessary conditions." To date, the most exciting are the findings of studies providing cooperative learning experiences for children; there is now a substantial literature reporting the positive effects of cooperative learning on children's attitudes, peer relationships, and school outcomes (e.g.. Johnson, Maruyama, Johnson, Nelson, & Skon, 1981; Johnson, Johnson, & Maruyama, 1983). Thus, studies of cooperative learning may provide settings in which to examine social influence processes and to test further the transmission-of-values hypothesis.

As noted above, it may be that the best way to examine whether the lateral-transmission-of-values hypothesis and the achievement process model derived from it *ever* occur is to find classrooms in which the expe-

---

[2]In his dissertation, Michael Frank (1984) is examining the effects of gain and loss contingencies on group processes within cooperative and individualistic groups. He is examining both negative and positive peer-influence attempts.

riences of the children are positive and in which there are theoretical reasons for expecting social influence variables to be important. Seemingly, cooperative learning studies provide such classrooms, for according to contact theory, positive intergroup relations should result. Therefore, the focus now shifts to the social and achievement processes of classrooms in which interventions have attempted to facilitate intergroup contact.

As suggested above, the achievement process predicted by contact theory may be quite similar to that predicted by the transmission-of-values perspective, for social influence variables may well play an important role in shaping peer interaction and achievement. Rather than yielding a different causal sequencing of variables, one could view contact theory as predicting the existence of two types of classrooms: those that facilitate social interaction and those that don't. Classrooms that don't facilitate interaction should be indistinguishable from those studied in examining the transmission-of-values perspective. In classrooms that facilitate interaction, however, the pattern might be very different; if social interaction is enhanced, the model might be more like that *predicted* by the transmission-of-values perspective.

The examination of achievement processes in schools using cooperative learning techniques has an additional benefit: It allows an exploration of how cooperative learning experiences affect the broader classroom environment. For example, do the benefits of cooperative learning treatments exert any enduring impact on the classroom? Do any benefits of cooperative learning accrue through structural changes independent of social influence and personal adjustment variables, or do they alter those variables in some way? Do they mediate the relation between background variables and achievement, or are any effects independent of such variables? Answers to questions such as these should help researchers understand more fully how and why cooperative learning interventions work.

An additional potential benefit of the approach examining classroom processes and cooperative learning interventions is that it may speak to concerns expressed by researchers adopting positions drawn from expectation states theory (e.g., Cohen, 1980). Expectation states theory suggests that cultural beliefs about the relations of variables such as race or ethnicity, sex, and age to competence are so strong that interventions such as cooperative learning will not alter them. Thus, even though children may show modest gains in achievement or increased intergroup liking, the basic nature of the classroom is untouched, and the relations of background and other status variables to achievement remain strong.

Translated back to the social influence model presented earlier, expectation states theory argues that cooperative learning interventions would have little or no effect on *relative* achievement and, therefore, would not appreciably alter the achievement process. Increases in peer acceptance should have only minimal effects on achievement and should not appreciably alter the personality and adjustment variables. Thus, the nature of the relation of background and achievement variables in cooperatively structured versus noncooperatively structured classrooms and of the relation of cooperative learning interventions to broader achievement processes can provide information about the accuracy of the expectation states perspective.

To summarize, an examination of achievement processes in desegregated classrooms that use cooperative learning techniques may provide information about whether there appears to be "lateral transmission of values" in such classrooms, about how cooperative learning interventions influence classroom achievement processes, and about the importance of concerns about the enduring effects of expectation states. The three conceptual views posit a model of school achievement that contains basically the same variables, yet they differ in specifiable ways. First, the transmission-of-values perspective seems to argue that cooperation is unnecessary; thus, cooperative learning interventions would simply mediate effects that already exist in the classroom. In effect, basic classroom processes would be unchanged by cooperative learning. Second, contact theory argues that the presence of variables such as positive goal interdependence act to facilitate certain classroom processes. Thus, contact theory seems to suggest that strategies such as cooperative learning act as catalysts to stimulate classroom processes, thereby changing substantially the nature of the achievement processes. Third, expectation states theory argues that cooperation is typically not very effective, for it doesn't alter basic status patterns. The relations of social class and ability with achievement ought to be unchanged. Likewise, social influence variables should still retain the effects of diffuse status characteristics such as sex and race. Therefore, interventions such as cooperative learning ought to affect school achievement processes in modest ways, at best, and may well act primarily to transmit the effects of other variables on achievement.

TRANSLATION OF THE CONCEPTUAL MODEL INTO A TESTABLE MODEL

In the preceding section, I have argued that a general model of school achievement processes can be used to contrast three conceptual views of how cooperative learning affects school achievement processes. In this section, the model is described in more detail. In its most general form, the theoretical model consists of four sets of variables; background, social influence, personal adjustment, and school outcomes. Of most interest are the relations among the social influence, adjustment, and outcome variables. In drawing from the earlier causal modeling analyses as well as from other analyses examining achievement processes in predominantly white classrooms (e.g., Bachman & O'Malley, 1977; Maruyama, Rubin, & Kingsbury, 1981), it seems that the "personality" type of adjustment variables are of questionable importance. Therefore, the focus of the present model is on social influence variables, attitudinal adjustment variables, and school outcomes.

Ideally, one would compare the achievement processes of children who have had cooperative learning experiences throughout their school years with the achievement processes of comparable children who have not had such experiences. Practically, the model most testable is one that contrasts the achievement processes of children who receive a cooperative learning intervention with those of children who do not. Such analyses can examine the achievement process up to and then after the intervention. (Having more than one postintervention follow-up is also desirable.) A diagram illustrating how such analyses could be done appears in Figure 1.

Again, ideally, the sample would be sufficiently large to examine the achievement processes of the cooperative-intervention children separately from those of the other children, and minority (or other "different") children separately from white children. Practically, sample-size constraints often preclude such analyses. A second, somewhat less desirable, approach is to dichotomously code racial/ethnic identification (white/other) and goal structure (cooperative/other) and to include those variables in the model. Racial/ethnic identification would be a background variable; goal structure would be a variable related to all of the postintervention variables.

Before focusing on the causal model, preliminary analyses should examine the effects of the cooperative learning treatment on the postmeasures and/or change scores. If the treatments show no appreciable effects, then the causal modeling analyses would most likely not be worthwhile. Note that even if the interventions are successful, altering classroom processes involves long-term changes that extend beyond the end of the interventions.

The model in Figure 1 contains the two background variables family social class (SES) and academic ability (ABL), family (FSUP), teacher (TSUP), and peer (PACC) support as social influence variables; attitudes toward "different" children (RATT) as a personal adjustment variable;

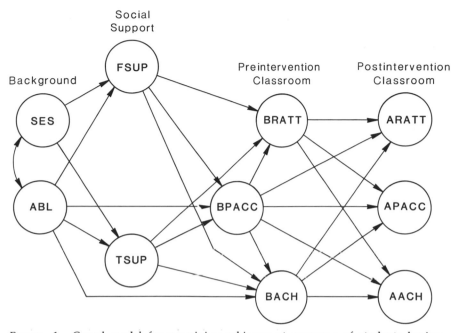

FIGURE 1. Causal model for examining achievement processes of students having cooperative learning experiences. SES = socioeconomic status; ABL = academic ability; FSUP = family support; TSUP = teacher support; BPACC = preintervention peer acceptance; BRATT = preintervention racial attitudes; BACH = preintervention school achievement; ARATT = postintervention racial attitudes; APACC = postintervention peer acceptance; AACH = postintervention school achievement.

and school achievement (ACH). Note that the variables of peer acceptance, attitudes toward "different" students, and school achievement are measured prior to and after the intervention, thereby providing a panel model that can take into account the stability of the variables.

All the straight arrows in the model depict hypothesized casual paths. The curved, double-headed arrow depicts a noncasual path. Note that many possible paths interrelating variables have been omitted (e.g., there is no path from SES to BPACC, to BRATT, or to BACH). The omitted paths are ones found nonsignificant in prior analyses of achievement processes or hypothesized to be nonsignificant by the theoretical perspectives. Likewise, each of the paths included in the model can be justified as either empirically supported by prior work or as needed to test hypotheses generated by the conceptual views.

The "causal" paths in the model can be described fairly simply. First, social class is viewed as noncausally related to ability; much of the correlation of social class with other variables results from its relation to ability (e.g., Maruyama et al., 1981). Because that relation is depicted as noncausal, any relation to other variables resulting from the relation to ability is viewed as spurious. After such relations are taken into account, social class is viewed as directly influencing only family and teacher support. Ability is viewed as directly affecting all the support variables and achievement. There is empirical support for each of these paths (e.g., Maruyama, 1977; Maruyama & Miller, 1980; Maruyama et al., 1981). Because children's family and teachers provide major sources of socialization, their support variables are each seen as affecting peer acceptance, school achievement, and attitudes. Consistent with the general framework, the support variable of peer acceptance is seen as causally prior to attitudes and achievement. Finally, peer acceptance, achievement, and attitudes are each hypothesized as influencing each other over time. These last nine paths are ones that help to examine the effects of the cooperative learning interventions. Note that it is these last three variables, which measure the children, that are repeated over time.

If the cooperative learning intervention is successful, both social relations and school achievement should change. If the changes were to affect all children equally, the covariance structure of the variables would not change, and therefore, the causal model would be no different from that found for a noncooperative classroom. Changes in means are most easily tapped through analysis-of-variance techniques; it is important to remind readers that the approach described here complements the approaches commonly used in experimental research on cooperative goal interventions. Major shifts in means, however, would very likely be accompanied by some shifting of covariance structures as well, for it is unlikely that all children would change equal amounts on each variable. Further, shifts in means may well result in later changes in covariance structures. For example, if attitudes toward "different" others became markedly more positive, it seems likely that patterns of peer relations would consequently change and that the nature of the relations of peer acceptance and attitudes to achievement would change as well.

Changes that don't affect all children equally should act to lower the stability of the attitude, peer acceptance, and achievement variables compared to noncooperative classrooms. Lowered stability would allow other variables to affect each of the postintervention variables. If such variables are included in the model, some of the causal paths should change. If such variables are omitted from the model, either spurious relations will appear to be causal in the model or the residuals will increase. In order to help disentangle the classroom processes, I would suggest (1) analyzing the cooperative and noncooperative classroom separately, and (2) analyzing all classrooms together with *cooperative* versus *not* as a dichotomous variable affecting the postintervention variables.

Before concluding this section, it is important to digress from the main theme and talk briefly about the methodology that would be used. The type of methodology is commonly known as causal modeling techniques or structural equation techniques. Such techniques include path analysis, cross-lag panel analysis, and maximum likelihood analysis of structural equations (MLASE). It is this last technique, MLASE, whose use is most desirable, for it can avoid many of the simplistic assumptions that are necessary with other techniques. A description of how they can be used to study achievement processes appears in Maruyama and McGarvey (1980). Provided there are multiple measures (three to four) of each of the variables in the model, MLASE provides a flexible method for examining relations among variables.

CONCLUDING DISCUSSION

Throughout this paper, I have attempted to argue for the potential value of applying causal modeling techniques to the study of cooperative learning interventions. As has been noted frequently, one of the shortcomings of the cooperative learning literature is the limited duration of many of the interventions. The approach described here is intended to examine how the effects of cooperative learning are related to classroom achievement and social interaction patterns. Further, in examining the nature of the relations, the three conceptual views described in this paper—namely, transmission of values, contact theory, and expectation states—are compared.

Interestingly, even though I have chosen to focus on an application of causal modeling techniques that focuses on achievement processes with cooperative learning interventions as an intermediate variable in the causal sequence, there are other possible applications of this methodology within the cooperation literature. Most notably, there are many hypotheses about why cooperative learning is effective and about the effectiveness of different cooperative learning techniques. Causal modeling techniques could also be used to explore the effects on school outcomes of variables such as the amount of reward or task interdependence, individual accountability, and so on (e.g., Slavin, 1980); the nature of the information available, of the learning task, of communication, and so on (e.g., Sharan, 1980); or the characteristics of the small-group interaction (e.g., Webb, 1982). (See also Johnson *et al.*, 1981,

1983.) Such an approach might look at classroom structure and demographic variables as background variables and the variables described above as mediating variables.

In concluding, I will attempt to speculate about what analyses of models such as the one proposed in this paper will find. As was noted earlier, the best test of social influence processes would come from measuring children who had a history of educational experiences that included regular "doses" of cooperative learning. The minimal condition for providing a good test of the occurrence of social influence processes would be provided when causal modeling techniques can be applied to a (large) sample that displays strong beneficial effects of the cooperative intervention. In either case, it is important to have available data that show some effects of cooperative learning; without such effects, it is difficult to know what different patterns of influence would mean.

Of course, an alternative view to the one presented above would be that there are few, if any, enduring effects of cooperative learning strategies, and that no sample will ever yield findings like those predicted. Given the effectiveness of cooperative learning techniques (e.g., Johnson et al., 1981), I suspect that is unlikely. Nevertheless, the question is empirical; only after findings from a number of studies have been accumulated will the processes become understood.

Perhaps a continued investigation of social influence processes will demonstrate that such processes rarely, if ever, occur in the heterogeneous classrooms produced by desegregation or mainstreaming. If so, attempts to examine the effects of cooperative learning interventions should focus on other classroom and school variables in attempting to understand the relation between cooperative learning and school achievement. Before we discard the social influence perspective, however, it needs to be given as many opportunities to be observed as possible, for as argued earlier, there are many studies documenting social influence processes in different situations.

In addition to the information discussed earlier, the dominant model of attitude- and behavior-change processes in social psychology involves both normative and informational social influence. Fishbein and Ajzen (1975) see behaviors as resulting from two distinct sources: the attitude toward the behavior and the subjective norm about the behavior. The attitude is drawn from beliefs about the consequences of the behavior, the subjective norm, from normative beliefs. From the present perspective, desegregation may allow children to form new beliefs about the appropriateness and/or the consequences of certain behaviors, which, in turn, may lead them to develop new attitudes and values. It is the acquisition of new beliefs about appropriate behaviors that are being called *informational social influence*. On the other hand, desegregation could also provide a new set of normative beliefs. If conforming to these normative beliefs is important, then the subjective norm from the Fishbein and Ajzen model is salient, and behaviors will follow from the subjective norm. This latter process has been called *normative social influence*. In summary, the dominant model of attitude and behavior changes includes both normative and informational social-influence processes. These processes do occur and can potentially occur in desegregated classrooms.

Given the number of perspectives and the amount of information supporting social influence processes, it seems reasonable to pursue such processes further. Such an approach may need two focuses. First is a continuation of the present work, attempting to see when such processes occur and how they operate. Second, perhaps, there is a need to alter the perspective that accompanies social influence research. There is seemingly a stigma attached to social influence processes, for they have been associated with assimilationist orientations to education. Yet, social influence can work in many ways. Thus, a second avenue of research should focus on tailoring such processes so that they support school achievement without forcing assimilation. This latter challenge is critically important, for the implementation of successful multicultural education strategies is a major challenge facing educators today.[3] Finally, what may be most important is that this chapter attempts to provide researchers with a different way to think about cooperative learning interventions. If cooperative learning researchers are willing to collect additional information and to expand their focus somewhat, there are gains to be made. Ideally, a clearer picture of the relation of cooperative learning to broader classroom-achievement processes will emerge from studies that both conduct interventions and collect data for examining the patterns of social interaction and achievement within the schools.

REFERENCES

Allport, G. W. *The nature of prejudice*. New York: Addison-Wesley, 1954.
Aronson, E. *The social animal* (2nd ed.). San Francisco: W. H. Freeman, 1976.
Asch, S. E. *Social psychology*. Englewood Cliffs, N.J.: Prentice-Hall, 1952.

---

[3]Perhaps group competition in cooperative learning can be used to increase social influence in a more pluralistic classroom.

Bachman, J. G., & O'Malley, P. M. Self-esteem in young men: A longitudinal analysis of the impact of educational and occupational attainment. *Journal of Personality and Social Psychology*, 1977, *35*, 365–380.

Cohen, E. G. Design and redesign of the desegregated school: Problems of status, power, and conflict. In W. G. Stephan & J. R. Feagin (Eds.), *Desegregation: Past, present, and future*. New York: Plenum Press, 1980.

Coleman, J. S., Campbell, E. Q., Hobson, C. J., McPartland, J., Mood, A. M., Weinfeld, F. D., & York, R. L. *Equality of educational opportunity*. Washington: U.S. Government Printing Office, 1966.

Cook, S. W. Motives in a conceptual analysis of attitude-related behavior. In W. J. Arnold & D. Levine (Eds.), *Nebraska Symposium on Motivation, 1969*. Lincoln: University of Nebraska Press, 1970.

Crain, R. L., & Weisman, C. S. *Discrimination, personality, and achievement: A survey of Northern Blacks*. New York: Seminar Press, 1972.

Deutsch, M., & Gerard, H. B. A study of normative and informational social influence upon individual judgment. *Journal of Abnormal and Social Psychology*, 1955, *51*, 629–636.

Fishbein, M., & Ajzen, I. *Belief, attitude, intention, and behavior: An introduction to theory and research*. Reading, Mass.: Addison-Wesley, 1975.

Frank, M. J. *A comparison between an individual and group goal structure contingency that differed in the behavioral contingency and performance-outcome components*. Unpublished doctoral dissertation, University of Minnesota, Minneapolis, 1984.

Gerard, H., & Miller, N. *School desegregation*. New York: Plenum Press, 1975.

Johnson, D. W., Maruyama, G., Johnson, R. T., Nelson, D., & Skon, L. Effects of cooperative, competitive, and individualistic goal structures on achievement: A meta-analysis. *Psychological Bulletin*, 1981, *89*, 47–62.

Johnson, D. W., Johnson, R. T., & Maruyama, G. Interdependence and interpersonal attraction among heterogeneous and homogeneous individuals: A theoretical formulation and a meta-analysis of the research. *Review of Educational Research*, 1983, *53*, 5–54.

Jones, E. E., & Gerard, H. B. *Foundations of social psychology*. New York: Wiley, 1967.

Jöreskog, K. G., & Sörböm, D. *LISREL IV: Estimation of linear structural equation systems by maximum likelihood methods*. Chicago: National Educational Resources, 1978.

Lewis, R., & St. John, N. Contribution of cross-racial friendship to minority group achievement in desegregated classrooms. *Sociometry*, 1974, *37*, 79–91.

Maruyama, G. *A causal-model analysis of variables related to primary school achievement*. Doctoral dissertation, University of Southern California. (*Dissertation Abstracts International*, 1977, *38*, 1470B.)

Maruyama, G. What causes achievement? An examination of antecedents of achievement in segregated and desegregated classrooms. In D. E. Bartz & M. L. Maehr (Eds.), *The effects of school desegregation on motivation and achievement*. Greenwich, Conn.: JAI Press, 1983.

Maruyama, G., & McGarvey, B. Evaluating causal models: An application of maximum likelihood analysis of structural equations. *Psychological Bulletin*, 1980, *87*, 502–512.

Maruyama, G., & Miller, N. Re-examination of normative influence processes in desegregated classrooms. *American Educational Research Journal*, 1979, *16*, 273–283.

Maruyama, G., & Miller, N. *Does popularity cause achievement? A longitudinal test of the lateral transmission of values hypothesis*. Paper presented at the Annual Meeting of the American Educational Research Association, Boston, April 1980.

Maruyama, G., Rubin, R. A., & Kingsbury, G. G. Self-esteem and educational achievement: Independent constructs with a common cause? *Journal of Personality and Social Psychology*, 1981, *40*, 962–975.

McGarvey, W. E. Longitudinal factors in school desegregation. Doctoral dissertation, University of Southern California. (*Dissertation Abstracts International*, 1978, *38*, 5097B.)

Newcomb, T. M. *Personality and social change*. New York: Dryden, 1943.

Sharan, S. Cooperative learning in small groups: Recent methods and effects on achievement, attitudes, and ethnic relations. *Review of Educational Research*, 1980, *50*, 241–271.

Slavin, R. E. Cooperative learning. *Review of Educational Research*, 1980, *50*, 315–342.

U.S. Commission on Civil Rights. *Racial isolation in the public schools: A report*. Washington D.C.: Government Printing Office, 1967.

Watson, G. *Action for unity*. New York: Harper, 1947.

Webb, N. M. Student interaction and learning in small groups. *Review of Educational Research*, 1982, *52*, 421–455.

V

Learning to Cooperate

SPENCER KAGAN

Over 50 years ago, Julius Maller (1929) concluded his classical experimental study of cooperation and competition with the following statement:

> The frequent staging of contests, the constant emphasis upon the making and breaking of records, and the glorification of the heroic individual achievement and championship in our present educational system lead toward the acquisition of the habit of competitiveness. The child is trained to look at the members of his group as constant competitors and urged to put forth a maximum effort to excel them. The lack of practice in group activities and community projects in which the child works with his fellows for a common goal precludes the formation of habits of cooperativeness and group loyalty. (p. 163)

Although in the recent past we have seen greater emphasis in our educational system on individualized instruction, the lack of cooperative group activities as an integral part of the educational experience remains, for the most part, conspicuously missing.

The systematic institution of cooperative group activities in schools and classrooms can result in a restructuring of the social system within which students develop. The remaining three chapters of this volume describe three different innovative approaches to the comprehensive institution of cooperation in schools. The approaches as a group represent a radical departure from the socialization role currently maintained by U.S. public schools. The need to institute cooperative, prosocial socialization experiences in schools is supported by examining the modern socialization void, the negative consequences of this void, and projected social and economic needs.

THE SOCIALIZATION VOID

Social forces in the last generation have radically changed the relative potency of the American family for the socialization of prosocial values among the nation's youth. There has been a mass exit of women from

---

SPENCER KAGAN • Department of Psychology, University of California, Riverside, California 92521.

full-time homemaker roles as they join the work force, as well as a wide-spread disappearance of the extended and large family. Rather than filling the socialization void created by these forces, commercially sponsored television has contributed to the void: As TV has entered center stage into American family life, it has commanded a restructuring of family activity away from social interaction and the opportunity for prosocial socialization. Too often, America's children only view rather than experience social interaction. And the social interaction represented on commercially sponsored television is often far from prosocial: Advertisements consistently point toward product acquisition, not positive interpersonal relationships, as the passport to fulfillment; in programming, violence rather than discussion is too often the favored mode of conflict resolution. As families have become increasingly individualistic and mobile, children have been separated from the stabilizing influences of long-term neighborhood and community support systems. Parent–child, grandparent–child, and teenager–child interactions within the family have been reduced dramatically as a function of the trend toward smaller and less extended families. Increasingly, children have been separated also from the career activities of their parents, a separation that denies them yet another important prosocial socialization experience. (See Bronfenbrenner, 1976, for a fuller discussion of these trends.)

At the same time, the schools have included remarkably few opportunities for prosocial socialization both within classrooms and within schoolwide activities. Each quarter, I ask my undergraduate students if they ever have worked together cooperatively with other students on an academic project. Over 90% have not, an indication that the entire schooling experience for those students is lacking in experience in cooperative interaction within classes. In typical classrooms, the students are expected to sit quietly and listen to the teachers (Adams & Biddle, 1970; Perkins, 1964). When interviewed regarding the results of "A Study of Schooling," probably the most comprehensive study ever made of American schools, John Goodlad, director of the study, stated,

> The average instructional day in a junior or senior high school includes 150 minutes of talking. Of this, only seven minutes is initiated by students. If I myself were in such classrooms hour after hour, I would end up putting my mind in some kind of "hold" position, which is exactly what students do. (Fiske, 1983, p. 1)

For the most part, students are not interacting with their teachers or their peers; little prosocial socialization occurs within typical classrooms. Although good data are not available on the frequency of cooperative or prosocial activities conducted at a schoolwide level, casual observation indicates that such activities are extremely rare.

CONSEQUENCES OF THE SOCIALIZATION
VOID

One of the clearest consequences of the socialization void is the alarming increase in crimes against property within the schools. Each year, over $200 million is spent repairing damage to school property in the United States. Each month over 100,000 U.S. teachers report having something stolen, and over 5,000 report being physically assaulted. Student–student crimes are extremely common: Each month well over 2 million students report a theft of their property in school; over .25 million report being physically attacked (Bybee & Gee, 1982).

Another consequence of the socialization void is the absence of cooperative skills among students. When placed in experimental game situations in which valued rewards can be obtained only through cooperation, American students consistently adopt nonadaptive competitive strategies. Nonadaptive competitiveness has been observed among American students at grade levels ranging from second grade through college (Edney & Harper, 1978; Kagan & Madsen, 1971, 1972; Madsen & Shapira, 1970). The failure of students to adopt cooperative behavior patterns when such patterns are necessary for reward maximization can be related to the absence of cooperative activities within the schools. Had students worked cooperatively in their classrooms and schools, they would recognize and adjust to situations in which cooperation is adaptive. Large-scale social failures to adopt adaptive cooperative strategies in areas such as rapid transit and arms control are long-term consequences of the prosocial socialization void.

PROJECTED SOCIAL AND ECONOMIC NEEDS

Although students generally do not work cooperatively together in school, they are expected to do so when they leave school to enter the work force. The social structure within schools is out of synchrony with the social skill needs of our highly flexible technological economy. It is hard to point to a job today that does not require cooperative interaction abilities; as Nancy B. Graves and Theodore D. Graves (Chapter 15) point out, 70%–80% of jobs today require "complex coordination of efforts and ideas."

Importantly, the emphasis on teamwork abilities will increase dramatically as America increasingly moves away from high-volume production toward flexible-system enterprises in which solving unique problems is the goal:

In high-volume production, most of a firm's value is represented by physical assets, while the principal stores of value in flexible-system enterprises are human assets. Specialized machines and unskilled workers cannot adapt easily to new situations. Flexible machines and teams of skilled workers can. Only people can recognize and solve novel problems; machines can merely repeat solutions already programmed within them. The future prosperity of America and all the other industrialized countries will depend on their citizens' ability to recognize and solve new problems, for the simple reason that processes that make routine the solution to older problems are coming to be the special province of developing nations. Industries of the future will depend not on physical "hardware," which can be duplicated anywhere, but on human "software," which can retain a technological edge. (Reich, 1983, p. 108)

The need to train students in cooperative social skills is supported also by urbanization trends. The urbanization of the world population is occurring at a logarithmic rate: If we take the percentage of persons living in localities of more than 20,000 inhabitants as a measure of urbanization, in 1800 about 2.4% of the world population was living in urban centers; by 1900, the percentage was about 10%; by 1950, it was 25% (Hauser, 1957). Population density demands increased social skills, but unfortunately, urbanization has been associated with increased competitiveness rather than with cooperativeness among the children of the world (Kagan, 1981). Cooperative experiences in schools are the only viable way to systematically socialize future generations to meet the needs presented by an increasingly urban, technological, and interdependent world.

In spite of the prosocial socialization void experienced by our youngest generation, as well as the other clear indications of a need for cooperative experiences in the schools, the schools for the most part have not moved from the position that their domain is exclusively intellectual development; moral development has been left as the responsibility of home, church, and community organizations. This dichotomy is not tenable. Classroom and school structures are *either* cooperative, competitive, or individualistic. The absence of a systematic program within the schools to promote cooperative, prosocial development amounts to a *de facto* decision to institute a socialization program that fosters competitive and individualistic, antisocial, and asocial development. There is no escape from the critical value question: How should the schools socialize our youth? The question is not whether our schools should enter the moral domain and include socialization programs; the only real question is what kind of socialization programs they will adopt.

The three chapters that follow represent steps toward the redefinition of the socialization role of the schools; they are attempts to fill the prosocial socialization void. The chapters provide models for creating schools and classrooms that can meet the socialization needs of our next generation. The chapters provide theoretical frameworks for introducing cooperative experiences into the schools, as well as numerous examples of practical cooperative activities, such as cooperative learning groups, cross-grade buddy systems, pupil-led school landscaping and beautification programs, the cooperative involvement of parents and other community members in school life, and school-sponsored family fun festivals. As we read about these cooperative programs, the lack of viability of traditional, exclusively competitive, and individualistic social structures in the schools is all the clearer by contrast. If we think of the efforts expended in the traditional system to get our students not to talk to each other and to sit quietly listening only to the teacher, we can only wonder why our very high alienation and dropout rates in schools are not higher. What is striking about the creative, innovative cooperative programs is that they are so very simple and natural. It is unnatural to prevent students from sharing what they know and from participating in improving school life. In the novel cooperative alternatives, there is a liberation and an empowering of the students: The students take the responsibility for what and how to learn, as well as how to share what they have learned. They become responsible to other students and to the school as a whole. These rich socialization experiences have the power to create an improved social environment. We are left to wonder not at the viability of the new cooperative approaches, but at how we ever could have settled for so long and so completely for the poverty of a pervasive reliance in the schools on competitive and individualistic structures.

REFERENCES

Adams, R. S., & Biddle, B. J. *Realities of teaching: Explorations with video tape.* New York: Holt, 1970.

Bronfenbrenner, U. Who cares for America's children? In V. Vaughn & T. Brazelton (Eds.), *The family—Can it be saved?* New York: Year Book Medical Publishers, 1976.

Bybee, R., & Gee, E. *Violence, values, and justice in the schools.* Boston: Allyn and Bacon, 1982.

Edney, J. J., & Harper, C. S. The commons dilemma: A review of contributions from psychology. *Environmental Management*, 1978, 2(6), 491–507.

Fiske, E. B. "Talky" schools need restructuring, study finds. *The Register*, Orange County, California, July 19, 1983, pp. 1–2.

Hauser, P. M. *Urbanization in Asia and the Far East.* Calcutta: UNESCO, 1957.

Kagan, S. Ecology and the acculturation of cognitive and social styles among Mexican American children. *Hispanic Journal of Behavioral Sciences*, 1981, 3(2), 111–144.

Kagan, S., & Madsen, M. C. Cooperation and competition of Mexican, Mexican American, and Anglo American children of two ages under four instructional sets. *Developmental Psychology*, 1971, *5*, 32–39.

Kagan, S., & Madsen, M. C. Experimental analyses of cooperation and competition of Anglo American and Mexican children. *Developmental Psychology*, 1972, *6*, 49–59.

Madsen, M., & Shapira, A. Cooperative and competitive behavior of urban Afro-American, Anglo-American, Mexican-American, and Mexican village children. *Developmental Psychology*, 1970, *3*, 16–20.

Maller, J. B. *Cooperation and competition: An experimental study in motivation.* New York: Teachers College, Columbia University, 1929.

Perkins, H. V. A procedure for assessing the classroom behavior of students and teachers. *American Educational Research Journal*, 1964, *1*, 249–260.

Reich, R. B. The next American frontier. *The Atlantic Monthly*, April 1983, 97–108.

14

A Program to Promote Interpersonal Consideration and Cooperation in Children

DANIEL SOLOMON, MARILYN WATSON,
VICTOR BATTISTICH, ERIC SCHAPS,
PATRICIA TUCK, JUDITH SOLOMON,
CAROLE COOPER, AND WENDY RITCHEY

INTRODUCTION

This chapter describes a project whose purpose is to develop and evaluate the effectiveness of a comprehensive school- and home-based program to enhance prosocial tendencies in young children. This project (called the Child Development Project) was initiated in response to what we see as some critical problems in contemporary society: inadequate levels of social responsibility and concern for others' welfare, accompanied by excessive self-centeredness and social alienation.[1] These phenomena may be reflected in such recent trends as increasing vandalism, violence, delinquency, and school discipline problems. Although there are undoubtedly multiple determinants of these trends, the project is guided by the assumption that they can be effectively ameliorated through strengthening children's tendencies to behave in more socially positive ways. The aim is to encourage children to be concerned about and responsive to the needs of others, without at the same time inappropriately sacrificing their own legitimate needs and interests.

Social science research has identified several processes that can help to increase social concern and responsibility and to decrease selfishness and aggression. The project has drawn heavily on these findings in developing both its intervention program and its assessment strategies. However, it expands on previous attempts to apply this knowledge in "real-world" settings, both in the duration and comprehensiveness of

[1]The Child Development Project is funded by the William and Flora Hewlett Foundation.

DANIEL SOLOMON, MARILYN WATSON, VICTOR BATTISTICH, ERIC SCHAPS, PATRICIA TUCK, JUDITH SOLOMON, CAROLE COOPER, AND WENDY RITCHEY • Developmental Studies Center, 130 Ryan Court, Suite 210, San Ramon, California 94583.

its intervention program and in the range and complexity of behaviors and mediating variables that are being assessed.

The intervention program is being delivered over a period of five years in three elementary schools and a preschool setting in a single San Francisco Bay Area school district. Over the course of that time, a set of mutually consistent program components, developed in collaboration with school personnel and parents, is being provided in schools, class-rooms, and homes.

The project's research efforts have a dual focus. The first of these is the description and monitoring of program implementation. The second focus is the evaluation of program effects on children's social behavior, and on an array of mediating skills and tendencies believed to be funda-mental to the appropriate performance of prosocial behavior. In addi-tion to following the groups of children receiving the program (begin-ning in kindergarten for some and two years prior to kindergarten for others), we will also longitudinally assess children in the same grades in three comparison schools in the same school district.

What follows are descriptions of the theoretical assumptions guiding the design of this comprehensive program and research effort, the program components and their rationale, the implementation ap-proach, and the research design and assessment strategy.

THEORETICAL MODEL

The intent in this project is to create a substantial and long-lasting im-pact on the development of prosocial behavior in children. By *prosocial*, we mean interpersonal behavior that is responsive to the legitimate needs of others as well as the self. Because the aim is to have as strong and general an effect as possible, we have constructed a theoretical model that incorporates an extensive and mutually consistent set of vari-ables having reasonable empirical and/ or theoretical support. This model takes into account four domains: (1) types of prosocial behavior; (2) the internal characteristics assumed to mediate the performance of prosocial behavior; (3) the likely environmental determinants of these internal characteristics; and (4) the potential mechanisms by which the environmental determinants might achieve their effects.

PROSOCIAL BEHAVIORS

The right-hand column of Figure 1 presents a general list of the catego-ries of prosocial behavior. Some of these focus on the benefit to the other and may involve an element of self-sacrifice (e.g., helping and

EXTERNAL/ENVIRONMENTAL DETERMINANTS

- Opportunities to learn prosocial behaviors
- Participation in prosocial activities
- Approval or reward for prosocial behavior
- Disapproval, punishment and/or absence of reward for antisocial behavior
- Communication of prosocial norms, values and expectations of family, school, community, and culture
- Nurturance, sensitivity, clarity, consistency, and responsiveness in adult—child relationships
- Opportunities for reciprocal interaction with peers

INTERNAL MEDIATING VARIABLES

Cognitive Factors
- Social understanding
  - Knowledge of the other's thoughts, feelings, intentions
  - Knowledge of the consequences of one's actions
  - Knowledge of alternative courses of action in social situations
  - Knowledge of social role relationships
- Concepts of justice or fairness
- Knowledge of appropriate behaviors in different situations
- Beliefs about the prosocial characteristics of self and others

Affective/Motivational Factors
- Commitment to prosocial values
  - Concern for others as well as the self
  - Commitment to justice and fairness
- Sympathy/empathy
- Emotional responses to one's own social/moral actions
  - Pride and satisfaction
  - Shame and guilt

Behavioral Competencies
- Communication skills
- Ability to negotiate
- Ability to perform particular prosocial acts

Personality Factors
- Self-control, impulse control
- Self-esteem
- Sense of efficacy
- Assertiveness
- Social orientation

PROSOCIAL BEHAVIORS

- Cooperating
- Compromising
- Comforting
- Helping
- Rescuing
- Donating
- Sharing
- Carrying out one's responsibilities
- Upholding prosocial values
  - Not hurting others
  - Not stealing or taking more than one's fair share
  - Telling the truth
  - Keeping one's promises
  - Being considerate

FIGURE 1. Hypothesized determinants of prosocial behavior.

rescuing), whereas others are essentially oriented toward equalizing the outcomes between the self and others (e.g., cooperating and compromising). As implied above, the goal is not merely to increase the frequency of these behaviors, but to help children develop ways of accommodating *both* their own needs and those of others. The *situationally appropriate* performance of these behaviors should indicate a general disposition to behave prosocially. The specific behaviors encompassed by each of these broader categories will, of course, differ according to level of development and environmental context.

INTERNAL MEDIATING CHARACTERISTICS

Several internal mediating characteristics are hypothesized to be fundamental to a multidetermined, general disposition to behave prosocially. These internal mediating variables are shown in the center column of Figure 1. Included are cognitive factors, affective/motivational factors, behavioral competencies, and personality factors. The model's focus on this range of mediating variables suggests an intervention approach that is somewhat broader than those suggested or taken by other theorists. For example, in emphasizing perspective taking and social problem-solving, Copple, Sigel, and Saunders (1979), as well as Spivak and Shure (1974), focused their interventions on cognitive factors. Kohlberg (1969), Turiel (1969), and Lickona (1974) also relied primarily on cognitive factors in their approaches to moral judgment. Hoffman (1982) stressed affective/motivational factors such as empathy and guilt, and the Feshbachs (1981) stressed both cognitive and affective/motivational factors in their intervention program. The intervention program designed by Pitkanen-Pulkkinen (1977) emphasizes self-control and social understanding and thus includes both personality and cognitive factors. The present model is an eclectic one that incorporates the perspectives put forth by these various theorists. In this regard, it is similar to the model proposed by Staub (1978), who also emphasized the importance of all the above-named factors—cognitive, affective, motivational, personality, and behavioral.

Among the cognitive factors believed to be important in prosocial behavior are the skills and beliefs necessary for effective social interaction. These include an understanding of others' thoughts and feelings, concepts of justice and fairness, abilities to conceive and assess the appropriateness of alternative courses of action, and beliefs about the prosocial characteristics of the self and others. Such beliefs and skills, however, do not themselves guarantee prosocial behavior. Indeed, some of them can be used to take advantage of others. Further, the relative importance of any individual factor as a significant predictor of prosocial behavior may well change with developmental level. For example, level of social understanding may be a major predictor of prosocial behavior for preschool children, but it may be a less useful predictor for older children because of ceiling effects.

Within the affective/motivational domain, the model emphasizes both enduring motivations and more immediate affective responses. The former include commitments to prosocial values such as concern for others. The more immediate responses include reactions to others, such as sympathy and empathy, and to one's own behavior, such as pride or guilt.

Many prosocial actions require specific behavioral competencies. The model assumes that individuals who can easily perform these actions will be more likely to do so. In addition, personality factors can limit or enhance one's tendency to behave prosocially. Figure 1 lists several personality factors (such as self-control and self-esteem) that seem likely to influence the disposition to behave prosocially.

EXTERNAL/ENVIRONMENTAL DETERMINANTS

Finally, as shown in the left-hand column of Figure 1, several environmental conditions are identified as major determinants of both the intervening dispositional properties and the actual performance of prosocial behavior. Although different theoretical perspectives stress the significance of different determinants, it seems likely that each is influential during development.

Moreover, although each of these determinants may independently affect certain aspects of prosocial behavior, widespread and long-lasting gains in prosocial development are most probable when all of the determinants are present in a mutually reinforcing system. Thus, all of those listed (opportunities for learning prosocial behaviors, participation in prosocial activities, and so on) have influenced the choice of interventions.

POTENTIAL PSYCHOLOGICAL MECHANISMS

The mechanisms postulated in several theories were considered when we assessed the potential importance of each of the external/ environmental determinants and decided which to include and in what ways to incorporate them into the specific components of the intervention program. To take one example, the hypothesized effects of *reciprocal peer interaction* on social development can be explained from the theoretical perspectives of Piaget and H. S. Sullivan (see discussion in Youniss, 1980) and of social learning theory. A social learning approach would explain increasing social skill as being due to the accumulated positive and negative outcomes of various peer-interaction attempts and approaches. A cognitive construction approach, on the other hand, would suggest that peer interaction provides the child with the opportunity to participate as an equal in decision making, to justify, defend, and modify his or her point of view, and to both influence and respond to others by persuasion, negotiation, and reciprocal give-and-take. From experience with reciprocal interaction, the child is seen as developing an understanding of the perspectives, beliefs, thoughts, and likely responses of others; as learning to assert, clarify, communicate, and negotiate concerning his or her own perspectives; and as coming to understand the importance of reciprocity and mutual accommodation. The mechanisms put forward by the different approaches are not contradictory; they merely focus on different aspects of the experience and on different outcomes. For each of the hypothesized environmental determinants of prosocial effects, the model assumes that all reasonable mechanisms may be operating. The specific interventions are therefore being structured so as to allow for the operation of as many relevant potential mechanisms as possible.

THE MODEL AND THE DERIVATION OF THE PROGRAM

The intervention program developed for this project consists of five major components: (1) cooperative activities, in which students work on learning tasks in cooperative groups and play cooperative games, and in which family members work or play together cooperatively; (2) regular participation in helping and sharing activities; (3) opportunities for children to experience others (adults as well as children) setting positive examples (i.e., being considerate, cooperating, taking responsibility, helping, and sharing); (4) role playing and other activities designed to enhance children's understanding of other people's needs, intentions, and perspectives; and (5) positive discipline, which includes the development and the clear communication of rules and norms that emphasize the individual's rights and responsibilities with respect to others, as well as discipline techniques that use the minimal force necessary to obtain compliance, and that explain the reasons for rules; emphasize the potential effects of one's behavior on others; provide firm, fair, and consistent guidance; foster nurturant adult–child relationships; and offer age-appropriate decision-making opportunities to children.

These components were selected because they seem mutually consistent, and because they represent aspects of the environmental determinants that seem likely to influence children's prosocial behavior, cognitions, motivations, and affects. Each component is individually well supported by prior research and/or theory, but the effects of this particular combination of components have not been previously investigated. Although the program is considered a unified whole in which all five components are important, the cooperative activities component will be discussed in a bit more detail than the others, in keeping with the focus of this book.

Each of the interventions is designed to have effects on generalized tendencies to behave prosocially. These effects will be achieved, according to the present scheme, through creating environmental conditions that will lead to the development and the maintenance of internal mediating characteristics (including the relevant cognitive, affective/

motivational, personality, and behavioral competency factors). A list of the environmental determinants that each of the components is assumed to incorporate is presented in Table 1. Each component encompasses several of them, with the largest number represented in cooperative activities. The internal mediating variables that each of the program components is assumed to influence are shown in Table 2. Cooperative activities, for example, are expected to produce effects with each of the four general types of variables shown in this table.

TABLE 1. External/Environmental Determinants That Interventions Are Assumed to Provide

Planned interventions	External/environmental determinants[a]						
	A	B	C	D	E	F	G
Cooperative activities							
Participation in structured cooperative groups	X	X	X	X	X		X
Exercises in group decision-making and interpersonal problem-solving	X		X		X		X
Helping							
Participation in prosocial activities	X	X	X		X		X
Setting positive examples							
Opportunities for observing prosocial behavior	X		X		X		
Activities to enhance understanding of others							
Role playing, affect identification, and related activities	X				X		X
Positive discipline							
Induction			X	X	X	X	
Communication of prosocial norms and values					X		
Age-appropriate rules and expectations					X	X	
Clear articulation of rules					X	X	
Consistent and fair enforcement of rules			X	X	X	X	
Involving children in setting rules and consequences	X				X	X	X
Moderate sanctions with stress on reparation and logical consequences				X	X	X	
Warmth and mutual consideration			X		X	X	

[a]A = opportunities to learn prosocial behaviors; B = participation in prosocial activities; C = approval or reward for prosocial behavior; D = disapproval, punishment, and/or absence of reward for antisocial behavior; E = communication of prosocial norms, values, and expectations of family school, community, and culture; F = nurturance, sensitivity, clarity, consistency, and responsiveness in adult–child relationships; G = opportunities to interact with peers.

TABLE 2. Hypothesized Influences of Planned Interventions

	Internal mediating variables			
	Cognitive factors	Affective and Motivational factors	Behavioral competencies	Personality factors
Cooperative activities				
Participation in structured cooperative groups	X	X	X	X
Exercises in group decision-making and interpersonal problem-solving	X	X	X	X
Helping				
Participation in prosocial activities	X	X	X	X
Setting positive examples				
Opportunities for observing prosocial behavior	X	X	X	X
Activities to enhance understanding of others				
Role playing, affect identification, and related activities	X	X	X	
Positive discipline				
Induction	X	X		
Communication of prosocial norms and values	X	X		
Age-appropriate rules and expectations		X		X
Clear articulation of rules	X			
Consistent and fair enforcement of rules		X		X
Involving children in setting rules and consequences	X	X	X	X
Moderate sanctions with stress on reparation and logical consequences	X	X		X
Warmth and mutual consideration		X		X

DEVELOPMENTAL CONSIDERATIONS

It is assumed that logical structures, motivations, and skills develop gradually and affect behavior unevenly, depending on the experience, temperament, and other characteristics of the child and the child's environment. Developmental factors are therefore considered in selecting the interventions to emphasize at different ages, and in determining the ways in which those interventions are carried out. For example, it would be inappropriate and possibly counterproductive to hold 3- and 4-year-olds responsible for the successful completion of chores in the same way and to the same degree as for 7- to 9-year olds. Although the present assumptions are generally inconsistent with a rigid stage theory in which each stage is homeostatically balanced, they do not prevent such stages from emerging should they exist.

The Program

Program Components

Most previous intervention programs have been relatively short-term and narrowly focused. Yet, it has been argued that major behavioral or motivational changes are unlikely unless more comprehensive and long-lasting interventions are provided. The intervention in this project will extend over five years, beginning in the preschool years for one cohort and in kindergarten for another, with the same children exposed to the program and followed for four (preschool cohort) or five (kindergarten cohort) years. The program will attempt to influence the children's social development through interventions in several settings: elementary schools, preschool settings, and homes.

Cooperative Activities

This component includes cooperative learning groups and other cooperative activities in classrooms and on playgrounds, and parallel activities in the home. Numerous prototypes of cooperative classroom organization have been developed, including those by Slavin (1980), Aronson (1978), Johnson and Johnson (1978), Sharan and Sharan (1976), and Kagan (1982). Although the approaches differ in several respects, they typically divide classrooms into heterogenous groups, each working on an academic task toward a common group goal. Because these procedures can become part of normal classroom routines, are consistent with academic emphases, can be easily structured for different developmental levels, and emphasize combined attention to the needs and contributions of others and of the self within the group, they seem very promising as a means of achieving the objectives of this project. Cooperative sports and games, in which children participate in playful group activities whose aim is to achieve a common goal (e.g., keeping a balloon in the air as long as possible), are also an important aspect of this component (see Fluegelman, 1976, 1981; Orlick, 1978, 1981, 1982; Orlick & Botterill, 1975).

Another element of this component involves exercises in group decision-making and interpersonal problem-solving. The children are provided with opportunities to develop and exercise negotiating and compromising skills through participation in group discussions aimed at solving particular problems or determining optimal courses of action. Some of this activity may occur in the context of the cooperative learning groups, but separate attention is also being given to the development of these skills. Less structured opportunities for equal-status peers to interact are also provided.

Home-based cooperative activities include many of the same elements. Parents are encouraged to hold periodic family meetings (Lickona, 1980) that include cooperative planning, decision making, and interpersonal problem-solving. Chores, responsibilities, or projects may be done cooperatively as an entire family or with family subgroups. Games, toys, and recreation provide other opportunities for family cooperation (Fluegelman, 1976, 1981; Orlick, 1978, 1981, 1982).

Cooperative activities incorporate several of the environmental determinants assumed in our model to be important in the development of prosocial characteristics (see Table 1). Thus, children in cooperative groups have many opportunities to learn prosocial behaviors and to participate in prosocial activities because, in order to achieve a group goal, it is often necessary to negotiate with, help, and encourage other group members. In addition, *approval* and *disapproval* (or reward, punishment, and nonreward) for prosocial and antisocial behavior will come about naturally in a cooperative group as the members work toward the group goal. Group members who help the group to reach its goals and to function in a smooth and pleasant manner (probably always an implicit goal) will usually receive the most approval from the other group members as well as from any adults who may be present. The expression of approval and disapproval is probably also an important way in which group norms, values, and expectations are communicated; for example, it is expected that adults and children involved in cooperative activities will show approval for behaviors that reflect such prosocial norms as fairness, consideration for others' views and opinions, and responsibility to the group. Finally, cooperative groups provide many opportunities for reciprocal peer interaction, especially groups that are composed of equal-status members, involve much collaborative activity, and are maximally directed by the members themselves.

Participation in cooperative activities is also expected to produce effects on each of the four general types of internal mediating variables shown in Table 2. Research on the effects of cooperative learning procedures has recently been comprehensively reviewed by Slavin (1983). Consistent with the hypotheses suggested in Table 2, Slavin summarized evidence that cooperative learning procedures positively affect children's understanding of others' perspectives (a "cognitive" factor in the terminology of the present model), their preferences for cooperative (as opposed to competitive) situations and their tendencies to make "altruistic" choices in reward distribution tasks (motivational factors), and their level of self-esteem and their tendency to believe that their own efforts determine their outcomes (personality factors).

Other effects of cooperative groupings on the internal mediating variables shown in Figure 1 are also anticipated. To the degree that cooperative groups involve mutual goal-setting, negotiating, consensus reaching, and collaborative work, effects would be expected on (1) the ability both to assert one's own position and to compromise with and accommodate to others' positions; (2) awareness of alternative possible courses of action; (3) concern for and empathy with others; (4) skill in communicating and negotiating; (5) skill in working cooperatively; and (6) appreciation of the value of collaborative work toward common goals.

HELPING ACTIVITIES

There is some research evidence (e.g., Staub, 1975) that children who are induced to help others, or who are given responsibility for others, subsequently exhibit spontaneous prosocial behavior. If helping activities are introduced in ways that are not unduly coercive, and that do not create resistance or resentment, children can learn the relevant skills, can learn that they are competent to help, and can begin to see themselves as valuable contributors to an interdependent social system. Several types of helping activities have been instituted in our program, including cross-age and same-age tutoring in schools and neighborhoods, the assignment of chores and responsibilities (with meaningful and visible effects) at home and at school, community service activities, and care of plants and pets.

SETTING POSITIVE EXAMPLES (MODELING)

There is much evidence—naturalistic and experimental—that children learn many social skills and behaviors through exposure to the behavior of others (Mussen & Eisenberg-Berg, 1977; Rushton, 1980; Staub, 1978, 1979; Yarrow, Scott, & Waxler, 1973). Certain aspects of the relationship between model and child increase the likelihood of the behavior's being imitated: the nurturance of the model, the degree to which the relationship is a continuing one, and the similarity of the demonstrated behavior to the child's existing behavioral repertoire. Although most of the research has focused on the *behavioral* effects of modeling, it seems equally reasonable to expect substantial effects of significant models on the consistent cognitive, affective, and motivational characteristics of children. The program thus seeks to highlight and emphasize not only certain behaviors, but also the associated attitudes, beliefs, values, and feelings. The program is also designed to help children to distinguish between those examples that should and those that should not be imitated.

Some desirable modeling occurs naturally just in conducting other aspects of the program. In order to create a generally prosocial environment, teachers and parents necessarily behave in cooperative ways, demonstrate consideration for the needs and feelings of others, and involve themselves in various helping activities. In addition to these examples, which do not require special or separate preparation, other more deliberate modeling activities are also being undertaken, sometimes with teachers, sometimes with older children. Audiovisual and curricular materials for use in the classroom, as well as TV programs and stories for home and school, are being selected (and developed) to provide other examples of prosocial behaviors. Attention is also being paid to ways of avoiding or minimizing exposure to negative models, and to minimizing the effects of such exposure when it does occur.

ACTIVITIES TO EHANCE THE UNDERSTANDING OF OTHERS

An understanding of others' thoughts, feelings, perceptions, and needs, together with an empathic or sympathetic reaction to them and an accompanying desire or inclination to help others, are considered essential to prosocial behavior (Feshbach, 1978; Ianotti, 1978; Mussen & Eisenberg-Berg, 1977). Consequently, an attempt is being made to train these skills, understandings, and orientations directly, through a component that involves role playing, affect identification, and related activities. This approach includes role plays of actual classroom and home occurrences as well as of hypothetical situations, games that involve understanding the perspectives of others, and the presentation of plays, stories, and audiovisual materials that portray people's feelings, intentions, and reactions to situations, and that involve simultaneous consideration of multiple perspectives and affects. In addition, some exercises help children to learn to distinguish between, and to behave appropriately in, situations calling for self-oriented behavior, those calling predominantly for other-oriented behavior, and those calling for coordination of one's own and others' needs.

POSITIVE DISCIPLINE

This component includes both specific approaches to discipline and more general aspects of the adult–child relationship. One aspect of positive discipline involves the clear and emphatic communication of prosocial norms and values. Children in this culture receive many inconsistent, mixed, or weak messages, and they often appear to be uncertain and confused about cultural values and guides for behavior. If children are to act in ways consistent with prosocial norms and values, they must know what the norms are, the reasons for them, and under what circumstances they apply. This information is being provided in the program in several ways: through verbal statements by adults and other children, through implicit and explicit themes in reading materials and other curriculur materials, through dramatic presentations, through school and family rules, and through comments, discussions, and the judicious use of sanctions in response to particular behaviors or events that arise in the course of daily activity.

Induction, another major aspect of positive discipline, involves discussing or pointing out to children the effects of their acts on others. Induction can be applied to positive as well as to negative acts, as a way of handling day-to-day encounters. There is some evidence that its use facilitates the development of prosocial behavior within this culture, particularly for young children (Dlugolinski & Firestone, 1974; Hoffman, 1977; Hoffman & Saltzstein, 1967; Zahn-Waxler, Radke-Yarrow, & King, 1979). Some theorists (e.g., Hoffman) believe that the consistent use of induction increases children's awareness and understanding of the needs and feelings of others, their own empathy with those needs and feelings, and their desires to be helpful and considerate to others. In both induction and the communication of norms, values, and rules, the explanation and discussion of reasons is essential. These help children come to understand that constraints and prescriptions are not arbitrary and not only that their own acts affect themselves, but that each operates within an interdependent social system.

Other aspects of positive discipline are intended to create an optimal context or setting in which prosocial characteristics can develop. Relationships with adults characterized by warmth, nurturance, and mutual consideration (or, more generally, settings in which people care about, help, and are considerate of one another) seem to be essential for the internalization of values and the development of self-control. Setting clear rules and expectations, with consistent and firm but moderate sanctions for misbehavior, teaches the child that there are definite values held by important adults. Child participation in rule setting and adults' use of the minimal pressure necessary for compliance should each promote acceptance and internalization of rules and values—the former through influencing the child's sense of commitment, the latter because compliance can be partially or wholly voluntary. The emphasis in discipline should be on ways of promoting the child's long-term internalization of values, rather than on obtaining unquestioning obedience in the immediate situation. It is, however, also important for parents (and other adults) to feel confident and secure in their disciplinary actions with children, as a way of conveying their own commitment to prosocial values.

Our general approach is not to provide teachers and parents with specific formulas or routines, but to help them achieve an understanding of the child as a developing individual with changing needs and abilities. This understanding should help the adults to focus on the child's reasons for particular behaviors (or misbehaviors) in particular situations, and to respond in ways that take into account the child's understanding of the situation and the child's needs, motives, and desires, as well as their own needs and the "actual" requirements of the situation.

PROGRAM IMPLEMENTATION

As of this writing (Summer 1983), the first year of program implementation has just been completed. Several aspects of the program have been gradually taking shape in the schools during the year, but many details remain to be worked out.

Our approach to program implementation has been heavily influenced by recent research on effective approaches to educational innovation and program development (e.g., Berman & McLaughlin, 1978). One principle guiding our activities has been that administrators, teachers, and parents must have major roles in planning the program if it is to be responsive to their needs and interests, and if it is to be willingly and consistently implemented. Several mechanisms have been developed for organizing their participation in creating and refining the program, within the framework of the general components and approaches just described. Efforts have also been made to establish indigenous support systems within each school (and, to some degree, between schools), and to develop systematic links among home, school, and the project. Finally, the role of the school principal is considered crucial in developing the sense of "ownership," and in promoting motivation and commitment among teachers and parents; the program staff have therefore tried to work closely with the principals in each of the participating schools.

INITIAL APPROACHES

It seemed essential that support for this program be genuine and broad-based within the participating schools and the surrounding communities, and that it not be seen as imposed by the "central office" and/or outside "experts." Therefore, one major criterion for the selection of the schools in which to conduct the program was the interest expressed by school district administrators, principals, and teachers. All of the school districts in two San Francisco Bay Area counties were surveyed to determine which of them met this and certain other criteria (e.g., an adequate number of elementary schools, relative homogeneity of student populations, relatively low turnover rates, the absence of other major educational change programs, and receptivity to the projects' research requirements). The two districts that best met these criteria were then explored more intensively, through a series of meetings with district administrators, school principals, and school faculties. After one of these districts was selected, further meetings were held with the PTA boards and other parents at those schools in which the principal and the teachers had expressed the strongest interest. In the fall of 1981, six schools were selected for project participation. These were then divided into two approximately equivalent groups of three schools, and one group was randomly assigned to conduct the program and the other to serve as a "comparison" group.

After the selection of the program schools, the program staff took steps designed to solidify and broaden understanding and acceptance of the program, and to help create a commitment to carrying it out. These steps included the initiation of regular meetings with two high-level school district administrators to maintain liaison and communication with the district, and of regular meetings with the principals of the three program schools to discuss implementation plans and procedures for their schools, including ways to maximize teacher and parent participation.

During the winter of 1982, in the school year before that in which program implementation was to begin, project staff members began spending significant amounts of time in each of the three program schools. Staff members established offices in each school and were available to teachers as helpers in the classrooms (e.g., assisting with small group lessons and with field trips). The purpose was to develop rapport with the school faculties and students, and to become familiar with the school and classroom atmospheres and practices. The project staff members also began attending all faculty and PTA meetings. These practices are continuing as the program is being implemented in the schools.

During the spring of 1982, a series of orientation meetings were held with the faculties and with parents in each of the three program schools, in order to help develop understanding of and interest in the program. Descriptions of the origins, rationale, goals, and components of the program were given at these meetings. In subsequent planning meetings, parents and teachers raised questions and concerns about the project and explored ways in which they could influence program development with the project staff. Meeting with parents, teachers, principals, and district administrators will continue for the duration of the project.

PROGRAM PLANNING AND REFINEMENT

As a mechanism for enlisting significant participation in program development by teachers, parents, and principals from the three program schools, "coordinating teams" consisting of four teachers, four parents, the school principal, and two project staff members, were formed in each school. Each team has major responsibility for planning and overseeing program development within its school. The teams give other teachers and parents in the school and the community information about the program and support them as they try program-related activities. The teams will continue to meet during the course of the project, with their membership changing from time to time.

The first task of the coordinating teams was to develop an implementation plan that (1) was consistent with the project's theoretical perspective; (2) included all five components; (3) involved both home and school in coordinated and mutually supportive activities; (4) spanned the kindergarten to Grade 6 range; (5) involved as many teachers and parents as possible; (6) was as consistent as possible from school to school; and (7) gave particular emphasis to the children in the longitudinal cohorts as they progress through school.

Parent and teacher participation in program development is important not only as a way of increasing their motivation and commitment, but also because they are in the best position to suggest activities or variants of activities that will be relevant to the specifics of a given school, classroom, or family situation. Intensive and continued project staff involvement in developing these activities is also essential, to make certain that all program activities will be theoretically sound, mutually consistent, and similar from school to school. Similarity across schools is also being promoted by regular communication among the coordinating teams, by regular across-school meetings of all teachers of children in the longitudinal cohort (kindergartners in the 1982–1983 school year, first-graders the following year, and so on), and by the fact that each of the three project staff members belongs to coordinating teams from two schools.

PROGRAM TRAINING AND THE START OF IMPLEMENTATION

Implementation of the program in the three participating schools began during the fall of 1982. Although special attention is being given to the program for the children in the longitudinal cohorts, the overall program is schoolwide. Program implementation started gradually (as expected) and has been building during the year, at a somewhat different pace and in a somewhat different sequence from school to school, according to the experiences, skills, and interests of the faculty and the parents in each.

The two project staff members assigned to each school have guided the implementation of the program by the teachers and the parents. They work closely with the school faculty; conduct periodic meetings and in-service training sessions to further develop the teachers' understanding of the purpose of each of the components and activities, along with competence in implementing them; demonstrate activities in the classrooms; observe teachers undertaking program activities and provide them with appropriate feedback; and encourage groups of teachers to observe and consult with one another so that they can generate mutual support and assistance as they undertake the program. These activities have been particularly intense with the teachers of the longitudinal cohort children (kindergarteners during the first program year). The staff members also meet periodically with parents (one from each class in each program school) who have volunteered to represent the classes and to provide liaison with the project.

The coordinating teams in the three schools have also played major roles in training and in disseminating information, in addition to their involvement in planning. Early in the year, each coordinating team, with all of the program staff members, gave initial training in the program components to the entire faculty of its school plus an equal number of parents (the representatives from each class), in two halfday sessions. Several types of material were introduced and first used in these training sessions:

1. Manuals that had been started the previous summer (with teacher assistance), describing some school activities consistent with each of the program components, were given to all teachers. These man-

uals are continuing to evolve along with the project and eventually will represent a full range of school activities within each of the component areas. The teachers were encouraged to become familiar with the activities at their own grade levels and at adjacent grade levels as well, so as to promote program continuity across grades.

2. The participating parents and the program staff had also begun to develop descriptions of program-relevant activities that can be done in the home. These descriptions, organized as sets of "activity" cards, were distributed to all the parents in the training sessions. Sets of these cards are maintained at each school and are available to all parents with children in the three program schools.

3. Other materials, giving descriptions and a rationale for each of the program components, were given to the participating teachers and parents and were incorporated in the training sessions.

Several other activities have provided information about program plans and have helped teachers and parents to develop the appropriate skills.

1. The parent classroom representatives have helped with program activities, have encouraged the involvement of other parents, and have provided information about program activities to other parents. Because they know and live near the other families in the class, the parent representatives provide a useful link between them and the project.

2. The project staff members have been offering a series of workshops that focus on the development of the skills needed to implement the various components to teachers and parents of children in the "cohort" grades, as well as to other interested teachers and parents. To date, these workshops have focused on cooperative learning, puppetry, involving children in helping, and discipline.

3. A library of relevant children's books, activities, curriculum guides, film resources, and cooperative game materials and equipment is being maintained for the teachers' and the parents' use.

4. Finally, the project publishes a bimonthly newsletter that is mailed to all parents and teachers of the program schools. This newsletter includes articles about program-related activities (including descriptions of specific examples among the project schools or families), book reviews, and activity suggestions, as well as pictures of children, families, and school and community activities. One program component has been highlighted in each issue.

The general strategy of the implementation plan is for parents and teachers to have a significant role in planning and decision making concerning program emphases and sequences in particular schools, and in developing or adapting specific activities and making them relevant to the needs of particular schools, classrooms, grade levels, and families. Under this plan, the project staff provides a basic and theoretically coherent framework for the program, including general prescriptions that detail the goals and requirements of program activities. We are very concerned about maintaining the appropriate balance of staff, teacher, and parent roles, and we will undoubtedly be making adjustments in this balance from time to time (and possibly from school to school).

SCHOOLWIDE ACTIVITIES IN THE FIRST PROGRAM YEAR

Numerous schoolwide events and activities were conducted as part of the program during the first year. An important element in many of these was that their planning and conducting required the active collaboration of most of the school faculty. Several of the program components were represented in these events and activities, particularly cooperative activities, helping, and setting positive examples. Each school initiated some community-service projects with broad student participation; these include UNICEF fund-raising efforts at Halloween in lieu of trick-or-treating, toy and food drives, and school decoration activities during the holiday season. The teachers were trained to use "new games" (cooperative, noncompetitive physical activities) in physical education, and many are using them on a regular basis with their students. A cross-age tutoring program was also started at each of the three program schools. In each school, 60–80 fourth-, fifth-, and sixth-graders were intensively trained to tutor kindergartners through third-graders in regular academic subjects. The tutors were assigned to work one-to-one with younger children beginning in January and February 1983.

"Buddy" programs were also started at two of the schools. In these programs, classes of upper-grade students (fifth or sixth grade) were paired with classes of lower-grade students (kindergarten, first or second grade), and pairs of students (one from the upper grade and one from the lower grade) were selected from these paired classes to be "buddies." The buddies then had several meetings a month, during which the older student might read to the younger one, give help with homework, or play games. One school conducted a "special-person-of-the-week"program, in which a student from each classroom was singled out to be feted each week by his or her classmates, particularly by having other students post instances when the student was helpful, kind, or cooperative.

Several activities designed to link home and school also occurred. A "family fun festival" (a day-long picnic and introduction to "new games") was held at each of the schools during the year. Cooperative campus beautification projects (landscaping, painting, and so on) were undertaken at all three schools, with active participation by parents, teachers, and students. Some activities focused on TV watching, including evening workshops for parents on ways to watch TV with children and to teach them critical viewing skills. The "coordinating teams" from all three schools also put out a monthly TV newsletter for parents that discussed ways to use TV to promote prosocial objectives, and that alerted readers to upcoming prosocial programming. A "neighborhood-study-time" program was begun in one school community: each of four parents opened his or her home one afternoon a week for students to do homework, to practice skills, and to help each other with schoolwork.

ACTIVITIES WITH THE "KINDERGARTEN COHORT" DURING THE FIRST
PROGRAM YEAR

In periodic meetings during the 1982–1983 school year, the program staff and all of the kindergarten teachers from the three program schools collaboratively planned a detailed curriculum for the kindergarten classroom program, discussed their successes and failures in the various activities, and gave each other suggestions and support. The kindergarten curriculum contains numerous activities and practices relevant to each of the five program components. Beginning in January, special emphasis was given to one component each month, and numerous activities relevant to that component were done in each class. For example, when the focus was on *helping*, the kindergartners made valentines for the parents who work as volunteer aids in their classrooms, made birdfeeders for the school, and worked to help keep parts of the school campus clean. They also learned about and met adult "helpers" in the community, including fire fighters, police, and postal workers. Some kindergartners were paired with fifth- or sixth-grade "buddies," who read to them several times a month, thus providing positive examples of helping. Finally, the teachers made large bulletin-board displays on which each child's name was posted when the teacher observed the child being particularly helpful or considerate. Although these activities were emphasized during one month, many of them continued throughout the remainder of the year.

The kindergarten teachers gradually increased their use of cooperative grouping in the classroom during the year, with a peak during the emphasis month. They also spent time helping children to develop the skills needed for effective participation in cooperative groups.

Some cooperative activities were structured so as to involve resource interdependence, some goal interdependence, and some reward interdependence, and some to involve two or all three of these types of interdependence. All of the program kindergarten classes engaged frequently in cooperative play activities (e.g., "new games" and cooperative jigsaw puzzles). Cooking and many art and craft activities (e.g., making placemats) were also done cooperatively. Although most of these kindergarten cooperative activities did not have a specific academic focus, academic content was often inserted (e.g., a cooperative post-office activity became part of a math lesson). As the children progress through the elementary grades, the academic content and focus of cooperative activities will increase.

The program staff members assisted, observed, and advised the kindergarten teachers on a regular basis. In addition to doing new activities derived from the program, the teachers attempted to adapt the program to and weave it into their existing academic, arts, and social curricula, often adding prosocial elements or a prosocial "flavor" to their accustomed activities. For example, the teachers often selected books or stories with prosocial themes for their reading-readiness program; followed their reading of the stories with discussions of the moral and prosocial implications for the children themselves (e.g., Rudolph the Red-Nosed Reindeer became the basis for a discussion about teasing); and organized follow-up activities that incorporated other aspects of the program (e.g., a cooperative art project, such as cooperatively drawing a scene from the story).

Special evening orientation meetings were hosted by the kindergarten teachers and the program staff at each school to acquaint the parents of kindergarten children with the classroom program and to introduce them to the home activities. Boxes of "recipe cards" describing activities relevant to each of the program components were distributed to the parents, as was a "home curriculum," suggesting objectives within each component area, and activities designed to help the parents achieve those objectives.

EVALUATION OF THE PROGRAM

Developing an optimal strategy for evaluating this intensive, multifaceted, long-term intervention program has been, and continues to be, a considerable challenge. The requirements of sound research design and methodology must be tempered by the political, economic, and practical constraints inherent in "applied" research, and yet the research must retain sufficient rigor to detect and distinguish program effects from those resulting from normal developmental processes and extraneous social influences. We have developed a methodology that we believe will allow us to evaluate this program in its applied setting, and that at the same time will yield information relevant to many basic substantive issues in social development. Following is a summary of the basic research design and assessment strategy.

SAMPLE AND DESIGN

As described earlier, the program is being administered in three elementary schools, with one group of children receiving it for five years, and a second group for four years. Each group will contain approximately 200 children (at its maximum) and will be paired with an equivalent group in three other elementary schools that are not receiving the program, but that are participating as a "comparison" group. In total, then, a longitudinal sample of about 800 children in six schools will be involved in the research. To create the "program" and "comparison" groups, the six schools were divided into two similar groups of three (in terms of relevant demographic characteristics); one of these groups was randomly selected to implement the program, the other to serve as the comparison group. The three comparison schools are receiving alternative services relevant to their educational programs but unrelated to prosocial development.

Figure 2 summarizes this longitudinal, quasi-experimental design. Cohort 1 consists of children who entered kindergarten in the fall of 1982 in both the program and the comparison schools. The children in this cohort will be followed through the fourth grade. Cohort 2 consists of children of early preschool age (approximately age 3) in the fall of 1983 who live in the areas of two of the three program elementary schools and two of the three comparison elementary schools. Those in the program school areas are receiving a special two-year preschool program conducted by parents and staff members, whereas those in the comparison school areas are participating in research activities. At the end of this two-year period, this cohort will be expanded by the addition of all other children entering kindergarten in the six project schools. The children in this cohort will be followed through the first grade. They will be assessed during and at the end of their preschool careers, as well as at several subsequent points during the elementary-school years.

Also, as indicated in Figure 2, two additional comparison groups are included in the research design. In the spring preceeding the implementation of the program, a cross-sectional sample of children,

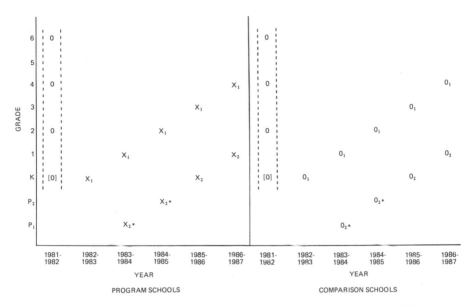

FIGURE 2.   Schematic of project research design. X_1 = first program cohort; X_1^* = preschool component of second cohort; 0 = cross-sectional comparison sample; 0_1 = first comparison cohort; 0_2 = second comparison cohort; 0_2^* = Preschool component of second cohort; P_1 = early preschool; P_2 = late preschool; [] = prior-year comparison sample.

ramdomly drawn from kindergarten and Grades 2, 4, and 6 in both the program and the comparison schools, was administered a set of measures of central "core" variables, which are also being assessed in subsequent years for the longitudinal cohorts. In addition to providing a "no-treatment" and no-prior-assessment comparison group for the longitudinal cohorts within each school, this sample yields cross-sectional data on developmental differences in social motivation and behavior, as well as additional information concerning the preprogram equivalence of the program and the comparison schools. Further, the subsample of children in kindergarten in 1981–1982 provides a prior-year comparison group for children in kindergarten during 1982–1983, the first year of the program (i.e., Cohort 1).

Assessment Procedures

The basic assessment strategy reflects a dual focus. First, the context and the process of program implementation are being documented. This documentation requires an assessment of the relevant aspects of the children's home and school environments, as well as monitoring of the nature and the extent of the implementation of specific program activities in the home and the classroom. Second, of course, is the ongoing assessment of the children's social motives, affects, cognitions, and behavior. Toward these ends, an extensive battery of measures has been compiled. Table 3 provides a general description of the major categories and methods of assessment being used in this project.

PROGRAM IMPLEMENTATION AND ENVIRONMENTAL CHARACTERISTICS

Two basic procedures are being used to assess the context and the process of program implementation. The first consists of extensive observations of program activities and general environmental characteristics (e.g., classroom structure and atmosphere, teacher–student interaction). These observations are being conducted each year in all six schools.

Second, teachers, principals, and other staff in the program schools are being interviewed each spring to provide feedback on program implementation and participation.

TABLE 3. Summary of Assessment Procedures

Focus	Method
I. Program implementation and environmental characteristics	
Classroom and schoolwide program implementation	Classroom observations; teacher questionnaires; teacher and principal interviews
Implementation of home program	Parent interviews and questionnaires; possible observation of parent–child interaction
Classroom atmosphere; teacher–student interaction; classroom dynamics	Classroom observations; teacher questionnaires; possible student questionnaires
Characteristics of home environment; child-rearing attitudes, values, and practices	Parent interviews and questionnaires; possible observation of parent–child interaction
II. Social development and program effects	
Social behavior	Individual-, class-, and school-level naturalistic observations in classroom and on playground; observations of behavior in structured small-group and individual tasks; parent interviews; teacher questionnaires
Social attitudes, values, and motives; social understanding; empathy; social perceptions and cognition; personality characteristics	Child interviews; child questionnaires; parent interviews and questionnaires; teacher questionnaires
School achievement	School records
School attendance	School records

PROGRAM EFFECTS AND GENERAL SOCIAL DEVELOPMENT

Our assessments of social development are focused equally on social behavior and on intervening cognitive, motivational, and affective variables. A primary assessment of "core" variables in each of these two categories (see Figure 1) will be conducted in the spring of the years when the students in the first longitudinal cohort are in kindergarten and Grades 2 and 4, and when those in the second cohort are in kindergarten. Cognitive, motivational, and affective variables are being assessed primarily through structured interviews. Social behavior is being assessed through (1) naturalistic observations of interactions in the classroom and on the playground; (2) performance in both structured and unstructured group tasks; and (3) interviews and rating scales administered to parents and teachers. (Some self-report instruments may also be used with the children when they are older, perhaps in the intermediate grades.) Finally, data on academic achievement, attendance, and related variables are being obtained from school records.

In addition to the "core" longitudinal assessments, a number of other assessments will be undertaken at various points throughout the project. Most of these will be conducted during the years when the "core" variables are not being assessed (i.e., when the children are in Grades 1 and 3). These assessments will apply different approaches to the measurement of some of the major "core" variables and will also include measures of additional variables that are in the same general domains, but that are not included within the "core" assessments (i.e., other variables concerned with empathic processes, social cognition, helping behavior, and interpersonal problem-solving). These additional assessments will also cover some related personality and motivational characteristics (e.g., sense of efficacy, self-esteem, impulse control, and fear of failure).

CURRENT STATUS OF RESEARCH ACTIVITIES

Research activity during this first year of program implementation has focused on the children of the first longitudinal cohort—kindergartners this year. Assessments of conditions existing before the program got under way were made with parent interviews and questionnaires, teacher questionnaires, and some classroom observations. Assessments of classroom atmosphere and program implementation in the kindergarten classroom have been made with an extensive, structured observation system (with each class visited twice by each of four observers). Other information about the implementation of and reactions to the program is being obtained from interviews with program-school teachers and principals, and from questionnaires given to the teachers and parents.

Initial information about the prosocial (and other) characteristics of the cohort children was obtained by asking the parents to do Q-Sort descriptions of them. The children's prosocial behavior at the end of the year was assessed through playground observations, teacher ratings, and observations of the children's performance in a series of four-person tasks. Assessments of their motives, perceptions, social understanding, empathy, and prosocial values (the "core" variables) were obtained through interviews in which children respond to described hypothetical situations and to some brief filmed sequences. (The variables measured in the interviews and the small-group tasks are shown in Table 4.) Although we are not including detailed descriptions of the instruments or procedures in this paper, we should indicate that they have been influenced by (and in some cases represent adaptations of) the work of Flapan (1968), Selman (1980), Solomon, Ali, Kfir, Houlihan, and Yaeger (1972), Solomon and Kendall (1979), Pepitone (1980), Eisenberg-Berg and Hand (1979), and others.

TABLE 4. Variables Assessed in Kindergarten Cohort Assessment—Spring, 1983

A. Interview variables
   1. *Norms*: The child's view of the relative importance of *personal achievement* vs. *helping others,* as she or he thinks it would be seen by his or her parents, teacher, and friends.
   2. *Reactions to interpersonal conflict*: The child's judgment concerning the appropriate actions to take in various interpersonal-conflict situations. Responses to these items are scored for the degree to which they reflect consideration for the other person's needs, as well as one's own, for the suggestion of mutual-benefit or compromise solutions, and for the specific actions suggested.
   3. *Helping and other prosocial values*: The child responds to hypothetical situations that pose a prosocial value (helping, keeping a promise) against self-interest (getting to a party on time, going to the beach). Both the initial response and the reasons given for it are coded.
   4. *Inquiry*: The child's understanding of the complexities of the helping situation; awareness that there are situations in which the person helped may have negative or mixed reactions to the help.
   5. *Reactions to one's own transgressions*: These items describe situations in which a child has committed a transgression that was intentional, was hidden from others' view, and was fairly serious. The children are asked about the reaction of the hypothetical transgressor in terms of feelings (e.g., guilt) and subsequent actions (e.g., punishment, reparation).
   6. *Social desirability:* The child's tendency to give responses that she or he thinks would be most valued by the adult interviewer (or by adults in general). These items are included primarily as one way of checking on the validity of the responses to the other items.
   7. *Social understanding:* Several aspects of social understanding are assessed from the children's responses to questions concerning several short sequences from a film

continued

TABLE 4. (*continued*)

(*Our Vines Have Tender Grapes*) that are shown to the child. The film shows several interaction episodes involving two children and some adults. Understanding of the different characters' feelings, motives, intentions, and views of each other are coded from the children's responses.

8. *Empathy*: Some of the children's faces are being videotaped as they watch the film sequences mentioned above. Their facial expressions will later be coded for emotional expressiveness consistent with the situations and the participants' experiences, as portrayed in those sequences.

B. Individual tasks

Two individual tasks are conducted during the course of the interviews: a helping task and a donating task.

1. *Helping task*: The child's helpfulness to the interviewer in picking up a box of spilled paper clips is rated.

2. *Donating task*: The child is given the opportunity to donate to children in a nursery school some stickers that have been given to him or her at the end of the interview. (The interviewer leaves the room when the child is donating but is able to count the number donated later.)

C. Small-group (four-person) task variables

A large number of variables is scored from these tasks. The following list is not complete but includes the major variables.

1. *Group-level variables*
   a. *Equality of participation*: Degree to which participation in a task is shared equally by the four group members
   b. *Behavioral coordination*: Degree to which group interaction is smooth and well coordinated
   c. *Group cohesiveness*: Apparent feeling of group "identity"; interest in one another's activities
   d. *Amount of collaboration*: Degree to which members of group work together on task(s)
   e. *Competitiveness*: Degree to which the group as a whole seems to construe the task as a competitive one
   f. *Arguing* over turn taking or distribution of resources
   g. Explicit mention of *strategies to maximize group outcomes*
   h. *Sharing and exchanging materials*

2. *Individual-level variables*: Variables representing individual behavior in the group task sessions are coded from videotapes made of those sessions. The coding system includes variables that fall into the following categories:
   a. *Evaluation of another's acts* (praises, putdowns, social comparison)
   b. *Status indicators* (copies, whispers, seeks attention)
   c. *Altruism* (comforts, protects, invites excluded child to play)
   d. *Aggression* (attacks another child, destroys group or individual project)
   e. *Control* (commanding and prohibiting)
   f. *Helping behavior* (offering or giving verbal or manual assistance)
   g. *Object exchange* (offering and giving objects, taking objects, suggesting trade)
   Also, eight stylistic ratings based on the videotapes are completed at the time of the videotape coding. These are 5-point ratings for each child of participation, extroversion, amiability, helpfulness, influence over others, assertiveness, bossiness, and competitiveness.

DATA ANALYSIS

The project presents a number of difficult analytic problems for which no completely satisfactory solutions exist (e.g., the units-of-analysis problem). The major data analyses will of necessity be numerous and complex and will be undertaken at several levels of analysis (i.e., individual, small-group, classroom, grade, and school). Thus, the evaluation of the intervention program will require an application and a comparison of several different analytic approaches. Although discussion of the numerous analytic possibilities is beyond the scope of this chapter, several major approaches may be outlined.

Within each year of the program, multivariate analyses of variance and covariance will be used to assess global program effects. These analyses will compare the program cohorts with each of the comparison samples: (1) the comparison-school longitudinal cohorts; (2) the within-school cross-sectional samples; and, for Cohort 1 in the first program year, (3) the prior-year (kindergarten) sample. In addition to investigating the treatment's main effects, some analyses will also be undertaken to investigate possible individual-by-treatment interactions.

It should be noted that the extensive data on variations in program implementation, general environmental characteristics, and so on will not only provide documentation of inevitable inconsistencies in program implementation but will allow us to take analytic advantage of these differences. Specifically, in addition to the major "between-group" analyses, extensive "natural variation" analyses will be undertaken in each program year to examine the effects of differences in program implementation and general environmental characteristics on the major outcome variables. Assuming that sufficient variation exists in program implementation, these analyses may provide suggestive information about the specific effects of particular program components on social development. In addition, some analyses of the effects of individual differences in exposure to, and participation in, the various program components will also be conducted, both within and across program years.

As implied above, from the second through the fifth program years, repeated-measures analyses will be undertaken to assess cumulative program effects both within and between samples. However, in addition to the analyses of program effects, extensive analyses will be undertaken within the comparison-school cohorts to examine developmental trends in social attitudes and behavior in the absence of planned "prosocial" interventions.

Finally, given the extensive network of various types of variables, a major analytic focus will be on identifying the patterns of relationships between environmental, internal mediating, and behavioral characteristics (e.g., through the use of structural equations), including changes in the interrelationships of these variables over time. The primary objective of these analyses will be to describe the processes underlying the observed variations in social behavior, and to examine the ability of various conceptual models to account for the observed patterns of relationship.

OVERVIEW: SIGNIFICANCE AND FUTURE DIRECTIONS

The project's major objective is a very practical one: to determine if children's cooperativeness, concern for others, and social responsibility can be enhanced through interventions delivered within existing social institutions. The comprehensive, theoretically consistent program that we have described is an attempt to demonstrate that it is possible to have a substantial impact on children's social development.

It should also be apparent that this project has the potential for making a major contribution to our theoretical and empirical knowledge of social development. First, the project will extend over several years and will focus on social development during an age range believed to be crucial in the establishment of social attitudes, beliefs, and behavior. Second, the assessments will be comprehensive and will provide information about a wide range of social behaviors, affects, cognitions, and motivations. This breadth of measurement, coupled with the longitudinal nature of the research, offers a rare opportunity to examine the complex patterns of factors underlying social behavior.

Along with the emphasis on maximizing the effectiveness of the intervention comes a concern with the dissemination and adoption of the program, or aspects of it. Regardless of the effectiveness of the program, it will not be widely adopted if it requires very extensive changes in existing institutional practices and/or a huge support network. Consequently, we have attempted to develop a program that is consistent with traditional academic goals and that can be used largely with existing curricular materials. We expect that different schools (or school districts) may find different aspects of the program appealing and relevant to their situations, and that therefore different subsets or groupings of the program elements will be involved in various adoptions. We do not see such differences in what various schools may decide to adopt as a problem. In fact, if these adoptions are carefully evaluated, the result could be a more complete understanding not only of the effects of the program, but of the different combinations and patternings of the program elements.

Finally, should the program prove effective, it is possible that the intevention may be extended to follow the cohorts through sixth grade, and that one or more follow-up investigations may be conducted after the children have been out of the program for several years. These extensions would make it possible to continue the assessments of social development into early adolescence, and thereby to assess the persistence of any program effects.

REFERENCES

Aronson, E., Blaney, N., Stephan, C., Sikes, J., & Snapp, M. *The Jigsaw classroom*. Beverly Hills, Calif.: Sage, 1978.

Berman, P., & McLaughlin, M. W. *Federal programs supporting educational change. Vol. VIII. Implementing and sustaining innovations.* Santa Monica, Calif.: Rand, 1978.

Copple, C., Sigel, I., & Saunders, R. *Educating the young thinker: Classroom strategies for cognitive growth.* New York: Van Nostrand, 1979.

Dlugokinski, E. L., & Firestone, I. J. Other-centeredness and susceptibility to charitable appeals: Effects of perceived discipline. *Developmental Psychology*, 1974, *10*, 21–28.

Eisenberg-Berg, N., & Hand, M. The relationship of preschoolers' reasoning about prosocial moral conflicts to prosocial behavior. *Child Development*, 1979, *50*, 356–363.

Feshbach, N. D. Studies on empathic behavior in children. In B. A. Maher (Ed.), *Progress in experimental personality research* (Vol. 8). New York: Academic Press, 1978.

Feshbach, N., & Feshbach, S. *Empathy training and the regulation of aggression: Potentialities and limitations.* Paper presented at the Western Psychological Association, 1981.

Flapan, D. *Children's understanding of social interaction.* New York: Teachers College Press, 1968.

Fluegelman, A. *The new games book.* Garden City, N.Y.: Headlands Press, 1976.

Fluegelman, A. *More new games book.* New York: Doubleday, 1981.

Hoffman, M. L. Moral internalization: Current theory and research. In L. Berkowitz (Ed.), *Advances in experimental social psychology* (Vol. 10). New York: Academic Press, 1977.

Hoffman, M. L. Development of prosocial motivation: Empathy and guilt. In N. Eisenberg (Ed.), *Development of prosocial behavior.* New York: Academic Press, 1982.

Hoffman, M. L., & Saltzstein, H. D. Parent discipline and the child's moral development. *Journal of Personality and Social Psychology*, 1967, *5*, 45–57.

Iannotti, R. J. Effect of role-taking experience on role-taking, empathy, altruism and aggression. *Developmental Psychology*, 1978, *14*, 119–124

Johnson, D. W., & Johnson, R. T. Cooperative, competitive, and individualistic learning. *Journal of Research and Development in Education*, 1978, *12*, 3–15.

Kagan, S. *Co-op Co-op: A single, flexible cooperative learning method.* Paper presented at Second International Conference on Cooperation in Education, Provo, Utah, July 1982.

Kohlberg, L. Stage and sequence: The cognitive-developmental approach to socialization. In D. A. Goslin (Ed.), *Handbook of socialization theory and research.* Chicago: Rand McNally, 1969.

Lickona, T. A cognitive developmental approach to interpersonal attraction. In T. L. Huston (Ed.), *Foundations of interpersonal attraction.* New York: Academic Press, 1974.

Lickona, T. Fostering moral development in the family. In D. B. Cochrane & M. Manley-Casimir, *Development of moral reasoning.* New York: Praeger, 1980.

Mussen, P. H., & Eisenberg-Berg, N. *Roots of caring, sharing, and helping*. San Francisco: W. H. Freeman, 1977.

Orlick, T. D. *Cooperative sports and games book*. New York: Pantheon, 1978.

Orlick, T. D. Positive socialization via cooperative games. *Developmental Psychology*, 1981, *17*, 426–429.

Orlick, T. D. *The second cooperative sports and games book*. New York: Pantheon, 1982.

Orlick, T. D., & Botterill, C. *Every kid can win*. Chicago: Nelson-Hall, 1975.

Pepitone, E. A. *Children in cooperation and competition*. Lexington, Mass.: D. C. Heath, 1980.

Pitkanen-Pulkkinen, L. Effects of stimulation programmes on the development of self-control. In C. Van Lieshout & D. Ingram (Eds.), *Stimulation of social development in school*. Amsterdam: Swets & Zeitlinger, 1977.

Rushton, J. P. *Altruism, socialization, and society*. Englewood Cliffs, N.J.: Prentice-Hall, 1980.

Selman, R. O. *The growth of interpersonal understanding*. New York: Academic Press, 1980.

Sharan, S., & Sharan, Y. *Small-group teaching*. Englewood Cliffs, N.J.: Educational Technology Publications, 1976.

Slavin, R. E. Cooperative learning in teams: State of the art. *Educational Psychologist*, 1980, *15*, 93–111.

Slavin, R. E. *Cooperative learning*. New York: Longman, 1983.

Solomon, D., & Kendall, A. J. *Children in classrooms: An investigation of person environment interaction*. New York: Praeger, 1979.

Solomon, D., Ali, F., Kfir, D., Houlihan, K., & Yaeger, J. The development of democratic values and behavior among Mexican-American children. *Child Development*, 1972, *43*, 625–638.

Spivak, G., & Shure, M. B. *Social adjustment of young children: A cognitive approach to solving real-life problems*. San Francisco: Jossey-Bass, 1974.

Staub, E. To rear a prosocial child: Reasoning, learning by doing, and learning by teaching others. In D. DePalma & J. Folley (Eds.), *Moral development: Current theory and research*. Hillsdale, N.J.: Erlbaum, 1975.

Staub, E. *Positive social behavior and morality: Social and personal influences* (Vol. 1). New York: Academic Press, 1978.

Staub, E. *Positive social behavior and morality: Socialization and development* (Vol. 2). New York: Academic Press, 1979.

Turiel, E. Developmental processes in children's moral thinking. In P. Mussen, J. Langer, & M. Covington (Eds.), *Trends and issues in developmental psychology*. San Francisco: Holt, Rinehart and Winston, 1969.

Yarrow, M. R., Scott, P. M., & Waxler, C. Z. Learning concern for others. *Developmental Psychology*, 1973, *8*, 240–260.

Youniss, J. *Parents and peers in social development: A Sullivan-Piaget perspective*. Chicago: University of Chicago Press, 1980.

Zahn-Waxler, C. Z., Radke-Yarrow, M. R., & King, R. A. Child rearing and children's prosocial initiations towards victims of distress. *Child Development*, 1979, *50*, 319–330.

15

Creating a Cooperative Learning Environment

An Ecological Approach

NANCY B. GRAVES

AND

THEODORE D. GRAVES

Introduction and Anthropological Background

We came to our interest in cooperative education as anthropologists, used to studying small societies as total systems. Consequently, when we began considering the process of socializing children to behave cooperatively, both in non-Western settings and in Western schools, we again did so from this holistic, anthropological perspective. We are of the opinion that learning in general, but particularly cooperative small-group learning, which involves coordination of effort with others, emerges out of the total social and physical environment within which the person is immersed. This "ecological" perspective guides our work in cooperative education, and in this chapter, we present a theoretical basis for this perspective and outline a program for implementing cooperative learning in a series of sequential steps within a restructured classroom context.

Our work in cooperative education grew out of years of studying the psychological and interpersonal changes that typically occur within non-Western societies under the impact of modernization. The communities we learned about and lived in all had variants of a subsistence agricultural economy that were beginning to change to a monetary base of cash-cropping and wage labor. Under the traditional social-economic system, it had been adaptive to work together cooperatively to share resources for common survival.

In the Cook Islands, for example, a group of men would typically

NANCY B. GRAVES AND THEODORE D. GRAVES • Consultants/Trainers in Cooperation, Creativity, and Change, 136 Liberty Street, Santa Cruz, California 95060.

cast a communal net, sharing the catch with everyone in the village. Gasoline outboard motors made individual fishing trips safer and more feasible, but a man was still apt to return home with far more fish than his family could consume before the fish spoiled. So he gave the surplus to his friends and relatives, knowing that tomorrow one of them would be sharing fresh fish with him. This process set up and reinforced bonds of reciprocity and interdependence that tied the entire community together. Under such conditions, social skills for cooperative work and conflict resolution evolve naturally: Your very livelihood depends on them. This is a perfect example of what the Johnsons call "positive interdependence," where everyone in the group sinks or swims together (Johnson & Johnson, 1975).

Then comes electricity, and those surplus fish get stored in the freezer rather than in one's neighbors' bellies. A cash economy comes and people begin "fishing in the stores." Bonds of reciprocity and mutual dependence break down; people can now afford to fight with their extended family and neighbors; social skills diminish through disuse. A typical Western school is introduced; and the children are taught that they must work on their own, that they must vie with others for the teacher's attention (behavior seldom allowed at home), and that helping their fellow students is "cheating." Eventually, if they work hard, they may win a scholarship and move to some urban center, where opportunities to "get ahead" are far greater than in the islands.

Through many seemingly unrelated avenues, the transition from a traditional interdependent community to an individualistic and highly competitive modern system gradually occurs, just as it has over the past 300 years in Western nations (cf. Merchant, 1980; Stone, 1975). In our research in the Cook Islands, for example, we were able to observe children even on the same island growing up in quite contrasting traditional and modern settings. We could then systematically record the differences in their prosocial behavior. Those raised in modern, nuclear households with formally educated, wage-earning parents were more egocentric and individualistic (as we in the West have come to expect to be typical of preschoolers) than those who were raised in traditional families with extended kin and who lived on the side of the island where most people still engaged in subsistence agriculture and fishing. The traditionally raised children were far more sociocentric, altruistic, cooperative, and socially responsible. (For the details of how these variables were measured see N. Graves & T. Graves, 1983.) From when these children entered school at age 5 or 6, up through Grade 3, the majority tested as generous and sharing on our measures, but by Grades 6 and 7, the majority were rivalrous and competitive. In addition, those adults, whose education, experience, occupation, and present family context were modern and Western, also displayed less prosocial behavior on our measures, and there were implications for their physical, social, and psychological health as well (N. Graves, 1978; N. Graves & T. Graves, 1978, 1979; T. Graves & N. Graves, 1976, 1979).[1]

These juxtapositions of old and new within the confines of a single island brought home to us the tremendous importance of environmental *context* in the development of prosocial behavior. We therefore came to the conclusion that the degree of cooperative behavior that emerges in a developing youngster depends on the "degree of fit" with the social and physical environment supporting and maintaining this behavior (N. Graves & T. Graves, 1983).

Thus, by an *ecological approach*, we refer to a systems model of learning in which cooperative behavior is an inextricable part of a total social context and arises spontaneously from interaction within the group.

An Ecological Perspective for a Program of Cooperative Learning

Drawing on these research findings and our own experience in introducing cooperative learning into ethnically mixed classrooms in New Zealand and California,[2] we have been refining a program of cooperative learning based on this ecological approach. We began by contrasting the contextual features of traditional cooperative village settings with those of a conventional Western classroom (Table 1).

Note the clear differences in the organization of physical space, in patterns of social interaction, and in the types of tasks, goals, and rewards that these two settings provide. Would it be possible, we asked ourselves, to develop *analogues* of these environmental features that

[1]The ethnographic research in the South Pacific that forms the immediate background for this demonstration project was funded by the Royal Society of New Zealand, the South Pacific Research Institute and the National Institute of Mental Health (Grant No. MH 30139-01-3). A year at the Center for Advanced Study in the Behavioral Sciences (1977–1978) provided the opportunity for us to begin to learn about the many classroom techniques for small-group cooperative learning that were already being developed.

[2]The current demonstration project, "Culture and Cooperation—Classroom Applications," is also being supported by NIMH, Grant No. PHS 5 R01 MH 30130. We are grateful to all these organizations for their past and continuing support. We also wish to express our appreciation to Professor David R. Thomas, Department of Psychology, University of Waikato, Hamilton, New Zealand, who currently directs the New Zealand phase of our study, for his stimulation and colleagueship over the last 10 years as our ideas for this project have jointly emerged.

TABLE 1. Comparison of Traditional Cooperative Settings and Conventional Western Classroom Settings

Contextual features	Conventional Western classroom	Traditional cooperative setting
I. Social structure		
A. Emotional bonds and group identity	A. No kin ties (even twins usually separated)	A. Kin-group membership creates strong emotional bonding beyond the nuclear family.
	No joint membership is emphasized; no group identity is emphasized.	Face-to-face interaction in cooperative activities in the village creates friendship bonds.
	The individual child is presumed to be the key unit, in school to gain knowledge and skills.	The children identify themselves first as members of their kin group, second as members of their village group.
	Children are expected to have a separate self-identity, or one connected to their nuclear family.	Many unrelated village members are well known even to young children because of their involvement in village activities.
	Emotional bonds are seen as irrelevant to the situation, except in terms of rapport between teacher and individual pupil.	
	Unless children have attended a neighborhood preschool from which the school draws, they may know no one as new entrants.	
B. Inclusiveness of group, range of personnel, roles	B. Usually only one adult; more frequently female than male; many strange, unrelated children	B. Household group consists of several adults in addition to the parents and many children.
	Community persons rarely visit the setting and have little range of role or function.	Other kin are nearby and are often involved in household activities. Children see a wide range of known, and usually related, people. Both sexes work close to home or family property. Children have many role models.
	Models are limited to teacher and principal.	

C. Distribution of authority and control	C. Centralized control in a single authority; rules applying to children, not to teachers Children are not expected to control or discipline other children. Children often do not share the school norms of appropriate behavior but acquiesce because they have no power. Self-regulation is related only to individual goals.	C. Diffuse, pervasive control: Many persons exercise control, and child is responsible for control over those younger than self. Shared norms of appropriate behavior. Shame over public misbehavior obviates need for much overt discipline. Group goals lead to self-regulation of behavior.
D. Social roles	D. Teacher: role of director, instructor, disciplinarian Pupil: role of learner, person disciplined, directed Teacher seldom participates in work activities of pupils. Children are seldom responsible for ongoing care of the classroom or planning the program. Children are segregated from younger children and have no supervisory duties	D. A variety of social roles: Child may be directed by others but also has opportunities to direct and nurture others. Multiplex roles for each person in various family, work and village groups Adults participate in the same tasks that they direct. Adult female caretakers are involved in basic subsistence work; children are needed to help with this work, with child care, and with home maintenance.
II. Goal and reward structure A. Group or individual	A. Individual rewards The pupils, and sometimes their nuclear families, reap the rewards of individual effort for personal goals.	A. Group rewards All achieve the benefit of group work, e.g., the meal, the improved home, the contented baby.

continued

TABLE 1. (*continued*)

Contextual features	Conventional Western classroom	Traditional cooperative setting
B. Intrinsic or extrinsic	B. Extrinsic rewards predominate. A calculated use of praise, attention, sometimes even affection promotes personal achievement. Mastery and sense of accomplishment are tied to approval and symbolic rewards such as grades. Children are doing what the teacher wants, rather than teaching themselves through observation and self-direction.	B. Intrinsic rewards predominate. Little manipulation of children with affection, praise, or special attention. Intrinsic reinforcement in being included in the group activity and in achieving a sense of mastery and accomplishment Children feel they taught themselves through observation, participation, and self- or other-child direction.
C. Monetary or "in-kind" rewards (wage labor or barter and exchange)	C. Children come from families in which work for monetary wages is the norm. Everything has a monetary value.	C. Children come from families where subsistence agriculture or fishing is the norm, and barter and exchange of goods and services is common.
III. Task structure and content A. Practical *vs.* academic tasks	A. Academic tasks Link to work in the "real world" is not always clear to the children. Their efforts are not seen as clearly needed by others, or as being of practical worth.	A. Practical tasks, i.e., "real" work where children's contributions are similar to those of adults and clearly needed for the welfare of the family or village
B. Concrete, tangible *vs.* abstract, ideational outcomes	B. Outcomes are abstract: ideational knowledge, eventually some sort of job far away in the future. Outcomes not always currently satisfying and relevant. Object relations are emphasized over human relations.	B. Outcomes visible, tangible: products, events, or the learning of interpersonal skills in group interaction Community recognition of concrete benefits to the group

IV. Physical environment

	Column 1	Column 2
A. Structure	Classroom space does not always include central area in which to congregate.	A. Villages have central meeting place or hall for communal gatherings and events.
B. Locational facilitation of face-to-face interaction	Separate individual desks and work spaces usually arranged so students face the teacher rather than each other.	B. Norms discourage high fences or plantings that cause privacy or isolation.
C. Sharing of material possessions	Each student has own equipment and separate books and materials for study.	C. Products from agriculture, sea, or forest shared among group. Personal possessions rare and few.
V. Social interaction style (competitive, individualistic, or cooperative)	Competitive or individualistic interaction favored over cooperation. Pupils pit themselves against performance of others or their own previous performance. Little coordination or accumulation of own with others' efforts; helping others in classroom is often seen as "cheating." Goals often mutually exclusive; concept of the "limited good" Teamwork is reserved for sports.	Cooperative interaction is common, with competition usually being between groups rather than between individuals. Cumulative or coordinated efforts toward a mutual goal; generosity and altruism toward group members; Considerable help from other children in common tasks Intragroup competition often takes the form of competing to give or do most for the group.

would be applicable in a modern classroom? To do so, we believed, would provide an ecologically more favorable setting for the introduction of cooperative small-group teaching methods. Too often, we have found, inadequate attention to preparing the contextual "soil" within which these methods are expected to take root has led to limited success. Cooperative methods introduced in isolation for one or two subjects during a small portion of the day seemed to lack social meaning for students. They may cooperate temporarily for the sake of external rewards or teacher approval, but it is questionable whether they would continue to cooperate if the contingencies and rewards promoting cooperative behavior were withdrawn, or if the children were faced with a new task and asked to structure it for themselves.

Western society has irretrievably lost many aspects of traditional life, and it would be naive to believe that these can be recaptured, even by analogy. Nor would this necessarily be desirable. But with 70% to 80% of jobs today requiring a complex coordination of efforts and ideas (Cohen, 1973; Naisbitt, 1982; Shallcrass, 1974), postindustrial society is already evolving, out of necessity, a synthesis of cooperative and individualistic approaches in education that will provide a more adaptive preparation for this new world of work than the highly competitive classroom.

Our most difficult task has been to get across to teachers and school staff the complete shift in perspective and attitude required for creating an environment supportive of cooperative learning. How can individual teachers build a total context that is basically cooperative and into which individualistic and competitive behavior can be incorporated? We are now suggesting that school personnel examine their program for consistency with five general guidelines characterizing an ecological approach.

First, teachers need to maintain a holistic rather than a piecemeal viewpoint: For each aspect of their day's activity they can ask themselves, "How does this fit with the atmosphere of a cooperative, helpful, supportive group that I am trying to promote? Or am I giving my students mixed messages?" For example, sports are one of the most competitive arenas in schools today. Many thoughtful physical education teachers are seeking ways to change the competitive aspects of sports or to mitigate their deleterious effects (Orlick, 1977, 1978, 1982; Sobel, 1983; Weinstein & Goodman, 1980). Teachers are considering whether the fun and excitement of such activities could be achieved in other ways.

Another way to make competition and individualism "fit" a cooperative environment, however, is to "reframe" (Watzlawick, Weakland, & Fisch, 1974) these behaviors within a basically cooperative context. Competitive motivations, such as striving for mastery and individual excellence as compared with others, can be reframed to change the conceptual or emotional viewpoint from which they are experienced. For example, children can be directed to consider how their talents can maximally contribute to the welfare and the success of the group as a whole. This change of viewpoint then changes all the associated experiences as well.

Second, teachers can expand the meaning of cooperation of students to include the wider settings of which they are a part. Children need to recognize that they can cooperate within a small group to complete an assignment, within the classroom to produce a play for an assembly, and within the school as a whole to put on a fiesta. They and their parents can cooperate on family projects or participate in neighborhood cleanups. Eventually, the children will want to learn what cooperation means on a state, national, or international level. The more we can expand the meaning of cooperation for students to include the wider settings of which they are a part, the more they will see how their cooperative skills are being developed in all these settings, as well as the relevance of this behavior to their lives. Thus, small groups do not operate independently of the connections that group members have to larger entities. They are like extended families within the clan of the entire class, which is part of a tribe, the school.

Third, because settings within the wider environment are related or are "nested" one within the other (Bronfenbrenner, 1979), something occurring on the playground or in the neighborhood will inevitably affect cooperative processes in the classroom. In a complex modern society, we are unable to produce the totally enveloping cooperative environment common to many traditional societies. But teachers can enlist a wider network of school staff members, parents, and community leaders in support of their efforts, making clear to them the ways in which they can contribute to the development of more prosocial behavior among students. The child development project described in the previous chapter involved teachers and administrators, parents, and community leaders in the planning and implementation of the cooperative program from the beginning. Students, too, can be asked how they experience the program, and in this way, teachers will learn what kinds of encounters children have that either facilitate or inhibit cooperative development.[3] This policy of incorporating as many different persons as

---

[3]Bronfenbrenner (1979) also noted that the practice of checking students' views and experience of classroom interventions provides the added advantage of "ecological validity" for a research design.

possible from different settings within which students are involved acknowledges that cooperative learning is not just a simple linear process but involves *reciprocal causation*, whereby everyone in contact with the students is affected and, in turn, affects the development of cooperation between the students.

Fourth, cooperation requires that more attention be paid to the *process* of interaction than does an individualistic or competitive activity. In a traditionally cooperative environment, an understanding of "how what *I* do affects *you*" is learned implicitly over a long time period. When we are seeking to *change* an environment to make it more cooperative, and when we have limited time, these interpersonal processes need to be made explicit. Furthermore, because parents and teachers have input into only a limited portion of their children's experiences, the relationship between these experiences and the desired cooperative learning needs to be emphasized and strengthened. This can be done most effectively not by preaching, but by helping students to arrive at the insight for themselves. In our workshops, we have taught teachers a discussion process that involves three stages: *identification* of the significant aspects of the situation that caused success or failure, *analysis* of those aspects in terms of how individuals experienced them and what their similarity is to previous experiences; and *generalization* to situations in the future, including possible changes to effect a better outcome (referred to as the "IAG" technique). For example, if one student puts down another in a discussion group, both can be helped later to recognize how that putdown interfered with the group's success in achieving their common goal and contributed to a growing animosity between them. Is that what they want to do in the future? In traditional environments, communication skills are seldom made explicit, but perhaps this may also make these societies more vulnerable to the disruptive changes of modernization.

Fifth, because we are attempting to create a cooperative social order in the classroom, where previously there were often only the most rudimentary structures for any kind of student interaction, we need to realize that the change process will be slow. It is necessary to have a *developmental perspective* that allows the most elementary building blocks of cooperative interaction to be practiced before more complex coordination efforts are attempted. How many of us can remember the Dewey-inspired projects in our own elementary years, in which one or two bright students did most of the work and perhaps resented it? In other cases, students did develop a cooperative interaction, but it was a haphazard process. Our teachers did not seem to know how to structure interaction for optimal results. Nor did they show us the interpersonal skills we needed, such as active and passive listening, modeling, tutoring, and conflict resolution techniques. Yet, they expected us to coordinate both goals and means, as well as our diverse personalities and their associated behavior patterns, to turn out a well-integrated final product. No wonder it is often assumed that committees will produce horses that look like camels!

Ideally, staff and teachers would learn the perspective and skills needed for cooperation by experiencing it themselves in a series of settings and situations, either by prolonged or repeated training sessions or by increased organizational development within the school system (Schmuck & Runkel, 1984). It is difficult for teachers to examine their customary classroom procedures in terms of optimal fit with a cooperative environment if they do not have in their background a model of an environment that says it is safe to be open, generous, helpful, friendly, supportive and unified with others in the classroom. Teachers also need to learn how to observe and be aware of how students are progressing in their development of cooperative behavior before demanding more than the students can handle. Negative experiences hinder the further growth of cooperative attitudes and behavior. On the other hand, teachers should be encouraged to be optimistic about all children's capability of learning cooperate, given a supportive and accepting environment and patience on the teacher's part.

To summarize, we see five general principles of an ecological approach to cooperative learning in a modern, complex society: (1) creating a holistic rather than a piecemeal viewpoint, that incorporates individualistic or competitive activities within a cooperative framework; (2) placing cooperative classroom activities within the larger system of which the class is a part; (3) enlisting a wide network of participants to contribute actively to students' prosocial development; (4) making more explicit the interpersonal processes among students; and (5) being patient, realizing that, with a sequence of well-structured learning experiences, change will proceed in stages.

STRUCTURING A COOPERATIVE LEARNING ENVIRONMENT

As we saw in Table 1, the structural features of natural cooperative environments as described in cross-cultural research (Ember, 1973; N. Graves & T. Graves, 1978, 1983; Munroe & Munroe, 1975, 1977; Ritchie & Ritchie, 1979; Weisner & Gallimore, 1977; B. Whiting & Edwards, 1973, B. Whiting & J. Whiting, 1971, 1975; J. Whiting & B. Whiting, 1973) contrast in every major respect with those of the conventional Western classroom. Although our description may not fit some modern, more humanistically oriented classrooms, there is considerable research evidence from other investigators that the features listed are the general norm (Aronson, Blaney, Stephan, Sikes, & Snapp, 1978; Gallimore, Boggs, & Jordan, 1974; N. Graves, 1975; N. Graves & T. Graves, 1978; Howard, 1973; Katz, 1971; Kirschenbaum, Simon, & Napier, 1971; McDonald & Gallimore, 1971; Sarason, 1971). To make the cooperative behavior that we wish children to learn both meaningful and consistently motivating, we must shift as many of these environmental parameters as possible.

Table 2 briefly illustrates how relevant contextual features gleaned from cross-cultural studies can be translated into *principles* of cooperative learning, which can then be implemented in a variety of ways in the classroom. As long as the principles are understood, especially from the perspective of direct experience in a group situation, the precise *content* of the implementation is limited only by the imagination of the practitioners involved. Once the framework is set for them, the students, too, turn out to be endlessly inventive in developing ways to expressing group identity, evolving and sharing roles, planning group goals, and so on. However, when teachers pay only lip service to the contextual principles and simply operate in terms of techniques, we have found that they often create double-bind situations for their students by undermining the cooperative process with old patterns of competition or individualism. Then, it is easier for the students to revert to the familiar habits of pleasing the teacher, competing for attention or grades, or dropping out of interaction.

We have called this process of restructuring the classroom environment *ground laying,* using the metaphor of preparing a garden by mulching, fertilizing, putting in good soil, and choosing the site carefully for the proper mixture of sunlight and shade. The first seeds are sown for cooperative interaction in this stage. It involves the entire class and pays particular attention to the integration of individuals into a meaningful whole.

The use of the principles laid down in Table 2 does not stop with the initial ground laying when students enter. It must continue throughout the school year, even as increasingly complex levels of coordinated academic effort are introduced. For those of us raised in an individualistic environment, the easiest thing is to ignore one another and proceed alone. For those trained to compete, the tendency for learning teams is to degenerate into small cliques or factions, which can destroy harmony within the class as a whole. It requires daily repetition of the concept of the class as a total social unit with interconnected behavior to avoid these pitfalls when small-group work is introduced. Furthermore, we suggest refraining from establishing long-term learning teams until a wider sense of group cohesiveness has developed within the class as a whole. Students can shift between groups of varying sizes and composition throughout the day until they have come to know all the class members and to feel comfortable working with almost anyone. In this way, they also discover different aspects of themselves through interaction within changing interpersonal environments. Like the Cook Islanders whom we observed, they develop multiplex roles and relationships and the ability to shift among these freely, as is appropriate to the situation.

As we discuss the specific principles outlined in Table 2, we remind the reader that we are taking a *systems* approach. Not every principle utilized here is unique to cooperative environments. Nor is every principle linked to certain specific outcomes in a unilinear causal connection. Rather, each principle affects a variety of outcomes conductive to cooperative behavior, and it is basically the *interaction* of these principles operating within the total system that promotes or facilitates cooperation. Perhaps, future research under more controlled conditions will isolate which factors have a more pervasive or potent effect on which outcomes. A truly cooperative classroom, we have observed, is like a gourmet dish created by a great chef. We cannot specify which ingredient produces our feeling of satisfaction and delight, mainly because it is the exemplary *blend* of ingredients that gives the superb effect, and one that develops at the dish simmers over a period of time.[4]

The cornerstone of any anthropological community study is an investigation of the group's *social structure*: What are the social components of this society, how are they organized, what roles and functions are important, and how do they articulate with one another?

Any social unit studied by an anthropologist usually has a clear sense of being an entity, and its members have an identity with it. In fact, one of the signs that a society is breaking down is that its members cease to identify with it and seek other reference groups. Yet, students in the modern classroom often fail to see their class as a unit, an entity

---

[4]We wish to thank the teachers and the administrative staffs who worked with us at the following schools for their inspiration and for examples of many of the illustrations of Level 1 principles cited here: Alianza Elementary School, Watsonville, California; Sylvia Cassell Elementary School, Alum Rock, San Jose, California; Bernard Ferguson Primary School and Ngaruawahia Primary School, Ngaruawahia, New Zealand; and Melville Primary School, Hamilton, New Zealand. We also greatly appreciate the help of the teachers who explored Levels 2 and 3 in small-group work at Calabasas Elementary School, Watsonville, California, and at Goss Elementary School, Alum Rock, San Jose, California, and Richmond Park and Hamilton West Primary School, Hamilton, New Zealand.

TABLE 2. Principles for Structuring a Cooperative Learning Environment (Level 1—Ground Laying)

Contextual features of the traditional environment	Cooperative learning principles	Implementation in the classroom
I. Social structure		
A. Close emotional bonds: Kinship or community membership	Principle 1 = group identity: Establishing a whole-group entity, whole-class cohesion, emotional ties, group unity	Bonding achieved through a. Getting acquainted activities b. Creating and adapting whole-group symbols c. Developing events that create unity experiences for the class
B. Inclusion of wide variety of personnel, roles, and personality types	Principle 2 = inclusiveness: Recognizing, valuing, and incorporating individual diversity into the whole with as little distortion of uniqueness as possible	Individuality incorporated by a. Celebrating the contribution of individual differences to the whole b. Providing occasions for learning and understanding students' family and cultural background c. Incorporating different ages and persons from the community into the classroom to provide a variety of experience and multiple role models
C. Distribution of authority and control Diffuse, pervasive control operated by many persons at many levels, shared norms, group action	Principle 3 = group norms and shared authority: Establishing a broader system of control involving more persons within and outside the classroom, dispersion of authority among students, joint institution of group norms and control procedures, directing others and learning how to be directed	Directing and following skills achieved by a. Class participation in establishing norms for cooperative interaction in the classroom, school, and community b. Opportunity for discussion and settlement of infringement of norms, or conflict situations c. Practice in organizing and directing others, beginning with younger children d. Practice with communication and conflict-management skills

D. Social roles

Multiplex, changing, whole-group participation

Principle 4 = shared responsibility for role performance; joint establishment and participation in the work load of the classroom; roles and functions for everyone; rotation of roles

Responsibility learned through

a. teacher's and students' cooperatively establishing roles and functions needed in the classroom

b. students setting up a rotating system so that all learn to participate

c. distinguishing between ongoing roles for daily routines and special roles for events—balance participation

d. taking advantage of special events to give individual talents recognition and acknowledgment

e. teacher's occasionally participating in chores alongside students

II. Goal and reward structure

A. Group goals and rewards more common than individual goals and rewards

Principle 5 = group goals and rewards: Demonstrating how everyone benefits from working together for common goals

Group goals incorporated by

a. relating goals of individuals to the goals of the group—be sure these do not conflict

b. discussing how each person contributes to and benefits from group goals—clarifying actions

c. leading students to select group goals that are meaningful to them

d. regularly following through with group goals, and rewards

e. involving parents and community members in setting wider group goals for students in neighborhood and at home

continued

TABLE 2. (continued)

Contextual features of the traditional environment	Cooperative learning principles	Implementation in the classroom
B. Intrinsic rewards More frequent than extrinsic rewards	Principle 6 = intrinsic rewards for learning: Developing pleasure from rewards inherent in the activity; clarifying the features of the activity that provide their own reward	Intrinsic rewards incorporated by a. avoiding external rewards and incentives as much as possible (e.g., stars and grades) b. establishing the importance of each activity as pleasurable in itself c. making explicit the fun and interest inherent in working as a group d. discussing the communication and empathic skills needed to make group work more fun e. spending time afterward in celebrating what students enjoyed about an activity, what they taught themselves in the process
C. Barter and exchange More common than monetary requirements	Principle 7 = exchanging talents, skills, and services: Learning what each has that may be of value to someone else	Exchange stimulated by a. having times set aside or special events where exchange and barter of physical objects and possessions are encouraged (Tom Sawyer style) b. discussing how one knows what other people like, want, or need c. setting up a service exchange in the classroom where students can contribute what they are good at and receive a service they would like (e.g., math tutoring for spelling drill)

	d. having students with special skills or talents teach that skill to the rest of the class or to selected students
	e. highlighting special attributes, experience, or knowledge of each member of the class so that students learn about what others have to contribute
III. Task structure and content Practical rather than academic; concrete, tangible rather than abstract, ideational	
Principle 8 = practical, relevant tasks: finding practical tasks on which to practice cooperative skills; making academic tasks as obviously practical and relevant as possible	Practical tasks incorporated by a. making "household chores" of the classroom occasions for cooperative effort b. emphasizing the cooperative nature of parties, field trips, special events c. tying cooperative efforts to group goals and needs; emphasizing relevance d. incorporating neighborhood, home, and community practical and relevant tasks into the class schedule as opportunities to learn cooperative skills e. giving practical, concrete outcomes importance through public recognition and acknowledgment of efforts f. teaching basic skills through applying them to relevant tasks for group goals, e.g., earning for classroom equipment, or cooking for parties
IV. Structure of the physical environment Physical location facilitates face-to-face interaction Few material possessions Sharing in scarcity and overabundance	
Principle 9 = an interactive physical environment: Restructuring space and material objects to promote cooperative interaction; sharing materials, equipment	Changing the environment by a. arranging work spaces to suit the nature of the task: huddled for highly interactive tasks, spaced wider for individual concentration

continued

TABLE 2. (*continued*)

Contextual features of the traditional environment	Cooperative learning principles	Implementation in the classroom
		b. gathering the class together closely in one group for class meetings, discussions, and planning sessions
		c. having students work out systems for sharing scarce materials and providing only the minimum necessary so as to encourage sharing
		d. providing central places for keeping shared materials within easy access to all students
V. Social interaction style: Cooperation Cumulative, coordinative, and creative more often than competitive or individualistic	Principle 10 = cooperative interaction: Establishing connections between individual members in their joint efforts	Connectiveness learned through a. practicing appropriate interpersonal skills that encourage rather than put down others
		b. incorporating experience with different types of cooperation: accumulation of individual efforts, coordination of joint efforts
		c. discussing the different types of cooperative effort and when each is appropriate; recognizing that coordination takes more complex skills
		d. placing competitive behavior in an overall context that is cooperative—"reframing" competition
		e. using intergroup competition only when cooperative patterns are well established

with a life of its own, even though it does evolve, willy-nilly, through the interaction of its members over the school year. Because a classroom does not have the emotional basis for unity and cohesion provided by kinship or community ties, particularly where children come to school from distant neighborhoods, teachers need to establish as quickly as possible a basis for class identity and bonding (Principle 1) that will serve as a foundation for coordinated class efforts.

Bonding can be promoted both by establishing reasons for cohesion that are based on common characteristics of the children regardless of background differences, and by having them experience activities or events that become part of the common memory of the entire class. These attributes and events can then be refreshed periodically by the use of memory repositories such as bulletin boards or scrapbooks, or by using class symbols, songs, or mottoes.

The successful implementation of Principle 1, however, is strongly tied to the implementation of Principle 2, inclusiveness. Students will show less interest in common bonding if they feel that their individual characteristics are denigrated, ignored, or downplayed. So, this bonding must recognize and value the *variety* found in the classroom as well. At the same time that the common characteristics of everyone are made explicit, a corresponding attempt must be made to highlight and value the unique contributions of individuals related to their talents, their ethnicity, their gender, their religion, their neighborhood, and their background experiences. One teacher incorporated both principles in developing a class shield. The students first drew pictures of their favorite activities and combined four of these on an individual shield. The class then got together to categorize the activities and to discover those that they held in common. These were combined creatively into a shield for the entire group. A T-shirt for each child with his or her own design on one side and the class design on the other became the next step.

A further development of the inclusiveness principle, which fits the ecological guideline of expanding cooperation beyond a single setting, is to incorporate a variety of persons into varying roles within the classroom, and to take students out of the classroom to work with other children in the school and persons in the community. Although this is often done in the name of enriching the environment for disadvantaged children, we think it has a more important effect in promoting cooperative behavior. Through coming in contact with a wide variety of teaching and learning styles, personalities, skills, and subject content, students learn to integrate disparate parts into a whole and to recognize that there are a variety of solutions to any problem. Like the Aitutaki child who has multiple caretakers and joins with adults and other children in village events and work parties, the students in a class that provides many role models develop flexibility, communication skills, and tolerance of differences. They become motivated to learn better ways of coordinating their behavior with that of others, as well as a sensitivity to others' styles, moods, and needs. They are also open to practicing group problem-solving, decision-making, and conflict resolution.

In a bilingual magnet school with which we have been associated, the students have the opportunity each Friday afternoon to pick a teacher other than their own and to enjoy learning something that is that teacher's speciality, such as embroidery, math puzzles, pottery, word games, and other academic or nonacademic activities. In addition, the older students also went to a science teacher with pupils from other classes, had a separate physical education teacher, spent daily lessons in second-language learning with a group different from their classroom group, tutored younger students from lower grades, learned art from local artists, and related to classroom aids and parent volunteers throughout the year. Because their homeroom was still the focus of the majority of their time and activities, and their teachers worked to establish a strong sense of class identity, the teachers whom we interviewed did not feel that these contacts reduced the effectiveness of their relationship to their own students. In fact, these experiences seemed to make the students easier to work with and more willing to be tolerant of one another. It became apparent that social ties were successfully being established throughout the school when the students asked us during the administration of a sociometric measure if they might include friends from other classes.

An important aspect of social structure for the anthropological investigator is the way in which authority and control are distributed: vertically, as in the typical bureaucratic pyramid, or horizontally, as in acephalic network societies, which have become the model for many modern corporate structures. In the latter form of social organization, authority and control are decentralized and are kept as close to those engaged in primary production activities as possible, as in the case of "quality circles."

Although centralization of authority is always a matter of degree the most cooperative social groupings appear to be those in which authority is diffused and shared as much as possible. The word *cooperation* has two meanings for many of us: "Why won't you cooperate with me?" (i.e., obey me and willingly do what I say) or "Let's cooperate to get this job done" (i.e., work together as a team). Learning to coordinate efforts appears to take place best in a relatively less hierarchical setting, and teachers in a "cooperative classroom" find themselves increasingly delegating their authority to the students themselves as they gain in group skills.

Principle 3, group norms and shared authority, assumes that the more opportunities students have to develop rules and norms of appropriate behavior, to be involved in the running of operations in the classroom and the school, and to practice both leadership and membership skills, the more likely they are to feel responsibility to the group for the consequences of their behavior and the outcome of events. Success in a small work group depends on both individual accountability and having the skill to involve other members. Simply manipulating the reward structure will not guarantee that students will understand how to be good group members or leaders or will be motivated to participate fully. During the ground laying stage, they can gain experience through contributing ideas for class rules and norms, adjusting these when they appear not to be working, developing systems or negotiation and sanctions for flagrant violations, organizing groups of younger children in simple tasks, serving on committees that mediate disputes, organizing playground standards, and participating in many other such activities. When small study groups are organized, they are quite prepared to make a list of how they believe they should act to further group goals. Without such whole-class experience, we have found that children either need extensive training in such skills or adopt a laissez-faire attitude that gradually undercuts productive effort.

Again, teachers have the most success when they continually make it clear to their students that it is *their* responsibility to create a pleasant and supportive working or play environment for each other, while guiding them in efforts to systematically bring this about without simply laying down the rules from an adult perspective. Out of experiences of failure, the children learn most effectively about the need for self-control. As in all aspects of teaching cooperative interdependence, it is useful to guide students through a review of their process, helping them to *identify* the relevant aspects of their experience, to *analyze* how these contributed to their success or failure, and to *generalize* from past to future situations. When teachers first attempt to help students become aware of their interpersonal processes, there is always some self-consciousness and awkwardness. But soon the students learn to apply these techniques for themselves. The students in one elementary school that we know of typically work out their own disputes without adult intervention. For example, they confronted a child displaying exclusive behavior (identifying), found out that he felt a need to do this because of the disruptive behavior of another child (analyzing), and then helpfully offered the disruptive child the option of being alone for a while

("Maybe you just need some space?") until he felt ready to return to the group on a nondisruptive basis.[5]

A fourth important aspect of any group's social structure involves the type and distribution of social roles. In modern societies, our role relationships are often isolated from each other: we are rarely teacher, friend, and co-worker to the same person. Non-Western, cooperative societies, however, frequently display these "multiplex" role relationships. Furthermore, one group member may be the leader in one situation and another the leader in the next, as when an Indian tribe has one chief for war and another for peace.

This shifting of roles appears to facilitate a shared responsibility for role performance (Principle 4), by allowing children both to observe and to practice a variety of role relationships in the same setting. Sharing roles contributes not only to the acquisition of more social skills, but also to an experiential understanding of others' problems and feelings when they are acting in various capacities.[6] Nothing produces more empathy among students for the problems of being a teacher than personal experience in teaching others.

We therefore urge that students be involved in deciding what classroom roles are needed, that these roles be as widely distributed within the class as possible, and that they be rotated frequently by some student-derived system conceived to be fair. Many teachers assign class roles such as monitor, student council representative, or window raiser, whereas others rely on volunteers. This practice has the disadvantage of preparing some children more than others for group responsibility, and their lack of preparation is then reflected in small-group work. Because many children resent working on some chores alone, some teachers have had success in setting aside a general work time when the whole class cleans up without specific roles, and in saving these for sporadic tasks spread throughout the day. Another solution is pairing students to do a task together. Then, they learn to take joint responsibility for its outcome. Finally, a profound motivator is teachers' "pitching in" as part of the group in communal tasks. Such participation echoes the cross-age work groups and participative leadership style found in cooperative communities. Caretaking and supervising younger students, again, contribute to responsible role performance.

---

[5]Thanks to Serena, a teacher at a school near Laytonville, California, for this graphic example of the cooperative group problem-solving of an interpersonal conflict.

[6]"Perspective taking" has been shown empirically to contribute to cooperative behavior (Aronson & Bridgeman, 1979; Bridgeman, 1977), although evidence of the contribution of "empathy" is less clear.

After examining the social structure, a second important focus is distributing goals and rewards. In most cooperative societies, we find many *group goals* around which individual efforts must be coordinated: casting a communal fishing net, putting on a communal feast, or preparing the soil in each others' garden plots. The rewards of these activities are usually relevant to the whole group and arise in large part out of the pleasure of working together. Achieving a high degree of excellence, as in a dance performance, is another common form of *intrinsic reward*. Finally, in these societies, people are bound together by networks of *exchange*: I work in your garden plot, and the day ends with beer and a feast for all of us who helped. Then, tomorrow, you will expect to join me in helping someone else prepare his or her plot, and so on.

From these observations, we derived Principles 5–7. Group goals and rewards enhance cooperation in a number of ways. Students who are rewarded when the *group* achieves its goal are motivated to work harder for the group and to help each other because the group incorporates their personal benefit (Principle 5). Merely to be included in the group, furthermore, constitutes an intrinsic reward. Most students go to school as much to be with their friends as to learn their lessons. Additional intrinsic rewards include the lightening of the labor among many helping heads and hands, the fun of social interaction along with the work, and the self-esteem that comes from mastery when one knows that one's skill is valued by others (Principle 6).

Within any work group, as within the society as a whole, there is a diversity of talents and expertise, so that an exchange takes place that enhances each participant, turns out a more complete end-product, and sensitizes the participants to the needs of one another. If I wish to barter or exchange something that I own for something of yours, I must understand what will be of value to you, whereas an exchange that involves monetary compensation means that I need to know nothing about you. Such interpersonal sensitivity in exchange helps to equalize status among participants and creates an atmosphere in which all feel valued and thus are motivated to contribute. Teachers can promote this atmosphere by helping children to intuit what others like, want, and need; by providing opportunities for the barter of material objects and, later, ideas and services; and by stressing the intrinsic pleasure of engaging in such exchanges (Principle 7).

In most cooperative societies, the bulk of daily activity revolves around practical tasks (collecting and preparing food, clothing, and shelter) or engaging in social activities (visiting, gossiping, singing, and feasting). In Western schools, the emphasis on abstract thinking probably makes it more difficult for children to learn cooperative social skills and group decision-making and problem-solving. Initially, students can learn to cooperate while performing routine classroom chores and such concrete tasks as decorating the classroom, landscaping the school, and planning and conducting fund-raising events, parties, trips, or assembly entertainments (Principle 8). They will increasingly use these skills in academic tasks as teachers make the subject matter as practical and relevant to the children's current life and interests as possible. For example, students can compose and write or dictate stories, which they later read to younger children at "story time." They can dictate daily journals on what is important to them and share from these in small groups (Landor, 1982). They can write letters both individually and as a class to public officials on issues about which they are concerned, use math skills to increase recipe measurements to provide enough for a class party, or calculate the costs of buying a piece of equipment for the classroom. When it comes to practicing routines such as multiplication tables or spelling rules, they will see these as comparable to routine domestic tasks, such as helping each other with washing the dishes. As they grow in communicative and social ability, as well as in their capacity to handle more complex cognitive materials, they can develop group projects that require more integrative, creative thinking and more sophisticated organizational skills.

Anthropologists typically begin their study of a social group by mapping its territory and showing how settlement patterns and the layout of homes influence social interaction. The available material resources and other aspects of the physical environment are also important in promoting or inhibiting cooperation.

Educators have already paid a great deal of attention to the way in which teachers structure the physical environment of the classroom and its effects on children's learning behavior. Principle 9 urges that these efforts be self-consciously applied to the development of an *interactive* physical environment. The way in which physical and social variables influence each other is important to understand. An example from our early days of consulting work may illustrate: A teacher had arranged her class in groups of six with individual desks facing inward in small clusters throughout the room. She was dismayed at the level of "noise" thus generated, in the form of conversations between students, and instituted many punitive rules against talking. We pointed out that she was giving double messages by placing the desks so that the arrangement encouraged discussion, and we suggested she might guide her students to develop norms for when they should talk for purposes of cooperative group work, when they should keep silent for wider class discussion in turns, or when they should listen to the teacher (using Principle 3). Imagine our dismay when next we visited her class to find all the students' desks arranged conventionally in long, straight rows! The teacher told us that the students had chosen this organization themselves. We later asked members of the class why they preferred their desks in this arrangement. One boy said, all too candidly, "She didn't want us in circles anymore and said we could have them this way or in rows slanting out from her desk like rays of the sun. We didn't want *her* being the sun!" Here, the teacher limited the alternatives available because she did not feel capable of developing in the students the group responsibility for monitoring their own interaction and wanted an arrangement that would increase her own control.

Face-to-face interaction is maximally facilitative for cooperative work, yet some teachers may not feel that they or their students are ready for this approach until communicative and social skills are more fully developed. In this case, Poirier's (1970) solution of "huddles," or moving desks or students together during cooperative work sessions only, may be preferred. With additional ground laying in the social aspects of cooperative learning, students may be able to handle free movement throughout the classroom, and teachers can also accustom themselves to distinguishing busy, productive noise in working groups from disruptive social interaction. Even in the best of circumstances, however, the classroom will be more alive with talk than one restricted to individualized learning.

Another aspect of the physical environment is the classroom materials and equipment. We noticed that in traditional settings where the homes had few possessions, of easily replaceable materials, there was far more generosity and sharing than in more modern homes with breakable china, fancy bedspreads, and personal toilet articles for each family member. When restructuring a school environment to encourage sharing and turn taking, it may be useful to take into account the effect of scarcity. Disputes over scarce materials can then be used to highlight discussions (using the IAG technique) of ways to structure interaction so that everyone has a turn, or to introduce the principles of division of labor. For special or expensive pieces of equipment that can be used only one at a time (such as computers or typewriters), student committees can work out time-sharing techniques, sign-up sheets, and so on. Again, practice in social skills and in making explicit the interpersonal issues involved is essential to making the interaction cooperative.

In addition, natural, replaceable materials can be used to promote a sense of participation and ownership among students. Students can decorate the room with shells, leaves, and plants. Older children can make their own class curtains and drinking cups, build storage shelves, or decorate with class murals. Often the natural environment of the school itself can be enhanced by student landscaping, gardening, raking, and leveling of play areas. By paying outsiders for many of these services, we deprive students of a sense of ownership and belonging in their environment as well as of many opportunities for cooperative interaction.

A school in rural New Zealand with 90% Maori children and a negative community image changed this image completely when it gained a Maori woman principal. She began by enlisting the children—and ultimately the community—in radically changing the entire *physical environment* within which they worked, using this change as a basis for establishing a strong total-group identity. For example, she involved both students and teachers in devising a school emblem. This was prominently displayed as a flag on a carved pole depicting Maori ancestors, in the central courtyard. Students and staff further beautified the yard by painting benches and play areas with bright colors, planting a rose garden, and painting murals on the walls of facing buildings that incorporated the natural environment by representing native trees and birds. The school then began holding ceremonies in this central, unified area to which parents, community members, and the founder's son were invited. Not only was cooperation engendered among staff and students, but parents and other community members began taking an interest in the school, and they contributed considerable time and money to its projects and its ongoing needs. Student attendance and study habits improved and vandalism ceased. Former students began to drop in after high school to help with recreation programs and service projects. The school was on its way to becoming a hub of activity in the community.

This example illustrates a major point that we wish to make clear: It is the *integration* of the principles of cooperative environments that is important, rather than the effect of any one principle or specific activity alone. Beautifying a school could make it a more formal, less comfortable place for community members, parents, and the students themselves. School assemblies are often more boring than unifying for the student body. Intrinsic motivation to be "one up" on another person could result in competition rather than cooperation. We have attempted to give a holistic picture of what an environment supportive to cooperation can be, and it is this whole that must serve as the model for a program of cooperative learning.

All of the preceding nine principles contribute to the development of cooperative interaction among students. In turn, because we are dealing with a total system, cooperative behavior by some will both provide role models for others and contribute to and reinforce aspects of the restructured cooperative-learning environment. In other words, a "cooperative interaction style" becomes part of a social environment that fosters cooperation in others (Principle 10).

Cooperative interaction can take three major forms: cumulative, coordinative, and creative. During the ground-laying stage, children can be introduced to the first two forms, and the third will occasionally emerge spontaneously in their play. It is easier for young children, or those with little experience in cooperation, to accumulate individual efforts to make a whole. For example, each child can contribute a separate monster drawing, and these can be combined by collage into a long mural. Later, the children may be able to jointly create a monster world, agree on what is to be in it, and then draw or paint the mural as a group. The latter activity requires more communication as well as cognitive skills such as integration of ideas, turn taking, and group decision-making. By the time the group graduates to academic tasks that involve more cognitively complex subject matter, they will have developed their social and communicative skills.

FOSTERING GROWTH IN COOPERATIVE SKILLS

We now come to a discussion of the order in which cooperative methods are introduced into a school, and to the specific cooperative skills associated with each. In Table 3, we have outlined a sequence of increasingly complex cooperative-learning activities on the left, and the interpersonal and cognitive skills that seem to be associated with them on the right. Level 1, ground laying, and Level 2, team building, teach similar skills and attitudes at, respectively, the whole-class and the small-group levels. As noted earlier, Level 1 activities continue through the entire school year and extend beyond the classroom and even the school. Level 2 activities may consist, particularly at the beginning, of subgroups of the whole working on particular class problems of organization, fund raising, enforcing of norms, and so on. However, when teachers feel their students are ready, they may wish to introduce exercises or games suitable to small groups rather than the whole class (such as Bavelas Five-Squares, communication exercises, and cooperative math puzzles), aimed at enhancing particular cooperative skills on

TABLE 3. Fostering Growth in Cooperative Skills

Types of cooperative learning activity	Cognitive and social skills learned
Level 1: Laying the Groundwork (Total class cohesion) Nonacademic games, activities, and events that integrate diverse individuals and promote identification with total class Establishing roles, functions, and group norms of appropriate cooperative behavior Introducing intrinsic and group rewards Integrating class with school and community	*Levels 1 and 2* Paying attention, listening, following instructions Being aware of needs of others Trusting others Accepting and valuing individual differences Taking turns and sharing Helping skills: how to ask, accept, reject, help nicely Speaking nicely to each other, making suggestions Communicating feelings Taking responsibility for own and others' behavior Coordinating efforts toward a common goal Monitoring group process
Level 2: Team Building (Small-group activities) Student committees or task forces dealing with classroom organization and functioning within the whole Short-term nonacademic activities and games for practicing team skills. These are more highly structured, with rules set by teacher. Subsequent discussion to identify, analyze, and generalize experiences	
Level 3: Simple teamwork (Aggregated individual effort) All team members working on same topic Dyadic tutoring and drill Individual evalaution with improvement of own record and/or intergroup competition Team rewards and acknowledgement	*Level 3* Simple group organization Interrogation skills Checking skills Tutoring skills, explanation, giving help when needed Communication skills: listen, paraphrase, reflect, support and encourage, verbal, nonverbal
Level 4: Coordinated Teamwork (Specialization, integration within small groups) Each team member assigned different parts of topic "Expert" groups formed from representatives of each team, studying same part of topic together Team members reconvene and teach each other their parts Individual or team evaluation	*Level 4* Complex role organization within teams Division of labor Teaching skills Interviewing skills Summarizing Synthesis of parts into whole

continued

Table 3. (continued)

Types of cooperative learning activity	Cognitive and social skills learned
Level 5: Group research and investigation (Specialization, integration within both small groups and total class) Class divides topics amongst study groups Study groups formulate researchable problem Division of labor within study groups Group product as an emergent Group members evaluate own and others' work	Level 5 Planning and developing own curriculum Developing and readjusting a personal perspective of the content area More complex decision-making and problem-solving Critical evaluation of own and group members' work
Level 6: Group creativity (Process determines product) Creative group problem-solving Discovery, invention, theory generation Creation of new paradigms	Level 6 Advanced divergent thinking Tolerance of ambiguity Suspension of judgment/premature closure Use of metaphor and analogy

which students need more practice. At first, these may have little academic content, but as interpersonal skills build, more learning games with specific course content can be introduced.

At the early stages, teachers will be careful to make it possible for each child to belong to several different groups of this kind with varying membership. Some of these groups will gradually grow into learning "teams" that work together for longer periods of time. At Level 3, these teams attempt no division of labor but work on the same topic (cumulative effort). Examples of such methods are TGT and STAD (Slavin & DeVries, 1979; Slavin, 1980), but teachers have developed many others of their own. Group incentives can be provided that give the team a sense of joint accomplishment but that are not so extreme as to split the classroom group into rival factions. We found that teachers who had been conscientious in the application of Level 1 principles prevented intergroup competition because it was disruptive to class unity and undermined good relations within the team. They preferred to have the teams strive toward bettering their own record and to give rewards that benefited the whole class, such as a special class activity once all teams passed a certain level in math or spelling.

When a learning team is simply accumulating individual efforts and students are helping each other to master the subject matter, complex roles within the group are usually unnecessary. The teams in some of the classes we visited that were using Level 3 methods evolved captains responsible for organizing and safeguarding the materials, and all members took responsibility for seeing that the members helped, encouraged, and listened to one another while discouraging putdowns and other negative communication.

Once students seem ready for more specialization and integration of knowledge, they can be introduced to Level 4, coordinated teamwork. If they have had practice in integrating practical ideas around the concrete tasks of classroom organization or special events, they are better prepared for this level and will move into it smoothly. If, however, they have not mastered the skills listed under the first three levels in Table 3, or if they have not had practice on practical class projects, students frequently find the challenge of integrating complex academic material in a group more than they can handle interpersonally. Examples of a well-known cooperative method at this level of complexity are Jigsaw (Aronson et al., 1978; Aronson & Bridgeman, 1979) and Jigsaw II, an adaptation that uses standard textbooks rather than dividng the subject matter onto learning cards (Slavin, 1980, 1983). Both are especially suitable for the study of social studies, literature, or the natural sciences. They require materials that need not be learned sequentially, and that can be divided into parts that ca be learned and taught independently. A bilingual version of Jigsaw has been developed for kindergarten through Grade 8 by the Hollister Project in California (Guerrero & Gonzales, 1983), and a sixth-grade black-studies unit was developed by a research associate in our current study (Rivera, 1983). However, once the Jigsaw principle is understood, teachers can develop their own versions. In a bilingual school, the use of six questions about a film studied in Jigsaw groups was shown to be more effective in students' retention of information than the same questions studied individually.

There is no attempt at Level 4 to integrate the information beyond the level of the small groups studying together, nor is there usually a group product. Group rewards or incentives may or may not be used, depending on the level of intrinsic pleasure derived from group work that has been developed within the class.

At Level 5, however, students apply to academic subject matter skills that they began learning at Levels 1 and 2 through practical class projects such as plays, assemblies, parties, or fund drives. Just as they searched for suitable methods of raising money for their class, they now decide on suitable topics for research. Their interpersonal skills are now well developed; they have become used to working together to achieve common academic goals at Levels 3 and 4. They are ready to handle more complex intellectual subject matter and plan their own curriculum.

The Johnsons' Learning Together model (Johnson & Johnson, 1975), although applicable to any level in our scheme, seems to give rise most often to coordinated teamwork somewhere between Levels 4 and 5. Two other examples that are clearly of the highly coordinated kind of group study typical of Level 5 are Co-op Co-op (cf. Kagan, Chapter 16) and Group Investigation (Sharan & Hertz-Lazarowitz, 1980). The former is simpler and less time-consuming than the latter.

Simple expansion of Level 5 can lead into the creative group problem-solving and theory-generation represented by Level 6, group creativity. If, at earlier stages, students have experienced brainstorming methods of generating and pooling ideas, either in the whole class or in small-group activities, they will be more ready for this stage. Spontaneous creative activity on the part of individual members of the group often occurs at Level 5. The difference here is that the group *sets out* to create new artistic, humanistic, or scientific material, using all the combined knowledge inherent in or accessible to the group. One method for structuring the procedure to enhance group creativity and productivity is synectics, an advanced type of brainstorming developed by William J. J. Gordon (1961) at MIT and elaborated more fully by Prince (1970). We have found this method to be successful among university students. High-school students could probably handle it as well.

In conclusion, the skills associated with each level of cooperative activity are those that we and other observers have found emerging among students working at each level, and that also appear to order themselves from simple to more complex. That more complex skills emerge at Levels 3, 4 or 5 does not mean children cannot work at those levels without experience at the lower levels. But it does mean that the task will probably prove to be harder, and that more remedial work, particularly on social skills, will be required.

In this chapter, we have taken an ecological perspective urging teachers and researchers to recognize the *interconnectedness* of students' experiences when designing a program of cooperative education. Only in this way can we provide a truly nurturant context in which cooperative behavior and attitudes can meaningfully develop.

REFERENCES

Aronson, E., & Bridgeman, D. Jigsaw groups and the desegregated classroom: In pursuit of common goals. *Personality and Social Psychology Bulletin*, 1979, 5(4), 438–446.

Aronson, E., Blaney, N., Stephan, C., Sikes, J., & Snapp, M. *The Jigsaw classroom*. Beverly Hills, Calif.: Sage, 1978.

Bridgeman, D. *The influence of cooperative, interdependent learning on role taking and moral reasoning: A theoretical and empirical field study with fifth grade students.* Unpublished doctoral dissertation, University of California, Santa Cruz, 1977.

Bronfenbrenner, U. *The ecology of human development: Experiments by nature and design.* Cambridge: Harvard Press, 1979.

Cohen, R. School reorganization and learning: an approach to assessing the direction of school change. In S. T. Kimball & J. H. Burnett (Eds.), *Symposium on Learning and Culture, Proceedings: 1972 Annual Spring Meeting, Ethnological Society.* Seattle: University of Washington Press, 1973.

Ember, C. R. Feminine task assignment and the social behavior of boys. *Ethos I,* 1973, 424–439.

Gallimore, R., Boggs, J., & Jordan, C. *Culture, behavior and education: A study of Hawaiian-Americans.* New York: Sage Publications, 1974.

Gordon, W. J. J. *Synectics. The development of creative capacity.* New York: Harper & Row, 1961.

Graves, N. B. *Inclusive versus exclusive interaction styles in Polynesian and European classrooms.* Paper presented for the Biennial Meeting of the Society for Research in Child Development, Denver, April 10–13, 1975. Available as Research Report No. 5 of the South Pacific Research Institute, Auckland, New Zealand.

Graves, N. B. Growing up Polynesian: Implications for Western education. In B. Shore, C. Macpherson, & R. W. Franco (Eds.), *New neighbors . . . Islanders in adaptation.* Santa Cruz: Center for South Pacific Studies, University of California at Santa Cruz, 1978.

Graves, N. B., & Graves, T. D. The impact of modernization on the personality of a Polynesian people. *Human Organization,* 1978, 37, 157–162.

Graves, N. B., & Graves. T. D. Children in a multi-cultural society: Building on cultural assets in the school. In A. Jelley (Ed.), *Children in New Zealand: The raw materials of our society.* Auckland: Auckland Headmasters Association Extension Course Lecture Publications Series, Vol. 16, 1979.

Graves, N. B., & Graves, T. D. The cultural context of prosocial development: An ecological model. In D. Bridgeman (Ed.), *The nature of prosocial development: Interdisciplinary theories and strategies.* New York: Academic Press, 1983.

Graves, T. D., & Graves, N. B. Demographic changes in the Cook Islands: Perception and reality. Or, where have all the *mapu* gone? *The Journal of the Polynesian Society,* 1976, 85(4), 447–461.

Graves, T. D., & Graves, N. B. Stress and health: Modernization in a traditional Polynesian society. *Medical Anthropology,* 1979, 3, 23–59.

Guerrero, M., & Gonzalez, A. *A cooperative/interdependent approach to bilingual education: Jigsaw teacher's handbook.* Hollister School District, Curriculum Center, 761 South Street, Hollister, Calif. 95023, 1983.

Howard, A. Education in 'Aina Pumehana: The Hawaiian-American student as hero. In S. T. Kimball & J. H. Burnett (Eds.), *Symposium on Learning and Culture, Proceedings of 1972 Annual Spring Meeting of the American Ethnological Society.* Seattle: University of Washington Press, 1973.

Johnson, D. W., & Johnson, R. I. *Learning together and alone: Cooperation, competition and individualization.* Englewood Cliffs, N.J.: Prentice-Hall, 1975.

Katz, M. B. *Class bureaucracy and schools: The illusion of educational change in America.* New York: Praeger, 1971.

Kirschenbaum, H., Simon, S. B., & Napier, R. W. *Wad-ja-get? The grading game in American education.* New York: Hart Publishing, 1971.

Landor, L. *The study of individual culture: Developing the habit of notation.* Paper presented at the International Conference on Universal Education: The growing child, an experience in transformative approaches to learning. Available through The Institute for Child and Society, Sonoma State College, 703 Seventh Street, Santa Rosa, Calif. 95401, 1982.

MacDonald, S., & Gallimore R. *Battle in the classroom: Innovations in classroom techniques.* Scranton, Pa.: Intext Educational Publications, 1971.

Merchant, C. *The death of nature: Ecology, women, and society in the scientific revolution.* San Francisco: Harper & Row, 1980.

Munroe, R. L., & Munroe, R. H. *Cross-cultural human development.* Monterey, Calif.: Brooks/Cole, 1977.

Munroe, R. L., & Munroe, R. H. Cooperation and competition among East African and American children. *Journal of Social Psychology,* 1977, 101(1), 145–146.

Naisbitt, J. *Megatrends: Ten new directions transforming our lives.* New York: Warner, 1982.

Orlick, T. *Winning through cooperation: Competitive insanity, cooperative alternatives.* Washington: Hawkins, 1977.

Orlick, T. *The cooperative sports and games book: Challenge without competition.* New York: Pantheon, 1978.

Orlick, T. *The second cooperative sports and games book.* New York: Pantheon, 1982.

Poirier, G. A. *Students as partners in team learning.* Berkeley, Calif.: Center of Team Learning, 1970.

Prince, G. M. *The practice of creativity: A manual for dynamic group problem solving.* New York: Harper & Row, 1970.

Ritchie, J., & Ritchie, J. *Growing up in Polynesia.* Sydney: George Allen and Unwin, 1979.

Rivera, M. *Blacks in the American West: A cooperative/interdependent Jigsaw approach to black history.* Unpublished manuscript of a program for sixth-graders, 1983.

Sarason, S. B. *The culture of the school and the problem of change.* Boston: Allyn and Bacon, 1971.

Schmuck, R., & Runkel, P. *The third handbook of organization development in schools.* Palo Alto, Calif.: Mayfield, 1984.

Shallcrass, J. Ultimately politics and power. *New Zealand Listener,* March 2, 1974, p. 29.

Sharan, S., & Hertz-Lazaraowitz, R. A group-investigation method of cooperative learning in the classroom. In S. Sharan, P. Hare, C. Webb, & R. Hertz-Lazarowitz (Eds.), *Cooperation in education.* Provo, Utah: Brigham Young University Press, 1980.

Slavin, R. E. *Using student team learning.* Baltimore: Johns Hopkins University Center for Social Organization of Schools, 1980.

Slavin, R. E. *Cooperative learning.* New York: Longman, 1983.

Slavin, R. E., & DeVries, D. L. Learning in teams. In H. J. Walberg, (Ed.), *Educational environments and effects: Evaluation, policy and productivity.* Berkeley, Calif.: McCutchen, 1979.

Sobel, J. *Everybody wins: 393 non-competitive games for young children.* New York: Walker, 1983.

Stayton, D., Hogan, R., & Ainsworth, M. D. S. Infant obedience and maternal behavior: The origins of socialization reconsidered. *Child Development,* 1971, 42, 1057–1069.

Stone, L. The rise of the nuclear family in early modern England: The patriarchal stage. In C. E. Rosenberg (Ed.), *The family in history.* Philadelphia: University of Pennsylvania Press, 1975.

Watzlawick, P., Weakland, J. & Fisch, R. *Change: Principles of problem formation and problem resolution.* New York: Norton, 1974.

Weinstein, M., & Goodman, J. *Playfair: Everybody's guide to noncompetitive play.* San Luis Obispo, Calif.: Impact, 1980.

Weisner, T. E., & Gallimore, R. My brother's keeper: Child and sibling caretaking. *Current Anthropology,* 1977, *18*(2), 167–190.

Whiting, B., & Edwards, C. P. A cross-cultural analysis of sex differences in the behavior of children aged three through eleven. *The Journal of Social Psychology,* 1973, *91,* 171–188.

Whiting, B. B., & Whiting, J. W. M. Task assignment and personality: A consideration of the effect of herding on boys. In W. W. Lambert & R. Weisbrod (Eds.), *Comparative perspectives on social psychology.* Boston: Little, Brown, 1971.

Whiting, B. B., & Whiting, J. W. M. *Children of six cultures: A psychocultural analysis.* Cambridge: Harvard University Press, 1975.

Whiting, J. W. M., & Whiting, B. B. Altruistic and egoistic behavior in six cultures. In L. Nader & T. W. Maretzki (Eds.), *Cultural illness and health.* Washington, D. C.: American Anthropological Association, 1973.

16

Co-op Co-op
A Flexible Cooperative Learning Technique

SPENCER KAGAN

Co-op Co-op evolved over a period of 10 years. It originated as a way of increasing the involvement of university students in traditional psychology courses by allowing them to explore in depth topics in which they were particularly interested. The use of topic teams (groups of students who cover closely interrelated topics and who develop a coordinated presentation to the whole class) evolved not out of a philosophical commitment to cooperative learning but as a practical solution to the problem of how to fit student presentations into the time usually allotted for a university course. As soon as the use of teams was introduced, however, it was immediately apparent that the teams were far more than a time-saving, practical solution. The teams increased student learning tremendously (as measured by the quality of individual papers), probably because they allowed student communication on topics of mutual interest; the sharing of references, resources, and ideas; and increased involvement in and investment in learning. For many students, knowing that they would share what they learned with other students appeared to be a far more powerful motivational device than the traditional letter grade.

When the teacher training program of the School of Education at the University of California, Riverside, decided in 1980 to train its student teachers in the theories and techniques of cooperative learning, they included training in Co-op Co-op. This allowed further development and refinement of the method; it was used with over 1,000 public school students. In the process of training of student teachers, it was discovered that training in Co-op Co-op could best be accomplished with an approach that differs from teacher training in other cooperative learning methods. The other cooperative learning methods each train teachers using either a "basic principles approach" or a "cookbook approach."

SPENCER KAGAN • Department of Psychology, University of California, Riverside, California 92521.

The cookbook approach is exemplified by the work of Robert Slavin and his associates at John Hopkins University (cf. Slavin, 1979), who have developed Student Teams-Achievement Divisions (STAD) and Teams-Games-Tournaments (TGT), and who have adapted Aronson's Jigsaw method so it can be used with ordinary curriculum materials (Jigsaw II). In training teachers, Slavin and his associates rely on a very detailed set of instructions for setting up cooperative classrooms, including mechanical methods for assigning students to teams and grades to students. This approach has a number of advantages, including facilitating research (when STAD or TGT is the independent variable, it is clear what has been done; if some other methods are used, the nature of the independent variable is open to considerable guesswork), simplifying teacher training (STAD and TGT teachers are trained in a fraction of the time required for Group-Investigation), and being almost "teacher-proof" (even very inadequate teachers can master the techniques of STAD or TGT). In contrast to the cookbook method is the basic principles approach to teacher training by the Johnsons (Johnson & Johnson, 1975b) and the Sharans (Sharan & Sharan, 1976). In the basic principles approach, an attempt is made to train teachers in basic principles that they can apply in a unique way to each class. The basic principles approach also has its advantages, including a greater flexibility and range of applicability and a greater opportunity for creative student and teacher input into the learning process.

Co-op Co-op was designed to incorporate the advantages of both the cookbook and the basic principles approaches by having teachers learn the basic principles and philosophy associated with a set of elements of steps. Little detail is provided, leaving considerable flexibility and room for student and teacher input, but certain critical steps are outlined that must be present if Co-op Co-op is to be used to full advantage. As will be seen, Co-op Co-op is philosophically linked to Group-Investigation, which places faith in the curiosity, intelligence, and expressiveness of students rather than in extrinsic points and competitive motives. On the other hand, Co-op Co-op is a very American expression, complete with a 10-step "how-to-do-it" guide.

THE PHILOSOPHY OF CO-OP CO-OP

Co-op Co-op is based on a philosophy of education that assumes that the aim of education is to provide conditions in which the natural curiosity, intelligence, and expressiveness of students will emerge and develop. The emphasis in this philosophy is on bringing out and nourishing what are assumed to be natural intelligent, creative, and expressive tendencies among students; it is an approach quite in contrast to traditional approaches, which assume that the student is a void into which educators must pump facts, theories, and methods. Co-op Co-op is based on the assumption that following one's curiosity, having new experiences that modify one's conception of oneself and the world, and sharing these experiences—especially with one's peers—are inherently satisfying, and that no extrinsic reward is needed to get students to engage in these activities, which are the most important forms of learning.

Co-op Co-op, therefore, is structured to maximize the opportunity for small groups of students to work together to further their own understanding and development—usually, but not always, in the form of producing a group product—and then to share this product or experience with the whole class so that the other class members also may profit. Thus the name Co-op Co-op: Students cooperate within their small teams to produce something of benefit to share with the whole class; they are cooperating in order to cooperate. There is, therefore, a fundamental difference between Co-op Co-op and cooperative learning methods such as STAD or TGT, in which students cooperate in teams in order to obtain more points as a team than do other teams. In those methods, students learn in order to win or to beat others, they cooperate in order to compete better. In Co-op Co-op, students learn in order to satisfy their own curiosity about themselves and the world and to share with others. In STAD or TGT, learning and cooperating are the means; the goal is winning. In Co-op Co-op, learning and cooperating are the goals.

As the foregoing brief discussion indicates, Co-op Co-op can be viewed as a way of operationalizing the ideas of progressive education as described by Dewey. It is experiential. As Dewey (1957) noted,

> A primary responsibility of educators is that they not only be aware of the general principles of the shaping of actual experience by environing conditions, but that they also recognize in the concrete what surroundings are conducive to having experiences that lead to growth. Above all, they should know how to utilize the surroundings, physical and social, that exist so as to extract from them all that they have to contribute to building up experiences that are worthwhile. (p. 35)

Further, Co-op Co-op embodies a democratic, cooperative philosophy. Again, as Dewey recognized,

> The way is, first, for the teacher to be intelligently aware of the capacities, needs, and past experiences of those under instruction and, secondly, to allow the suggestion made to develop into a plan and project by means of the further suggestions contributed and organized into a whole by the members

of the group. The plan, in other words, is a co-operative enterprise, not a dictation. The teacher's suggestion is not a mold for a cast-iron result but is a starting point to be developed into a plan through contributions from the experience of all engaged in the learning process. The development occurs through reciprocal give-and-take, the teacher taking but not being afraid also to give. The essential point is that the purpose grow and take shape through the process of social intelligence. (p. 85)

The Elements of Co-op Co-op

The essence of Co-op Co-op is to allow students to work together in small groups to advance their understanding of themselves and the world, and then to provide them with the opportunity to share that new understanding with their peers. The method is designed to be simple and flexible. Once a teacher grasps the philosophy behind Co-op Co-op, he or she may choose any number of ways to operationalize the technique in a given classroom. Nevertheless, the inclusion of certain elements or steps increases the probability of success of the method. The 10 most essential elements or steps of Co-op Co-op are described below.

Step 1: Student-Centered Class Discussion

At the beginning of a class unit in which Co-op Co-op is used, the students are encouraged to discover and express their own interest in the subject covered. An initial set of readings, lectures, or experiences prior to the student-centered class discussion is helpful in stimulating and generating curiosity about the topic to be covered. The aim of the discussion is not to lead the students to certain topics for study; rather, it is to increase their involvement in the topic by uncovering and stimulating their curiosity. The class discussion serves also to allow the students to know the nature of the interests in the topic held by other students in the class. The discussion should lead to an understanding among the teacher and all the students about what the students want to learn and experience in relation to the topic or unit to be covered. In Co-op Co-op, learning is not seen as progress toward a predetermined, teacher-defined goal; it is a process that flows out of the interests of the students.

This first step in Co-op Co-op may take more or less time, depending in part on the extent to which the students have differentiated interests related to the topic. The importance of the initial student-centered discussion cannot be underestimated; it is unlikely that Co-op Co-op will be successful for any students who are not actively interested in a topic related to the unit, and who are not motivated to learn more about the topic.

Ideally, if the student-centered initial discussion is successful in uncovering and stimulating the curiosity of the students, the students will see learning as an opportunity to find out more about a topic that they wish to explore; the students identify with the learning process. They become more intrinsically motivated and increase their sense of internal control. A second major reason for the initial discussion is so that students can see that their own learning can be of use to their classmates. As they listen to other students express what they would like to know, the students discover that they can be instrumental in the goal attainment of others, and thus that knowledge can lead not only to the satisfaction of their own curiosity but also to helping others.

STEP 2: SELECTION OF STUDENT LEARNING TEAMS

The students may be assigned to teams or may be allowed to select their teams, depending on the goals of the class. If the teachers have as their goals increasing the probability of cross-ability-level peer tutoring and improving cross-ethnic relations, they will find it useful to assign the students to teams in order to maximize heterogeneity among the students. Methods for maximizing heterogeneity within student teams have been worked out and described in detail (Slavin, 1979, pp. 98–100). On the other hand, if the development of preexisting student interests is of greater concern, the teachers may allow the students to select their own teams on the basis of their interests. There are potential pitfalls, however, in allowing the students to select their own teams: The students may group in teams that are homogeneous with regard to ethnic and achievement levels, with the potential for reinforcing stereotypes and polarizing the classroom social climate. In general, by maximizing the heterogeneity of the students within the teams, the teachers increase the probability of establishing positive peer tutoring, improving ethnic and social relations, increasing role-taking abilities, and improving self-esteem among the students. Nevertheless, teams assigned by the teacher on the basis of heterogeneity increase the need for team-building experiences, especially at the secondary levels, in which cross-ethnic and cross-ability-level relations among students may be quite poor.

STEP 3: TEAM BUILDING

Team building can be used for a variety of purposes, including (1) helping the students get acquainted; (2) demonstrating to the students that each person is a unique and valuable member of the group; (3) building trust among teammates; (4) training the students in effective methods of interaction within groups, such as division of labor or social roles and effective communication skills and styles; (5) demonstrating the benefits of cooperative interaction and the necessity of working together in situations of positive interdependency; (6) fostering team identity; and (7) producing an atmosphere in which the students feel free to be warm, empathetic, and genuine. Different team-building tasks commonly used in classrooms can be divided according to their goal. For example, games such as "This Is Me" and "What Would I Do with a Million Dollars?" aim primarily at disclosure and values clarification. In contrast, "Lost in the Desert," although containing elements of value clarification and disclosure, aims primarily at fostering a sense of mutual interdependency and teaching students the synergy principle, that is, that a group product is often superior to the product that can be produced by an individual team member working alone.

A number of team-building exercises have been described in detail (Johnson & Johnson, 1975a). The number and type of such exercises to be used with Co-op Co-op depend on the needs of a particular classroom. In general, more team building is necessary among secondary-level students than among primary-grade students because, in traditional classroom structures, cross-ethnic and cross-ability-level relations among students deteriorate with successive years in school. Whereas primary students, especially in the earliest years, readily accept assignment to heterogeneous teams, secondary students often resist such grouping. Co-op Co-op cannot proceed successfully until the members of the student teams feel that they are "on the same side," that is, until they have a strong, positive team identity.

Several team-building techniques have been designed especially for Co-op Co-op. They are designed to quickly introduce students to each other and to overcome resistance among students to identifying with a team made up of students different from themselves. Two of these techniques are Interview and Roundtable Brainstorming. Interview quickly introduces students to each other in a positive context. Roundtable brainstorming quickly produces a strong, positive team identity, a willingness to work in teams, and a sense of the mutual interdependence of the teammates and the need for cooperative interaction. Instructions for interview and roundtable brainstorming are presented in Appendix A.

STEP 4: TEAM TOPIC SELECTION

After the team members have developed trust and communication skills sufficient for them to work together, they are allowed to select the topics for their team. Before doing this, the teams are reminded (usually via a handout or the blackboard) which topics the class as a whole has indicated are of greatest interest, and it is pointed out that the team can cooperate most fully in realizing the class goals if they choose a topic related to the interests of the class. Further, the teammates are encouraged to discuss among themselves the various topics so that they can settle on the topic of most interest to themselves as a group. As the teams discuss their interests and begin to settle on a topic, the teacher circulates among the teams and acts as a facilitator. If two teams begin to settle on the same topic, this can be pointed out, and the teams can be encouraged to reach a compromise, either by dividing that topic in two, or by having one of the teams choose some other topic of interest. If no team settles on a topic in which there is considerable interest or for which there is a need, this, too, can be pointed out, and the students can be encouraged to respond to the need.

If this fourth step of Co-op Co-op is carried out successfully, each of the teams will settle on a topic and will feel identified with its topic. The teachers can facilitate a spirit of class unity by pointing out how each of the topic presentations will be of importance to the class as a whole, and how each individual will benefit from the work of his or her teammates and classmates via the minitopic presentations and the team presentations.

STEP 5: MINITOPIC SELECTION

Just as the class as a whole divides up the learning unit into sections to create a division of labor among the teams within the class, so does each team divide its topic to create a division of labor among the students within each team. Individual students are encouraged to select minitopics, each of which covers one aspect of the team topic. Minitopics may have some overlap, and the students within teams are encouraged to share references and resources, but each minitopic must provide a unique contribution to the team effort. As the students settle on minitopics, the teachers may need to be more or less involved, depending on the level of the students. The teachers may require that minitopics meet the approval of the teacher because some topics may not be appropriate to the level of a given student, or because sufficient resources may not be available on a given topic. It is acceptable and natural for some students to make a larger contribution than others to the total team effort because of differences in abilities and interests among students, but all members need to make an important contribution. This can be accomplished by various means, including (1) allowing the students to evaluate the contributions of their fellow teammates; (2) assigning an individual paper or project to the students on their minitopics; and (3) having the teachers monitor the individual contributions. If the minitopics are selected properly, each student will make a unique contribution to the total group product or experience, and so individuals will have peer support for mastering their minitopics.

Step 6: Minitopic Preparation

Once the students have divided the team topic into minitopics, they individually gather resources in an attempt to learn as much as possible about their particular minitopics. They each know that they are responsible for their particular minitopics and that the group is depending on them to cover an important aspect of the team topic.

The preparation of minitopics takes different forms, depending on the nature of the class unit being covered by Co-op Co-op. The preparation may involve library research, some form of data gathering, the creation of an individual project, interviews of experts, the planning of an individual contribution to a group project, or introspection. All of these activities take on a heightened interest when the students know that they will be sharing the fruits of their labor with their teammates.

Step 7: Minitopic Presentations

After the students have gathered their resources and have organized the materials on their individual minitopics, they present what they have learned or created to their teammates. The minitopic presentations and their discussion within teams is an extremely important element of Co-op Co-op. Minitopic presentations and discussion within teams are done so that all of the teammates are afforded the knowledge or experience acquired by each, and so that they can actively discuss the topic as a panel of experts. The students know that the minitopics, like the pieces of a jigsaw puzzle, must be put together in a coherent whole for a successful team presentation to the entire class. It is in the process of interacting with peers over a topic of common concern that some of the most important learning may occur.

In preparation for the minitopic presentations, the teacher may review the principles of active listening, interviewing, and supportive questioning. A division of labor within the teams may be encouraged so that one teammate may take notes, another may play the role of critic, another may check for points of convergence among the minitopics, and yet another may check for points of divergence. After the students actively discuss the minitopic material, time is allowed for the students to further research and/or rethink their minitopics individually and to deal with the questions raised during the team discussion of the minitopics. Then, they report back to their teams so that the team can integrate the new material.

Only if the team actively synthesizes the minitopic material will the team presentation to the whole class transcend a panel presentation. If there has been a thorough discussion and integration of the material gathered by each teammate, the team (and the class) will reap the benefits of the synergistic principle: The team presentation becomes far more than the sum of the minipresentations.

STEP 8: PREPARATION OF TEAM PRESENTATIONS

It is important that the students distinguish minitopic presentations from preparation of the team presentation. It is tempting for students to rush prematurely to discussions of how to share the material that their team has gathered. Such discussion should follow the synthesis of the material; the students need to formulate a clear idea of the most important ideas. Ideally, the format for the team presentation will emerge naturally as the students gain closure on their topic. Once understanding is obtained, communication of that understanding is the natural next step.

The teams are informed of how long their presentations will be, and they are encouraged to plan a presentation that will be interesting and informative. Nonlecture formats such as debates, displays, demonstrations, skits, and class involvement are encouraged. The use of blackboards and handouts is also encouraged. Some teams find it useful to make a media presentation such as a slide show. Panel presentations and lectures are discouraged; they generally reflect a lack of higher level integrative cooperative work.

Depending on the level of the students, formal practice sessions may be useful. Teams may make arrangements with other teams to give them feedback following a formal practice presentation, with the aim of improving their presentation to the whole class. This form of between-team cooperation is encouraged, as it between-team sharing of references and resources.

STEP 9: TEAM PRESENTATIONS

During the time allotted for the team presentation, the teacher gives control of the classroom to the team. The team members become responsible for how the time, the space, and the equipment of the classroom are to be used during their presentation. They are encouraged to make full use of the classroom facilities, including rearranging student seating if that will facilitate their presentation.

One of the greatest difficulties that students have with their first team presentation is managing time. This becomes especially critical if several team presentations are to be made on the same day, so there is generally a need to appoint a class timekeeper who is not a member of the presenting team.

The team may wish to include a question–answer period and/or time for comments and feedback as part of its presentation. In addition, the teacher may find it useful, following the presentation, to lead a feedback session and/or to interview the team so that other teams can learn something of what was involved in the process of developing the presentation. Particularly successful teams are held up as a model: Through the interview process, the teacher uncovers elements that might be useful to other teams in future units to be covered by Co-op Co-op.

STEP 10: EVALUATION

Evaluation in Co-op Co-op occurs at several levels: teacher and class evaluation of team presentations; student/or teacher evaluation of individual contributions to the team effort; and teacher evaluation of the individual paper or project of each student on his or her minitopic, if assigned. In addition, the teachers may wish to elicit comments from the class in order to evaluate each Co-op Co-op unit after all teams have made their presentation on that unit.

Following each team presentation, the teacher may guide a class discussion of the strongest and weakest elements in the content and the format of the presentation. A more formal evaluation of the team presentation may be made in writing by the classmates and/or the teacher. It is helpful if the teachers circulate an evaluation form well before the team presentations are made so that the students know how they will be evaluated by their classmates. In some classes, the teacher may want the students to develop or to contribute to the evaluation form. An evaluation of the contribution of individual students to the team effort can also be done by her or his teammates, either formally or informally. If the students write a paper on their minitopic, they receive feedback on this as well.

Co-op Co-op can run well with anything from great to no emphasis on grades. Some teachers and students find it comfortable to derive individual grades from the minitopic papers, the minitopic presentations, and the team presentations. Others prefer to make learning and sharing their own reward. The teachers may choose to allow the class to determine the weight to be assigned to each of the graded elements of Co-op Co-op. A structural analysis would lead to the conclusion that unless the students have some input into the evaluation of the individual contribution of their teammates, the problem of the free rider will arise. That is, some students might make little or no contribution to the group, figuring that they will receive whatever grade the group receives. In fact, however, Co-op Co-op has been carried out successfully with no such teammate evaluation; apparently, intrinsic motivation and/or informal peer pressure can be sufficient. The extent to which an extrinsic grading system must be employed probably depends partly on the charisma of the teacher, the nature of the subject, the extent and types of the external demands on the students, and the intensity of the students' interest in the topic.

ALTERNATE FORMS OF CO-OP CO-OP

It is possible to use Co-op Co-op in a very brief format in which the teams have only 10 or 15 minutes to prepare a short presentation of 5 minutes or so, or in a very long format in which the teams have a year to prepare very detailed presentations. It can be very helpful to have the teams stay together for two or more presentations; over time, the weaker teams model themselves after the stronger teams if given the opportunity, and the successive presentations become stronger. The Co-op Co-op unit may complement an ongoing learning unit that is taught in a traditional format, or it may be the only treatment of a unit. Co-op Co-op can be used in a group-investigation format, in a format that emphasizes insight and disclosure, or in the acquisition of basic information (in which case the teams have as their goal the mastering of content or methods and then teaching that material to the other teams). In some cases, there may be a formal group product, such as a thesis, an experiment, a mural, or a slide show; in other cases, there may be no formal product but only a sharing of feelings following a group discussion. Co-op Co-op is designed to be a flexible method of allowing students to learn cooperatively across a variety of content areas.

EFFECTS OF CO-OP CO-OP

Although Co-op Co-op has been used successfully in a great many classrooms, a rigorous, formal, empirical analysis of the effects of Co-op Co-op has not been completed. There are available, however, two sets of empirical data that can be used to provide a preliminary, informal evaluation of the effects of Co-op Co-op. The first set of data consists of the elicited and spontaneous written statements of university students following the use of Co-op Co-op in upper-division undergraduate courses. The second set of data consists of an analysis of the cooperativeness of high-school students following the use of Co-op Co-op and traditional classroom techniques. This latter set of data is summarized in Chapter 11 of this book and so is not reviewed here; the high-school experience is reviewed in the present chapter only at the discursive level.

THE UNIVERSITY EXPERIENCE

Co-op Co-op is easiest to use at the university level, and the results at that level are most uniformly positive. Students at the university level have been selected for high ability and motivation, and they often appreciate the opportunity to explore a topic of interest in depth. Further, they are less hesitant about speaking before a class, and in many university settings, there are no strong race-relations problems to overcome. Although most students at the university level have never worked in cooperative learning groups, when given the opportunity most welcome it. Some find the opportunity to work together to prepare a presentation for their peers the perfect outlet for creative energy that is generally kept in check by class structures that reduce the job of the undergraduate university student to memorizing facts in order to perform well on a multiple-choice exam made up by the textbook publishers.

A preliminary, informal evaluation of Co-op Co-op at the university level is provided in two forms: (1) anonymous statements of students about the technique, elicited directly by asking them to write down the positive and negative aspects of their experiences with Co-op Co-op; and (2) statements of students about the technique that were written during an anonymous university-administered course evaluation. These latter statements are spontaneous with regard to Co-op Co-op because the course evaluation form made no note of evaluating group work, but many of the students spontaneously described the impact of their team experience.

ELICITED STUDENT COMMENTS

Following a 10-week Co-op Co-op experience, in each of two undergraduate university classes, students were asked to submit a statement of the positive and negative aspects of the Co-op Co-op experience. An attempt was made to have the students describe their experience in an unstructured, open-ended way, as it was assumed that the students' free expression would be most revealing. The instructions were as follows: "Please write a few paragraphs describing your experience with teams as used in this class. Try to make your statement as balanced as possible, including both positive and negative experiences. Focus on both the academic and the social aspects of the experience, and try to say it the way it was. There is no need to sign your statement."

The unedited verbatim responses of 10 students are presented in Appendix B. The responses were selected to cover the range of statements, from the most positive to the most negative. The set of responses is not truly representative because fewer than 5% of the total responses received were strongly negative, but one strongly negative response (Response 8) is included to represent the range of responses received.

Most of the students indicated that the Co-op Co-op experience led to both increased learning and improved social relations. Some of the students, however, did not include increased academic learning as one of the consequences of the Co-op Co-op experience, focusing instead exclusively on the beneficial social aspects of the experience (see for example, Response 5). Although the students almost always indicated that the increased communication with peers facilitated academic learning, one student did imply that the group presentation detracted from individual learning (see Response 1). Interestingly, that student gave the strongest positive statement of the beneficial interpersonal and intrapersonal effects of the cooperative group experience. Clearly, each individual brings to a team unique needs and interests, and in turn, the Co-op Co-op experience has different effects.

Many students indicate informally during class that the Co-op Co-op experience has reversed a negative opinion that they had formed about group work (see Responses 1 and 7). Interviews with students regarding the lack of success of previous group experiences almost always reveal the "free-rider" problem. One group grade is given, and a few students do most of the work; generally, the best students feel imposed on by this group structure. In contrast, almost all students are quite pleased and surprised to find everyone contributing in the Co-op Co-op format. Occasionally, however, the free-rider problem can occur in Co-op Co-op (see Response 8). The relative absence of free-riders in Co-op Co-op is probably attributable mostly to the inclusion of minitopics, which ensures that each team member will be responsible for a unique portion of the group presentation, and to teammate evaluations.

Two problems that emerge in the student comments are leadership issues and group size. Experience indicates that groups larger than seven members are too large and should be avoided if possible. The leadership issue arises if one group member attempts to be too dominant. As indicated in the comments of Respondent 5, this situation can lead to an important although painful learning experience for the student who is not aware of the adverse effects of his or her dominance; the Co-op Co-op groups provide a very real experience in democracy.

SPONTANEOUS STUDENT COMMENTS

The University of California, Riverside, employs a course evaluation format administered at the end of each academic quarter. As part of this course evaluation procedure, the students provide anonymous descriptions of their class experiences. In courses using Co-op Co-op, although the response form does not mention team experiences, many of the students spontaneously evaluate the team experience. All of the comments made about the team experience in two undergraduate classes are presented in Appendix 3; they represent about half of all responses for those classes.

These brief, anonymous comments about Co-op Co-op, like the more detailed elicited comments, reflect a positive attitude toward the cooperative learning experience. The comments indicate that, for at least some students, Co-op Co-op had an important impact on how the students thought of themselves and of learning. The students mentioned that they had had the opportunity for "experiencing rather than thinking about," and that they had used their heads as a "thinking tool instead of a repository." Co-op Co-op can provide an environment in which personal development, social development, and academic learning are mutually supportive. By respecting the intelligence, the interests, and the expressive capacities of students, Co-op Co-op allows students to "enjoy a sharing and community effort" and, in the process, to "become aware of the facilities within themselves."

THE HIGH-SCHOOL EXPERIENCE

The high-school experience with Co-op Co-op is not as uniformly positive as the university experience. At the high-school level, there are numerous problems not encountered at the university level. By high school, many students are turned off by the traditional educational experience to such an extent that they are not motivated to learn or to participate in a group learning project. There is often a very high rate of absenteeism, especially in inner-city schools, which is a very difficult problem to deal with, especially if the group project demands the prolonged and consistent participation of all team members. Race relations are also often very poor, and there is the problem of achievement-level differences among students, which can be extreme by high school, especially in required classes in schools that have a policy of allowing almost all students to advance a grade each year, regardless of failing or near-failing performance. The assignment of students to teams in such cases often means placing students together who differ radically in their levels of achievement and motivation.

Given this set of problems, the success of Co-op Co-op at the high-school level is, to a fair extent, dependent on the flexibility, the commitment, and the creativity of the teacher. If a teacher is hesitant about the use of racially mixed groups, the ability of students to work together, or the ability of students to present a team project, that hesitancy is communicated to the students, and it reinforces their own hesitancies. In such cases, Co-op Co-op can fail. In other cases, however, high-school teachers and students have responded in very positive ways to the challenge of Co-op Co-op. Although no formal evaluation of Co-op Co-op at the high-school level has been conducted, there are numerous examples of the successful use of the method.

One particularly successful team presentation involved a unit on the Vietnam war for a history class. Each student on the team did enough research to be able to write an accurate "letter home" from a participant in the war. An impressive aspect of this team effort was that each team member took the role of a very different type of participant: One letter was from a war hawk, another from a conscientious objector serving as a medic, a third from a highly religious soldier, and so on. The students worked together to make a synchronized slide and tape presentation so that appropriate slides accompanied the tape of each student reading a letter. This case illustrates several principles that can be used to overcome common problems at the high-school level. First, when there is hesitancy to stand up and speak before a class, a tape and/or slide presentation can be appropriate. Second, in cases of extreme ability-level differences, a presentation format can be found that allows each participant to contribute to the presentation at his or her own level. Third, when there is a wide discrepancy among the team members with regard to point of view, a presentation format can be found that accommodates that range of perspectives: In the discussion of the war from a variety of perspectives, important learning took place, a type of learning seldom encountered in the traditional classroom structure.

CONCLUSION

Co-op Co-op represents only one of many possible cooperative learning methods. It is attractive because it is flexible and relatively simple, while embodying a philosophy of education that affirms the intelligence, the creativity, and the prosocial tendencies of students. It is designed to give the control of learning back to the students, so that they become actively involved in choosing what and how to learn and share.

There are some problems with Co-op Co-op at the university level, mainly surrounding issues of leadership and the occasional free-rider. Nevertheless, the university experience is generally quite positive, sometimes dramatically so. At the high-school level, the experience with Co-op Co-op is more mixed, demanding more creative involvement of the high-school teachers. Co-op Co-op at the high-school level, though, can be a very rewarding method; it can lead to depth of understanding and a more prosocial orientation among students than traditional, whole-class methods.

REFERENCES

Dewey, J. *Experience and education*. New York: Macmillan, 1957.

Johnson, D. W., & Johnson, F. P. *Joining together: Group theory and group skills*. Englewood Cliffs, N.J.: Prentice-Hall, 1975. (a)

Johnson, D. W., & Johnson, R. T. *Learning together and alone*. Englewood Cliffs, N.J.: Prentice-Hall, 1975. (b)

Sharan, S., & Sharan, Y. *Small-group teaching*. Englewood Cliffs, N.J.: Educational Technology Publications, 1976.

Slavin, R. L. Student team learning: A manual for teachers. In S. Sharan, A. P. Hare, C. Webb, & R. Lazarowitz (Eds.), *Cooperation in education*. Provo, Utah: Brigham Young University Press, 1979.

CO-OP CO-OP TEAM BUILDING TECHNIQUES

Part I: Interview

Interview is designed to introduce teammates to each other in some depth and classmates to each other superficially. It is designed to provide students some basis for relating to others with common interests or experiences, to give students the opportunity to feel received, and to overcome initial resistances that some students have to participating in groups.

Steps of Interview

1. Teacher has students gather in teams.
2. Teammates count off 1, 2, 3, 4 or more, one per teammate.
3. Teacher informs students it is the job of 1 to interview 2, 3 to interview 4, etc., for five minutes. The aim of the interview is to gather information that will be used to introduce each person to his or her teammates. Interview topics may be suggested such as hobbies, unusual experiences, favorite movies, life goals, etc. Interviewing tips may be provided, such as how to follow the lead of the other person rather than suggesting topics of interest to yourself.
4. Introductions are carried out within groups. That is, rounds are made so that each interviewer has one minute to present to the group the person he or she has interviewed.
5. Steps 3 and 4 are repeated with students shifting roles: 2 interviews and presents 1, 4 interviews and presents 3, etc.
6. The team engages in a discussion attempting to discover the "positive essence" of each of the teammates so that the teammate can be described in an adjective or a very brief phrase, such as, "gutsy," "adventuresome," "caring," or "nature girl." Students are instructed to look for themes in the interview material that help them capture the positive essence of the person.
7. Team members introduce their teammates to the class by having teammates make rounds stating the adjective or phrase that best captures the positive essence of each team member, and providing a sentence or two of explanation.

Alternate Formats for Interview

Short Format Eliminate team discussion (Step 6), and for Step 7, have each teammate tell the most interesting positive thing they learned about one other teammate.

Repeated Format Begin team meetings with a focused round of Interview each week. The first week could focus on hobbies, the second week on movies, the third on unusual experiences. As students become ready, "deeper" topics can be approached, such as "happiest moment," "saddest moment," "a time I was really mad," or "someone or something dear I lost."

Part II: Roundtable Brainstorming

Roundtable Brainstorming is designed to create a positive team identity and a willingness to work in teams. It is used to overcome the initial resistance to working in teams that is often found in desegregated classrooms, especially at the secondary level.

A number of steps should be followed in order to ensure that each group will feel that each of its members can make a positive contribution and that each group will experience improvement over the successive trials.

Steps of Roundtable Brainstorming

1. Have students sit in a circle at a table (or if their chairs have the desktop built on, have them pull their desk chairs into a circle so they have a common work space in the middle).

2. Instruct students to clear the work space of everything but one pencil and one piece of paper.

3. Write the names of the teams on the blackboard with lines after them for team scores. (Students should have named their teams prior to roundtable brainstorming.) The blackboard should look something like this:

Team Name	Trial 1	Trial 2	Trial 3	Trial 4
Indians				
Chiefs				
Warriors				
Braves				

4. Present the teams with a problem that is specially designed to relate to the academic content of the class, but that meets two critical tests, as follows:

    (a) The problem must be very simple. Remember, this is a team-building exercise, not a test of skills, and the success of all members is critical. If the problem is such that any members of a team cannot be successful on at least several rounds, roundtable brainstorming will have effects *opposite* those intended.

    (b) There must be numerous correct solutions to the problem.

Some examples of problems that are appropriate for roundtable brainstorming are the following:

    (a) Write as many words as you can from the word *teamwork* (1 point can be given for one-letter words, 2 points for two-letter words, 3 for three-letter words, etc.).

    (b) Write as many pairs of numbers as you can that add up to 21.

    (c) Write as many reasons as you can for wars.

5. Have the teams race to obtain as many correct answers as they can in one minute. Tell them that it is a race and that their scores will go up on the board afterward. Indicate, however, that they must follow certain rules in this race:

They must each take a turn, passing the paper and pencil around their roundtable in a circle. Members are not allowed to skip a turn without trying for at least 10 seconds to produce a correct answer. This last element is critical, as it ensures that all students will contribute to the group product and that they will feel they are valuable members of the group. If some team members delay for very long, the problem is too hard. *Remember*: the problem should be very simple; the positive effects of roundtable brainstorming come from the involvement of the students in a race in which they all participate.

6. Following the one-minute race, teams are asked to score their own papers and to count the number of correct solutions. The team score, the sum of correct solutions, is put on the blackboard as follows:

Team Name	Trial 1	Trial 2	Trial 3	Trial 4
Indians	15			
Chiefs	12			
Warriors	19			
Braves	7			

7. The teacher then interviews the most successful team and sets them up as a model for the other teams. That is, he or she walks over to the team and has all of the other teams focus their attention on the leading team. The interview consists of complimenting the team for the excellent performance, asking the team members how they worked and to what they attributed their success, listening carefully to what they say, paraphrasing it, and looking over their work to determine if the team relied on some cooperative format that might be followed by other teams. If so, the teacher points this out to the whole class. For example, whereas an unsuccessful team paper following the "21" exercise might look like this:

$$
\begin{array}{cc}
1 & 7 \\
+20 & +14 \qquad \text{etc.} \\
\hline
21 & 21
\end{array}
$$

a successful team might have a worksheet that looks like this:

$$
\begin{aligned}
7 + 14 &= 21 \\
8 + 13 &= 21 \\
9 + 12 &= 21 \\
10 + 11 &= 21 \\
\text{etc.}
\end{aligned}
$$

The most efficient cooperative method probably will not evolve on the first trial, but within a few trials, teams will become amazingly cooperative and efficient. Following a number of trials, when all the teams have been getting good scores, the cooperative principle can be pointed out, or the teacher can have the teams discover it via discussion. Finally, an academic principle can be pointed out as well, such as the fact that adding a number to one side of a plus sign and taking it away from the other does not change the total.

8. Following each trial, the teacher interviews the most improved group, stressing the basis of their improvement, and the leading group as well if they have made some conceptual advance. The focus is on improvement and the basis of success, so less efficient teams spend their energy on modeling themselves after leading teams, not on feeling bad about their performance. The weaker teams receive positive attention from the teacher and the class on the basis of their improvement.

9. Change the roundtable brainstorming game slowly. For example, if one day the problem is two numbers that sum to 21, begin the next day with two numbers that sum to 35. Only after all the teams reach near maximum efficiency is it time to change to three numbers that sum to 21. And only after the teams have evolved some rather complex strategies on that type of problem (such as changing the first number in the sum and the last; or the first and second only, using zero; or changing all three) is it time to move on.

It is the race aspects of roundtable brainstorming and the participation of all team members in an exciting effort in which there is progressive improvement that will produce a strong cooperative spirit and positive team identity.

10. All content areas can be adapted. For example, if the problem is three-letter words from *teamwork*, the next day it could be four-letter words. Or if the problem is reasons for wars one day, it can be made more specific on the next, like "economic reasons" or reasons for a specified war. Whereas the cooperative principle is often clear in math and may be masked in the social sciences, it can be found. For example, a successful team might include economic, social, political, philosophical, cultural, and linguistic reasons for war; a less successful team might not cover all the bases. A second trial might deal with a question about economic productivity that could in a similar way include economic, social, political, philosophical, and cultural elements, and the inclusion of all these elements by the successful teams can be held up as a model for other teams to follow.

APPENDIX B

ELICITED STUDENT COMMENTS ABOUT CO-OP CO-OP

1. "In the beginning of the quarter I was not motivated to be in my senior year of college, let alone do college work. In a way, it was like, 'Oh no, I have to work with another group of people I don't know.' Yet that in and of itself became a motivating factor for myself. I actually began getting into my college work as well as the group presentation—I was lifted out of a beginning-of-the-year depression, by working with other people whom I didn't know that well in the beginning. This in turn has given me new friendships as well as renewed self-confidence.

"All in all, the group was an important part of this quarter for me. I feel I have grown (interpersonally) from working in this group of persons; they were inspirational to and for me."

"To be very honest, I can say that I did not learn about the topic of suicide by presenting the topic. I believe I could have learned more by concentrating on my paper, which may have been more comprehensive. I believe the group was more concerned with presenting the topic in an interesting way so that the class would be captivated."

2. "I really enjoyed working in the child abuse group. The idea that we could use each other's material for cross-references was the most productive aspect, I thought. Everyone shared and contributed whatever was of interest to another—that was neat. I also thought it was a good experience to work with others who were as intensely interested in a particular topic as I was. Putting the presentation together was actually a really fun way to share our research and to learn from others; it's a good idea. The only aspect that I did not particularly care for was the time restriction (for our presentation); however, overall I thought the project was fun."

3. "I enjoyed working in a group. I feel that I learned so much more. The group presentations are very helpful because they have all been very informative and interesting. In our group, we did not have any problems organizing or working as a group."

4. "The idea of doing a group project really helped bring together some resources for the project and individual papers. A lot of personal sharing takes place so that everyone gathers more information on the subjects being covered. The main disadvantage in our case was the fact we had more than one 'leader' to start and everyone had their own idea how the whole production could go. We did finally get the whole thing together, so it really ended up working toward a positive end. I think the sharing of information was the most valuable thing we received."

5. "I really liked working with a group! Most of all I enjoyed getting to know the other psychology students at UCR. Many of those people became good

f.iends and all were instrumental in introducing other personalities into my experience."

"I also, rather painfully but positively, learned a very important fact about working in groups—a "leader" cannot do everything and must allow group members time to give group input. Depending as opposed to nondepending on group members leads to both a more positive group experience and a group output. More importantly, dependence on members leads to more positive feelings among the group!

"It was fun! I hope you keep it in your classes."

6. "My personal opinion of the group presentations is that they were very effective. I felt that I learned more by being part of a group than I would have if I had worked on my own. There does, however, need to be a limit on the number of people per group. Our group had nine members, all of whom worked well, but it was difficult to set times when all nine members could get together. The relatively close interaction by the members made learning about suicide both informative and enjoyable. All of the members contributed significantly and there was a great deal of exchanging of ideas and information from the research that was done.

"There were also close personal ties which developed through the group. These ties led to study groups which helped each other prepare for tests even if there had not been tutors.

"Needless to say, the groups were definitely a help rather than a hindrance."

7. "Good Points

   a. Changed my attitude toward group activities. Before, I hated groups, now, they're okay.
   b. Allowed me to get a broader view of my paper topic.
   c. Discussion time can be used for group preparation.
   d. Got me acquainted with classmates.
   e. Helped in my research.

"Bad Points

   a. Not quite enough guidance as to specific content of the presentation.
   b. Requires extra meeting time.

"Overall, I enjoyed the group presentation experience. Our group was a good one in that everyone did some work and our sessions were generally positive. Doing the group activity had a transfer of positivity to the classroom because I was acquainted with more people than I would normally. Therefore, when I didn't understand or missed some course material, I had someone to go over it with."

8. "The cooperative educational experience was a frustrating one for me. The group members seemed to show a lack of common goals from the beginning and a genuine lack of solidarity. (The only solidarity shown was a desire to compete with other groups—halfheartedly expressed toward the end. Really competition between individuals seemed to be replaced by competition between groups.)

"To further clarify the lack of common goals, some group members were simply not as highly invested as others, saying that they'd prefer to spend their time studying for the tests and doing their papers, as the presentation just wasn't worth that much toward the final grade. Their goal was to "get by" the presentation—that's it—reserving their best efforts and ideas for their own work.

"There was a lot of absenteeism among group members—in one case, one member didn't show up at all the night before the presentation! There was a real lack of pride in their contribution to the group, and again, it just seemed to be a low priority in their lives. Two members of the group wound up doing the bulk of the work for two reasons: (1) we really enjoyed the topic and (2) fear—getting up in front of the entire class and being unprepared jackasses wasn't a pleasant visualization.

"Maybe if the cooperative thing could be optional, "teams" could be composed of members who really wanted to be team members, while those just along for the ride could do their own thing. There's some residual resentment, too, that those who coasted shared the class grade for the presentation with those who worked far harder."

9. "My experience with the study groups was very beneficial. After the initial introductions were exchanged and we, the members of our topic group, relaxed enough to allow some ideas for possible topics to be generated, I found myself in a surprisingly rich "think tank" environment. Each member of my group had different interests and different educational paths through which their individual interests had become knowledge within a field of study. In focusing our interests into a salient presentation topic, we were able to discuss, quite credibly, broad ranges of knowledge. Each person was able to learn from the other's reasoning for why a particular topic was interesting to them; that is, each was able to learn from the background thinking, personal experiences, educational experiences, and unanswered questions of the others. As a group, we were often able to provide answers to the others' questions. We pooled our knowledge much as is done in a "think tank," and, by the time we had discussed numerous topics, we were able to settle on a topic new and interesting to all. Obviously, in pursuing research on my aspect of our topic, I was able to gain intellectually from the new information; I was also able to gain from the research of the others when we got together to discuss our progress and review each other's findings. The groups are enriched environments where one might learn something if one's not careful.

"I could tell, too, that the others in the class experienced their groups in a similar fashion by the clarity and understanding with which the others presented their individual and group topics."

10. "The first time I heard the words *group presentations* mentioned in my abnormal psychology class, a chill went up my spine and I was flooded with feelings of fear, anxiety, and uncertainty; 'I'll have to get my hair cut!' and 'It's the Scarsdale diet horror all over!' and 'I'd better stock up on the acne medicine.' When groups were being organized and topics assigned, I found myself stuck in the largest group in the class (seven people) with the exciting and intriguing (ha, ha) subject of organic brain syndrome as our topic. But as we began to meet and

discuss our ideas, the tension subsided, friendships developed, and an air of *intense* motivation began to creep over our group. Sure, there were problems and obstacles, but we conquered them as a team, drawing on our pool of resources. I actually became motivated to learn, to experience, and to trust and depend on other human beings. But the ultimate reward was seeing fellow classmates respond to all our hard work and preparation; they laughed, they were interested, and they expressed their appreciation. It was the best 'natural high' I've ever experienced. In retrospect, I came away not only with an *understanding* of the facts of our subject but, more importantly, with a new confidence in myself as a human being, able to interact with others as a means of accomplishing a common goal. American education is doing a great job at filling our heads with facts and figures but it is failing miserably in teaching individuals how to be human beings; and the concept of 'group presentations' in the classroom seems a very effective and logical stride in the direction of overcoming this hurdle.''

SPONTANEOUS STUDENT COMMENTS

1. "This has been the most enjoyable psych. class I have had at UCR. I think I benefited the most from the team project because it allowed the students to do some independent research on a topic they were really interested in."

2. "The format of group presentations was very beneficial and allowed for in-depth research."

3. "The oral projects were fun and much knowledge was gained. The oral projects were neat in that they gave us all an opportunity to meet fellow class members."

4. "The group presentations helped tremendously in that we could concentrate on one specific topic and go into detail."

5. "The group project, while nerve wracking and slightly disjointed as a learning experience, was enjoyable and productive educationally."

6. "The group presentation format is effective. Not only do you learn your area but others also, in a very interesting way."

7. "I liked the style of the team topics and feel it was an invaluable experience."

8. "Course was well integrated. I enjoy the sharing and community effort in this class."

9. "I felt that the teaching method required me to be more creative and put much more thought into the class material."

10. "Topic teams concept is a good one. It forces new responsibility on students and allows opportunity for experiencing rather than just studying about. Very rewarding class."

11. "I feel that I have learned more about psychology and about myself from this course than from any other course I have taken. The class format was new and exciting; it let the students become the teachers."

12. "I did not enjoy the set up of the class. I would have liked the class better if there had been regular lectures, rather than class presentations."

13. "The team approach is a novel way to teach a course. It gives the student a chance to use his head as a thinking tool instead of a repository. Sufficient time was allowed for team presentations and Professor Kagan stopped to help students over the rough spots."

14. "The course organization offered the advantage of students actively directing their own learning. It had the disadvantage of incomplete or unclear descriptions of psychotherapies if a group presentation was weak."

15. "The student topic teams were a great idea. You had the perfect mix of instructor lecture and topic team lectures."

16. "At first I was taken aback by the idea of a group presentation, but in the end I liked it a lot and feel I learned a lot."

17. "It is a good experience to speak in front of a group and to work with others to organize a presentation."

18. "I very much appreciate the structure of the class presented by Prof. Kagan; it allows the students to become aware of the facilities within themselves, which I feel is necessary."

Index

Ability
  group composition and, 165–167
  interpersonal relations and, 163–164
Academic achievement
  comparison of methods and, 321–325,
    336–337
  conflict versus concurrence and, 115
  contact theory and, 354
  Co-op Co-op and, 449
  cooperative learning and, 6, 9–11, 75,
    114, 355–359
  desegregation and, 351–352
  ethnic differences and, 268
  expectation states theory and, 355
  factors in, 352–353
  group composition and, 165–167
  group relations and, 168–169
  interdependence and, 105–112
  interpersonal relations and, 147,
    153–161, 164–165
  Jigsaw method and, 233, 234, 239,
    240, 243–244
  peer tutoring and, 150–151
  predictors of, 351
  research on, 148–151
  small-group mathematics instruction,
    213, 215, 219–221, 224
  standardized test scores, 293–295
  structural bias theory, 278–279,
    289–295
  Team-Assisted Individualization, 188,
    192–193, 196–203
  See also High-achieving students;
  Low-achieving students
Action research, 2
Activity structure, 22
Affect
  cooperative learning groups and,
    118–119
  grouping methods and, 126
  group interaction and, 130
Age level
  Jigsaw method and, 245
  role-related cooperation and, 30

Age level (*cont.*)
  structural bias theory, 285–286,
    295–297, 301–304
Algebra instruction, 214
Anthropology, 403–404
  See also Ecological approach
Argumentation
  communication and, 138–140
  defined, 99
Assimilation
  cooperative learning and, 256, 270–271
  definitions of, 264–265
  opposition to, 266–267
  pluralism and, 270
  prejudice and, 267–268
  values and, 265
  See also Ethnic differences
Attendance (school), 13
Attitudes, 188–189, 220, 221
Attributional analysis, 272–273

Behavior
  cognition and, 128–129
  goal structures and, 103–104
  grouping methods and, 126
  other-orientation and, 55–56, 60–61
  self-orientation and, 50, 55
  small-group mathematics instruction,
    213
  socioeconomic class and, 48–49
  Team-Assisted Individualization and,
    189, 191
  time on task and, 116
  See also Interpersonal behavior
Between-team reward structures, 86–87,
  92–93
Between-team task structures, 84–85
Bias. *See* Structural bias hypothesis
Biological Sciences Curriculum Study
  (BSCS), 238
Brainstorming, 222–223

CAI. *See* Computer-assisted instruction
Calculus instruction, 213